Series Preface

This series of books is addressed to behavioral scientists interested in the nature of human personality. Its scope should prove pertinent to personality theorists and researchers as well as to clinicians concerned with applying an understanding of personality processes to the amelioration of emotional difficulties in living. To this end, the series provides a scholarly integration of theoretical formulations, empirical data, and practical recommendations.

Six major aspects of studying and learning about human personality can be designated: personality theory, personality structure and dynamics, personality development, personality assessment, personality change, and personality adjustment. In exploring these aspects of personality, the books in the series discuss a number of distinct but related subject areas: the nature and implications of various theories of personality; personality characteristics that account for consistencies and variations in human behavior; the emergence of personality processes in children and adolescents; the use of interviewing and testing procedures to evaluate individual differences in personality; efforts to modify personality styles through psychotherapy, counseling, behavior, therapy, and other methods of influence; and patterns of abnormal personality functioning that impair individual competence.

IRVING B. WEINER

Fairleigh Dickinson University
Rutherford, New Jersey

(*continued on back*)

Interventions for Children of Divorce

CUSTODY, ACCESS, AND PSYCHOTHERAPY

William F. Hodges
University of Colorado

A WILEY-INTERSCIENCE PUBLICATION

JOHN WILEY & SONS

New York · Chichester · Brisbane · Toronto · Singapore

This book is dedicated with love to Linda, my wife

Library of Congress Cataloging-in-Publication Data:

Hodges, William F.
    Interventions for children of divorce.

    (Wiley series on personality processes)
    "A Wiley-Interscience publication."
    Bibliography: p.
    Includes indexes.
    1. Children of divorced parents—Mental health.
2. Custody of children. 3. Custody of children—
Psychological aspects. 4. Child psychotherapy.
5. Divorce therapy. I. Title. II. Series.
RJ507.D59H63 1986   306.8′9   86–13239
ISBN 0–471–81354–0

Printed in the United States of America

10 9 8 7 6 5 4 3 2

Preface

This book is designed to provide mental health professionals, lawyers, and judges with principles for working with children of divorce. Within the context of a theoretical understanding of how separation and divorce affect children, evaluation of custody, access, and therapeutic interventions will be presented. The book's ideas are based on theory, research, and clinical experience.

The approach of the text attempts to present an integrated theory of development. The focus is a cognitive/dynamic one guided by Piaget's cognitive concepts and neoanalytic developmental theory related to separation-individuation. For the uninitiated, these theoretical orientations are briefly summarized in Chapter 1. The text can be used as a guide for how children make sense of the world, based on their cognitive abilities at different developmental stages. The reaction to divorce will be presented in terms of the systems context of family, school, community, and the broader culture to demonstrate why children in different settings respond differentially to marital conflict and the separation of their parents.

The development of these conceptualizations are based on the research literature, my own clinical experience, and the clinical experience of all of those clients and professionals who have contributed to my understanding of children of divorce. I am aware that there are a variety of areas in which my opinions are not held by others. Those areas are identified.

The reader may be tempted to skip over Chapters 1, 2, and 3 to get to the "meat" of the clinical enterprise, providing services. I would urge you to spend time with the first sections. The book has included implications for clinical interventions. These implications are set off in italics. Intervention is likely to be more effective if informed about the research and theory on the effect of specific stressors and characteristics of the child and family.

After a brief introduction of theory and terminology, Chapters 2 and 3 review in detail the literature and my clinical experience on the relationship between developmental stages and adjustment to the divorce of parents. Because individual assessment of developmental stage is not possible, the material on children's response is organized by chronological age. Certainly some of the variation that can be seen at each age may be accounted for by different developmental stages of children at the same age. Recommendations for clinical intervention and parental consultation are included in those chapters.

Chapters 4, 5, 6, and 7 on mediation, custody, and visitation may seem like an unusual addition to a book on intervention since that term tends to generate images of psychotherapy. It has become quite clear in my own practice that an understanding of intervention requires knowing the effects of the different ways families reach their present status and consequences of chronic, post-divorce conflict and visitation problems.

Chapter 4 is a plea to consider mediation as an alternative to the adversarial court procedure. Divorce mediation is still in its infancy, and the research base is quite limited. Even with those limitations, the available evidence suggests that mediation is superior to court battles for most families. Chapters 5 and 6 deal with custody evaluation. While this book is not intended to be a definitive work on how to do custody evaluations, understanding the basic principles is likely to improve clinical service through an appreciation of the experience of the parents and children and what may have gone wrong developmentally in the process of divorcing.

Access and visitation are likely to be major issues for parents consulting a mental health professional concerning problems in the divorce. Both parents and children act out the anger and hurt around this transition time. The most controversial aspect of Chapter 7 has to do with recommendations for visitation time as a function of age. For prevention, the knowledgeable clinician who can facilitate negotiation for custody and access can be a most helpful interventionist. Intervention for children of divorce includes effective processes for deciding post-separation access.

Research on single parenting and remarriage form a separate literature from that of divorce. Yet when clinicians are working with families of divorce, issues of single parenting (Chapter 8) are often major. With the high rate of remarriage (perhaps as high as 75 percent within five years of the divorce), working with families of divorce means working with remarried families (Chapter 9).

Chapter 10 reviews school-based programs, which tend to be group oriented, and other group approaches.

Chapter 11 on consultation with parents is unique for this kind of book. The chapter provides a model of consultation that clearly defines the child as the client and the parent as a collaborator in helping this child. This strategy reduces defensiveness on the part of the parent and can increase the helpfulness of intervention.

Chapter 12 presents models for working individually with children of divorce, using the information from prior chapters as a base for defining what interventions are needed. Family therapy with families of divorce, single parents, and remarriage are then discussed in Chapter 13.

When I finished my review of the literature and my own experience, it was apparent that there were large gaps in the data base for helping children. A final postscript summarizes the unanswered questions for interventions, the answers to which would improve the professional's ability to be effective in helping children of divorce.

I would like to express my appreciation to clients (adults and children) who have helped me understand their experience of divorce and what would be helpful to them. Dr. Lanning Schiller, a clinical psychologist in Boulder, Colorado, who has extensive experience in custody evaluations has given me invaluable editorial assistance and I have given him inadequate citation for ideas on the chapters on custody and visitation. Finally, my deep appreciation goes to Linda Hodges, my wife, for her support, encouragement, and most important editorial assistance.

I would also like to thank the following for permission to reprint material: Author Richard A. Gardner and Jason Aronson, Inc., Publisher, for text from *Psychotherapy with Children of Divorce*, copyright 1967; author Stuart L. Kaplan and *Family Process* for two figures from "Structural family therapy for children," copyright 1977, Volume 16, pages 75–83; and The Associated Press for the syndicated article, "Husband disputes ex-wife's visitation rights to two cats," copyright 1984.

WILLIAM F. HODGES

Boulder, Colorado
September 1986

Contents

CHAPTER 1

Introduction

Evaluation and intervention require a full understanding of what one might expect of children at different ages. It is appropriate to ask the following questions:

Is this behavior pattern typical of children of this age, older, or younger?

To what degree are problems this child is manifesting potentially due to father custody or joint custody?

Are explosions on the part of the child on Friday and Sunday evidence of harmful visitation?

It is to answer these types of questions that research literature and clinical experience are potentially useful.

The research literature is generally quite poor by scientific standards. In a review of the literature of about 250 studies on children of divorce, Dr. Walter Prowansky found only 22 research studies with acceptable standards of design with control groups. Given the quality of research in this area, this book will be subject to extensive revision as the data are expanded. Even in the 10 years that I have been doing research in this area, my opinion about a variety of issues has changed. For example, psychoanalytic theory on optimal visitation patterns for very young children suggests limited visits. Experience with children in day care, however, demonstrates that with predictable visitations on a regular basis, very young children can tolerate without apparent harm (one must be very cautious in this area) much longer visitations than theory would suggest.

Few studies exist on visitation at all. From 1945 to 1975 there was not a single research article on visitation patterns and their effect on children. There were several theoretical statements about what visitation should look like for young children, but no empirical evidence. Since that time, there have been a half dozen articles on visitation, although few, if any, on infancy and preschool age children.

What are the typical problems in the research literature?

1. Many reported studies are actually case histories. Case histories are potentially useful in communicating individual reactions to divorce and particular intervention strategies. An understanding of particular children can in-

form one's understanding of the research literature. Many examples have been used in this text to illustrate a point. In the absence of research, the case history is the only source of information available.

The case history is a rich source of information that can be used to generate hypotheses for the research. The research literature contains numerous examples of proposals from case histories being confirmed in the research literature. The role of family conflict on child adjustment is one such example.

Case histories do have some problems, however. The absence of quantified data makes it impossible to determine whether the reader would come to the same conclusions as the author. One has no choice but to accept the author's conclusions, perhaps with a grain of salt. It is also impossible to compare one study with another. How could one reconcile apparent contradictions between studies without information about the measures and bases for conclusions?

2. Most of the studies do not have control groups. While comparisons within groups of children of divorce can provide useful information, statements about the effects of divorce on children are difficult to evaluate without a control group of children from intact families. If preschool age children respond to divorce with anger, regressive behavior, tantrums, and whining, is that behavior significantly different from what would be expected in a child of that age from an intact family? If teenagers turn to peer groups for support after parental divorce, is that dependency on the peer group greater than would be expected of the peer group orientation of teens from intact families? Without such control groups, such questions cannot be answered.

Even when there are control groups, potential confounding variables such as income level, must be controlled, either statistically or by matching. Since true experimental control cannot be accomplished in divorce research (people cannot be randomly assigned to get a divorce), all designs are essentially correlational.

With correlational designs, it is always possible that cause and effect are reversed or the relationship is interactional. For example, when it is discovered in the literature that children who have fathers that visit infrequently are also less well adjusted, it is tempting to conclude that infrequent visitation caused the child's maladjustment. It is just as likely that visitation with a maladjusted child is less rewarding and that the maladjustment "caused" the less frequent visitation!

Mental health professionals should be cautious about assuming that all causes flow from the parent to the child. Troublesome behavior on the part of the child often leads the parent to respond in less warm, supportive ways.

3. Much of the research is based on very small sample sizes. Thus, many studies cited in this book are based on a small group of children. Bias in the sample may be a greater likelihood with these small groups. How were the participants recruited? What was the motivation of the parents for deciding to permit their children to be in the study? These are troublesome questions.

4.   Even when sample size is adequate, biases in socioeconomic status, cultural bias in different areas of the country, initiator status for the divorce, and motive for participation may all play a role in the data. While data provided by parents and teachers are useful, each source of data might have its own source of bias. Even observation may either miss important but low frequency behavior or cause changes in the behavior.

THE IMPORTANCE OF TERMINOLOGY

Terminology is important to this text because words both reflect subtle attitudes and shape interventions. Consistent with recommendations made by a variety of professionals, this text avoids the term "broken home." Not only does such a term imply damage or inadequacy, but it interferes with strategies designed to build an alternative structure of the family that can be healthy for all members.

There is ample evidence that children in our culture flourish best in a home with two loving parents and parents that love their children. The assumption, however, that failure to provide that structure for children dooms them to maladjustment is simply not supported by the evidence. The developmental tasks are different when divorce occurs than for an intact family. The term "intact family" is unfortunate since it suggests the term "broken" by implication. While the term "nuclear family" is a way of describing a family in which both biological parents of the children are living together, the concern was that an insufficient number of people would recognize nuclear family as an alternative. Thus, intact family will be used in spite of its unfortunate implications.

In a similar way, remarriage presents problems of terminology. Satir (1972) referred to such families as "blended" families to reflect the coming together of two prior families. The literature often refers to "reconstituted" families. This term is technically correct, but has the unfortunate connotation of less-than-fresh orange juice. For the purpose of this text, the term "remarried" families will be used.

THEORETICAL ORIENTATION OF THE BOOK

Understanding the recommendations for interventions discussed in this book does not require elaborate theoretical study; the area is simply not that well developed. Two theoretical bases have been helpful here:

1.   The object relations theory of ego analytic thinking. From this theory comes the description of separation and individuation of the child from the parents and the developmental stages of working on that process.

The bonding between child and each parent and the effect of premature breaking of that bond presents difficult developmental tasks to the child.

2.   Jean Piaget's cognitive theory. Piaget provided a structure for understanding the child conceptualization of the world including object permanence, cause and effect, egocentrism, time perspective and empathy.

Each of these theories will be discussed briefly in this section. It is assumed that most readers will have at least a passing acquaintance with both theories.

Development from Object Relations Theory

When considering the impact of divorce on child development, the nature of separation from one or both parents raises questions about the nature of the bond and the ability of the child to separate from one or both parents and establish the individuation process. Mahler, Pine, and Bergman (1975) suggested the following phases in development in that process, reviewed here in their relevance to the present topic of the parents' divorce:

1.   *The normal autistic phase.* The newborn infant is in a sleeplike state. The child is relatively unresponsive to external stimuli. Separation from primary caregivers during this time is likely to have an impact only if the biological needs of the child are disrupted. The emotional stability of caregivers following the separation and divorce may be of importance in terms of how the child progresses through the next stages.

2.   *The beginning symbiotic phase.* During the second month the infant begins to become aware that there is a "need-satisfying object" in the world. The infant acts as if the mother (typically) and child were an omnipotent system. The child begins to "split" the world into bad and good experiences. This is the precursor to the problem of developing rigid, splitting of good and bad perceptions of people at a later time. Trauma in the caretaker at this time or separation from a need-satisfying object could result in pathological splitting.

3.   *The normal symbiotic phase.* In the third month, the child develops a bond with the caretaker (usually the mother), but a sense of self is still not clearly developed. If the child is experienced with joy and warmth, the child will develop pleasure in interacting with the world. If the parent is stressed and chronically anxious as a function of marital discord and separation, the child's symbiotic nature may result in a lack of joy and chronic tension in the child.

a.   Development of body image. According to Mahler et al. (1975), at 4 to 5 months, the child begins differentiation, the self is seen as separate from the primary caregiver. The social smile is an indication of both the separation process and the bond with that caregiver. The child may develop transitional objects, which are generally soft and smooth such as blankets, that serve to bridge the child's need to be in contact with the mother when she is not present. By six months, the child is playing with the mother and the environment and learning to recognize objects.

Transitional object such as a soft blanket can be used with older infants and toddlers to bridge separations for significant caregivers. Parents should be encouraged to permit the use of such objects particularly after separation from both parents due to marital separation and the necessity for employment on the part of the mother.

   b.   The early practicing period. From 7 to 10 months the child is now able to move away from the parent. The child is able to practice independence only in close proximity to the primary caregiver. The caregiver becomes a stable "home base" for the child. Physical contact with the caregiver results in "emotional refueling." With this refueling, the child develops independence from the caregiver and the parent often feels ambivalence in this moving away. Parents who are suffering from the loss of a marital partner may have more difficulty allowing the physical and psychological separation of the infant.

7-10 months

   c.   Rapprochement. By the middle of the second year, the child both moves away from the parent and wishes to be reunited. The child becomes afraid that separation will result in loss of love. If the parent is not psychologically available during this phase, the child's fear may seem to be realized. Availability of the primary parent during this period will result in clear reality testing, optimal cognitive functioning, and effective coping by the beginning of the third year. From this theoretical point of view, it is clear how important the primary caretaker is to the child's development and how over- or under-involvement would inhibit optimal separation and individuation. According to Mahler et al. (1975), severe separation anxiety in the third year (a common developmental phase beginning about nine months or so) may be a sign that object constancy (that is, that a person continues to exist when absent) is not developing appropriately. The lack of a secure base in the parent-child relationship may increase the likelihood of such a problem.

2½ yrs

   d.   Consolidation of individuality. The child develops lifelong individuality and object constancy. The child can cope with separation for fairly long periods of time (hours, not days) even though tense. The child is able to merge "good" and "bad" images of the parent into a single, integrated perception. This phase occurs at about three years of age and includes the skills of verbalization, fantasy, and reality testing.

3yrs

Numerous authors have pointed out that development through childhood continues to raise issues relating to separation and individuation. In western culture, the onset of school requires a separation from parents and the ability to maintain a sense of self as separate from the parent for large parts of the day. If the parents do not provide a solid, stable base from which to make that separation, the child may have more difficulty with it. The onset of adolescence is another stage in which the child must begin again to separate and individuate. Only if the base of love and affection is secure can separation, rapprochement, and increasingly more mature individuation occur. Marital discord at this phase may result in a child who spends more time at home and is less able to separate from parents.

Development from Piaget's Cognitive Theory

Piaget's theory does not focus on individual differences, so that applications to stressful life events such as marital discord, separation, and divorce are more inferential than under the object relations theory. Ault (1977) has given an excellent and readable summary of Piaget's basic theory. The four phases of development from Piaget's view, again related to the concerns of this book, are:

1. *The sensorimotor period.* The child learns to use the sensorimotor apparatus, to integrate information from different sensory systems and to develop simple mental representations of external objects. Beginning with simple reflexes, the child learns to experience the external world, to recognize its characteristics and manipulate it. By 1½ years, the child is able to search for hidden objects. By two years of age, the child is able to think about a task prior to acting. Object permanence, as in object relations theory, is a major task of this age, although the theory focuses on inanimate objects rather than the emotional bond with the parents.

Frequent contact with both parents is particularly important from 8 months of age on, in order to help the child maintain an image of each parent during separation as continuing to exist. Pictures, tapes, phone calls, and frequent visitation can facilitate object permanence.

2. *The preoperational period.* Around two years of age, the child begins symbolic functioning. According to Ault (1977), symbols are demonstrated from behaviors such as the search for hidden objects, delayed imitation, symbolic play, and language. Such symbolic ability can help the child cope with the stress of parental separation and exposure to new situations such as a new home and school. The child develops concepts of classes, ordinal position, and conservation (e.g., that the number of objects is not changed by their position). Because symbolic functioning is limited and the child is not able to mentally manipulate several symbols simultaneously, the child's ability to understand the meaning of the divorce is limited. Parents can both underestimate and overestimate the ability of the child to use information at this age. A child

will make errors of causation ("Daddy left because I was bad.") or have difficulty remembering what a long-absent parent looks like. The child may have difficulty in understanding that parent-parent relations belong to a different category of relationships than parent-child relations. "If mommy is mad at daddy and can divorce him, will she divorce me if she is mad at me?"

3. *Concrete operations.* At 6 or 7 years of age, some very important cognitive changes occur that permit the child to handle a parental separation with greater ease. The child can now solve a variety of tasks through mental operations. The child can mentally check out hypotheses about cause and effect and is less likely to feel the cause of divorce. The child can understand the difficulty in the parental relationship. Time perspective becomes infinite, and the child can understand that divorce is forever. The child can do simple problem solving mentally, permitting more effective coping.

4. *Formal operational thinking.* The final stage in Piaget's theory is formal operations: the child can perform true logic and abstract thinking, including imaginary proposals. Typically beginning around the onset of adolescence, the child is now able to hypothesize about parental relationships and mentally try out various ideas to see if they work. As will be discussed in Chapter 2, the ability to empathize is limited at first. Later in adolescence, however, the child is able to develop an understanding of why parents might behave the way they do. This ability at abstract thinking can give the adolescent important coping skills in dealing with parental divorce.

THIS BOOK'S ORIENTATION FOR CLINICAL INTERVENTION

The book's basic themes both in understanding the effects of divorce and in developing interventions relate to the following:

1. Given an understanding of the age, gender, socioeconomic status, temperament, parenting history, family conflict, and other potentially relevant variables, what would one expect would be this child's understanding of the world?

2. What *is* the nature of the child's understanding of the world?

3. In what ways is that understanding distorted because of developmental needs or cognitive limitations?

4. How is the coping of the child maladaptive, given the developmental tasks with which the child must cope?

5. What kind of experiences can be given to the child to correct misunderstanding about the nature of the world and provide the child with alternative modes of coping?

The development of these conceptualizations are based on psychological theory, research literature, and clinical experience.

CHAPTER 2

The Response of Children to Separation and Divorce

Almost all children, regardless of age, experience the divorce of their parents as a major stressful event. Only children who have been physically abused or have observed spousal abuse tend to be relieved that the fighting is over. Adults have difficulty understanding why children mourn over the loss of a marital relationship in which parents were chronically angry at each other or unhappy—Why can't the children see that everyone is better off now? Children are often unable to see the advantages of divorce until several years later. Even children who report that their parents are happier and that a reconciliation would never work often report fantasies of the family getting back together.

Children of different ages have different cognitive abilities to make sense out of what is happening to their lives. In part, this determines the differing emotional reactions shown by children of different ages.

Young children also have some common misperceptions based on their assumptions about the nature of the world. First is the assumption that parental love for the child is wired in by nature. When children obtain information that leads them to come to the conclusion that the parent does not love them, they have to try to make sense out of that contradictory information. The usual resolution is for the children to decide that they are so unlovable as to violate a law of nature. Thus, abandonment by a noncustodial parent is a particularly devastating experience. With the death of a parent, the child can mourn the loss without loss of self-esteem. With abandonment, the child is constantly faced with the possibility of unlovability. It takes a fairly mature child (for that matter, a fairly mature adult) to have the perspective that the parent has limitations in the ability to love, rather than the child is unlovable. More on the impact of abandonment will be discussed in Chapter 7.

A second unfortunate perception is that parents' love for each other is forever. When parents get divorced, it can shake the foundations of what children believe is true about the world. Younger children in particular have difficulty having this basic assumption shaken and destroyed. If this assumption is false, what other assumptions about the world are also false? Can parents divorce children? If Mom quits loving Dad, can she quit loving me? It is this question that leads some children to attempt to be especially well-behaved in order to preserve their relations with their parents. Since it is difficult for a young child

to maintain such control for long periods of time, anxiety attacks in anticipation of rejection may result. Other children become so panic stricken by the
imagined rejection by a parent, that they misbehave outrageously in order to
get the rejection over with.

*Extreme behaviors of excessive misbehavior or unusually cooperative behavior
after marital separation may mask fear of abandonment.*

Chronic family stress or parent separation? There is a tendency to assume
that it is the separation from the noncustodial parent that is responsible for
the negative effects of divorce on child development. While that separation
can be quite stressful for the child and both children and parents focus on the
separation as a major loss, professionals working with children of divorce
must remember that divorce typically occurs in the context of a chronically
unhappy marriage. It may be that chronic conflict that leads to adjustment
problems rather than the divorce per se.
In our culture, children would seem to flourish best in families in which
both parents love each other and love the children. Children do not inevitably
become maladjusted if those conditions are not met, but the developmental
tasks are more difficult. Chronic stress within the home also presents the child
with tasks that might interfere with the ability to cope with day-to-day stress.
Nye (1957) compared the adjustment of children from both divorced and
unhappy intact homes and found that unhappy intact homes presented greater
difficulties for normal adjustment than children from divorced homes. Raschke
and Raschke (1979) in evaluating 289 children from the third, sixth, and eighth
grades reported that children from intact families with high levels of family
conflict showed significantly lower self-concepts than children from families
with low levels of conflict. They found no significant difference in self-concept
from intact, single parent, and remarried families.

*Keeping the marriage together for the sake of the children when there is chronic
conflict in the family is probably ill-advised.*

Since mental health professionals have been giving that advice for years, it
is worth knowing that there is research substantiating that view.

THE EFFECT OF DIVORCE ON ADULTS

In addition to the impact of chronic stress on the life of the child, it should
be remembered that the parents, too, are under long-term stress. Parents may
have limited ability to be helpful to their children during the chronic conflict
prior to the divorce and the adjustment period immediately after the separation.

Bloom (1975) in an epidemiological study of Pueblo, Colorado found that divorce was a much more powerful predictor of psychiatric hospitalization than was socioeconomic status. Admission rates for psychiatric hospitalization was nine times greater for men from the separated and divorce category than from the married category. Approximately 7 percent of all divorced males in the study were hospitalized for psychiatric reason in any given year. The percentage for women was about 2 percent. The question of cause and effect can be raised by this study. Did divorce increase vulnerability for psychiatric hospitalization or do men at risk for psychiatric hospitalization have greater difficulty maintaining a marriage? The answer to both questions is yes. There is substantial evidence to support the contention that divorce is a major stressor in people's lives.

Bloom, Asher, and White (1978) have summarized a large number of studies that document the overwhelming negative effect of divorce on adults.

The suicide rate for divorced men is three times higher than married men. Risk of death by homicide is far higher for divorced people than for other groups.

Car accidents average three times higher for the divorced than for the married. These rates double between the six months prior to and the six months after the divorce.

Death rate by disease, where it is particularly difficult to reverse the cause-effect explanation, is also much higher for the divorced category.

The widowed and divorced have higher age adjusted death rates for all causes of death combined than for married people of equivalent age, sex, and race. Particularly, death by tuberculosis, cirrhosis of the liver, malignant neoplasm of the respiratory system, diabetes mellitus, and arteriosclerotic heart disease are higher for some divorced groups.

Why do men have more trouble than women with separation and divorce? There is no clear research evidence on this issue, but a variety of possible explanations offer themselves. Women are more likely to experience stress prior to the separation (Caldwell, Bloom and Hodges, 1984). Men are in more stress after the separation (Hodges and Bloom, in press). Women are more likely to retain custody (historically about 90 percent nationwide) and the residence of marriage. Women are more likely to see talking to others as a benefit to handling stress and are more likely to have a highly developed social support system. Social support has been demonstrated to serve as a mediator in reducing stress of divorce (Caldwell and Bloom, 1982). Thus, women typically have less loss and have better coping skills for dealing with the stress of divorce. Feminists have proposed that men have a better deal in marriage (typically contributing less than half of the work load), while women have a better deal outside of marriage. Finally, women are twice as likely to instigate the separation and the "dumper" is likely to have higher self-esteem than the "dumpee."

Women are more likely to be distressed about marital conflict prior to the separation than men. Men have much more difficulty recovering from the divorce than do women.

As joint custody and father custody (discussed in detail later in the book) increase in frequency, research studies will need to reevaluate the relative adjustment of adults to divorce. Androgynous men may be able to cope more effectively with the stress of separation and divorce and maintain high levels of contact with the children.

Having children increases the stress of marriage and lowers marital satisfaction. Having children also increases the anger and post-divorce conflict (Bloom, Hodges, and Caldwell, 1983). Parents are required to continue contact for the sake of the children and are likely to resent the contact of the exspouse with the children. While this continued conflict has negative effects on the children (discussed later in this chapter), it is understandable from the point of view of the parent. Many parents get a divorce to protect the children, when they would not do so to protect themselves. (This is the opposite viewpoint from "keeping it together for the sake of the children.") Also, if a parent decides that a spouse's behavior is detrimental for that parent's own development, it is not surprising that the parent would decide that the same person could be damaging to the development of the children.

Fear and anger on the part of parents are a natural response to divorce and dealing with those feelings must be a part of the clinician's strategy for intervention.

In addition to the parents' emotional reactions to the divorce, the child's life may be more chaotic after the divorce, contributing to adjustment problems. This chaos is semi-independent of the reaction to the divorce itself. Hetherington, Cox, and Cox (1979) noted in their study of preschool children that family life after the divorce was extremely disorganized for at least a year: meals were served at irregular times and mother and children were less likely to eat together; bedtimes were erratic; young children were read to less than children from intact families; and children were more likely to be late to school. Noncustodial fathers were less likely to eat at home, had more trouble sleeping, and had difficulty with shopping, cooking, laundry, and cleaning.

The mental health professional should not overinterpret the loss due to the separation and divorce. Chronic conflict prior to the divorce, parents who either did not love each other or had substantial ambivalence about each other, continued conflict after the separation, and parents under significant stress and less available to the children for emotional support may all play a role in making separation and divorce a stressful life event for the children.

THE REACTIONS TO DIVORCE AND CHILD DEVELOPMENT

It is important to evaluate age-related reactions to divorce in order to antic- ipate typical needs of children at different ages. Such anticipation can provide guidelines for prevention and for assessment of reactions that require more intrusive intervention because of their abnormality. The following sections will review the research and clinical evidence for short-term effects of separation and divorce up to two years. Chapter 3 will discuss the limited number of studies on longer term effects and the role of other stressors.

Birth to Two Years of Age

There has been almost no research on the effect of divorce on infants. The primary problem associated with doing research on the immediate impact of divorce on infants has to do with the long delay from separation to divorce. Even though many states have relatively short waiting periods, couples often take much longer to resolve the divorce process. For example, in Boulder, Colorado, couples have a 90-day waiting period between filing for and ob- taining a nonadversarial divorce. Yet couples take an average of 13 months from separation to divorce (Bloom, Hodges, Caldwell, Systra, and Cedrone, 1977). Most studies of the effect of divorce on children do not identify po- tential participants in the study until the filing for the divorce which may be a long while after the separation. Infants may move to toddlerhood during this period. More studies of families at the point of separation are needed.

Mothers are more likely to obtain custody of infants. Given that they are likely to be in better psychological condition and have been more involved in infant care, such custody arrangements makes sense in the average home. The average quality of fathering of infants in the United States is quite limited. It has been estimated that fathers may spend less than a minute a day with in- fants under three months of age (Rebelsky and Hanks, 1971) and up to an hour a day across infancy (Pedersen and Robson, 1969). Thus, separation from the father in a typical home may present little stress for the infant.

How upset the custodial mother is about the separation and divorce may be far more important in determining the effect of the separation on the in- fant. Mothers who are tremendously upset will upset the infant. In addition, the routine and responsiveness to the infant may be extremely disrupted.

Parents with infants should pay particular care to (1) maintaining routines and (2) reducing the exposure of the infants to emotional upset on the part of the parent.

Often, parents have difficulty in obtaining high quality day care for infants. A mother previously unemployed will almost always have to seek employment since poverty (or at least a reduced standard of living) is an almost inevitable consequence of divorce. Inexpensive child care is difficult to find. A mother may find herself losing one sitter and going to another on a frequent basis.

Research on institutional care where the child's physical needs are provided for but there is only a minimum of social interaction, play, and opportunity for exploration, has suggested that children are quite adversely affected (Provence and Lipton, 1962). Prior to 3 or 4 months of age, there was no major difference between institutionalized and noninstitutionalized infants. After four months of age, the institutionalized infants were showing much less vocalization, including cooing, babbling, and crying. A rigid stance rather than molding of the body to the arms of an adult was evident. By 8 months of age, there was less interest in toys and loss of interest in the external environment. The faces were less expressive and body rocking was much more common than for children raised in families. There was no language development at one year of age for the institutionally raised infants. Other research with infants have found anaclitic depression in infants in institutional settings with a dull, listless response to the environment (Spitz, 1946).

Another early study (Rheingold, 1956) looked at the effect of two different types of institutional settings. The first type had many different caregivers. In the second setting, only one person played the role of mother eight hours a day, five days a week, for eight consecutive weeks. In addition to having one person provide care, the babies in the second setting received more affection and stimulation. After the eight-week intervention of affection and stimulation, infants were tested. Infants cared for with a warm, consistent caregiver were much more socially responsive to the person in the mother role and to strangers than did children with multiple caregivers. There was no apparent affect on perceptual motor skills.

Mussen, Conger, and Kagan (1979) reviewed the literature on the influence of good child care outside of the home on infant development. They concluded that children raised in a consistent, nurturant environment with another adult will develop attachments to that adult and will not have delayed development. Such children attach to both the mother and day caregiver and show stranger anxiety and separation anxiety at the usual times. At 20 months, these children will also prefer the mother to the caregiver when bored, tired, or anxious. Mussen et al. (1979) recommended that in order for a day care center to be adequate for infants, there must be one caretaker for no more than three to four infants or five or six toddlers. In addition, the day care setting needs to expose the children to a variety of stimulation and opportunity to develop new skills. They have found that children under such conditions will develop in a similar way as they would have if they had remained at home.

Infants can handle day care quite well, provided that caregivers are warm and affectionate, provide a stimulating environment with opportunity for skill development, and provide continuity over time. Parents should try to maintain the same caregivers and avoid day care services with high staff turnover.

Tessman (1978) reported that children who had experienced early, total abandonment by a parent were characterized later by grief and sadness, with longing for the relationship. She described searching behavior where the child looks at the faces of people in shopping centers or the grocery hoping to have instant recognition of the parent about whom they had no memory.

Herzog (1980) reviewed the treatment of 12 boys between the ages of 18 and 28 months whose presenting complaints were a syndrome resembling night terrors. In every case, the parents had been divorced or separated within the previous four months and the mother had custody. In every case, Herzog had been consulted within three weeks of the onset of the symptoms. A characteristic pattern included falling asleep with lesser or greater difficulty and waking early in the night, terrified, disoriented, and calling for help. Often, the child would cry for his father. In eight of the twelve cases, there had been a change in sleeping arrangements. In four cases, the son and mother were sharing the same bed. In the other four cases, the son and mother were sharing the same bedroom. Each child perceived that the return of the father would stop the night terrors. Herzog interpreted the problem from the point of view of castration anxiety, narcissistic injury, fear associated with aggression mobilized by the loss of the father, and "father hunger." While it is not wise to generalize from such a small sample, certainly the total concentration around recent father loss and the high frequency of changed sleeping arrangements is strongly suggestive.

In boys aged 18 months to 30 months, night terrors after divorce may reflect anxiety about father loss. Reassurance, increased father contact, and removal of the boys from the mother's bedroom may facilitate reduction in the terrors.

The only research study on separation in infancy and later personality development was done by Kalter and Rembar (1981). This study lookd at (1) the marital status of families of children in an outpatient psychiatric service across a wide age range and (2) the diagnosis of the children. Such retrospective studies present problems of interpretation since conclusions are limited to children who ultimately develop psychiatric problems and receive treatment for it. The results do suggest, however, that particular types of problems are created by earlier divorce. Separation of parents during infancy as compared to separation of parents at other ages was related to the child having problems with parents that did not involve aggression when the child was in latency (6 to 12 years of age). In addition, adolescent boys with separation during infancy were less likely to have problems with peers around aggressive issues.

Two to Three Years of Age

Psychoanalytic theory has proposed that this period is a particularly sensitive time for divorce. Gardner (1976) stated that the younger the child, the more adverse the impact of divorce. Longfellow (1979), in her excellent review of the literature, concluded that preschool children (including the two- to three-year-olds) may have particular difficulty handling the divorce of parents. Toomin (1974) argued that the loss of the father at the 18- to 36-month period had critical implications for the separation-individuation process. Children at this age who are dealing with how safe it is to separate from a parent may find the partial or complete disappearance of a parent a frightening experience. Only when the child has a safe, trustworthy base can exploration occur. When that base is threatened, either by the separation from the noncustodial parent or by chronic emotional upset of the custodial parent, the child's ability to explore and separate may be severely hampered.

Two- to three-year-olds were evaluated in a study of children from 2 to 18 done by Wallerstein and Kelly (1975). They studied 131 children from Marin County, California during their parents' divorce. The children were referred by a variety of professionals in the community for help with normal reactions to divorce. In this study, children were followed for 10 years, providing a rich data base. Unfortunately, there was no comparison group of children from the same community from intact families.

The study reported that preschool age children from two to three showed regression, irritability, aggression, and tantrum behavior. Regression included loss of toilet training, separation anxiety, masturbation, and the use of transitional objects (i.e., the use of blankets or dolls as reassuring objects). Since these behaviors are fairly common during the "terrible twos," it is not surprising that children under stress would also demonstrate similar coping skills. Although their data is based on a very limited number of children at this age (9), the uniformity of reactions to the separation is impressive. Wallerstein and Kelly noted that the most severe reactions occurred when children were not provided an explanation of the disappearance of the absent parent. By one year later, for all but three of the children, the major problems with aggression, fearfulness, and possessive behavior had disappeared.

Parents underestimate the ability of 2- to 3-year-olds to understand and utilize information about what is going on around them. Parents should be counseled to tell children about what happened to the absent parent and why.

Three to Five Years of Age

As for younger children, children of this age have a limited (but not zero) ability to cognitively make sense out of the loss of one parent. As previously noted, the loss of a parent through separation and divorce can lead the ego-centrically oriented child to assume that it is his or her unlovability that led to the separation. It is not surprising that children of this age have difficult understanding and appropriately coping with separation and divorce.

From psychoanalytic theory, the concern for developmental processes at this age is the disruption to the oedipal phase of development, in which children are developing stronger identification with the same sex parent, sex role identification, and greater moral understanding and identification with parental values. Consistent with that theoretical position, Biller (1981) noted that learning appropriate sex-roles is more critical before than after six years of age. Boys with father loss prior to age six have more trouble obtaining a masculine identity than boys with father loss after six. Some writers have noted the likelihood of powerful guilt feelings if separation and divorce occurred during this period (Rohrlick, Ranier, Berg-Cross & Berg-Cross, 1977; Toomin, 1974). The effect of separation and divorce on sex role identification will be discussed in detail in Chapter 8 on single parenting.

One major problem that is common at this age is the tendency for children to be used to help the parent handle his or her own pain. Children commonly move into the parental bed after the separation. Seldom does the parent who is practicing this behavior report it to the mental health professional. Rather, the other parent usually raises concerns. The mental health professional should routinely ask where a 3- to 6-year-old child sleeps.

The argument is not being made that having a 4-year-old son move into the mother's bed after a separation results in the child winning the oedipal conflict and being forever fixated at the phallic stage of development. There is a risk of sexualizing the relationship between the child and parent at an age when the child does have increased interest in the sexuality of the parent. Perhaps the greater risk is the increased dependency that is supported by such behavior. Children who move into the parental bed are much more likely to continue substantial levels of immature dependency on the parent. Parents will go to extraordinary lengths to try to convince the mental health professional that such a move is not possible: "He is too upset to sleep alone"; "She crawls into my bed in the middle of the night and I wake up in the morning with her there." I suggest getting a lock on the bedroom door and encouraging the child to knock. If the parent is frightened that they will not hear the child cry out with a nightmare (common at this age range), I suggest an intercom.

Children who are sleeping with either parent need to be moved out of the parental bed. When the child is significantly upset and tries to move into the parental bed, the parent should provide reassurance and return the child to his or her own bed, stay with the child, and encourage sleep by sitting with the child until sleep comes, perhaps calming the child with a back rub. Then the parent should return to the parental bed.

Several research studies have looked at the reaction of 3 to 5 year olds to the divorce of their parents. McDermott (1968) reported on the earliest study done on preschool age children. His study evaluated 16 nursery school children of divorce, age 3 to 5. Extensive weekly records were kept by the teachers for several months around the separation. The records were not kept for the purpose of the study, although it is likely that the recordkeeping was affected by the teachers' knowledge of the situation. Ten of the 16 children were acute management problems, eight showed sad, angry feelings, two seemed lost and detached, and three of the girls showed "pseudo-adult" behavior involving constricted and bossy behavior. Regression was commonly observed and boys showed more aggression and destructive behavior.

Wallerstein and Kelly (1975) reported that regression was no longer a common response in 2- to 3-year-olds. Perceptual motor skills had been sufficiently overlearned so that stress did not result in loss of skills. Aggressive behavior, irritability, and whiny and tearful behavior were common. Fantasy developed as a coping skill. Of the 11 children in this study, 7 were evaluated as worse one year later. For almost all of the children who were worse, it was in the direction of lowered self-esteem, greater inhibition, sadness, and neediness. While the sample is limited, these data do raise the question of whether the 3- to 5-year-olds are more vulnerable to the effects of separation and divorce than younger children.

One of the problems with limited samples is that chance distribution of certain types of children can influence the interpretation of data. In this case, all but one of the seven children who were worse a year later had fathers with serious problems and fairly harsh disciplinary child-rearing strategies prior to the separation. It is difficult to know whether it was the harsh treatment before the separation, the loss of structure caused by the separation or the effect of separation on children of this age that accounted for the poor adjustment reaction of children of this age.

Hetherington et al. (1979) were able to elaborate on a variety of issues of the reaction of children to separation and divorce when at the preschool age. The study looked at 24 boys and 24 girls from divorced homes and compared them with a matched set of 24 boys and 24 girls from intact homes. The children from homes of divorce were matched by selecting children from intact homes who were similar on parental age, parental education, length of marriage, sex of child, age, and birth order. Matching studies do not rule out alternative explanations of the data since it is always possible that a nonselected variable (for example, parental conflict) is one in which the two groups differ and is more important than the ones that were selected. When a person is researching an area that cannot be under experimental control, however, such matching is far better than no comparison group. For example, although the Wallerstein and Kelly (1975) study provides rich data for further exploration, it is difficult to know whether in Marin County, California, the whiny and dependent behavior in 3 year olds of divorce is greater (or how much greater) than for 3 year olds without the separation experience.

Another important aspect of the Hetherington et al. (1979) research is the extreme care she took to gather information on the children: interviews, structured diaries, observation in the laboratory, observation in the home, parent rating, personality battery for the parents, observation of the child in the preschool, peer nominations, teacher ratings, and assessment of the child's sex role, cognitive performance, and social development. Children were assessed two months after separation, one year later, and two years after the separation. This study found that preschool age children, with an average age at divorce of 3.79 years, did develop more negative behavior than children in intact families. Boys had statistically significantly more trouble handling the divorce than girls. While girls were returning to the level of adjustment of girls from intact families by one year after the separation and problems had disappeared by two years, boys were still having significant problems at two years, although the level of problems was declining.

For women who were married to upper class men, the drop in income was profound, moving to lower middle class. Poverty was seen as delaying restabilization.

One of the major contributions of this study is the careful analysis of parent-child interactions. Coercive interactions were common between mother and child. Boys were particularly difficult for mothers to handle. Preschool boys would ignore an instruction from the mother and obey that same instruction when given by the father. Since preschool boys in this culture are intensely preoccupied with sex role identification, it is likely that the reluctance of boys to obey mothers is related to sex role identification. Mothers who had custody of only boys had particular difficulties and, two years after the divorce, had low self-esteem as a parent. The boys tended to be out of control.

Wallerstein and Kelly (1975) noted that feelings of responsibility can occur for children this age, but Hetherington et al. (1979) indicated that for children of this age such feelings are rare. My own clinical experience has suggested that feelings of responsibility are relatively uncommon. There are two major reasons why a child of this age would assume responsibility for the divorce of his or her parents:

1. Children of this age are relatively egocentric and tend to see most things as revolving around them. It is easy for a child to turn a fight over financial matters into "You should not have bought me that jacket."

2. Assumption of responsibility may be an attempt to gain control over the situation. If the child had done something that caused the divorce, then the child could undo the divorce by reversing the behavior. Thus, some children become unusually good after the divorce in an attempt to reverse the "cause" of the noncustodial parent leaving home.

Regardless of whether a child is being egocentric or is trying to assume control over the divorce, the child will be better off if the parents insist that the child did not cause the divorce and does not have the power to reverse the process.

In the Kalter and Rembar (1981) study, in which they looked at the diagnoses of out-patient psychiatric clinic children as a function of sex and age at the time of parental separation and divorce, they found that if separation occurred from 3 to 5.5 years of age, boys later had more school-related problems and less anxiety and depression than boys experiencing divorce at other ages. Adolescent boys who had experienced separation at preschool age showed less aggression toward parents and siblings than boys who experienced separation later. Girls who experienced separation during this preschool time did not have differential diagnoses during latency, were more aggressive toward parents and peers during adolescence, and had greater academic problems than did girls with separation of parents at other times. Why anxiety and depression are lower for boys if divorce occurred at this age is unknown. An expectation, at least from psychoanalytic theory, would be for greater anxiety, rather than less. For aggression, the results are easier to explain. Since boys became less aggressive and girls became more aggressive, the results suggest that later sex role stereotypic behaviors are reduced by father loss by divorce at this age.

Relatively few studies have looked at cognitive and social functioning for preschool age children. These variables are much more commonly investigated for school age levels. Guidubaldi and Perry (1984) evaluated intellectual, academic, social, and adaptive behavior for 115 kindergarten children in a suburban school district. Single parent status due to divorce and socioeconomic status was investigated to see which variable was more important in predicting behavior. There were 26 children from single parent homes (23 percent of the sample). They measured the Peabody Picture Vocabulary Test, Draw-A-Person, Bender Visual-Motor Gestalt Test, Wide Range Achievement Test, Metropolitan Readiness Test, general academic ratings, Sells' and Roff's Scale of Peer Status, The Kohn Social Competence Scale, and the Vineland Social Maturity Scale.

Socioeconomic variables predicted school-entry competencies. High socioeconomic levels were associated with high intellectual levels, academic performance, and personal-social development. Single-parent status was, however, the most consistent predictor variable and predicted academic, visual-motor, and social development. Correlations ranged from .19 to .42. Single parent status was a stonger predictor than socioeconomic status on 7 of the 12 nonintellectual criteria. Single-parent status did not predict the intellectual measures. When multiple correlations were performed, single parent status did add predictive variation over that provided by socioeconomic status on six of the seven academic variables, suggesting that single-parent status does make a difference in academics. There were 16 other predictors and seldom did they add any additional predictive value. The study concluded that the negative effect of divorce on child development was not mediated entirely by economics.

Given the intense reactions to separation and divorce that McDermott (1968), Wallerstein and Kelly (1975) and Hetherington et al. (1979) reported, I decided to further evaluate this group in terms of determining individual differences (Hodges, Wechsler, and Ballantine, 1979). Which children were at risk for maladjustment and which were likely to cope well with the stress? The participants were 52 preschool children: 26 from intact families who had never experienced the separation of their parents and 26 who were presently living in maternal-custody homes. The mean age was 4.3 years. The children were enrolled in five different preschools in Boulder, Colorado. This population was predominately white and middle class. Data included direct observation of the children in the preschool, a behavior checklist filled out by the custodial mother, and a behavior checklist filled out by the child's preschool teacher.

The first hypothesis to be tested was that children from divorced homes would manifest greater problems than children of intact homes (particularly aggression, withdrawal, dependency, and other signs of immaturity). However, few statistically significant differences were obtained. These results were startling in light of the previous studies! The findings were obtained in spite of the fact that both parents and teachers reported the belief that divorce had a profound impact on child behavior. Only 9.5% of the divorced mothers reported a negative change in the child's behavior following the marital separation.

When the data for children in the divorce group were analyzed, those children who were more likely to have problems could be identified. The younger the parents and the lower the father's income, the greater the teacher-rated general maladjustment of the child. The greater the number of moves, the greater the amount of aggression in the child. This last correlation was .65 ($df = .24, p\langle .01$). In a multiple regression analysis, it was clear that younger parents, lower income, and number of moves were all the same variable. It is the young parents who have not yet settled into a career and who move frequently. More on the role of economics and other stressors will be presented in Chapter 3.

It is younger parents with fewer resources such as a lower income and less geographic stability whose preschool aged children are likely to have more difficulty with their separation and divorce.

The research may not have shown the greater level of problems for preschool children of divorce as compared to children from intact families because of sample bias. It is impossible to determine what biases led parents of either type of family to decide to participate.

MINIMAL EFFECTS.   There is a possibility that cannot be ignored that for this population, divorce did not have a measurable effect on child behavior. There is evidence to suggest that children are not always adversely affected by the divorce of their parents. In an unpublished study done in Boulder, Colorado with similar results, Audrey Kick and I evaluated the effect of marital status of parents on the behavior of Head Start Children. Staff were convinced that divorce led to greater behavioral and emotional problems in their preschool age children. We obtained a zero correlation ($n = 26$) between marital status of the parents and year-long requests for consultation around behavioral and emotional problems.

ATTRIBUTION OF CAUSATION.   Why would parents and teachers assume that divorce leads to behavior problems in preschool age children when for Boulder, Colorado there is no evidence to support that view? When a child from a divorced home has emotional or behavioral problems, the general assumption is that the problems were caused by the divorce. Statements such as "that child is aggressive, because he comes from an intact family" are unlikely to be made—even though they may be truer than assumptions that behavior problems in a child from a divorced family were caused by the divorce.

ATTRIBUTION OF DAMAGE. Because of the assumption that divorce will inevitably damage the child, parents and teachers can be overly concerned about the child's welfare. Children who receive messages that they are to be pitied for the plight that they are in may develop long-term problems, while getting short-term support.

THE SOCIAL ENVIRONMENT. In Boulder, Colorado, the divorce rate is 60 percent, substantially higher than the national average. Thus, divorce is a common event and children report that many of their classmates have experienced the divorce of their parents. One reason why children of divorce in the Hodges et al. (1979) study were not seen as having greater problems may have to do with the common experience of divorce in that community. Divorce, while still likely to be a serious loss for children, may not be seen as depriving or unusual in a community where divorce is common. One bit of supporting evidence for this interpretation was the findings of a follow-up study (Hodges, Buchsbaum, and Tierney, 1984) using the same measures, but obtained in Denver, Colorado, 30 miles away and with a significantly lower divorce rate. In that study, the more typical findings of greater aggression, dependency, poorer on task behavior in preschool, poorer general adjustment in preschool, and more acting-out aggression toward the parents at home were obtained. Boys of divorce were less happy, more distractable in preschool, and less well adjusted at home than were girls of divorce.

In summary, for most studies and in most communities, separation and divorce tends to predict greater problems in preschool children of divorce, particularly for boys. The egocentrism of children of this age may lead them to assume the divorce is their fault. Economic problems in the family particularly puts families of divorce at risk for children with adjustment problems.

Five to Six Years of Age

For Wallerstein and Kelly (1975), the 14 children in the 5 to 6 age range also showed aggression, anxiety, restlessness, whininess, moodiness, irritability, separation problems, and tantrums. These children were old enough to understand some of the changes due to the separation. The study reported that some children did not seem to be adversely affected by divorce events. The most vulnerable group of five children were diagnosed as developing childhood depressions with unhappiness, anxiety, denial, feelings of rejection, and sleep disturbances, phobias, compulsive eating, aggression, and dependency.

Adams (1984), summarizing seven major studies supported by the National

Institute of Mental Health, noted that children under 6 years old when their parents were divorced were three times more likely to need psychological help than older children.

Seven to Eight Years of Age

There is a major shift in cognitive ability that occurs around seven or eight. Children move from a preoperational logic in which cause and effect are difficult to understand to concrete operations (Piaget) where a greater understanding of the nature of the world is obtained. One particularly important shift is the development of an infinite sense of time. The ability to think about the future develops slowly during the preschool time. By the age of 7, the child can understand the concept of "forever." Indeed this understanding is why death phobia is so common at this age. In terms of the implications for divorce, the child is now able to understand that the parents intend to remain divorced forever. In terms of visitation, the child is able to tolerate long visitations and understand intuitively the return to the custodial parent. From a theoretical point of view, this greater ability to handle the information about divorce should result in reduced long-term, negative consequences.

From a theoretical point of view, a divorce that occurs during the child's latency period should have less impact on development than one that happens during the child's preschool or adolescent periods. Certainly the possibility of delayed oedipal resolution due to prior marital conflict is a predictable outcome. Academic achievement may be affected (this age is the beginning of Erikson's (1963) age of acquiring a sense of industry), and the development of appropriate peer relations may be harmed. The importance of the developmental tasks of this age, consolidation of previous stages, and the learning of peer relations and less self-centered orientation to life all suggest that the latency stage is not irrelevant to development and several theorists have emphasized the importance of stability in the lives of children (Erikson, 1963; Sarnoff, 1976).

One advantage to the child of this age is the presence of school. Peers are more likely to be available as social support (and distractors) and the child comes in contact with a variety of adults who are not in turmoil because of the separation and divorce. In addition, the child has the opportunity to meet other children who are coping with the same stressors of marital disruption. For the younger elementary age child, the limits in the ability to understand the feelings of other children makes it difficult to take advantage of the experience of other children, however. By 10 or 11, empathy is more developed, but still reserved for people who are better known. As will be discussed in Chapter 10 on school-based intervention, training children in self-awareness and empathy for other children can be particularly helpful at this age.

Wallerstein and Kelly (1976a), in evaluating 26 children in their sample in this age group, reported sadness, grief, depression, and fear of the future. At this age, depression looks more like the sadness and grief of the adult. Prior to this age, depression in children looks more withdrawn and shut down rather than tearful. Deprivation feelings and intense feelings of loss in relationship to the noncustodial father were common, particularly for the younger boys (as would be predicted from psychoanalytic theory). Boys, more than girls, expressed anger at their mother for either causing the divorce or requiring the father to leave. One-quarter of the children felt pressure from an angry mother to reject the father. In school, more than half of the children had behavior changes sufficient to be reported to the interviewer by the teacher. Very few children reported fantasies of having caused the separation. In terms of the one year follow-up, these children did look less disturbed than was true for the younger children. Of the 26 children in this sample, 23 percent were worse one year later and 50 percent were improved or continued previous progress. The intense pain had been replaced by sad resignation. A third of the boys continued to wish for reconciliation. Anger in the child was particularly likely where the parents continued to battle.

One major behavior that is common at this age is an active wish for reconciliation. Wallerstein and Kelly (1976a) reported that almost all of the children entertained such wishes. Indeed it is a rare child that does not wish for reconciliation. Such wishes would seem to be true even for children exposed to constant fighting between parents. Only for older and more introspective children would the statement come some time after the separation and divorce that the parents are happier now and a reconciliation would not work.

Children should be encouraged to not provide information back and forth between households. They should also be encouraged to negotiate directly with each parent concerning rules in that household.

What makes that rule difficult to follow is the obvious need to provide protection to the child. It is sometimes difficult to evaluate when stories about the other household are putting the child in the middle (which is exactly where some children want to be). It is also difficult to know when it is necessary to encourage such stories in order to evaluate whether the child's welfare is endangered.

One major problem that begins at the 7 to 8 year old range is the development of conflicts of loyalty. Children often respond to ambivalence by choosing one side or the other, splitting their conflict in order to simplify it. Even adults have difficulty tolerating two contradictory feelings simultaneously.

Children should be encouraged to avoid choosing sides in the conflict. Since the child tends to identify with each parent, a child cannot choose one parent as right and another as wrong without some loss of self-esteem. Even when it is clear that one parent was irresponsible, the child should be encouraged to consider parents as both good and bad.

Felner, Stolberg, and Cowen (1975) evaluated the school maladjustment problems of children from 5 to 10 years of age who had significant early school adjustment problems. Children were matched on sex, grade, city versus country, socioeconomic level (a particularly important match), repeat in grade, and prior intervention. Of the 800 children in the first study, 108 had a history of parental separation or divorce and 32 had a history of parental death. The children who had experienced the separation and divorce of parents were higher than children from intact families on restless behavior, obstinate behavior, class disruption, and impulsiveness. Children who had lost a parent by death were higher on "unhappy or depressed" and "moody." An additional analysis of 950 children in a new sample, showed that children with parental histories of separation and divorce were significantly more maladjusted than the controls and showed heightened levels of acting out and aggression. Children who had experienced the death of parents also had significantly higher total maladjustment scores and were higher on shyness, timidity, and withdrawal.

Professionals who compare the mourning by the young child to the divorce of parents to the mourning about the death of a parent may make incorrect comparisons. The two types of situations produce significantly different reactions in children with divorce leading to increased aggression and disruptive behavior and death of a parent associated with depression.

Nine to Twelve Years of Age

Children of this age assume more responsibility for handling the household. Parents in intact families in the United States culture underestimate the ability of children to assume responsibility for household chores. Single parents must have the child help clean the house and take care of their own rooms. Sometimes major responsibilities concerning the babysitting of younger siblings occurs because of the difficulty in affording day care.

Another major cognitive shift is occurring in the 9 to 12 age range. While children are capable of empathy responses as low as one-and-a-half years of age, the ability to understand the perspective of parents does not begin to become sophisticated until the child enters the concrete operational stage of elementary school. In this age, the child improves substantially in the ability to see the world from someone else's point of view. This empathy is still quite limited to those people that the child knows quite well. The average elementary school age child will participate in vicious teasing. Yet children of this age can be enormously caring and concerned about the pain that their parents are going through in handling the divorce. This concern leads to *parentification of the child*—a major problem of the 9- to 12-year-old range. Parent and child reverse roles. The parent who is lonely and demoralized by the divorce finds a sympathetic ear in the child. The pattern of using the child to unload the pain of the working day and the loneliness of the evenings begins.

As was previously mentioned, it is common that children of this age are given increased family responsibilities. Parentification leads to excessive dependency on the part of the parent about the responsibility of the child. One child, showing significant depression, was coming home from school, cleaning the house, cooking dinner, and then after dinner listening to the mother complain about all the things that went wrong at work that day.

Parents should be encouraged to use someone other than a child to unburden their problems, concerning the difficulties of the day or the loneliness of the nights. While children of divorce should be given more responsibility to help the family cope with the amount of work, parents should take care to avoid burdening the child to the point of eliminating play.

Children with these burdens do not become identified as problems. They are super-responsible children. If they do come in contact with a mental health professional, it is usually because they have either developed a psychosomatic illness or depression. They are pseudo-mature rather than truly grown up. Because the maturity is not developing in a normal fashion, it is not truly balanced. The major problem from the point of view of mental health is that these people grow up into very responsible, joyless adults.

One mother described her 11-year-old daughter as extremely helpful around the house. In the course of therapy, the mother revealed that she routinely shared her adult problems with her child. The mother was urged to find friends to take that role. In an effort to encourage the daughter's spontaneity, the mother suggested a slumber party. (There is little sillier than 11-year-old-girls at a slumber party, unless it is 11-year-old-boys.) When the slumber party started, the daughter indicated that she had cleaned the house. She warned her guests to take care of the house, again assuming her responsibility role. The mother told the daughter that the mother would watch after the house. The daughter started to relax, and giggles were soon coming up from the basement where the slumber party was held.

Wallerstein and Kelly (1976) reported that the 31 children of this age (i.e., 9 and 10 year olds) in their sample responded to the divorce of their parents with poise and courage. They characterized the children as showing soberness, clarity, and empathy for the parent. The single feeling that stood out as differentiating these children from younger children was the conscious, intense anger. About half of the children were angry at their mothers and about half angry at their fathers. A large number were angry at both parents. The anger was often directed at the parent who was seen (often accurately) as initiating the divorce. Fear of abandonment was common in about one-fourth of the children. Shame was a common response to the news of the separation. The Wallerstein et al. (1976) sample showed a shaken sense of identity as well as loneliness and loyalty conflicts. Some children reported somatic symptoms, such as headaches and stomach aches. One half of the children of this sample declined in school performance (see the later section on the effect of divorce on school performance).

About half (14 of the 31) had fallen into a depressive behavior pattern and 7 others were openly distressed. About a quarter of the children (8 of 31) developed fierce loyalty conflicts aligning themselves with one parent against the other. At the five year follow-up, this loyalty conflict had disappeared.

Wallerstein et al. (1976) reported that one year later, understanding was greater. The responses to the separation were much less intense. About half of the children (15 of the 29 available for follow-up), were doing well, although not without some bitterness about the divorce. Of the total group, 10 maintained a strong level of anger at the noncustodial parent, and about a quarter were more distressed than at the initial interview.

Krantz, Clark, Pruyn, and Usher (1985) evaluated the cognitive appraisals of 26 boys and 26 girls of divorce, children who ranged from 8.5 to 12 years old. These children were an average of 2.5 years post-separation. The measures included a semi-projective measure of perceptions about divorce which asked the child to respond to possible thoughts a child of divorce might have in 13 problematic situations that were described. A measure of the ability of the child to generate alternative solutions to three divorce-related problems was also obtained. Reports by parents and teachers on the child were also obtained.

Boys who generated more coping alternatives had fewer behavior problems at home or school. The more adaptive the boys' evaluation of the divorce, the better their post-divorce adjustment at home. Adaptive beliefs included a positive or mixed evaluation of the divorce, optimism about the future, or acceptance of the divorce. No relationship was found between adaptive evaluations and adjustment at school. Girls in general had high levels of coping and adjustment.

Late latency boys, who can be helped to accept the divorce, to be more optimistic about the future, and to increase alternative problem strategies, are likely to show improvement in adjustment.

Of course, the opposite relationship may be true. Boys who are better adjusted can solve problems better.

In another study of adjustment of 9 to 12 year olds, Wyman, Cowen, Hightower and Pedro-Carroll (1985) compared 98 children of divorce with 170 demographically similar children from intact families on perceived competence, trait anxiety, and social support. The child of divorce had higher anxiety, lower perceived cognitive competence, and fewer social supports. For both groups, greater social supports correlated with a more positive self-view and lower anxiety.

In two studies of elementary school children, aged 6 to 12 (and therefore not matching the organization of this chapter), Bernard and Nesbitt (1981) obtained no significant differences in disruption and anger when children of divorce were compared with children from intact families. The authors used the Children's Emotion Projection Instrument, a measure that gave children a series of vignettes and asked the children to identify the main character and tell the counselor how they would react if they were that child. In study number one, while age differences were obtained on measures of aggression, assertion, and avoidance, the children of divorce ($n = 19$) did not differ in scores from children of disrupted families ($n = 8$), on these dimensions. Children from intact families ($n = 79$) offered *more* aggression responses and resignation/acceptance responses than children from divorced or disrupted families. In study two, with 35 children from divorced families and 35 matched children from intact families, no significant differences were obtained, except children from intact families obtained higher resignation/acceptance scores than did children of divorce. The authors interpreted their results as indicating that divorce is an unreliable predictor of adjustment. The problem with this interpretation is the unique aspect of the instrument. There is no way to evaluate whether this assessment tool is a valid measure of adjustment.

Copeland (1985) studied children of divorce, ages 6 to 12 and their mothers. For boys, mothers who described themselves as more angry and hostile also described their sons as having more behavior problems. Boys rated as having more behavior problems reported themselves as more confused about the separation and feeling more guilt than boys with fewer behavior problems.

For girls, mothers who described themselves as angrier, more hostile, confused, bewildered, tense, and anxious also described their daughters as having more behavior problems. As for boys, girls who reported more guilt were the girls with more behavior problems.

In this type of study, it is, of course, impossible to determine cause and effect or to determine the degree to which response biases may have accounted for the relationship between self-description and child description. Mothers, for example, who described themselves in a negative way may have been more negative in how they would describe anyone, including their own children.

Stolberg and Bush (1985) analyzed 82 mother-child families of divorce with children from 7 to 13 years old. Families were 9 to 33 months post-separation. In a path analysis of post-divorce child adjustment, three paths were most useful.

One pathway suggested that mothers with more children described better post-divorce child adjustment. Well-adjusted mothers had better parenting techniques. Better parenting techniques predicted better social skills, prosocial activities, and less internalized pathology in the child.

Promoting improved parenting techniques post-separation is likely to improve post-divorce adjustment (particularly regarding internalized pathology) in the child.

In the second pathway, younger children had more life changes. Higher life changes were related to greater externalized psychopathology and less prosocial skills. These results were consistent with Hodges, Tierney, and Buchsbaum (1984) for preschool children, to be discussed in Chapter 3.

Reducing life changes for the child, particularly the younger child, is likely to reduce externalized pathology (such as aggression).

The third pathway is the effect of overt marital hostility which predicted both externalized and internalized pathology and fewer social skills in the children. Extensive discussion of the role of parental conflict will be discussed in Chapter 3.

Reducing conflict between parents may reduce psychopathology in the child and increase social skills.

Adolescence

With the onset of adolescence, another cognitive change occurs. The child moves from Piaget's concrete operational period to formal operational logic. This move means that the child gives up the relatively concrete approach to solving problems and attempts to obtain solutions on a more abstract level. It is important to understand that the child must give up concrete operational thinking before becoming effective at the formal operational level. In addition to this major cognitive change, the child has several tasks of adolescence involving proving that he or she is an individual and not a clone of the parents. These characteristics of adolescence have several implications for understanding the response to separation and divorce:

1. *Egocentrism is high.* This egocentrism leads the adolescent to assume that everyone is just as preoccupied with his or her experience as he or she is. Adolescents tend to see everything revolving around their experience and cannot easily see the world from someone else's point of view.

2. *Empathy goes down.* The child can no longer use the concrete operational empathy of understanding the parent, but the ability to appreciate the parents' points of view has not yet developed at a more abstract level. This lack of understanding (and sympathy) on the part of the early adolescent is hard for most parents to accept. Certainly parents undergoing separation and divorce do not find the support that the later elementary age child was giving. It is not until 15 or 16 years of age that the formal operational logic has developed to such a point that the child is likely to start appreciating the parental point of view.

3. *Separation-individuation again becomes an issue.* The egocentrism and empathy reduction of early adolescence typical in the United States culture is functional for the task of separation from parents. Parents are typically ambivalent about allowing their children to grow up. If the early adolescent were in touch with that ambivalence, combined with their own ambivalence about the same issue, separation would become significantly more difficult to accomplish. Thus, it is important for the adolescent to be oblivious to the pain

of the parent. When the pain is about separation from a marital partner, the adolescent is presented with an even more complex problem.

Wallerstein and Kelly (1974) reported on 21 teenagers in their program that experienced recent separation and divorce. They reported that all of the adolescents tried to withdraw from the family to protect themselves from the pain. The withdrawal manifested itself in increased social activities or prolonged periods of staying away from home. It is difficult to evaluate the implications of this withdrawal without a control group from the same community since increased time away from home is a common characteristic of adolescence.

When the adolescent reaction to marital separation of parents is withdrawal, it is particularly difficult for the clinician to differentiate that behavior from typical adolescent independence. The clinician should take particular care in evaluating whether adolescent depression is in need of intervention.

An unpublished research study that I did with a graduate student, Janet Lemmon, evaluated adolescent friendships as a function of the marital status of the parents. Our study did not look at the immediate reaction to separation since the population of teenagers from single parent homes had been in single parent homes for varying lengths of time. The study showed that adolescents who had experienced the divorce of their parents spent more time at home and had fewer friends than adolescents from two parent families. Direct comparison with the data in the Wallerstein and Kelly's (1974) study is not possible. However, the possibility is raised that separation from parents is easier when the adolescent does not have to worry about the psychological well-being of the parent.

Sorosky (1977) noted that the younger the adolescent when divorce takes place, the more likely the teenager will experience the divorce as a personal abandonment and loss of love. There is ample research evidence to demonstrate that, as with younger children, autonomy in the adolescent is supported by a warm, safe environment.

4. *The adolescent makes judgments on an absolute basis.* Ambivalence is handled by splitting. A person is judged as either all good or all bad. Judgments are made on absolute basis. Thus, loyalty conflicts are likely to increase as the adolescent makes judgments about who was right and who was wrong. The ability to see both parents as having admirable qualities and sharing responsibilities has not yet developed. Wallerstein and Kelly (1974) refer to the "precipitous deidealization" of the parent (what an eloquent phrase!) as a response to the divorce. The child moves from seeing the parent as near perfect with few flaws to seeing the parent as seriously flawed and unworthy of respect. The overvalued parent is now the target of rage and underevaluation.

The degree to which parents and therapist encourage the child to experience ambivalence and to see people as complex beings that are not all good or all bad, the better the child will be able to solve the complex relationships of adolescence.

It is difficult to predict which parent will be picked as the enemy. Some adolescents will pick the parent who leaves, but others will blame the remaining parent for not being lovable enough (or supportive enough). Wallerstein and Kelly (1974) reported that by one year later virtually all of their adolescent sample had been able to separate themselves from the loyalty conflicts. My clinical experience indicates that severe loyalty conflicts may continue well beyond the year, particularly when the custodial parent continues to be deeply hurt and bitter and there is limited contact with the noncustodial parent.

McLoughlin and Whitfield (1984) in an Australian sample of teenagers of divorce also reported continued anger toward the noncustodial father, particularly for girls when the father was involved in adultery. In that study, the length of time between marital separation and the interview was not reported. The lack of contact of some adolescents prevents the adolescent from obtaining disconfirmation of the custodial parent's point of view.

To reduce severe loyalty conflicts, parents should avoid exposing their adolescents to the bitter anger they may feel. Some regular contact (even if limited in duration) should be encouraged to give the adolescent an opportunity to reduce splitting.

Because adolescents have difficulty with their own sexuality, they often blame the parent who had an affair. This concern raises another problem of adolescence—sexuality.

5.   Adolescents have difficulty with their own sexuality and the sexuality of parents. Wallerstein and Kelly (1974) noted that parental dating forces teenagers to be confronted with their parents' sexuality, particularly when the father was dating someone not far from their own age.

Because teenagers have difficulty with parents' sexuality, parents should minimize the teenager's exposure to that sexuality, particularly during the first year of adjustment to the divorce.

Sorosky (1977) noted that the father leaving the home can be viewed as a sexual rejection by an adolescent daughter. The teenage boy who is made the "man of the house" may have difficulty dealing with the closeness of the relationship with the mother.

This anxiety about the parents' sexuality is increased when parents enter themselves into pseudo-adolescent behavior. Many parents who divorce when their own children are teenagers have not dated since they themselves were late teenagers and may revert back to those behaviors. An adolescent daughter or son may find themselves apparently competing with their parents. Parents who have not dated for such a long time often were reared in sexually less permissive times and experience some guilt over their own sexual behavior. Some mothers can resent a daughter's attractiveness and youth and respond with excessive controls, inviting defiant acting-out (Sorosky, 1977). Such guilt can be translated into excessive permissiveness for the teenager. I had one parent who, when confronted with "You're sleeping with your boyfriend. Why can't I?" gave her 15-year-old daughter explicit permission to have sex with boys.

In addition, the teenager is faced with information about the parents' sex lives that would never had occurred without the divorce. As Sorosky (1977) pointed out, the parents are no longer safe sex objects. The father who is dating a woman much younger (a not unusual pattern) may provide a pseudo-peer relationship with the teenage daughter or son, and thus lose healthy generational boundaries.

It is important that parents of adolescence not handle their own guilt with excessive permissiveness. Adolescents need to be told that adults and teenagers have different rules. A variety of behaviors that are acceptable for adults are not acceptable for teens.

6. *Self-esteem goes down.* The early adolescent's self-esteem is particularly vulnerable. Self-esteem in children tends to rise until age 12 and then drops until 18 years of age (Simmons, Rosenberg, and Rosenberg, 1973). When teenagers describe themselves, they are more negative than they were when younger. Feelings about how acceptable the self is is a major issue. Since the child identifies with both parents, continuing parental conflict that includes character assassinations is likely to substantially reduce self-esteem.

As for all other ages, whatever the therapist can do to encourage parents to decrease fighting or to decrease the exposure of the child to that fighting, the better off the child is likely to be.

Another response to divorce during adolescence noted by Wallerstein et al. (1974) and other clinicians is delayed entry or accelerated entry into psychological adolescence. Those children with delay entry may refuse to engage in the separation from parents, remaining excessively dependent. Wallerstein and Kelly (1974) reported one case of heightened parentification in which a young teenage boy took over control of his mother, checking her social activities, monitoring her telephone calls, and requesting the check at restaurants. Such teenagers do not develop the peer relations that are helpful to them in the individuation process.

Accelerated entry into adolescence tends to manifest itself in early introduction into adult pleasures, that is, sex, drugs, and alcohol. Parents undergoing separation are often so preoccupied with their own pain that they do not provide adequate supervision. An example is when one thirteen-year-old boy came home drunk at 4 A.M. his mother only expressed surprise that he got home so late. As mentioned earlier, other parents permit excessive freedom because they feel sorry for the pain that the adolescent experienced as a function of the divorce.

Many teenagers who act out sexually and by using drugs may simply be wishing for external controls to be placed on them. As one teenager said to me, "I wish I had been raised a Catholic." Since religion had not been a major part of her upbringing, I was surprised and asked why. She answered that the Catholic Church provides guidelines for how to behave. Whenever she asked her parents what to do, they told her to do whatever she thought was best. With wisdom beyond the typical teenager, she said that she was too used to freedom to accept the structure of the church now.

In terms of normal development, research findings indicated that teenagers develop the most mature levels of autonomy with a democratic level of control (Conger and Petersen, 1984). Complete freedom and high levels of authoritarianism develop teenagers who are excessively dependent or excessively rebellious (Mussen, Conger, and Kagan, 1979). A democratic level of control is one in which there are clear guidelines for behavior, but the teenager participates in the development of the rules and the consequences for breaking them.

Sorosky (1977) noted that prior to the divorce, teenagers are sometimes put in the role of trying to hold the marriage together. When these attempts fail, the anger may be directed at the parents with strong aggression.

Teenagers are often quite concerned about the future. Money is a common preoccupation on the part of teenagers (Wallerstein et al., 1974). Since the parent battle often centers around finances, it is not surprising that the adolescent also becomes concerned with whether there will be enough money for clothing, dates, or college. Indeed, those children who experience the sharpest drop in quality of living have the most trouble (Desimone-Luis, O'Mahoney & Hunt, 1979). More on the issue of economics will be presented later in Chapter 3.

Another major concern about the future involves the possibility of their own future marriage succeeding. Remember that children who are experiencing their parents' divorce during adolescence are all seeing a marriage of some duration break up. How can you ever be sure that a marriage will last? The answer, of course, is you cannot be sure.

Adolescents can be reassured that for their own future, they are not doomed to repeat the mistakes of their parents. They can learn from their parents' mistakes.

When this author asked a group of seventh grade boys and girls in a "family change group" whether they wanted to marry when they grew up, they indicated, without exception, that they did. They did, however, decide that the major error that their parents had made was marrying too young and that they would wait significantly longer. Similar responses were obtained in the McLoughlin and Whitfield (1984) Australian adolescent sample.

Teenagers also worry about the statistic that the children of divorcing parents are more likely to divorce themselves. This statistic has been interpreted by some mental health professionals as evidence that divorce produces serious harm in the development of the child so that the ability to form long-term, intimate relationships is damaged. Indeed, Wallerstein and Kelly (1974) noted that the parents in the 60 divorced families in their study typically showed an absence of love, compassion, and intimacy. Teenagers may have something to worry about if they do not learn how to negotiate relationships in a more effective manner and how to share love and affection. There is, however, a more parsimonious explanation for the higher divorce rate among children of divorcing parents: children whose parents got divorced are more likely to consider divorce as a solution to an unhappy marriage than are children from intact families. In contrast to reports of adolescents worrying about marrying, in the McLoughlin and Whitfield (1984) Australian sample, 84 percent of the adolescents planned to marry and were optimistic of a happy marriage.

College Students

Almost no research has been done on the reaction to divorce of parents during late adolescence or college. Bales (1984) reported on the pilot research of Hagestad, Smyer, Cooney and Klock who interviewed 39 college students at the University of Pennsylvania who experienced the divorce of their parents while in college. More than half of the students reported a decline in emotional health, depression, stress, and a sense of insecurity. Themes common to younger children were also found here, including increased vulnerability, stress, anger, and worries about parents and their future. School breaks and holidays were described as a nightmare for many students.

About one-half of the students reported improved relationships with mothers and more than one-third noted improved relations with their father. When a deterioration in a relationship did occur, it was more likely to happen between fathers and daughters. Of the daughters who reported being angry, 43 percent said that their fathers were the sole target of the anger, while 14 percent said that their mothers were the sole target. Unlike younger children, most of the college students accepted the divorce, with only 15 percent believing that the parents should have stayed together.

Farber, Primavera, and Felner (1983) obtained information about the reaction of college students to divorcing parents by questioning 83 clinical directors of college mental health centers. The indirect nature of the data makes it more difficult to determine reliability. The problem with using service providers as informants is that their biases and distortions may influence their report. They saw female students as more likely to seek counseling for the divorce of parents. A long list of problems were seen as statistically more likely for college students facing the divorce of parents as compared to students from intact families: difficulty concentrating on studies, drug use, sleep problems, eating problems, withdrawal, dependency on roommates, difficulty with intimate relations, depression, anxiety, sexual identity problems, fears of abandonment, financial difficulties, loyalty conflicts, and feelings of insecurity. Thus, even at the college age with late adolescence there is considerable distress over the separation and divorce of parents.

Comparison Studies Over Childhood

As part of our separation and divorce program, my colleague Bernard Bloom and I (Hodges and Bloom, 1984) evaluated the parental reports of the behavior of 107 children from 1 to 18 years of age who were an average of 1.8 months after separation when the parents joined the study. People participating in the study were solicited by a deliberately ambiguous offer to participate in the University of Colorado Separation and Divorce Project. People who participated had reactions to the separation that ranged from significant distress to no distress. The parents provided descriptions of the children at entry into the study, at 12 months later, and at 18 months later (now 20 months post-separation).

Consistent with the studies previously discussed, younger children were reported as exhibiting more acting out than did older children. Older children were seen as having more depression. Boys were described as having more problems than girls on all measures at the initial interview and all measures except depression at 6 and 18 months.

Our study had extensive questions and long-term follow-up, but was obviously flawed by the nonrandom nature of the participants, all of whom were volunteers. Whether a person chose to answer the advertisements for the project was out of our control.

Another study tried to compensate for this common problem. Levin (1984) used data from the Health Examination Survey, Cycle II (children from 6 to 11) and Cycle III (children aged 12 to 17). These data were obtained for a major program of the National Center for Health Statistics. The data was based on a representative, probability sampling design of loose clusters of people in landbased areas. The sampling universe was all noninstitutionalized children residing in the United States excluding Hawaii and Alaska and American Indian Reservations, a universe of 24,000,000 children. Cycle II data were collected from July 1963 and December 1965. Cycle III data were collected from 1966 and 1970. Even though the data analysis is recent, it should be remembered that divorce had different meaning and context 15 to 20 years ago and interpretation of the results should be tempered with that realization.

Data included results of physical, psychological, and dental examinations as well as additional medical data such as audiometry, electrocardiograms, height, weight, and blood samples. Cycle II data were completed on 7119 children (96 percent of those designated in the sample). For Cycle III data, 7514 children were tested (90 percent of the sample).

Since there were a large number of variables, data were reduced to a smaller number of factors. Variables were eliminated if there were little variation. Then subsets were obtained that were theoretically meaningful.

Levin used five models for testing the data. Model A assessed the effect of parental marital status with the effects of child's age and sex removed. Model B measured the effect of marital status after a set of variables had been controlled, all of which were likely to be correlated with marital status such as age-of-mother at birth-of-child, birth order, education, and income. Model C did not include marital status as a variable. Model D added the interactive effect of family structure variables with each of the variables in Model B. Model E contained all the control variables, marital status variables, and all the interaction variables. Marital status variables were: intact, headed by divorced mother, headed by separated mother, headed by widowed mother, headed by remarried mother, father present but mother absent, and headed by relative.

The findings indicated that marital disruption did not exhibit any important effect on physical and health outcomes. Marital status did have some impact in the areas of cognitive and intellectual performance, parental monitoring, and social-emotional areas. The amount of variance explained varied from 2 to 4 percent. When other independent variables were controlled (Model B), the effect of household type was reduced to less than one percent in every case.

When all variables were taken into account simultaneously and children of divorce were compared with children from intact families, (Model E) Levin obtained some surprising results. Children age 6 to 11, living with divorce mothers, performed better on intelligence (IQ) tests and achievement tests, had fewer academic problems, fewer nose and throat problems, and were monitored more closely by their parents than were children living in intact homes. For children 12 to 17, the pattern was similar, but not as clear. Boys from divorced households had better oral hygiene, were slimmer, and had better overall health as compared to boys from intact homes. Girls in divorced homes had poorer oral hygiene, somewhat more ear and hearing problems, and poorer overall health. For both sexes, teenagers from divorced homes had more academic problems and required more resources for exceptional children than teenagers from intact homes, but did not have greater emotional problems. IQ scores were higher for teenagers from divorced homes, but academic achievement was lower. Health monitoring and sharing in the decision-making process was greater for teenagers of divorce than teenagers from intact homes.

Studies in which Age Was Not Taken into Account

McDermott (1970) reviewed the intake records of 1487 children up to the age of 14, who were evaluated at the University of Michigan's Children's Psychiatric Hospital from 1961 to 1964. Of these children, 116 were from families of divorce and 1349 were from intact families. McDermott found that duration of presenting problems were shorter for children of divorce than children of intact families. Most had had the problem for one to two years and were 6 to 12 years of age. Home and school maladjustment were given as diagnoses more often for children of divorce than children of intact families. Children of divorce were also characterized as running away from home more often and as having very poor home and school behavior. McDermott classified 34.3 percent of the divorce group as depressed, but did not give a comparable statistic for children from intact families. He noted that one common problem in divorced families was the conspiracy of the mother and child to recreate the absent father by having the child identify with the father's traits.

In contrast, Morrison (1974) looked at 127 children who had already been diagnosed as having psychiatric problems and found few differences for children of divorce as compared to children from intact families. Children of divorce were twice as likely to have problems with enuresis after age five as were children from intact families, but no other differences were found, including no differences in level of depression. Also, in contrast to McDermott's data, children of divorce had a longer duration of presenting problems.

Studies Indicating No Lasting Effect of Divorce on Child Development

The prior discussion of my research (Hodges, Wechsler, and Ballentine, 1979) suggested that children in some communities may not be adversely affected by divorce. Other studies have indicated that divorce did not result in measurable maladjustment. There is a moderately large literature that has deemphasized the effects of divorce on children.

Santrock (1975), using careful controls, also reported the effect of early divorce on fifth and sixth grade boys and found few differences in moral development. Burchinal (1964) tested 1566 seventh and eleventh graders in Cedar Rapids, Iowa and found few significant differences as a function of the marital status in the home. Reinhard (1977) reported little effect of divorce during adolescence. Landis (1960) reported that college students who had experienced the divorce of their parents from ages 5 to 8 were less upset (not more) than peers who had experienced the divorce of their parents at a later age. Pitts, Meyer, Brooks, and Winokur (1965) found no relationship between divorce in childhood and any diagnostic category as compared to a control group. Gregory (1966) reported no effect of childhood divorce on 1056 adult psychiatric patients with a control group matched for age and sex. Adult neurotics were significantly less likely to have lost a parent before five.

SUMMARY

There is evidence of broad effects of marital separation and divorce on child development. Young children are likely to demonstrate aggression and other acting out behavior. Teenagers may show more withdrawal and depression. Children of divorce demonstrate a wide variety of strengths as a function of divorce. If the child is able to cope adequately with the stress of marital disruption and separation, the child may learn to be independent and more mature.

In the next chapter, the research on long-term effects of divorce and the role of other stressors will be reviewed. In particular, the role of economics, conflict, reconciliation, abandonment, and cumulative stress will be presented.

CHAPTER 3

Long-Term Adjustment to Divorce, The Role of Stress and Child Development

Relatively little research has been done on the effects of divorce on child development over time. Post-separation events have a profound effect on child development. For example, parental conflict and economics have already been discussed in the context of Wallerstein and Kelly's (1974, 1975, 1976a, 1976b, 1977, 1980c) research and the research study of Hetherington, Cox, and Cox (1979). Some of that research will be discussed in the context of developmental changes in children post-divorce.

LONG–TERM ADJUSTMENT TO DIVORCE

Six Months to Two Years Postseparation or Divorce

According to Wallerstein and Kelly (1975), approximately two-thirds of children 2½ to 3¼ years old showed substantial improvement one year later. (It should be noted that the sample size was nine). Gone were the regressions, aggression, fearfulness, possessive behavior, and heightened questioning. Still present was an apparent neediness in relationships, manifested by a readiness to accept and reach out for strangers and wanting to sit in a stranger's lap and hold hands.

For preschool children, 3¾ to 4¾ years old (11 children), seven were worse off one year later, suggesting that this age is particularly vulnerable to parental separation. The difficulties one year later were in the direction of increased inhibition and constriction in play, fantasy and behavior, lowered self-esteem, sadness, and neediness. Again a need for physical contact, individual attention, and approval was evident. They agreed with McDermott (1968) that the children were unable to handle their anxiety and depression through play. Play was characterized by seriousness, sadness, and a sense of helplessness. When they looked at the parents of the children who were worse off one year later, they found that six of the children had fathers with psychiatric disorders and all seven fathers were harsh disciplinarians.

For the oldest preschool group (5 to 6 years of age), Wallerstein and Kelly (1975) reported that 5 of the 14 children in the study looked significantly worse one year later (36 percent). Four of the five were girls, demonstrating some of the problems of limited sample size. Other research has clearly indicated that boys at this age (indeed, at all ages) are much more vulnerable than girls.

For early latency age children, Kelly and Wallerstein (1976a) reported on the course of adjustment for 26 children who were 7 and 8 years of age. By one year later, the pain experienced initially had largely disappeared and was replaced by sad resignation. They reported that by one year later, 50 percent had improved in adjustment, 15 percent had consolidated the difficulties initially seen, and 23 percent were worse in adjustment. For later latency children (31 children aged 9 and 10), Wallerstein and Kelly (1976b) reported that about 21 percent were still adversely affected one year later.

For adolescence, Wallerstein and Kelly (1974) reported on 21 teenagers over time. They reported that within a year following parental separation, most of the adolescents were proceeding toward the tasks of that stage of development at an appropriate pace. Those teenagers who experienced entry into adolescence with a history of long-standing difficulties had more trouble. The precise percentage of adolescence doing well at one year was not reported.

Hodges and Bloom (1984) evaluated the parent report of 107 children from 1 to 18 years of age over a period of 20 months beginning an average of two months post-separation. The study found that the Disruptive Behavior Scale was higher for younger children than older children at the 6 and 18 month interviews (8 and 20 months post-separation). Depression increased with age at both the initial and six month interviews. Boys were having more difficulties on all four scales (Depression, Disruptive, Agitation, and Total score) at initial interview and all scales except Depression at 6 and 18 months.

The age of the child also made a difference in the reaction over time. Rated maladjustment increased as a function of time (over the 18 month follow-up) for children below eight years of age. Beyond eight years of age, while mean scores still increased over time, the increases were not statistically significant. This increase in problems for younger children is similar to Wallerstein and Kelly's (1976a) findings for young preschool children and the lower level of problems for older children over time is also similar to their findings. Direct comparison is not possible, however, since they did not report the use of objective measures or inferential statistics and our study was based on parent report rather than direct contact with the children.

The results in Hodges et al. (1984) also indicated that parents who were separated or remarried at the 18 month follow-up described their children as worse off than did parents who were divorced. These findings for separated parents are consistent with the view that when parents are separated, but not divorced, it may be a particularly vulnerable time for children (Kalter, 1977).

Parents who remain separated without either reconciling or divorcing may be creating an additional stress for the child. The mental health professional may benefit the adjustment of the child by encouraging parents to decide what they want to do with the relationship.

The failure to finish the work of divorce or to reconcile leaves the child wishing for reconciliation and fearing the divorce. The child is unable to obtain closure in either direction. The findings for remarriage are also consistent with the review that remarriage is a time of particular stress, destroying hopes for reconciliation, requiring new role demands, and leading to significant aggression and withdrawal. Parenting problems is the most common area of problems in second marriages (Messinger, 1976). Additional discussion of the problems of remarriage will be discussed in Chapter 9.

Professionals who suggest to divorcing parents that the reaction of children to the divorce will disappear in a few months are doing the clients a disservice. Particularly for preschool and early school age children, there is reason to believe that a significant number will be seen as worse off for the next one to two years. For older children, the adjustment level may not deteriorate, but improvement may not occur.

Hetherington et al. (1979) reported on a two-year follow-up of preschool age children of divorce and a matched group of children from intact families. They noted that by one year after divorce the girls had returned to a level of adjustment similar to the girls from intact families, while the boys from divorced homes, even at two years, were only approaching the level of adjustment of boys from intact families. By two years, one-fourth of the fathers and one-half of the mothers said that the relationship with the child was better than ever. Parents were having difficulties with affection with the child, were inconsistent in discipline, and had poor control over the child. Positive behaviors were rarely rewarded. The divorced mother was giving children twice as many commands as mothers from intact families. While the father was indulging, the mother was giving coercive commands.

Ten Years Post Divorce

Kurdek, Blisk, and Siesky (1981) evaluated the reaction to divorce of 58 white, middle-class, 8- to 17-year-old children whose parents had been separated for four years. They then evaluated the adjustment levels two years later (i.e., at approximately six years postseparation and divorce). By four years postdivorce, the children did not seem to be experiencing severe problems in regards to the divorce. However, the children's reactions toward the divorce were still primarily negative. They found that the children's understanding of the divorce was not related to their feelings about the divorce, a finding that suggests that cognitive factors in understanding the divorce may not play as important a role as previously thought. The custodial parents' evaluation of the children's level of adjustment was related to the children's feelings about the divorce rather than understanding. Well-adjusted children were older and experienced infrequent visitations from the noncustodial parent (more on this latter finding in Chapter 7 on visitation). Well-adjusted children had an internal locus of control (i.e., saw themselves as in control of their own lives), had parents who had been separated for a relatively long time (especially true for the older children), and had a custodial parent who was low in personal competence. Why low personal competence in the parent was related to good adjustment in the child is not clear. Modeling would predict the opposite. Perhaps having an incompetent parent forces the child to develop competence.

By six years postdivorce, children were not generally experiencing severe problems with regard to the parents' divorce. Children were now less likely to blame themselves for the divorce and did not think their parents would reconcile. The well-adjusted child was older, had parents who were not recently divorced, had an internal locus of control and a high level of interpersonal reasoning. Again, as found for the four year data, these children were better adjusted if they experienced infrequent visitation from the noncustodial parent. Since other data indicate that frequent visitation is best for the child, it is difficult to interpret the relationship with infrequent visitation. Kurdek et al. interpreted that finding to indicate that diminished contact might reduce hopes of reconciliation and increase awareness of parental incompatibility. One additional possibility is the reduced level of conflict that occurs with rare contacts. Bloom, Hodges, and Caldwell (1983) indicated that parents are considerably angrier post-divorce than nonparents (couples without children). While the Kurdek et al. (1981) study did not co-vary parental hostility in these analyses, it may be the case that infrequent visitation reduced such conflict. Another possibility is that older children are better adjusted *and,* with adolescence, visit less with the noncustodial parent.

Wallerstein and Kelly (1980c) provided information about adjustment levels in their five year follow-up. Some of their statistics are quite sobering. Five years later, 40 percent had poor relationships with their fathers and 25 percent had poor relationships with their mothers. There was no longer any age effect of divorce. Children doing well came from families with low parent conflict, good quality of parenting, *regular* visitation (in contrast to the findings of the Kurdek et al. (1981) study) absence of feelings of rejection by the noncustodial parent, personality strengths, a supportive network, and the absence of anger and depression. They reported that it was not possible to predict postdivorce functioning based on knowledge of predivorce functioning. In their sample, 37 percent were characterized as moderately to severely depressed. Postdivorce visitation was very important to the child and a good father-child relationship predicted high self-esteem. It should be noted that demonstrating cause and effect is extremely difficult in child development. It may be that fathers can maintain relationships with children who are happier with themselves. They reported that best adjustment for girls 5 to 12 years of age occurred when there was low conflict at home, the mother was not lonely, and they had good peer relationships. Younger girls were vulnerable to psychologically disturbed mothers. Older adolescent boys and girls were affected by the psychological intactness of the father. One of the more distressing statistics provided by Wallerstein et al. (1980c) is the finding that 80 percent of the children had not been provided with adequate explanation or assurance of their continued care after the separation and divorce.

Regardless of the age of the child (except for infants) parents should be encouraged to provide their child with some explanation of the divorce, information about what is going to happen in term of living space, when visitation is going to occur, how holidays are going to be arranged and what the future is going to look like. In addition, for parents with the resources for interpersonal skills, the parents should be urged to encourage their children to talk about the divorce and to ask questions.

One study looked at reaction to separation over a five year period. In a longitudinal study an ethnically mixed New York City sample of 1034 families were evaluated for the effects of marital disruption as reported by the mother (Rickel and Langner, 1985). From 25 to 50 percent of the subsamples had experienced marital disruption. When marital separation had originally occurred was not reported. At the time of the original assessment, children from fatherless homes as compared to children from intact homes were characterized as having greater levels of: the Underdemanding Scale (significant for Hispanics), Delinquency, Total Impairment, and Total Symptoms. On nine scales, presence of a surrogate father (a boy friend or stepfather) in divorced homes predicted more pathology than divorced or intact. Five years later, the negative effect of a surrogate father had largely disappeared as had the effect of father absence. At the five year evaluation, father absence led to greater reports of delinquency than father surrogate families which in turn were greater than reports for intact families. Rickel and Langner suggested that a presence of surrogate father might be initially disruptive, but the effect would seem to diminish over time (but not disappear altogether).

Ten Years Post Divorce

Wallerstein (1984) provided a report of a 10-year follow-up of the 30 children who were between the ages of 2½ and 6 at the point of the original study. These 30 children, 14 boys and 16 girls, were part of the 34 preschool children in the original study. Custody had been found to be quite stable over the 10 years. Of the 30 children, 90 percent had remained in the custody of their mothers. Over half were living in remarriage homes, usually occurring within three years of the breakup. Three children had experience a second divorce by the custodial parent. Six children had had some legal problems. One-third lived within an hour's drive of their father, revealing a surprising stability in geographic mobility, a result that may have occurred as a function of the counseling program. Of the remaining, many fathers had moved some distance, with half of the total sample of fathers out-of-state.

Most of the children claimed no memories of the predivorce family. Almost none of the children remembered their emotional reactions to the divorce. No child remembered being frightened even though this feeling was the most common response at the time. These children who were preschool at the time of the divorce did not carry painful memories of the divorce. This lack of memories was in sharp contrast to the reaction of older children who reported vivid memories of the separation and their pain.

The follow-up of preschool children 10 years later indicated that these children were not preoccupied with the reasons for the divorce and few had clear ideas of why the divorce occurred. Few children were caught up in the bitterness between the parents.

While the children were not caught up in the memories of the pain of the divorce experience, over half of them still talked wistfully of life in the intact family. One-quarter disapproved of divorce. About half still had reconciliation fantasies, although these fantasies were seldom seen as realistic.

Over half of the children had close, trusting, open relationships with their mothers. Many children appreciated their mothers for how hard it was to be a single parent. Almost all children were aware of economic issues. A subgroup of children were angry at the mother and felt that she was not physically or emotionally available.

In terms of relationships with the fathers, all but one child continued to value the father. This valuing was independent of how much visitation occurred. The angriest children were those who had experienced severe economic deprivation as a result of failure on the part of the father to pay child support that he could afford.

In a speech including data not yet published, Wallerstein (1983) reported on additional information on the 10-year follow-up of their research participants age 2 to 18. There had been no increase in delinquency, school dropouts, or abortions. Only two children were on welfare (again indicating that the population studied was relatively affluent).

Fine, Moreland, and Schwebel (1983) obtained data from 100 introductory psychology students who had experienced the divorce of their parents seven or more years previously and compared the answers to self-reports questionnaires with 141 students from continuously intact families. The average time since divorce was 10 years. They found that young adults from divorced families perceived the relationship with fathers and mothers less positively than did participants from intact families. Girls from both types of families perceived their relationship with mothers more positively than did boys. By seven years postdivorce, there was no relationship between age at time of divorce and any dependent measures. Perceived predivorce father-child and mother-child relationships were predictive of the current perceived parent-child relationship. Since the predivorce relationship was retrospective, it is not possible to determine the degree to which the present relationship colored the memory of predivorce quality.

In this study, there was no indication that the parent-child relationships were unhealthy. Indeed, participants from divorced families rated their relationships with their parents as essentially average in quality (participants from intact families did rate their relationships as above average).

Factors that were seen as reducing the negative impact of divorce on the father-child relationship, postdivorce, were the perception of a positive predivorce family life, a higher quality predivorce father-child relationship, parents who had more frequent contact with one another (in contrast to the Kurdek et al., 1981, study), and higher socioeconomic status. Factors that improved the relationship between the mother and children of divorce were a more positive perception of the predivorce mother-child relationship, better adjustment of the participants at the time of the divorce, and parents who maintained a higher quality relationship after the divorce.

Vess, Schwebel, and Moreland (1983) evaluated the effects of divorce on sex role development for college students. Students ($N = 84$) who had experienced the divorce of parents prior to age 10 were compared to students from intact homes ($N = 135$). There were no overall differences in the two groups in sex role development. Surprisingly, boys with fathers who left before age five were more masculine and had fewer feminine traits than boys whose fathers left later. Girls with earlier separation were also more feminine. For girls, high postdivorce conflict was related to more feminine behavior. These results are in a different direction than much of the research on single parent homes and difficult to interpret.

Wallerstein, in a speech (Conference on divorce, fall, 1983) enlarging on the 10-year follow up (Wallerstein and Kelly, 1984) reported that those girls who were 10 to 18 in the original study and now were 20 to 28 had a subgroup that were cohabiting with men who were often significantly older. There was no comparable group among the boys.

Mitchel (1983), in evaluating 50 Scottish late adolescents who had experienced the separation and divorce of parents during latency, (7 to 13 years of age), found that the majority had not been given any explanation as to the reason for the divorce, even several years later. Most were upset by the separation, but some hid the response from the custodial parent. Anger was a common response against both parents. Fourteen percent had changes in custody (eight times for one girl). Few of the teenagers accepted a parent's new partner as a stepparent, a common finding for remarriage and adolescents.

It is likely that children of both sexes need a warm intimate relationship with adults of both sexes, for self-esteem, normal sex role development, and normal adult sexuality. While a friend of the family or relative can perform that role, Big Brothers or Big Sisters can also facilitate that learning.

Hetherington (1972) investigated the behavior of adolescent girls who had lost fathers at an earlier age as a function of death or divorce and compared them to a matched group of teenage girls from intact families. The interviewer was a young adult male. Girls who had lost their fathers by death sat as far away from the interviewer as they could get. Girls from intact families sat a middle distance from the interview and girls who had lost their fathers through divorce sat as close to the interviewer as possible, knees almost touching. The interview data from the girls and mothers confirmed the same view. Girls who had lost their fathers by death dated less and seemed frightened of men. Girls who had lost their fathers by divorce dated more often and were more sexually active. It is as if the girls who had lost their father by divorce were using sexuality to regain a relationship with a man.

Slater, Stewart, and Linn (1983) looked at 217 adolescents, an average age of 16.6 years old. About one-third had come from divorced homes. Boys from divorced homes had better self-concepts and better perceptions of family environment than boys from intact homes. For girls, the opposite findings were obtained. If parents were divorced, the family was seen as having more control, more conflict, and more achievement orientation than was true if the parents were not divorced. Boys then seemed to have a relatively positive view of the divorced home and girls a relatively negative view.

Adult Adjustment with Childhood Divorce

Chess, Thomas, Korn, Mittelman, and Cohen (1983) reported on data from the New York Longitudinal Study for 132 subjects (from intacted and separated homes) from 87 middle and upper middle class families that had been followed from early childhood to 18 to 22 years of age. Of the 132 young adults, 35 experienced permanent separation of parents, most leading to divorce. The other families remained intact. Separations had occurred before 5 years of age for 10, between 9 and 13 for 10, and between 14 and 19 for 11. There had been two maternal and nine paternal deaths.

Consistent with the other research found in this chapter, they found that parental conflict at age three years was correlated with young adult adaptation ($r = .28$, $p < .01$), although this study is the first that indicated that a relationship may exist over such a large numbers of years. Surprisingly, they found that neither separation, divorce, or parental death were related to adult adjustment. The death-related results have to be taken with caution given the small number of death-related families. The sex of the child did not affect the correlations obtained. There was also no relationship between age of separation and later young adult adjustment. In an additional report on the same data base, Thomas and Chess (1984) noted that difficult temperament at age 3 also predicted adult adjustment at about the same level ($r = .29$) as did parental conflict.

How can one reconcile the absence of findings in this study with other evidence previously discussed (and in research that follows) that divorce does have long-term effects? Since there is evidence in the following section that economics is a crucial variable, it should be noted that the New York Longitudinal Study was based on a relatively affluent population and the availability of such resources may offset any aversive consequences of separation and divorce.

Langner (Adams, 1984) tracked 75 children of divorce and 125 children of intact families for 16 years. The effects of race and social class were controlled, a relative rarity in this area of research. As young adults, the two groups were found to have the same rates of depression and marital troubles. Adults whose parents had not separated had *twice* the arrest rate of adults who parents had divorced—certainly data at odds with the expectation of an increase in delinquency with divorce that some researchers have had in the past.

If parental divorce occurs by 16 years of age, there is a greater risk for divorce in adult life. Glenn and Shelton (1983) found that the divorce and separation rate for adult women whose parents divorced during their childhood was almost two-thirds higher than for women with intact childhood homes.

Several studies looked at the adjustment of college students when divorce occurred during adolescence. Raschke (1977) evaluated family structure and social and personal adjustment in 207 college students from colleges in an urban area in the southeastern United States. Family structure (i.e., intact versus single parent versus remarried) was not related to social and personal adjustment. For students from intact and single parent families (mostly divorced families), if the student was happy while growing up, then adjustment tended to be high. Age at which divorce or death of parent occurred was not related to college age adjustment.

Gregory (1965) evaluated all students admitted as freshmen over a five-year period at Carleton College in Northfield, Minnesota. The study included 127 students who had had a previous loss of a parent through divorce (41) or death (86). He then matched these students by gender and time of entry with a group of students from intact families. The low percentage of loss by divorce is typical of studies done in the 1950s and 1960s. Students from divorced families had consulted a college psychiatrist significantly more often than had students from intact families. There was no differences in use of counseling services for students who had lost a parent by death as compared to divorce, as a function of the gender of parent lost, or whether loss had occurred prior to or after age 10.

Farber, Felner, and Primavera (1985) obtained a wide range of measures for 65 late adolescents ranging in age from 17 to 23 who had experienced the divorce of their parents after the age of 12. Measures of adjustment (the State-Trait Anxiety Index, the Zuckerman Multiple Affect Adjective Checklist and the Tennessee Self-Concept Scale), demographic information, the Coping Response Repertoire, the Survey of Social Support, Hassles of Divorce Survey, and the Family Environment Scale were all obtained. The participants were students enrolled in an introductory psychology class at Northwestern University. In spite of claims that the full range of socioeconomic levels were represented, the question must be raised about potential biases in the sample since only college students were involved.

Adolescents of divorce in college who lived farther from home were more anxious, depressed, and hostile that adolescents of divorce living closer to home. Women were more depressed than men. Greater state anxiety (how anxious do you feel right now?) was present for adolescents whose parents had been separated for shorter periods of time.

Using self-blame was a consistent predictor of adjustment. Adolescents who more frequently blamed and criticized themselves were also more anxious, depressed, and hostile. High levels of anxiety were also related to denial of seriousness of the situation and seeking of support. Participants who rated their family as less cohesive and more conflict filled were also reporting more anxiety. Those who reported higher levels of stress related to divorce and change in the family were more anxious, depressed, and hostile. The authors concluded that the postdivorce environment was the most consistent predictor of postdivorce adjustment for adolescents.

Booth, Brinkerhoff, and White (1984) looked at the impact of childhood divorce on the courtship of 365 college students. Parental divorce was related to a slightly greater increase in courtship activity. If there was acrimony during and after the divorce, the courtship behavior was even more frequent. If the custodial parent remained single, courtship behavior was more frequent than if the custodial parent remarried. The authors interpreted the findings as reflecting the modeling of parental behavior. The perceived quality of courtship relationships was poorer if there was postdivorce conflict and if there was a decline in parent-child relationships postdivorce as compared to no conflict and continued good relationships. Women were more likely to be cohabiting if there was postdivorce conflict or if there was poor parent child (mother or father) relationships. The age during childhood when the divorce of parents occurred had no effect on courtship behavior.

Several other studies have looked at adult dating and marriage behavior as a function of childhood divorce. Kulka and Weingarten (1979) reported that adults from childhood homes of divorce were less likely to marry than adults from other homes. In contrast, according to Hepworth, Ryder, and Dreyer (1984), divorce of parents was related to accelerated courtship. The death of a parent also led to accelerated courtship, but there was a greater tendency to avoid intimacy. With death of parent in childhood, the number of sexual partners was least. With childhood divorce of parents, there was a greater number of sexual partners than for other groups. Adults whose parents stayed together were in the middle in terms of sexual behavior. These results are quite similar to Hetherington's (1972) and Wallerstein et al. (1980c) research on the effect of divorce on adolescents.

Schooler (1972) analyzed the interview material for 3101 civilian employed men interviewed by the National Opinion Research Center in 1964. The responses of men whose parents had divorced or separated before the men were 16, men who had lost a parent by death, and men whose parents remained married were compared. Men who were from divorced homes were, in adult life, more anxious, more distrustful, and less cognitively flexible. The scores were poorest on these dimensions when there were no adult males in the household. If the men had lost a parent by death, they were less cognitively flexible, more authoritarian, less receptive to innovation, less anxious, more concerned with extrinsic as opposed to intrinsic job values, and less likely to make intellectual demands on their use of time. Once again the research indicates that death of a parent and loss of a parent through divorce have very different outcomes.

Grossman, Shea, and Adams (1980) compared 33 college students of divorce with 261 students from intact families on measures of ego identity. Almost all of the students of divorce had experienced divorce between the ages of three and seven. In that study, no differences in ego identity as a function of marital status of parents were obtained. In fact male students who had experienced divorce were higher in identity scores than students from intact families. When the mother had remarried, there were no differences in comparison with students who were from intact families. The higher ego identity scores for males of divorce is difficult to interpret. While one could argue that divorce can strengthen coping processes, males typically are found to have more, not less, trouble. The authors noted that the data indicates that at least for their measures, there was no evidence that negative effects of divorce continue into young adulthood.

OTHER LONG-TERM PROBLEM OUTCOMES
FOR CHILDREN OF DIVORCE

One of the interesting phenomena in the literature on the effects of separation and divorce on child development concerns the likelihood that certain undesirable outcomes such as delinquency, serious academic problems, depression, and suicide are increased as a function of divorce. The literature and clinical experience previously reviewed in this chapter have not indicated that these three outcomes are common. While increases in aggression are mentioned, no researcher has indicated that delinquency was a frequent outcome. While drops in school performance for a year or so has been noted for children in elementary school, increases in drop-out, academic failures, and chronic school discipline problems have not been mentioned by investigators. Wallerstein and Kelly (1980) noted that depression was common for children five years after the divorce, but no mention of increase in suicide rates was made. Yet when one reads the research and theoretical literature in each of these areas, there are numerous references to "broken homes" and the effect of single parent families on suicide and delinquency.

Why do the two literatures not overlap in terms of understanding the effect of separation and divorce on children? First, there is a problem of definition of populations. Broken homes and single parent families are not synonymous with separation and divorce. A family can be a single parent family for a variety of reasons including the decision not to marry, abandonment, death of parent, or prolonged work-related separations, such as in the military. Each of these types of single parent households is likely to have its own set of developmental tasks to solve. Second, there is a problem of base-rates. While suicide may be a relatively rare event in terms of absolute numbers for children, it is a common cause of death for children. The frequency may be too small to show up in the small sample sizes typically used in research on divorce and children. The question of whether the risk of suicide increases for the children who experienced the divorce of their parents remains.

Finally, and perhaps most important, the prior research is based on correlations. Any time correlations are used to prove a point of causation, one has to be cautious about interpretation. It is always possible that a third variable "caused" or interacted with both correlated variables to lead to the relationship. For example, aggression in the child may be increased by having parents who fight frequently. The separation and divorce are more likely with fighting parents, but the separation and divorce may not, in itself, increase the aggression at all. As will be discussed in some detail, economics tend to be highly correlated with marital status and economics is a powerful predictor of many problem behaviors. Evidence for each of these problem areas, delinquency, poor academic performance, and suicide will be discussed in the following sections.

Delinquency and Divorce

For a long time, there has been an assumption in the literature that broken homes cause delinquency, dating back to the Cambridge-Somerville study (Glueck and Glueck, 1950). In none of this research was a differentiation made about the cause of single parenting and economics was not controlled. No studies were found that looked at delinquency with the reason for single parenting taken into account. Since this research is based on single parenting rather than divorce, the research will be discussed in Chapter 8 on single-parenting. In summary of that research, it would seem that family type accounts for a trivial amount of the variance in delinquency. Economics plays a major role.

School Performance

It has also been assumed for a long time that separation and divorce were major causes of academic problems, in terms of poor grades, poor school attendance, greater discipline problems, and greater likelihood of dropping out. As with the research on delinquency, research on divorce and school performance has been characterized by poor design.

One extensive study of 18,000 elementary and secondary school children in 14 states was conducted by the National Association of Elementary School Principals (NAESP) and the Institute for Development of Educational Activities (IDEA) (Evans and Neel, 1980; NAESP, 1980). The study looked at single parent versus two parent families. At the primary level, 38 percent of the one parent elementary school children were low achievers as compared to only 24 percent of two parent children. At the secondary level, of the one parent children, 34 percent were low achievers as compared to 23 percent of two parent children. One parent students were more likely to be late to school, truant, and receive disciplinary action than were children from two parent families. At the secondary level, three times as many single parent children were expelled as children from two parent families. Children from single parent families were twice as likely to drop out of school as children from two parent families. While the study noted that one parent families were much more likely than two parent families to have low income, the measure of low income was admittedly crude and it was not used to look at the role of income in the data. The report suggested that schools establish a recordkeeping system to keep track of changes in students' family status.

This report, which has considerable status given its prestigious sponsors, has been criticized by the National Committee for Citizens in Education (American Personnel and Guidance Association Guidepost, 1980). This committee and its spokesperson, Phyllis L. Clay, noted that the report was misleading in several ways. Data were limited to school records, which may be self-perpetuating in terms of myths. Correlation was interpreted as cause. Reduced income, higher mobility, and lower teacher expectations may all play a role in the relationship. Finally, the interpretation of the statistics may be misleading. While three times as many single parent children were suspended from school, this statistic referred to only 11 children—only one-sixteenth of one percent of the single parent elementary school children in the study.

In fairness to the original report, recognition of the small numbers was given and awareness of the role of economics was evident. Ourth (1980) in communicating the NAESP report to schools noted that a stigma is often attached to separation and divorce. He also questioned whether the worst is automatically expected of a child whose parents have separated. Perhaps one problem with the NAESP report is that when the media reported on the research results they tended to omit such caveats. Two years later, Ourth and Zakariya (1982) noted that scare headlines such as "Kids from Broken Homes Fare Poorly in Schoolwork," did not take into account the danger of labels and stereotypes.

In a follow-up analysis of the same data, Zakariya (1982) summarized the work of Wayne A. Barton on the effect of economics (as crudely measured by participation in subsidized school lunch and Title I programs). With this crude measure of economics, one parent children constituted 41 percent of the lower income group while making up only 17.5 percent of the total sample. Family income and sex of the student had a greater effect on achievement rank than whether the child came from a one or two parent home. Barton found, however, that when economics was held constant, two parent children still had higher achievement than one parent children. Follow-up analyses of 241 children showed that one parent children had higher rates of absenteeism, but no differences in discipline referral or suspension than for children of two parent families. In addition, Barton found that children from two-parent households had a more positive relationship with their teachers and a more positive attitude toward themselves and their peers than did children from one parent families. It is not clear from this second half of the study with new interview data, whether controlling for economic differences between the two groups would have made a difference in the interpretation of the results.

Teacher expectation of poorer performance for children of divorce may lead to teacher ratings that evaluate these children as poorer. There is ample evidence that teacher expectation affects how much the child will learn.

Santrock and Tracy (1978) showed 30 teachers a videotape on the social behavior of an eight-year-old boy. Half of the teachers were told that he came from a divorced home and half were told that he came from an intact home. Teachers rated the child perceived as from a divorced home as less happy, with poorer social adjustment, and poorer coping with stress than the child perceived as coming from an intact home. Kellam (1977) also found that teachers rating of children social adaptation could be predicted from knowledge of the child's family background. Since single parent status is highly correlated with income, background, and familial marital status both lead to teacher expectation of poor school performance.

While the aforementioned research argues that little is known about school performance and family marital status, there is some research that indicates that children of divorce do have more problems in school. Shinn (1978) reviewed 54 studies on academic performance and single parent families. Of these studies, 28 were judged adequate in terms of methodology. Of these 28, 16 showed some detrimental effects of father absence, 9 found no effects, and 3 found mixed or positive effects. Children from single parent families were an average of 1.6 years behind in achievement and about .9 standard deviation units lower in IQ. Shinn noted that financial hardship, high levels of anxiety, and low level of parent-child interaction were important causes of poor academic performance for children in single-parent families.

Given evidence that financial hardship, anxiety, and low levels of parent-child interaction may play a causative role in poor academic performance for children of divorce, the mental health professional should encourage child-support payments, work to reduce anxiety in the child, and help the family determine how to increase the quantity and quality of parent-child interactions.

The most carefully done study investigating the effects of divorce on academic performance was done by Guidubaldi, Cleminshaw, Perry, and Mcloughlin (1983). They obtained a sample of 341 children from divorce homes and 358 children from intact homes, matched on age, sex, and school. Children were randomly selected from the school. IQ and socioeconomic variables were controlled statistically. Two first graders, two third graders and two fifth graders were selected from each school. Extensive differences between children from divorce and intact homes were obtained, always favoring the children from intact homes. Children from intact homes were better on 14 of the 16 classroom behavior ratings, were absent less often, had higher peer popularity rating according to parent and teacher, had higher internal locus of control, and had higher full scale IQ's and Wide Range Achievement Test reading and spelling scores. Grades in reading and mathematics were higher. Children from intact homes were less likely to repeat a school grade. Even when socioeconomic status was removed statistically, the relationships remained.

Boys from divorced families were particularly likely to have difficulties with greater behavioral, social, and academic difficulties in comparison to girls from divorced families and boys from intact families. Girls from divorced families were found to have greater difficulty in very few areas, suggesting little divorce-related maladjustment. Older children of divorce were also more likely to have difficulties as compared to younger children.

Children of divorce who had gained a stepfather in early childhood were not handicapped in cognitive functioning. If there was no father substitute, then there was some cognitive deficit. Statistical control of economic factors was not rigorous, since other economically-related variables could have some impact (for example, drop in income may be more important than absolute income). This study, however, does suggest that children of divorce are at risk for problems in school.

When carefully controlled studies are performed, school performance would seem to be affected by parental separation and divorce. Children may need extra emotional support, psychotherapy, structure, and tutoring to avoid reduced academic performance.

My own clinical work in Boulder, Colorado found a high level of referrals made for boys in the seventh grade, a transition year from elementary to junior high. These boys from homes of divorce had a great deal of difficulty with the increased academic demands, greater level of homework, increase emotional distance of the teachers, and greater temptations of alcohol and drugs.

More discussion on the effects of single parenting and child performance in school can be found in Chapter 8 on single parenting. That chapter also will present evidence of differences in cognitive functioning as a function of having an absent parent.

Suicide

Adam, Lohrenz, and Harper (1973) looked at the suicidal ideation of 114 college students who had used campus mental health services, 50 from intact families, 35 who had lost a parent by death, and 29 who had lost a parent by divorce. In this sample, 50 percent of those who had lost parent by death and 41 percent of those who had lost a parent by divorce had had serious suicidal ideation, as compared to 10 percent of the controls. Of the 12 suicidal attempts in this populations, 10 of them were students of death or divorce.

Dorpat, Jackson, and Ripley (1965) reviewed 114 consecutive committed suicides and 121 attempted suicides in King County, Washington. This early study was still using "broken home" as a category, but divorce was the most common cause of parent loss. Of those who complete suicide, 50 percent were from parent loss homes, but 63.9 percent of those who attempted suicide were from parent loss homes. For those who attempted suicide, divorce of parents was the most common cause of parent loss. For those who completed suicide, death of parent was the most common cause of parent loss. In the attempted suicide group, 42.7 percent had lost both parents while 22.8 percent of completed suicides had lost both parents. The high percent of loss of both parents does make both of these groups atypical.

Crook and Raskin (1975) matched 115 depressed inpatients with a history of attempted suicide on age and sex with 115 nonsuicidal depressed patients and 285 normal subjects. The suicidal group had a significantly higher level of parental loss due to desertion, divorce, or separation prior to the age of 12 (the age set by the study) than the other two groups. Parental death was not related to suicide or depression.

Stein, Levy, and Glasberg (1974) evaluated 330 patients in a large metropolitan hospital. A total of 165 suicidal men and women were matched with a control group for hospitalization, age, sex, ethnic group, and time of admission. Childhood separation was defined as separation from a parent, parent surrogate, or sibling for six months or more prior to 17 years of age. While the definition of separation is broadly defined and did not test the effect of separation or divorce, per se, the results have potential implications in terms of the effects of divorce. White subjects who had made a suicidal attempt were more likely than those who had not made a suicidal attempt to have had a parental separation during early childhood (birth to 7 years of age) or during the entire childhood (birth to 17). Black men who had made suicidal attempts as compared to Black men without suicidal attempts were more likely to have had early parental separation. Black women who had made suicidal attempts were more likely to have had entire childhood parental separations as compared to Black women without suicidal attempts.

In summary, there is evidence that divorce in childhood may increase school problems independent of economics and may increase the likelihood of adult suicide, particularly suicide attempts, but delinquency would seem to be much more influenced by economic factors than by separation and divorce.

OTHER STRESSORS IN THE LIVES OF CHILDREN OF DIVORCE

One way of understanding the long-term effects of divorce on children is to consider what is happening in their lives during that time. Predivorce marital discord and the separation and divorce itself may be stressors that most children are capable of handling. The role of a few additional stressors was previously discussed in the context of research on children of particular ages. This section will focus on research on economic factors, research on family conflict, reconciliation, and repeated separations, research on the cumulative effects of stress, and, finally, the effects of quantity and quality of parenting.

Economics

There is substantial evidence that families of divorce are adversely affected in the economic area. Flynn (1984), citing recent government statistics, noted that the single parent family is the most significant new factor contributing to the nation's higher poverty level. Single parent families are mostly headed by women (90 percent of custody is mother custody), and women earn 59 cents for every dollar earned by men. Flynn noted that 75 percent of the poor in this country are women and children. Three years after divorce, only 19 percent of divorced fathers continue to pay child support payments. Even if support is paid, the amount of the award generally covers less than half the actual cost of raising a child. After divorce, the woman's income drops by 73 percent while the man's increases by 42 percent. Families of divorce and particularly mother-custody families, suffer financially. Even when the father has custody or does pay child support, the ability to pay for two households can not be done at the same level of income as one household.

Bane (1976) noted that female-headed families with children are considerably worse off economically than female-headed families without children. In 1974, 51.5 percent of all children under 18 in female-headed families and 61.4 percent of all children under 6 in female-headed families lived in families with incomes below the poverty line.

Research on preschool children (Hodges, Wechsler, and Ballantine, 1979) demonstrated that low income in children of divorce predicted maladjustment, while lower income was not related to adjustment problems for children who were from intact families in the same school as the children of divorce. A follow-up study using a new sample of preschool children (Hodges, Tierney, and Buchsbaum, 1984), found that perceived inadequacy of income and low total income predicted adjustment problems, independent of the parents' marital status. Rated inadequate income predicted greater withdrawal and anxiety-depression in preschool children. Since reduced quality of living is an almost universal consequence of divorce, it is not surprising that families of divorce are adversely affected by increased poverty.

The latter study also obtained an interaction between marital status of parent and economics; rated inadequacy of income interacted with marital status to predict level of anxiety in the preschool child. For children from intact families, rated adequacy of income had no effect on levels of anxiety-depression. For children of divorce with adequate income, the level of anxiety and depression was the same as for children of intact families. Children of divorce with families with rated inadequate income had substantially higher levels of anxiety-depression than the other three groups.

Desimone-Luis, O'Mahoney, and Hunt (1979) evaluated 25 children aged 7 to 13 whose parents were members of the Parents Without Partners. Parents filled out the Louisville Behavior Checklist. With that scale, five children were identified as deviant children. Of approximately 30 demographic variables, only economics predicted maladjustment. The parents of all five children who were classified as deviant reported a drop in income of at least 50 percent immediately following separation. For the 20 nondeviant children, only one-fourth had experienced a 50 percent drop in income. While based on a very small sample size, these differences were statistically significant. Of additional interest is the fact that the deviant children were all between the ages of 6 and 9, while the nondeviant children were likely to be between the ages of 10 and 13. These results suggest that economics play a role in maladjustment in children. However, the small sample limits generalizability of the findings.

Colletta (1979) also found major effects of economics. This study of 72 mothers of divorce looked at father absence, income, number of children, and sex of child. Low income mothers in single-parent homes made more demands of their children than did middle-income mothers, both for greater self-care and for obedience. Low income divorced mothers were less likely to help their children with tasks such as dressing. Thus, Colletta's data suggest that income levels might predict parenting styles that might affect children.

Herzog and Sudia (1973) argued, based on their review of the literature, that the negative effects of father absence on child development would be eliminated if the economic deprivation of divorce were eliminated. Blechman (1982) reviewed the literature on single parenting and the risk for maladjustment for the child. This review of the literature presented a convincing argument that prior research has so many methodological flaws, it was difficult to evaluate the effect of single parenting, independent of many other correlated and potentially confounding variables. Economic factors in particular tended to be uncontrolled. The greater frequency of identified problems in families of divorce may be due to the reduced resources of these families for solving family problems in a nonlegal manner. Even when matching for socioeconomic status was used, samples were not comparable. Matching families by income necessarily selects families from the lower end of the income range in intact families and in the upper end of the income range for families of divorce. Blanchard and Biller (1971) found only 11 income-matched children from divorced and intact families from a pool of 297 children.

Thus, the behavioral problems of divorce may in part be a side effect of the economic conditions of divorce. Jauch (1977) noted that the poverty in homes of divorce may lead to child abuse, child neglect, delinquency, and child pathology, rather than divorce per se causing these problems.

Given the strong evidence that drop in income and in standard of living may play a major role in adjustment problems in children, helping professionals should do everything they can to encourage child support payments and other economic supports to families of divorce.

Parental Conflict

Goode (1965) reported that 48 percent of the women in the sample felt that their former spouses should be punished for their behavior. These feelings reduced little in intensity over time. Cline and Westman (1971) in an early article on the impact of divorce on children, reviewed 105 consecutive divorces in the Dane County, Wisconsin Family Court over a two-year period. Thirty-one percent (33 cases) had repeated conflicts requiring from 2 to 10 court interactions. Money and child rearing were equally represented as the basis for these conflicts. Eighteen of the 33 couples were still involving in predivorce conflicts. Six of the couples had maintained some amorous contact. Such continued sexual contact after divorce is a not uncommon phenomena and reflects the strong ambivalence common in divorcing couples.

Children will deliberately work to force parents to interact in order to facilitate a reconciliation. Children wishing reconciliation will become most anxious when parents do not interact. Even hostile interactions are less anxiety provoking than silence. One child asked his mother, "Is it O.K. to call my dad's new girl friend mother, too?" The mother, who had not talked to her ex-spouse in six months, was on the phone in seconds, complaining that he was trying to eliminate her role as mother. The mother was asked what her son expected her to feel in response to his question. The question was probably asked in order to get the mother to call her ex-spouse. Indeed, it was likely that he was anxious about his father's new relationship and wanted to get his parents talking again. This case history is an excellent example of the importance of encouraging parents to keep the children out of the middle even when children place themselves there. The mother's response should be that what the son called the woman at his father's house was between his father and himself, but that she did not want to ever hear the other woman described as "mom."

Mental health professionals should watch out for child-instigated conflicts between parents. The child may need active encouragement to stay out of parent fights. The child may also need strongly supported information that reconciliation is not going to occur (if, indeed, this information is correct), in order to discourage efforts on the part of the child to force contact. Parents can reduce such efforts by interpreting the behavior to the child and refusing to be baited by the provocative behavior (easier suggested than acted on).

Almost all clinicians and researchers agree that interparental conflict has adverse effects on child development. Jacobson (1979) evaluated children from ages 3 to 13 in 30 families and looked at the amount of hostility that occurred between the custodial mother and ex-spouse. Jacobson found that for the preschool children ($n = 21$), interparental hostility preseparation predicted higher levels of aggression, fearfulness, and inhibition in the child postseparation.

Porter and O'Leary (1980) evaluated 64 children who had been referred to a child psychological unit. Overt marital hostility was correlated with many behavior problems in boys, but not in girls. They raised the possibilities that parents may be more protective of girls, avoiding shouting in their presence. In addition, girls may cope better with stress than boys. For example, girls in the study came from more discordant marriages than boys, suggesting that more marital hostility did not lead to referral for girls.

Hansen (1982) looked at the effects of interparental conflict on preschool children's adjustment to divorce. In this study, 36 preschool children in mother-custody homes were evaluated. The mothers provided information concerning the quality and quantity of interparental conflict. Aggression was divided into two categories, aggressive anger (yelling, throwing things, name calling, pushing and shoving, and slapping and hitting) and nonaggressive anger (focusing on feelings, logic, and old issues and using facial expressions, expressing anger in a calm voice). Higher levels of aggressive expression of anger after the divorce correlated with increased adjustment difficulties at home, but less difficulties at school. Higher levels of nonaggressive expression of anger between parents was related to a greater amount of nonaggressive discipline measures used on the child, a greater amount of affection the mother reported giving to the child, and a reduction in the level of conflict between the mother and child.

Hansen found that conflict between parents over child-oriented and non-child-oriented issues had an adverse effect on child adjustment. Conflict over visitation was correlated with higher levels of anxiety in the child. Hansen also found that the content of the interparental conflict predicted child adjustment problems, but perhaps the problems themselves created the child's adjustment problems, rather than the conflict over the problem. Conflict over drinking, drug abuse, and finances all predicted problems in the preschool children.

Tierney (1983), also looked at preschool children of divorce. Here, the primary research focused on visitation patterns, but also evaluated conflict between parents. The sample included 67 preschool children. Total conflict between parents as reported by the mother correlated significantly, although not strongly ($r = .26$, $df = 55$, $p < .05$) with the preschool child's scores on the Louisville Behavior Checklist as reported by the mother. Conflict as reported by the father was much more related to Louisville Behavior Checklist scores, $r = .48$, $df = 28$, $p < .01$. The relationship with conflict over visitation followed the same pattern, .28 ($p < .05$) if conflict was reported by the mother and .57 ($p < .001$) if level of conflict was reported by the father. Specific areas of maladjustment in the child as a function of interparental conflict included: school and cognitive problems, irritability, immaturity, aggression, hyperactivity, sensitivity, and inhibition.

Johnston, Campbell, and Mayes (1985) looked at age-specific distress of 44 children aged 6 to 12, who were involved in parental postseparation disputes over custody. This sample had a high level of conflict, with 88 percent of parents physically aggressive toward one another. Behaviors had ranged from slapping, pushing, spitting, biting, and throwing objects to threatening with guns and knives. These events occurred on the average of once a month. Children had witnessed more than half of the abusive incidents.

All the children were acutely distressed by the fighting and very frightened of violence. Younger latency (6 to 8 year olds) tended to be submissive. Many tried to stop the fight. About half of the older children took sides in the fighting. Many children tried to avoid the fighting by leaving. One-fourth of the children responded with aggression. The authors felt that 40 percent were passive in their adaptation and 40 percent merged with the angry parent and were enmeshed in the dispute. The children often worked at being good, conforming, and patient.

In another report on the same data (Johnston, Gonzalez, and Campbell, 1985), the following variables predicted maladjustment in the child: role reversal of the child with the father, total disagreements between parents, and complaints by parents of the child's involvement in the dispute.

Emery (1982), in an excellent review of the relationship between interparental conflict and children of divorce, noted that there is a relationship between discord in intact marriages and severity or frequency of behavior problems in children. However, many of these studies were methodologically flawed. The review noted that a stronger association between marital discord and child adjustment are found in clinic samples as opposed to nonclinical samples. While Blechman (1982), as previously noted, believed that economics was the uncontrolled variable linking divorce and child maladjustment, Emery suggested that interparental conflict was the principal explanation for an association between divorce and childhood adjustment problems. Emery noted that several researchers found that children from divorced but conflict-free homes were less likely to have problems than were children from conflictual, nondivorced homes. One longitudinal study found that many of the problems in children from broken homes were present before the separation occurred.

Zill (cited in Adams, 1984), in a national survey of 1423 children found that children of divorce had fewer behavioral problems than children from intact families who had chronic conflict. Children from 12 to 16 who lived with fighting parents were one-and-a-half times more likely to be antisocial, including lying and bullying, than children living with a divorced parent.

This author has treated aggressive boys from conflict-filled families by working on the parents' conflict rather than the child's anger. Helping angry parents to communicate is a major accomplishment. Facilitating communication and reducing conflict through couple counseling can eliminate adjustment problems in children, even without the child ever being seen in therapy.

A significant percentage (but less than half) of parents in intense conflict can be convinced to reduce that conflict when it is demonstrated to them how it is hurting the children. Couple counseling can be effective in reducing interparental hostility and facilitate more adjusted behavior patterns in the children.

It is often useful in such couple counseling to bring step-parents or cohabiting mates into such counseling for three reasons: (1) these individuals often play a significant parenting role and need to be included in plans for the child; (2) the presence of the significant other can help a parent who is keeping the relationship alive through conflict to accept the divorce; and (3) the two parents can be reassured that the new person is not going to replace them in the parenting role. Particularly important in working with aggressive children with high levels of interparental conflict is to encourage the parents to get together on what shall be disciplined and to use a nonphysical form of punishment.

Any reduction in conflict is likely to be helpful. Any message to the child that the parents are trying to get together on rules or structure is likely to be of benefit. Even simple agreements on how much television watching is all right, what time bed time is to be, or what afternoon snacks are acceptable is likely to be viewed by the child as evidence of cooperation. Aggression levels are likely to decrease.

Reconciliation

The role of reconciliation has not been discussed frequently in the research or clinical literature. Clinicians have too frequently overlooked the impact of parents' reconciling, perhaps assuming that since children typically are wanting reconciliation, reconciliation was not a stressor. One 3-year-old child, for example, reacted relatively well to the parents' separation, but went to pieces after reconciliation. She cried frequently, showed extremely reactions to parental discord, and shadowed her parents everywhere. She now knew what she would feel if they separated again! Jacobson (1978b) found that if the divorce was characterized by previous parental separations, the child showed significantly more withdrawn and immature behavior. This research also supported the idea that repeated separations are very hard on children. One study with preschool children (Hodges, Tierney, and Buchsbaum, 1984), found that the total number of separations prior to divorce correlated .43 with ratings of dependency in the preschool child.

Repeated separations and reconciliations are very difficult for children. Encourage parents to stay in one state for a period of time and decide what they want to do. Parents who are truly ambivalent about divorce should consider staying together until deciding. If the conflict is so severe that chronic tension or danger of violence is present, separation may be healthier for the children (as might be true for divorce).

Abandonment

As previously mentioned, abandonment is a particularly difficult stress for children of separation and divorce. It is far more likely that fathers will abandon their children, although mother abandonment may be on the increase. Abandonment would seem to be more likely when there is minimal bonding between the abandoning parent and the children. Certainly the level of bonding between traditional fathers and infants tends to be poor in the United States. Even at the elementary school age, fathers spend only about 20 minutes per week in quality time with their children. As the feminist movement and increased androgyny in men increases shared child care (as reflected in increases in father custody and joint time custody), the rate of father abandonment should decrease. Traditionally, fathers have had instrumental roles involving discipline and wage earning. Only recently have they shown interest in birthing, early child care, and bonding.

Lack of bonding is only one reason for abandonment. Some parents find the sense of loss and pain so overwhelming that they avoid the children to reduce the sense of loss. Thus, one subgroup of abandoning parent is intensely bonded to their children, but are unable to tolerate the sense of loss that is generated with every separation. The bonding may be combined with dependency that intensifies the sense of loss or may be due to an inability or unwillingness to complete the mourning of the lost relationship.

One father asked this author whether it was best for the children for him to withdraw from parenting. The mother had remarried and the children liked the new stepfather. The mother would have preferred for the biological father to disappear from the scene so that she could reform a nuclear family (a common fantasy and not possible, as will be discussed in Chapter 9 on remarriage). The father said that he loved the children, but was willing to give up his need to be with them if the children would benefit. The clinician should always be careful with requests such as this, since the father may be signaling that he is engaged in harmful behavior with the children and wants to withdraw to reduce his guilt and protect the children. In this case, there was no evidence of such a dynamic and the father seemed to be genuinely attached to the children. My suggestion was that his children could accept love from more than one family. Their identity would always be connected in some way to their identification with him. Abandonment by him would be harmful to their self-esteem. He was very relieved at this advice.

Children are better off getting some of their needs met than none of their needs met, even if the partial satisfaction of needs leads them to wish for more. Abandonment should be strongly discouraged unless severe pathology exists and psychological and physical protection of the children are not possible.

A noncustodial parent may abandon the parenting role because the parents are engaged in an intense and bitter battle. Some parents find the rage at the other parent so noxious that avoidance of the whole family seems to be the only solution. Custodial parents have been effective in blocking (passively or actively) access to the children that noncustodial parents have given up.

Mental health professionals are seldom contacted by abandoning parents for help with reestablishing contact with the children. When abandonment is discovered in the context of therapy for other reasons, the professional might explore whether abandonment occurred because of prior scripts of abandonment, lack of bonding, excessive dependency needs, depression at the loss and incomplete mourning, or anger at the custodial parent. While it is likely to helpful to the child to encourage reengagement, the clinician must evaluate the probable impact on the parent.

Wallerstein and Kelly (1980c) reported that 9 percent of the 60 noncustodial parents of the 3 to 18 year olds ($N = 131$) in their sample were having no contact with the children. As mentioned previously, this low percentage may be due to the intervention program in which the parents and children participated. Fulton (1979) found a 28 percent abandonment rate in his sample of 419 parents. This rate was considerably higher than in the Wallerstein and Kelly study. Tierney (1983) in a sample of 67 preschool age children obtained an abandonment rate of 24 percent. Tierney suggested that this high rate might be due to the more tenuous nature of the bonding between fathers and children when children are at the preschool level.

Chapter 2 discussed the common experience of the child of abandonment. The children saw the abandonment as personal rejection, regardless of the actual motivation by the abandoning parent. In addition to this sense of rejection, the continued existence of the absent parent keeps the possibility of some day obtaining that love ever present. Tessman (1978) talked about the "searching behavior" of such abandoned children. They will look into the faces of strangers in shopping centers, looking for the abandoning parent. These children are often characterized by early abandonment and do not know what the absent parent even looks like, but they assume that instant recognition will be possible. One ten-year-old child rode all over town on his bicycle on the day his stepfather was to adopt him, in the hopes that he would see his biological father. He had not had contact with his father since he was 2 years of age. No one knew of the location of the father or had had contact with him since the divorce.

Another problem of abandonment is the possibility that the child will develop rescue fantasies to avoid the sense of rejection. "My father would be here, if he could. Circumstances prevent him from seeing me. If he were here, he would not make me go to bed at 10 o'clock. He would let me go to the rock concert." The custodial parent often feels unappreciated and resents the child's idealization of the abandoning parent. Attempts on the part of the custodial parent to tear down this fantasy is greeted with great resistance, since the child will be vulnerable to depression if acceptance of the abandonment occurs.

Rosenthal (1979) presented several case histories of children dealing with the sudden disappearance of a parent because of marital discord. Of the families that they worked with, 80 percent completed therapy and the children showed symptomatic improvement. After a two to three year follow-up, the children with interrupted therapy had severe learning and behavioral problems in school. The children showed sadness, longing for the absent parent, anger, and fear of loss of the other parent. The clinicians found that the relationship with the remaining parent was more important than the feelings about the absent parent in predicting adjustment in the child.

The child who experiences the abandonment by the noncustodial parent will need particular help in dealing with the blow to self-esteem. The child needs to be encouraged to interpret the abandonment as a problem of the noncustodial parent rather than due to the unloveability of the abandoned child. The child must also be encouraged to give up fantasies of rescue by the abandoning parent. In order to give up the fantasies, the child needs to have help in accepting the implied rejection.

The Effect of Cumulative Stress on Preschool Children of Divorce

Given the evidence of the research, not all preschool children are at risk for maladjustment as the result of the separation and divorce of parents. The evidence in the literature shows that economics and parental conflict affect adjustment to divorce. Hodges et al. decided to research what additional factors might predict which children were likely to have problems. It was predetermined that geographic mobility, low income, and young parents were likely variables that predicted risk (although the age of the mother did not hold up as a predictor in later research). Those findings led to two other related variables, (1) stress in the preschool child's and parents' life, and (2) the quality and quantity of parenting.

If geographic mobility and low income predict maladjustment in children of divorce, there are two likely pathways in which the effect occurs: (1) The child is directly affected by the stress on the family; and (2) The parents are so stressed that they are less available to the child for emotional and physical support. Hodges et al. (1984) looked at 44 boys and 46 girls, 30 from divorced families and 60 from intact families, in terms of the amount of stress on the child and custodial parent. Children from the two types of families did not differ in age of the child, age of parents, education of parents, or fathers' income. Divorced mothers were more likely to be employed than nondivorced mothers. In this study, divorced mothers were a mean of two-and-a-half years past the final separation that led to the divorce. Custodial mothers were asked to fill out a parents checklist of child behavior for the past month, a Child's Life Events Inventory (Coddington, 1972a, 1972b), which evaluated stress in the child's life for the past two years, and the parent's Life Events Inventory (Rahe, Meyer, Smith, Kjaer, and Holmes, 1964; Rahe, 1968), also reported for the past two years. Teachers at the children's preschools were asked to fill out a teacher child behavior checklist.

Total Parent Life Events correlated with Total Child Life Events, $r = .58$ $df = 88, p < .001$, indicating a high degree of overlap, which is not surprising given that the events were occurring in the same family. First, the ability of demographic indices of stress (geographic mobility, income, adequacy of income, and age of mother) to predict adjustment were investigated. Coming from a divorced home predicted greater distractability and more acting out. While marital status of parents did not predict other problems, there were other findings in which the demographic indices predicted problems, independent of the marital status of the parents. A greater number of moves predicted higher levels of aggression. Inadequate income predicted poor ability to stay on task, anxiety-depression, and total teacher rated maladjustment. Lower income was related to the child seen as more fearful and depressed. Older mothers (as compared to younger mothers in Hodges et al., 1979, study) had children with higher levels of poor task persistence and anxiety-depression.

It should be noted that while inadequate income and geographic mobility predicted maladjustment independent of marital status, families of divorce are more likely to have these stressors. In the Hodges, et al., study, families of divorce moved more often, had higher rated inadequacy of income, and had lower income than did intact families.

Mental health professional should be cautious about assuming that separation and divorce alone predicts maladjustment in preschool age children. Other stressors, particularly economic ones, may interact with divorce to predict problems. Separation and divorce leads to stressors that can cause problems independent of the stress of the separation, that is, lower income and geographic relocation.

The next question raised by the Hodges, et al. (1984) study was whether stressful life events in the life of the child or stress in the life of the parent was a more potent predictor of maladjustment problems in the child. In those analyses, parent life events accounted for most of the variance in explaining adjustment in preschool children as compared to other predictors. In no case did higher child life events predict adjustment better than did parent life events. High level of stress in the parents, independent of marital status, predicted dependency, poor ability to stay on tasks, and distractability in the child. These findings suggest that the stress on the parent may indeed have more effect on the child than does direct stress have on the child.

When type of stress was looked at to determine if desirable and undesirable stress made a difference or whether other kinds of losses predisposed children of divorce to adjustment problems, surprising results were obtained. There was no relationship between total undesirable life events and adjustment. Total desirable items (i.e., good things happening to the child) correlated -.40 (*df* = .27, *p* < .02) with acting out, indicating that the fewer desirable life events, the more the acting out toward parents. When type of stress was evaluated using Sandler and Ramsay's (1980) scales, only the Family Troubles Scale (reflecting economic problems and family arguments) predicted maladjustment, in terms of higher dependency. There was no evidence that prior losses predisposed the preschool child of divorce to greater levels of problems. Again the importance of economic factors is clear.

Clinicians should be aware that stress on the parent is more important than stress on the child in predicting adjustment in the child. Lack of positive events rather than greater number of negative events predicts maladjustment in the child of divorce.

Quantity and Quality of Parenting and Adjustment in Preschool Age Children of Divorce

In an analysis of the same population of study participants, Hodges et al. (1983) looked at quantity and quality of parenting. Mothers were asked to report on how often they gave one-half hour of direct, undivided attention to the child. By this very narrow definition of contact, quantity of contact with parents was unrelated to adjustment in children of divorce, while numerous relationships were found for children from intact families. There was no difference in time between mothers of divorce and mothers of intact families. For children of divorce, number of days per week that someone other than a parent cared for the child had a low to moderate correlation with the Anxious scale -.39, (*df* = 29, *p* < .02), indicating that there was less anxiety if the child spent more time with nonparents. This finding is intriguing, but since it was not predicted, caution should be exercised about its meaning. It is tempting to speculate that greater time in day care might reflect less time at home with an anxious parent. Visitation frequency was not correlated with any of the adjustment scales.

For quality of parent-child interaction and marital status, mothers in divorced homes described themselves at the same level of warmth and strictness as mothers in intact families. There were almost no differences in the use of different kinds of discipline (spanking, yelling, withdrawing privileges, affection for good behavior, use of guilt, or love withdrawal, and rewards of food, money, or special prizes). Parental warmth and permissiveness were correlated with a variety of child adjustment measures in both types of families. For both divorced and intact families, mothers' descriptions of themselves as less warm were related to descriptions of the child as having problems in misbehavior, being distractable, and generally being maladjusted at home. For both types of families, a less strict home life was correlated with the child seen as less anxious or fearful at home. Satisfaction with the relationships with the child and enjoyment of time with the child were related to a variety of adjustment measures. One should be cautious to assume cause and effect here. It is easier to enjoy a well-adjusted child, so the relationship is probably interactive rather than a simple cause and effect.

Remember that these children are over two years post-separation. There is considerable evidence that life tends to be quite chaotic for the child immediately after the divorce, with unpredictable feeding and bed times, disruption in routine and high parent unavailability.

SUMMARY

It is the context in which divorce occurs that determines whether separation and divorce adversely affect child development. For preschool children, cumulative stress on the parent of divorce predicted child adjustment better than stress on the child. Higher quality of parenting was related to good child adjustment regardless of type of family marital status (a relationship likely to be interactional). Economic factors such as low income, inadequate income, sharp drop in income, continued family conflict, prolonged separation, repeated separations and reconciliations, and total abandonment by the non-custodial parent are all factors that affect that context.

CHAPTER 4

Divorce Mediation: An Alternative to Custody Evaluation

Not one of the books on divorce, children of divorce, or child custody published before 1981 include mediation as a topic (Brown, 1982). Mediation as an alternative to custody disputes is clearly a very recent phenomena. The first formal private divorce and family mediation center was established by Coogler (1978), an attorney and family counselor, in 1974. He formed a national association, the Family Mediation Association. Another national organization, founded as the result of differences with Coogler's organization, is the Academy of Family Mediators (Brown, 1982). The Society of Professionals in Dispute Resolution is another national organization of people concerned with mediation and has a broader basis of membership with interest in helping conflicts in a wide variety of settings.

Reconciliation refers to the process of couples working out their differences in order to maintain their relationship. Conciliation is a method to help families either reconcile their differences or separate in the least destructive way (Irving, 1980). There is a general recognition that the adversarial court system is not well-suited for helping families resolve how to split up resources and how to protect the bonds between parents and children. Indeed, Brown (1982) argued that it is the worse possible approach to helping divorcing couples. The legal system has been slow to accept alternatives because the long history of trial law in the United States has guided procedure.

Divorce mediation in which parents work together with one or more mediators in as nonadversarial a climate as possible would seem to be one approach that would deemphasize conflict. In this model, the needs of both the parents and the children take precedence over blame. While there has been a great deal of excitement (at least in the nonlegal community) about this alternative model, there has been no research on whether the children are better adjusted or happier as a result of using this model as opposed to contested, court decided issues. Not surprisingly, the legal community has had concerns about mediation. One major concern has been whether the rights of each participant is best served by mediation. There is concern that mediation is practicing law by nontrained individuals. In addition, many lawyers have divorce cases as a major source of income and some lawyers have worried about whether mediation would result in a substantial reduction in income.

One major historical root for divorce in North America is the concept of fault. The adversarial system developed out of a history of requiring that the court find one person at fault for the divorce by "sinning" against the other. When no-fault divorce came into common use, the roots of finding one spouse at fault and "winning" over the other continued. Lawyers are enjoined to represent the interests of the client, not the family. Lawyers have been heard to say that if they do not get everything they can for their client, they are performing malpractice. Therefore, any strategy that increases the likelihood of a judge giving more resources or property or the children to one parent is fair game even if such a move is not in children's best interest or if the conflict so destroys the relationship between parents as to permanently affect their relationship. The adversarial relationship in court also implies that justice is best served when the lawyers on each side are of equal competence. Lawyers differ widely both in competence and style. When the parent with the most "competent" (vigorous and competitive and knowledgeable) lawyer wins the greater resources, the best interests of the child may not be served.

Irving (1980) felt that North America is the most litigation prone area in the world. Irving noted that Japan with a population about half of the United States has a population of lawyers that is about 3 percent of the number of lawyers in the United States. Restoring harmony rather than winning disputes characterizes the Japanese court orientation. Irving also noted that China has had an orientation toward mediation for centuries. Seldom do civil disputes ever reach the courts. The preference for using community mediation dates back to Confucius, whose teachings focused on preserving harmony and discouraging confrontation.

Mediation may be particularly needed in North American culture, because the culture has developed a style of handling disputes that may be harmful to the family of divorce.

In this chapter, the basic principles of mediation as outlined in the literature will be presented along with discussion of what little research there is on the effectiveness of mediation. Some of the concerns about mediation will also be outlined.

THE HISTORY OF MEDIATION IN WESTERN CULTURE

There are two major historical roots to mediation in Western culture. The first is religious in origin. Beth Din, the Jewish religious court, has a history of thousands of years and has had a major orientation toward conciliation between adversaries (Irving, 1980). As Irving noted, the Beth Din led to the Jewish Conciliation Board, founded in 1920. The purpose of the arbitration courts is to provide an impartial third party that can help mediate disagreements without using the civil courts. Brown (1982), in an extensive review of mediation history and principles, noted that early Quakers in the United State practiced mediation and arbitration. The Quaker arbitration and mediation sometimes included marital disruption.

The second, more modern historical root of mediation is in the area of negotiations. Mediation became a major way of handling disputes between management and labor. The same techniques could be used for disputes between marital partners getting a divorce.

The earliest conciliation service in North America was the Los Angeles County Conciliation Court which was started in 1939 (Irving, 1980). The purpose of this court was to preserve and promote family life, to reconcile families, and to provide amicable resolution to family controversy. Professional counselors began in California in 1954. For the next 20 years, an average of 1000 families a year were reconciled although 25 percent separated again within one year. Irving (1980) also noted that in the Toronto Family Court, 75 to 80 percent of families who were considering the court procedure, were able to settle their controversy through mediation. In 1981, California, maintaining its lead in innovations in the area of divorce and child welfare, passed a law that required that in every contested custody case, mediation must occur prior to the court hearing the case.

BASIC ASSUMPTIONS UNDERLYING MEDIATION

All mediation would seem to have similar foundations. Mediation attempts to provide a setting in which the couple can feel that the divorce does not require a win-lose battle. Each parent should feel that (1) his or her needs can be met, (2) the other person has needs too, and (3) the welfare of the children takes precedence over hurt, anger, and need for retaliation.

Girdner (1985a) noted that mediation is based on the assumption that the two parents have relatively equal power. Where the parents do not have equal power, there is a danger that agreement may come at the expense of fairness. The role of the mediator is to empower each participant to roughly an equal level so that relatively fair mediation can occur. Girdner noted that concern about women being less powerful in such circumstances has led some feminists groups to lobby against institutionalized mediation.

In cases in which passivity, dependence, acquiescence, or guilt leads one person in a mediation to give up power (and perhaps to have consistently given up power throughout the entire marriage), the mediator has to be particularly careful to empower that person to assume an equal right in the resolution.

Any arrangement that victimizes a member of the family should be unacceptable to the mediator. Thus, the mediator can refuse to accept agreements even where the parties have agreed (Brown, 1982). Brown cited an unpublished paper by Lohman in using a criteria of fairness saying that the bargain would be acceptable to the extent that each party would accept the reverse situation.

Girdner (1985a) suggested that the mediator set an example by avoiding talking about custody. Instead, Girdner suggested focusing on how the two families are going to parent two separate households.

Ricci (1985) discussed the distinction between entitlements and empowerments in balancing power. Entitlement refers to the belief in a natural or legal claim to something either by law or according to custom. Empowerment is the ability to exercise those claims. According to Ricci, the mediator must use power-balancing interventions to strengthen the weaker positions and to counteract dominant positions. Thus, the mediator should identify each person's entitlements and help them negotiate for their own best interests. Second, the mediator must objectively describe the pattern of interaction. Finally, the mediator must identify where and when to intervene.

Ricci described two potentially self-defeating patterns that women use in dealing with mediation. First, they may base entitlements on a role of peacemaker who is self-sacrificing and yielding to the husband's demands in order to have a harmonious relationship. Second, women who feel betrayed and thus feel "entitled" may demand rights that are more appropriate to the old "fault" divorce.

Ricci (1985) felt that it was useful to begin mediation by asking the couple to identify their greatest fears around mediation and to build assurance to reduce those fears and rebuild mutual trust. These traded assurances help reduce fears of manipulation and power plays. For example, the mother may work toward financial independence and the father may underwrite the majority of the cost for the planning toward that independence.

According to Brown (1982), mediation is based on five basic beliefs: (1) the availability of mutually acceptable solutions; (2) the desirability of mutually acceptable solutions; (3) that the other party should be valued and respected and has the right to be heard and understood; (4) superordinate goals that transcend special interests and are in the common good of the children and family; and (5) the fairness and integrity of the mediator.

Coogler's Structured Mediation

Coogler (1978) outlined four major areas of settlement in his structured mediation program: (1) division of marital property; (2) spousal maintenance; (3) child support, and (4) custodial arrangements. The structured program itself consists of five two-hour sessions. Additional sessions may be added if they are needed. The nonprofit organization that he founded in 1975, the Family Mediation Association, has a clear set of rules, subject to revision as research provides additional information about the best way to proceed.

Coogler's (1978) book provided a set of very useful appendices. Two orientation booklets that explain what mediation is and how the legal system works are provided in their entirety. The appendices also set out 45 rules on how the mediation is to proceed, including arbitration if the mediation is not successful. A guide for negotiating and drafting marital settlement agreements as well as forms used by the Family Mediation Association are also provided.

An impasse in mediation occurs if the mediator declares one, if either party declares one and the mediator agrees, and by either party regardless of the mediator's judgment if 10 hours of mediation have occurred. Clearly then the pressure is to have both parties stay with mediation for at least 10 hours to try and obtain a settlement. Coogler outlined several stages in the five session, ten hour mediation process:

1. *Orientation.* This stage is designed to provide information to the clients. It includes two identical packages of material, including: orientation information; the rules; forms for personal data, financial data, monthly expenses, emergencies, future goals, seasonal expenses, and debts; an analysis of expenditure; a predivorce or postdivorce mediation-arbitration agreement; a temporary custody and maintenance agreement; and a release for audiotaping for research.

2. *First hour of the first two-hour session.* After putting each spouse at ease and explaining the general procedure, the parties are asked to reach agreement on procedure. The mediator looks for opportunities to reinforce even this level of agreement.

The first session works on developing an agenda including temporary support and custody arrangements, identification of and division of marital property, spousal maintenance, child support, and child custody and visitation arrangements. The mediator then reviews the budgets and asks to complete omitted information. Again the focus is on finding even the simplest tasks on which the couple can cooperate. A temporary settlement agreement is signed to maintain the status quo during mediation. A written and signed agreement concerning sensitive issues, such as a removal of personal items from the residence is made.

3. *The second hour of the first two-hour session.* If there is no controversy over custody, discussion during the second hour concerns visitation arrangements. If it is needed and both parties are willing, an additional session beyond the 10-hour program may be scheduled to work out custody and visitation with the children present.

The marital property is also discussed. The basic assumption on division of marital property is a 50-50 division followed by a discussion as to why it might be fair to make a different division. At the end of the second hour, the couple begins consideration of support. If the budgets exceed the family income, the family must find additional sources of income or reduce the budget. The focus is on each individual's responsibility, not how the other spouse can solve that problem.

4. *Third through sixth hours.* The focus during this time is division of marital property, support, and custody arrangements. If couples cannot com-

plete these issues by the first four hours, the mediator must consider whether it is useful to continue or to declare an impasse. This decision is crucial by the end of the sixth hour. Most couples decide to extend the time by adding four or more hours.

Coogler, Weber, and McKenry (1979) noted that the amount of child support necessary should be determined prior to the question of custody. Thus, money is not used as manipulation in the mediation.

5. *The seventh hour.* If agreement has occurred by the end of the sixth hour, the couple meets with an advisory attorney for the seventh hour. The mediators summarize for the attorney the agreements reached, checking with each party for accuracy.

6. *The eighth hour.* The advisory attorney brings the final settlement agreement to this session. Usually only minor changes are required at this stage.

7. *The ninth and tenth hours.* When custody is in dispute and all other issues are resolved, the issues of custody and visitation are reserved for the ninth hour. Visitation is decided before custody. An agreement is made prior to this meeting as to whether the children will participate in this discussion and why. Children need to be told at the meeting explicitly *by each parent* that they have permission to express what ever they wish in this meeting.

When children participate in mediation sessions, the ground rules and reasons for the meeting need to be explained in age-appropriate language. The children need explicit, verbal permission from each parent to say what they wish. The mediator should verify with the children that this communication was accomplished.

Coogler (1978) provided theoretical discussion of how mediation works. He felt that achieving resolution of conflict requires that (1) the physical well-being of each party be maintained, (2) feelings of self-worth of each party be maintained, (3) each party respect or tolerate the opposite party as a person (not requiring approval of that person's morals or values), (4) all relevant facts and options be considered and used in reaching a resolution, (5) the consequences of all available options be considered before resolution, and (6) the resolution be chosen by both parties, even though other choices were available.

Coogler gave recognition to cooperative, individualistic, and competitive motivations and wants to develop a structure that supports cooperative motivation. The mediator accomplishes this support by establishing a spirit of cooperation. The mediator looks for any indications of cooperative behavior and compliments any instance of such behavior.

Demands for meeting individual needs and for winning need to be deemphasized in mediation and cooperation needs to be supported.

If the couple comes in early after the separation, escalation may not yet have occurred and cooperation is relatively easy to establish. If mediation is delayed until the battle has already begun, developing the proper atmosphere supportive to mediation is considerably more difficult.

Once the decision to divorce has been made, couples should be encouraged to begin mediation as early in the separation process as possible to avoid escalation. If the decision to divorce has not been made, couple therapy could be used to aid in making the decision.

Irving's Mediation Procedure

Irving (1980) proposed that the goals of mediation are to help the family come to a amicable settlement, to protect the children's interests as primary, and to help parents and children understand that divorced couples are always mothers and fathers. Irving recommended that even when the couple has already resolved the issues about the children, it would be useful to have the couple mediate in order to be sure that the welfare of the children are protected.

Irving proposed that prior to mediation, an agreement must be made to exclude the mediation process from the adversarial process. The agreement must exclude all meetings, information, and offers that occur in mediation from a subsequent court proceedings. A precondition of mediation is that the mediator cannot be called to testify or produce documents in the courtroom. This agreement makes it possible for the parents to consider alternatives without worrying that such consideration would be used against them later. In addition, it frees up the mediator to not worry about how the process could be undermined by the adversarial process. Irving also provided a useful example of the form that includes what issues would be discussed, what the criteria for resolution would be, whether the agreement is binding (usually not), how long mediation would be tried before court action would occur, and how fees will be handled. The form is used by the lawyers, the clients, and the mediator. Irving recommended that the mediator meet privately with the lawyers, accountants, or any other relevant people in order to clarify the rules and maximize the fact-finding phase of the mediation.

Prior written agreements that exclude mediation proceedings from any subsequent litigation is highly recommended to avoid legal manipulations or paranoia from rendering mediation ineffective. Clear communication in writing about guidelines and rules provided to the clients and their lawyers can protect the clients' rights and the well-being of the mediator.

The mediator's role is to provide advice and to help the couple identify areas of disagreement and to settle those disagreements. Irving felt that the major areas of mediation for divorcing couples are custody, visitation, and maintenance. Other mediators have also emphasized division of property as a major goal of mediation.

Since mediation has communication as its base, support for improving communication between family members lies at the core of mediation. The mediator monitors the communication patterns and clarifies for the family how to correct faulty communication. As in family therapy (and mediation is not therapy), the mediator encourages family members to communicate directly and with each other. The mediator may provide information, alternative choices, and advantages and disadvantages of particular options. Neutrality must be maintained, however, and sides should not be taken. The decisions are made by the family members, not the mediator.

In order to encourage communication between family members, the mediator should ask family members to direct concerns and questions to the family member involved and to give answers directly to that other family member. By avoiding the role of translator, the mediator gives training in direct communication.

Irving (1980) divided the mediation process into three phases:

1. *The initial phase: exploration.* In this phase, each individual family member is asked to tell their story. The mediator empathizes with each in order to communicate acceptance, understanding, and support. The focus is to determine where each person stands and what each person wants to accomplish. In addition, the mediator wants to understand each person's feelings, self-perceptions, and unique problems. This phase may be held with individual family members and the mediator. The behavior of the mediator in this phase is to provide emotional support and to help identify the problems.

2. *Second phase: problem solving.* In this phase, the focus shifts from the mediator to the family. Joint interviews with the couple or entire family are held. Each person is asked to explain that his or her goals and wants. The mediator reviews what each person has said and how that person is understood by the other family members. When ambiguous communications occur, the mediator helps the family to clarify the exact meaning. When an impasse occurs, the mediator reframes the conflict by broadening the perspective and offering alternatives. The behavior of the mediator in this phase is to obtain sufficient factual information to find a solution, develop and identify all possible alternatives, and evaluate the probable outcomes of each alternative.

3. *Final phase: resolution.* The final phase is highly structured. The purpose of this phase is to detail what each party will do in the general form of a contract. If anyone violates the agreement, there is immediate feedback. Crisis intervention or individual therapy (outside of mediation) is recommended if one or more family members have such high levels of resentment as to prevent proper separation. The behavior of the mediator in this phase

is to help the couple select one of the alternative solutions to each problem, develop an agreement as to the steps to implement that alternative, and formulate a way of following up on the success of the agreement.

Irving also recommended setting firm minimum limits for mediation and a fluid, maximum number of sessions. Generally, two sessions are recommended. When the maximum number of sessions has not resulted in agreement, there are three options:

1. Adversary through the courts;
2. Binding arbitration; and
3. Advisory arbitration.

In the case of arbitration that is advisory, unlike mediation, the arbitrator's report would be available to the court if one or more parents did not accept the advice. Irving saw arbitration as less desirable than mediation (because it removed the responsibility for arriving at a decision from the parents) but more desirable than the courts. In order to preserve the confidentiality of mediation, Irving recommended that if the mediation was not successful and the conflict moved to arbitration, the arbitrator should be someone new. Under arbitration, no information is confidential and the participants should understand the change in the rules.

Haynes' Divorce Mediation

Haynes (1981) came to divorce mediation as a professor of social welfare with a history in labor mediation. Haynes' model of mediation is carefully spelled out in his book (Haynes, 1981) on mediation.

As part of the decision as to whether mediation should occur, Haynes noted that it is important to determine whether the couple is sufficiently along in their development of thinking about divorce that true mediation can occur. If either party is still working toward reconciliation, the mediation is likely to be ineffective.

Mediation begins with a separate meeting with each party to discuss division of resources. Each person is asked to develop a list of family expenses for the past year and to estimate a budget for the new life. After the economics have been agreed on, the mediator defines property items that have emotional value to either or both of the parties. Once the areas of economic resources and wants in terms of items are defined, the mediator identifies areas of common agreement. The symbolic issues are then identified. Using labor statistics, the mediator helps both parties understand the likelihood of a drop in the standard of living. Hopefully, this will reduce postdivorce resentment over the financial consequences of divorce. The mediator strikes trades for items of emotional value. The process is designed to help each party respect the other, perceive the process as fair, and keep their own dignity.

Haynes used Federico's (1979) Divorce Adjustment Process model to determine at which stage of divorce that the couple is operating. Federico's stages as described by Haynes were:

1. *Deliberation.* The possibility of divorce has been raised by one or both of the parties. The initiating party may try one of two strategies to make the decision the fault of the other spouse.

a. *Provocation.* The initiator tries to force the other spouse to make the decision. Sometimes an affair that is "accidently" discovered can have this purpose.

b. *Sabotage.* The initiator provokes the other spouse until the other spouse retaliates in anger. The angry response is used by the initiator to justify leaving. It would be the role of therapist, not mediator, to identify and work with these strategies.

2. *Litigation.* Once the lawyer is contacted, the couple may try to work out the relationship.

3. *Transition.* The period of transition follows the physical separation. The period is characterized by irrational behavior that can be very upsetting and lead to feelings of overwhelming panic. During this period, the therapist may be required to repeat ideas over and over. The mediator, too, may have to repeat ideas several times.

4. *Redirection.* This period occurs when the couple as individuals are able to make decisions independently of the other. This period involves learning mastery over skills formerly performed by the spouse, giving up fantasies about sex with the other partner, feeling financially secure, giving up bitterness and anger, and looking toward new relationships.

While the therapist may have specific roles for each of these stages, the mediator has a limited set of goals that are not therapy-oriented. In the first three stages of divorce development, the mediator has problem-solving as a goal. In the fourth stage, empowerment or skill development are the primary goals.

In discussing custody mediation, Haynes suggested refocusing the mediation from custody (which he defined as residential or physical custody) to maintaining joint parental responsibilities for the children. Haynes tries to maintain a coparenting orientation. Joint physical custody apparently was a rare outcome for Haynes, but is likely to be more common now, in eight of recent research on the effectiveness of joint custody (see Chapter 5).

Haynes also focused on access as opposed to visitation. Haynes was concerned that requests for joint physical custody indicated that the couple was not ready for divorce and were trying to maintain their relationship.

For custody mediation, the parents are asked to complete three tasks: (1) list why the children should live with them; (2) list the accommodations that they are willing to make to facilitate the other parent having access to the children; and (3) list the accommodations that the other party would have to make that parent willing to let the other spouse have custody. Haynes felt that the lists generated could tell which parent really wants custody and which might be using custody requests as a bargaining tool. While I feel that this technique would be highly useful as part of the custody mediation process, my own experience is of a greater number of parents who both genuinely want custody and who feel deep attachment to the children.

The ultimate goal of mediation is to provide the child with direct and open lines of communication with each parent. Haynes worked toward helping the parents get out of the role of mediating between the children and the other parent. The parents and children were encouraged to contact each other and discuss issues directly. The techniques of encouraging such communication was given in several examples and was clearly derived from family therapy. Of course, when the issues are between the parents (rather than between parent and child), the children also need to be kept out of the middle.

Haynes described some very useful process variables in mediation.

1. *Referral.* The source of referral can be used diagnostically to predict the stage of the divorce adjustment process that one or both parties are in. Being referred by an external source rather than a therapist or another mediator is likely to be a good predictor that the couple is ready for mediation.

2. *Blockages.* Resistance to the fee or to the process may indicate that one or more persons is not ready for mediation. If the couple needs a therapist(s) rather than mediator, it is important to either change to that role or refer the couple elsewhere.

3. *Power.* The basic assumption of mediation is to equalize power. Haynes saw power as developing through control of income, rejection of the other partner and resistance of a settlement.

As have other developers of models of mediation, Haynes outlined steps for the sessions:

1. *The first session.* Credibility of the mediator, explaining the process, clarifying the expectations, and developing empathy are all goals of the first session. A data base for mediation is acquired. The first session is typically one hour and subsequent sessions are likely to be one-and-a-half hours. The appendix to his book provides sample handouts explaining the process. It also contains a sample budget form. Mediation begins with a "monologue" that tries to establish the goals of the first session. Therefore, a list of useful questions and helpful wording for collecting the basic data is also included.

2. *The second session involves review of the budget.* Unequal power distribution is a source of focus.

3. *Individual interviews.* In individual interviews, Haynes has each party fill out an individual interview form designed to review perceptions of the

marital disruption and strength of each party. As part of this process the mediator will legitimize feelings and set goals. As part of the negotiation process, the mediator develops a family profile of data about basic living arrangements, initiation of the divorce and feelings about it, strengths of each party, resources, feelings, power, self-esteem, and goals shared and not shared.

4. *Negotiating sessions.* Based on work by Morley and Stephenson (1977), Haynes defined four major components of negotiation. First, there must be some joint decision making. Second, each party has mixed motives with a wish to reach agreement and an investment in the original emotional relationship. Third, each party has a different order of priorities for the same set of items. Finally, the process requires talking prior to acting.

The mediator begins these sessions by indicating the areas of agreement or near agreement. This process sets the tone for the negotiation. Then the mediator slowly works through the items of minor disagreement, alternating items that require minor accommodations from each spouse. This process develops a spirit of give and take. Trading becomes a common strategy. Haynes provided an relatively extensive set of case studies that are helpful in demonstrating his principles and providing specific techniques.

All major forms of mediation include power equalization, emotional support for reaching preliminary agreements and trades on minor and major issues.

Musetto's Family Therapy Mediation

Musetto (1980) described an intervention into custody and visitation disputes that he developed over the last 10 years that used family therapy strategies for helping the families. When Musetto began to help with custody and visitation problems, he observed that the problems were similar to the marital and family problems that occurred in practice. His approach, although referred to as family therapy, is essentially family mediation. The entire family is seen together to help them assume responsibility to solve the problem in a constructive way. Family accountability is the theme of the therapy.

This approach is nonjudgmental in that it does not make rulings about who is right or wrong, and raises the issue of failed responsibilities. Families are seen as having responsibilities toward each other, including the responsibilities of the children to the parents.

The family is informed that the entire family will be interviewed together, that a sliding scale fee is charged, that more than one session is usual, and that the purpose of the sessions is to reduce hostility. Three or four sessions are usually required to reach a compromise.

After explaining the purpose of the meetings, the therapist provides one major ground rule: Everyone is to be heard without interruption. A family background and history of each spouse is taken. A marital history is taken with a focus on what factors prevent a resolution of the conflict.

It is recommended that family history be obtained to determine the family system issues that interfere with resolution of the conflict.

Musetto describes a series of underlying motives that can keep the dispute from being resolved, such as any factors that might prevent a parent from being granted custody (e.g., drug abuse, alcoholism, sexual or physical abuse, psychosis, or previous neglect of the children). Musetto did not consider psychopathology in the parent a sufficient criteria, in and of itself, to rule out custody.

The role of the clinician is to create an environment of communication and cooperation. Musetto indicated that a custody struggle is an expression of the parents' concern for the children. The positive connotations of each member's behavior are supported. Paradoxical prescriptions are used to reduce resistance to change (see Chapter 13 on family therapy).

The therapy is focused on helping the parents see how their problems are affecting the children. Parents may be asked to meet alone and work out a compromise. Further compromise is built on common grounds of agreement, for example that children should have contact with both parents. Two case histories that demonstrate the use of family therapy techniques in custody mediation are provided.

Unlike other custody mediation techniques, if the parents cannot obtain agreement, the therapist then makes a recommendation to the court. The mixing of these roles is seen by others writing about mediation to have the potential problems of (1) increasing anger in the sessions and (2) using the therapist for the adversarial battle.

MEDIATOR BEHAVIORS

Vanderkool and Pearson (1983) analyzed the behaviors of two-person mediator teams of mental health professionals and lawyers in the Denver Custody Mediation Project. The mediators had been trained in workshops led by Kessler, Milne, and Coogler using written materials by Black, Joffee, and Haynes. Analysis was from 35 taped mediations and 22 written summaries for 15 mediators. The following is a summary of the patterns of mediation found:

1. *Orientation.* All mediators worked on an atmosphere to support mediation and to build trust. Two styles were used, an informal egalitarian one and a more formal, task-oriented one. Empathy for each party was emphasized.

2. *Defining issues.* Five issues were typically addressed: custody, visitation, division of property, child support, and spousal maintenance. Issues were defined and clarified. Some structure was useful, but nonstructured approaches tended to interfere with mediation. Children, grandparents, and new

spouses were often included. Children were typically interviewed separately and information shared with the parents. All signs of generosity and agreement were reinforced. Small issues were addressed first to set the stage for bigger ones.

3. *Resolving divorce issues.* Emotional responses had to be ventilated and controlled. Interruptions, ascribing motives, and denigrating were forbidden. Reframing behaviors in more sympathetic terms was helpful in reducing rage by providing new ways of looking at the other spouse's motives. Reframing was also used to move from "custody" to "time sharing." Brainstorming was used to create alternatives. If a solution satisfying to both parties was not obtained, compromises were negotiated.

Vanderkool and Pearson found that the mediators most effective in reaching a joint agreement in mediation were those who were highly directive, active, and in control of the sessions.

SHOULD THE CHILDREN BE INCLUDED IN THE MEDIATION?

Drapkin and Bienenfeld (1985) proposed that in general it is useful to include the children in the mediation process. Children may be relieved to have a third party trying to include their feelings. By including the children, the mediator maintains the focus on parenting. This approach is particularly important when the parents are engaged in a bitter battle and claim that the children are doing fine.

These authors felt that there were two situations in which including the children was not appropriate. The first situation occurs when both parents see the children's needs in the same way and have similar plans for how to meet these needs (rare in court ordered mediation). The second situation occurs when the children are under 3 years of age.

In seeing the children separately from the parents, a type of play therapy may be the most supportive environment. In other words, instead of asking questions of the child, a supportive environment was developed in which the child could be self-expressive. Children should be carefully informed about why they are seeing the mediator. Young children should be allowed to explore in a informal setting with play materials. Children between the ages of 6 and 10 do better if given a chance to be physically active while talking. Paper, colored pens, and small, bendable family dolls, and child-sized table and chairs are all recommended. Other play therapy techniques include family dolls (setting up the child's family structure and asking questions about the family), three wishes (useful for children 3 to 5), and imaginative stories. The limits of confidentiality should be carefully explained, particularly limits about child abuse.

In individual contact with children, the mediator should be very careful to explain that what is being said is not confidential, particularly if someone is being hurt.

Children between the ages of 10 and 18 are interviewed more directly. The mediator should ask specific permission to share concerns that the child has with the parents. If the child fears punishment or anger, the mediator should share general impression and observations, but not verbatim remarks.

MEDIATION AND JOINT CUSTODY

Most mediators have a philosophical preference for joint parenting (Girdner, 1985a). Volgy and Everett (1985) cautioned that requests for joint custody may not be made in good faith, but may reflect a strategy to force concessions and may be made to exert control over the other spouse. In addition, there are pragmatic issues that should be considered prior to the mediator deciding whether to encourage joint residential or physical custody:

If the parents are quite different in their values and attitudes regarding parenting, how well do they tolerate the differences?

How stable was the emotional functioning of parents prior to the separation?

How much trust do the parents report in the other's parenting ability.

How motivated are the parents in supporting access of the child to the other parent?

What is each parents' capacity for parenting, now and in the future?

Volgy and Everett (1985) proposed the following systematic criteria for evaluating joint custody is a reasonable outcome for mediation:

1. *External family boundaries.* When the predivorced boundaries were closed, sharing time was difficult between parents and children. In cases where the boundaries were excessively open, chaotic functioning could result.

2. *Intergenerational family ties.* The presence of enmeshment is a danger signal for disruption to joint physical custody. Under such family dynamics, grandparents may intrude into the parent-child subsystem and sabotage the authority of the parent. Unhealthy alignments with parents against the other parent can also interfere with effective joint physical custody. Excessive disengagement also works against effective joint physical custody. The parents cannot work together sufficiently well to provide the structure that the children need.

3. *Structural decoupling.* In 50 percent of the cases identified as joint physical custody failures, there was excessive intrusiveness or retaliation by

one or both parents. Joint custody was a way of holding on to the old relationship or to control the other parent through the children.

4. *Structural recoupling.* The parent-child system must be balanced so that authority of each parent is not too enmeshed with intergenerational loyalties so as to be able to stand on its own. The effectiveness of integration of new relationship with the children will depend in part on whether *both* parents can develop new social contacts.

5. *Internal subsystem boundaries.* New boundaries within the parent-child systems must develop. Joint custody works best when both parents assume similar executive parental roles with each subsystem.

RESEARCH ON THE EFFECTIVENESS OF MEDIATION

As noted by Johnston, Campbell, and Tall (1985) there has been no research on which subpopulations mediation might most help. The few studies of outcome have made claims of success from 48 to 80 percent. Brown (1982) also quoted unpublished studies of reduction in costs of 75 percent and decreases of relitigation by one-third in mediation as compared to adversarial approaches.

Bahr (1981) evaluated the economic efficiency of mediation from published and unpublished documents concerning the programs of four areas. In evaluating the cost to taxpayers, the study found that courts with a mediation service cost about 10 percent less than a court without mediation service in Los Angeles, 50 percent less in Australia, 50 percent less than a custody evaluation in Minnesota, and about 10 percent less in Toronto. Bahr estimated that $9.6 million in court costs and $88.6 million dollars in legal fees would be saved yearly in the United States if court mediation were available everywhere.

Mediation was also a factor in compliance with court orders. In Minnesota, 26 percent of those using traditional child custody determination returned to court within two years. Only 10 percent of those using mediation returned to court. As Bahr noted, these results were confounded by the lack of random assignment to conditions. More difficult cases may not have been referred for mediation. For Wisconsin, the figures were 34.3 percent return to court for traditional custody study families and 10.5 percent for mediation. For Connecticut, there was no data on the adversarial group, but for mediation more than two-thirds said the agreement had been maintained.

The Irving, Bohm, MacDonald, and Benjamin (1979) study attempted to look at postdivorce adjustment. This study did involve random assignment to mediation or custody study. At a six week follow-up (which is far too brief a time for thorough evaluation) of 228 clients, three times as many mediation than adversarial divorcing couples reported that things had gotten "much better" (25 percent as compared to 9 percent).

Mediation is likely to have high satisfaction rates, lower relitigation rates, and significant savings in cost to the parents. When mediation is unsuccessful, the overall total cost is likely to be higher.

Koopman, Hunt, and Stafford (1984) reported on comparisons of structured mediation sample (Coogler's 1978 model) with 31 agreements, and a nonmediated sample from the same jurisdiction with 31 agreements. Both samples were compared with other published data on Connecticut, lawyer-initiated, adversarial cases (162 cases). They did not report any statistical analyses, but descriptive statistics were useful in getting a feel for the consequences of the different approaches. An additional problem was that the data for first two groups were collected in the central east coast region so that geographic locale was also not controlled.

In this study, mediation produced high levels of joint legal custody (88 percent) as compared to the nonmediated (0 percent) and Connecticut samples (4 percent). Joint physical custody was also h gher in the mediated group, although rarer (11 percent), as compared to the nonmediated sample (0 percent). Maternal residential custody was most common for both groups. Mediation also produced high levels of detailed visitation agreements (96 percent) as compared to the other two groups (38 and 8 percent, respectively). One consequence of mediation was the undifferentiated allocation of alimony and child support for 38 percent of the cases compared to 0 percent for the nonmediated group.

Koopman et al. (1984) suggested that mediation provides for "best interests of the family" as a model that is likely to reduce relitigation around child-related issues, finances, education, residential location, and medical and life insurance security. In addition, they noted that 100 percent of the mediation agreements acknowledged that development means change and all agreements provided arrangements for mediation for future changes.

In the initial analysis of the 61 couples who completed mediation in the Denver Custody Mediation Project, Pearson (1981) found that 51 couples went beyond one session. Of those, 30 (54 percent) came to a final agreement. The mean number of sessions was 4.2, taking 5.6 hours. Of those who agreed, 75 percent (70 percent in the final evaluation) chose joint custody typically with primary physical custody with one parent and generous visitation with the other. Of those who did not agree, 21 percent accepted joint custody. In a randomly assigned control group, only 14 percent chose joint custody and only 8 percent of those who rejected the offer for mediation chose joint custody.

Pearson and Thoennes (1982) found some evidence in reduced cost for mediation, although not always, with about $200 saved. The state saved from $5,610 to $27,510 per 100 cases mediated. Time was saved only if mediation was successful. Personal satisfaction with the mediation was high with two-thirds highly satisfied. Even with unsuccessful mediation, 81 percent would recommend mediations to others.

In a longitudinal analysis of the Denver Custody Mediation Project (Pearson and Thoennes, 1984), participants were interviewed as soon as they were identified as in a custody dispute and accepted mediation, three months following final orders, and six months after the second interview. The short-term effects included: high user satisfaction, better reported relationships between former spouses, more satisfaction, and higher compliance with orders than was true for the adversarial group. More visitation, more joint custody arrangements and more generous visitation terms were reported for the successful mediation group. The long-term (nine months post-decree) effects, as compared with the adversarial group and unsuccessful mediation group, were: those with successful mediation felt more optimistic about solving future problems with the ex-spouse without going to court, more satisfied with the decree, reported fewer serious problems, and reported more compliance with the terms of the order. They also reported more enjoyment of joint custody and more visitation.

Successful mediation as compared to the adversarial approach would seem to result in some financial advantage, significant improvement in problem solving, better relationship with the former spouse, more compliance with court orders, and greater support for long-term visitation frequency than the adversarial approach.

Additional analyses of the same data base (Pearson and Thoennes, 1985), added additional samples to the Denver project. Other interviews included: 300 individuals interviewed five years post-mediation (mediation occurred in 1978 or 1979); 100 individuals who had contested the divorce through the courts in 1981; 100 noncontested divorce cases from 1981; and a sample of individuals who had contested divorces in 1978.

Surprisingly, for the mediated and nonmediated 1978 samples visitation frequency seemed to be higher if the divorce was processed through the courts in an adversarial manner (80 percent regular visitation) than through mediation (60 percent regular visitation), when data was reported by noncustodians. When the data was reported by custodial parents, 60 percent of the adversarial group reported regular visitation and only 46 percent of the successful mediation reported regular visitation.

For the 1981 sample, when the custodial parents reported, 30 percent of the mediation group, 30 percent of the adversarial group, and half of the noncontesting group reported that visitation was rare or never took place. When noncustodian parents were reporting, none of the successful mediation group reported infrequent visitation and about 30 percent of the nonagreement mediation group and 30 percent of the adversarial group reported infrequent visitation. Thus, whether or not successful mediation improved visitation frequency postdivorce depended on who you were talking to!

Child support for the 1981 sample was becoming irregular by one year regardless of the group to which the individual belonged. Nonpayment of supported was a problem for successful and unsuccessful mediation groups and contested and noncontested groups. The increase in problems over time was greatest for the adversarial group.

In terms of reports of visitation problems, for the prospective study population, the noncontesting group initially reported about half as many visitation problems as the contesting groups (45 to 50 percent of the cases had three or more problems). By the final interview, nine months later, all groups were reported three or more problems in about 30 to 40 percent of the cases, except for the noncontested group which was at about 25 percent.

WHEN IS MEDIATION LIKELY TO FAIL?

Johnston et al. (1985) reported on factors that led to a mediation impasse. They found that the greater the number of levels or components of an impasse, the more complex and entrenched the divorcing family was.

The authors also identified several personality characteristics that lead to chronic battles: (1) The borderline disorder causing a characterological need to fight; (2) the obsessional parents, who enmeshed the ex-spouse and others in minute details, and (3) a smaller number of paranoid, psychotic parents who had projections and symbiotic ties with the children. They indicated that these problems were a remarkably small percentage of families who had reached impasse. Factors that they listed were:

1. *Unholy alliances and coalitions.* Mutual friends, extended kin relationships, and family of origin conflicts were sources of alliances. Displaced conflict occurred with a divorced spouse who had remarried or had a cohabiting relationship and had that relationship fail. They also found coalitions with helping professionals who were fueling the fight. It was not unusual to find a mental health professional, who after hearing only one side of the story, encouraged an uncompromising aggressive position. The adversarial stance of the legal system through tactics of the attorney also fueled the fight. Even when the attorney made charges out of context and in the most unfavorable light possible, spouses saw the strategy as coming from the other spouse, not the attorney.

When externally fueled disputes were identified, the authors recommended encouraging the divorcing parties to divest themselves of the individuals encouraging the battle. If it is not possible to get the divorcing parties to recognize the interference and disengage themselves, the authors would ask permission to work directly with the external agents, seeking to work with those most open to change.

2. *Character pathology.* When an impasse occurred they found that a large majority of disputing parties had indicators of character pathology. These patterns did not always fit the traditional diagnostic categories. In a significant number of cases, the disturbed behavior occurred only in the area of the divorce relationship. The people seemed to be well adjusted in other areas. Of

course, such encapsulated areas of pathology may well have played a significant role in the divorce itself. Several subtypes were identified:

a. *Legacy of a destructive marital relationship.* From a family system perspective, the "mutual crazy making" of some families leads them to habitually provoke, attack, and regress around the weakest areas of psychological functioning. Unhooking the spouses from each other is advised, both to avoid the traps and to take responsibility for not attacking the other's defenses.

b. *Traumatic or ambivalent separations.* There are two types of traumatic for ambivalent separations. In one type, the ex-spouses have negative and polarized views of each other with no grounding in current reality. They are so anxious about the crazy or dangerous behavior of the other that they act out their fears and fight to protect the children from imaginary dangers. Traumatic separation involving sudden abandonment, discovering secret plotting, secret affairs, and explosive incidence of violence are examples of traumatic separation that tends to increase such distorted views of the other spouse. Under such circumstances, the spouses avoided each other and an opportunity to disconfirm the distorted view could not occur.

With traumatic separations, the therapist would try to help the spouse search for reasonable explanations for the suddenness of the separation. The therapist tried to provide a safe arena for the exchange of factual information and improved communication. The other type involved maintaining an idealize image of the other and engaging in a constant search for reconciliation. The idealized image is likely to break down with trial reconciliations.

The authors saw both types as separation-engendered. These couples sometimes went through periodic separations and reconciliations in which they got closer to intimacy followed by explosive anger. Deep erotic attraction was combined with hostility and dependency. For many, the marriage was their first love experience. The ambivalence was sometimes related to complementary and opposite personality styles, which led to attraction as well as problems.

For the spouse with idealized images, the spouse was confronted with the dichotomy between the idealized view and wish and the reality. Separation was encouraged by drawing clear boundaries and business-like roles.

3. *Intrapsychic elements.* Certain intrapsychic conflicts, such as feelings of rejection, loss, humiliation and helplessnes, anger and loneliness, were generated by the separation and loss.

a. For many the battle was a defense against narcissistic injury. Wanting custody was a way of addressing the narcissistic injury and labeling the other spouse as wanting.

b. For others, the conflicts were a defense against experiencing a sense of loss.

c. For some, the arguments were expressions of a need to ward off a sense of helplessness.

d. Defense against guilt motivated others.

Girdner (1985a) indicated that mediation may not be appropriate for enmeshed or autistic couples. The stage of divorce can influence whether the couple is ready for mediation. When mediation might be an injustice to one or more parties, Girdner suggested referral to a therapist prior to mediation.

OPPOSITION TO MEDIATION

Brown (1982) noted that not everyone is uniformly enthusiastic about mediation. Some have claimed that the adversarial method is quicker and cheaper. (However, no data are provided to support those claims.) Several people have noted concerns about the ethics of lawyers who represent both parties in a dispute resolution. (This practice violates the code of ethics for lawyers.) Others have claimed that mediators may be practicing law without license.

There have been concerns that mediators may be too ready to accept agreements rather than fairness and that power equalization may not occur. Girdner (1985a) has cited cross-cultural research that indicated that unequals reach settlements that reflect the inequality.

Finally when mediation fails, the expense of the divorce increases. If the failure of mediation goes to mandatory arbitration, the new arbitrator must be paid and if the process goes to court, the cost of mediation is added to the cost of an adversarial divorce. In the absence of generally recognized standards of practice, these issues are yet to be resolved. Brown (1982) has provided an extensive review of these issues.

SUMMARY

The available evidence suggests that mediation is far superior to court resolved battles, for the well-being of both the parents and the children. Relitigation, post-divorce conflict, and costs are likely to be lower. Mediation would seem to be less effective when coalitions of family and friends are formed, when there is severe psychopathology in one or both of the parents, or when couples are enmeshed or autistic.

Effective divorce mediation is conceptually difficult and although it uses some of the same theoretical skills as psychotherapy, the interventions are very difficult. Since skill and knowledge are required, formal training and supervised experience are recommended.

CHAPTER 5

Custody Evaluations: Prior Considerations

Ninety percent of custody arrangements are made through stipulated agreements. In only 10 percent of the cases does a judge or referee decide who shall get custody. As Weiss (1979) pointed out, even though judges decide only a small minority of custody cases, the criteria they use leads to expectations on the part of lawyers and parents about what kind of arguments are likely to win in court should custody be contested. In addition, court decisions determine expectations about what is reasonable in terms of who gets custody and how much visitation is reasonable. Those 10 percent of cases that do end up in court can produce an inordinate amount of anger and pain. Mental health professionals can do a variety of things to insure that the evaluation for custody goes smoothly and the aftermath is less conflict ridden.

Custody evaluations are extremely difficult to do well. The ability to predict postdivorce behavior based on behavior seen during the emotional upset around the separation and negotiations for divorce is relatively poor. Custody evaluation, done well, is tremendously time consuming and expensive. One of the problems in basing a professional career on serving newly separated and divorcing families is that the cost of dividing up a household, setting up two separated households, and legal fees leave the family with little to spend on mental health professional services.

THE HISTORY OF CHILD CUSTODY

Foster and Freed (1978) in their review of the historical antecedents of custody set the first concern for the welfare of the child in custody. According to them, the first instance occurred in 1817 when Shelley, the poet, lost custody after Harriet's suicide because he was an atheist and because of immoral conduct.

Prior to 1920, however, children were considered property of the father and if a divorce occurred, they were typically given to the father. In the United States, the father's right to custody was never absolute (Foster et al., 1978). Generally, it was assumed that the father was best for the child because of the ability of the father to provide protection and nurturance as well as maintenance and education (Weiss, 1979). Several changes occurred during the late 1800s and early 1900s that led to changes in that attitude. With the movement from an agrarian society to an industrial society, the labor force led fathers to become primary wage earners in factories. Women became primary child care providers in the home (Clingempeel and Reppucci, 1982).

During the early 1900s, Freud's theory of child development became popular. People were increasingly aware that early childhood was strongly influenced by the emotional bond between the mother and the child. In addition, in the latter part of the nineteenth century, there was an increasing attitude that the family protected the child from an impersonal world. Mother love become an important aspect of child development (Weiss, 1979). In England, the Guardianship of Infants Act of 1925 gave equal rights for custody to both parents (Ricks, 1984). At the same time in the United States, Judge Cardozo wrote a child custody opinion based on "the best interests of the child." This criteria for child custody rapidly became accepted throughout the United States. Today, almost all states use this criterion for child custody.

It should be noted that the best interests of the child is seldom used as the sole criterion for deciding custody. For example, Derdeyn (1975) noted that the interests of the biological parents are given greater weight than those of the child. According to Derdeyn, the compromise accepted by the court is to give greater weight to the parents' needs. Surprisingly, Felner, Terre, Goldfarb, Farber, Primavera, Bishop, and Aber (1985) found that in a unnamed northeastern state, only 15 percent of lawyers and only half of the judges included best interests of the child as one of the five most critical factors in deciding custody.

The best interest doctrine that currently prevails still gives the judge or referee a great deal of discretionary power. Deciding which parent is in the best interests of the child can lead judges to use criteria that include "fault." The advent of the "no fault" divorce was enormously helpful in reducing the amount of anger and pain associate with being able to obtain a divorce. Certainly elimination of the requirement that one adult must have broken some moral code in order to obtain divorce has made it easier over the years to obtain a divorce. It has probably also contributed to the increase in divorce rate (and perhaps reduced the maladjustment of children that were previously required to live in a miserable, unhappy intact home).

The view that one parent "caused" the divorce and that fault should be punished is not uncommon. According to Weiss' (1979) recent review of laws associated with custody, only one state appeared to direct a judge to consider marital fault in custody. Another state, by omitting parts of the Uniform Custody Code, permits a judge to take into account the "moral behavior" of each parent. The Uniform Custody Code adopted by many states specifically stated that conduct of a parent that did not directly influence the child should not be considered as part of the custody evaluation. As noted by Weiss (1979), judges may be influenced by evidence of immorality (which may simply reflect that a parent is sexually active outside of marriage). In addition some judges are reluctant to award custody to a parent who has had an affair that was the precipitating event that led to the divorce. Such an award can have the appearance of rewarding "immoral" behavior.

Considerable concern about the role of cohabiting relationships as presumptive evidence for awarding custody to the other parent was generated by the Illinois case of *Jarrett versus Jarrett* (Minton and Elia, 1981). In a state supreme court decision, a mother lost custody of her three children because she had been cohabiting with a man for the past four years. Given the sharp increase in cohabiting relationship nationwide in the last decade, this court decision could affect the lives of many custodial parents. The Supreme Court of Illinois decided that such cohabiting relationships had potential for future harm on the character of the children and that the mental and emotional health of the children could also be adversely affected. This decision was made without regard to the quality of the relationship between the mother and the cohabiting "pseudo-stepparent" or the relationship of either with the children. Other states have indicated that such relationship does not automatically disqualify a parent from custody (Minton and Elia, 1981). In a follow up report on this case, (Minton, 1983), it was noted that the United State Supreme Court declined to reverse the decision.

The Illinois Supreme Court later qualified its decision in the Jarrett case. Remarriage on the part of the parent who had cohabited in the past would eliminate the disqualification. Later, the disqualification of custody for a parent with a cohabiting relationship was ruled to apply only if all other factors were equal (Minton, 1983).

TERMINOLOGY

It is not possible in two chapters (Chapters 5 and 6) to describe all the problems and suggested solutions that could be helpful in making custody decisions. Indeed, entire books have been written on how to do custody evaluations (Group For the Advancement of Psychiatry, 1981). The purpose of these two chapters is to help mental professionals understand (1) the issues that affect children around custody evaluations and (2) some of the consequences of those decisions. Prior to review of custody evaluation process and research review on the effects of various custody decisions, some definitional terms are useful.

Sole Custody

Historically, the legal responsibility for the child is given entirely to one parent. Usually residential custody is included in the custody arrangement. Prior to the development of joint custody arrangements, mothers obtained custody in about 90 percent of the cases, fathers in about 7.5 percent of the cases, and others (usually other family members) in about 2.5 percent of the cases. Frequency of custody nationwide since the advent of joint custody arrangements has not been published.

Joint Custody

The general public confuses the issues of legal responsibility and physical location of the child. In many jurisdictions, joint custody technically, refers to legal responsibility, not physical location. It is possible for parents to have joint responsibility for the rearing of the children, even though the children have primary residence with one parent.

Presently, about 26 states have developed joint custody statutes and many other states are considering such laws (Reppucci, 1984). Judges are usually permitted to order joint custody if either parent wants it and sometimes in cases where neither parent requests it. Eight states have the presumption of joint custody. Many states have assumed that neither parent is automatically better, that it is often difficult to determine which parent would be better for the child, and that if there is no loser in the custody battle there will be less postdivorce conflict. Little research is yet available to evaluate these assumptions. It may be that joint custody will reduce abandonment by one of the parents in hurt or anger after the divorce, but the evidence is not yet in.

When parents are in constant conflict, joint custody gives equal power to each parent and no ready method of resolving disagreements. One potential problem of joint custody may be that continued litigation postdivorce may increase. States that require mediation for such conflicts are likely to significantly reduce relitigation. Conditions under which joint legal responsibility *and* joint time might work will be discussed later in this chapter.

Split Custody

Under this type of arrangement, one or more children go with one parent and the rest go with the other parent. Most mental health professionals recommend against split custody on the grounds that such an arrangement could compound the sense of loss for the children. However, Chasin and Grunebaum (1981) recommended split custody if the children are chronically destructive to one another. Ramos (1979) referred to a combination of split physical custody and joint legal custody in which siblings live with different parents and apart from each other some of the time and live together and with one of the parents for a significant portion of the time.

Split custody could be considered if the interactions between siblings are destructive. If split custody does occur, it is important to arrange visitation in such a way as to provide an opportunity for the children to interact. One problem of split custody is the possibility that the children will feel rejected in not being chosen to go with a particular parent and feel jealousy about the chosen child. It is important that if split custody is being considered, the needs of the children be paramount rather than the parents. Under most conditions it is most appropriate to keep the children together.

Guardian *Ad Litem*

A guardian *ad litem* is an attorney appointed by the court or jointly agreed on by the two parents to serve as representative for the children's interest in the divorce proceedings. While such representation can be very helpful to the children, lawyers often do not like the role. The client is not an adult. Payment can be difficult. Many lawyers are not trained in what issues are in the best interests of a young child. In addition, the cost of litigation is increased and another layer of complexity is added to the case.

Theoretically, the guardian *ad litem* role can provide increased legal protection for the rights of the child. In practice, there has been little use of the role in court. Pearson, Munson, and Thoennes (1983) reviewed 100 contested child custody cases in Denver, Colorado for the years 1972-1976 and 60 cases in 1966 (prior to the passage of the Uniform Marriage and Divorce Act). Of the 146 cases reviewed, only 7 cases involved the appointment of a guardian *ad litem,* all after the passage of the Uniform Act. These 7 cases made up only 4.8 percent of the total sample and 4 were made by the same judge. It was clear from their data that the guardian *ad litem* role was used in particularly difficult cases, since in five of the seven cases, a third-party custody award was made. The judges apparently used the lawyer in that role more as a fact finder and less as an advocate.

When guardian *ad litem* lawyers were appointed, they played different roles, including no role at all. Pearson, et al. (1983) found that in three of the seven cases the guardians were inactive. For the other lawyers, the roles ranged from a "psychologist's mouthpiece," to fact finder, to advocate. A guardian *ad litem* may be particularly useful when neither parent is psychological healthy and abuse or neglect are real possibilities.

The Tender Years Doctrine

The tender year doctrine refers to the assumption that the young child's best interests are served by being with the mother. In the United States, concern that very young children were best served by being with the mother dates back to 1830 (Foster and Freed, 1978), but did not become common until the 1920s. The age defined as "tender" has been variously interpreted by different courts. Some courts have set the range at birth to 6 years of age, others to 9 years old, and still others to 12. Weiss (1979) noted that the upper age in which the tender years doctrine applied seemed to increase over time.

If the presumptive criterion is placement with the mother, the father must prove the mother unfit, rather than simply that the father is a better parent. In some states, the doctrine is now used as a tie breaker when all other factors are equal (rarely are all other factors truly equal). Several states repealed the tender year doctrine during the 1960s and 1970s. For example, California formally repealed a tender years doctrine in 1973 and required that custody occur according to the best interests of the child (Weiss, 1979).

The change in attitude concerning the tender years doctrine occurred because (1) the doctrine was clearly discriminatory against fathers, (2) there was a growing recognition that fathers could make very adequate parents even for very young children and, (3) it was recognized that the majority of custodial mothers became employed.

There is no evidence that gender of parent defines quality of parenting for a child of any age. Gender should never be presumptive evidence of competence at anything.

The Reversion Doctrine

The reversion doctrine has been used to support the biological parent's rights over that of a guardian (Goldzband, 1982). Thus, if a step-parent adopts a child as part of a remarriage and the custodial biological parent dies, the courts are likely to award the custody of the child to the noncustodial biological parent. It is clear that this doctrine may come in direct conflict with the best interests of the child. Some courts have indeed given the child to the adoptive parent, so the reversion doctrine does not always hold up.

Hoorwitz (1982) noted that biological parental rights do not tend to prevail in custody decisions in which there was a surrender of the child, abandonment, persistent neglect, or unfitness. The criterion of "extraordinary circumstances" has been added as a requirement before best interests of the child can be evaluated independent of biological parents. In addition to the above criteria, the courts have added conditions that would be traumatic to the child, unfortunate and involuntary interruptions of custody over an extended time, and attachment of the child to various adults.

PROBLEMS IN ACCEPTING CUSTODY ASSESSMENTS

Beware the False Custody Battle

Not every request for a custody evaluation is made in good faith. Lawyers sometimes complain that a client has not provided them with all the information that they need to provide an adequate case. Then, during the hearing, the lawyers learn crucial facts that change the entire thrust of the arguments and leave the presentation weak. Lawyers, like everyone else, hate to lose. They can get very angry at a parent who fails to mention physical abuse or major battles that have been observed by others. Yet the failure to mention these problems may be an indication that the parent was only going through the motions of a custody battle and did not want to win. As painful and as expensive as these battles can be, why should a parent develop a false custody battle?

1.   The custody battle is a continuation of the anger that the parents have felt toward one another. (Why should I let you win anything?) One referee told of an agonizing case where there was much bitterness between the parents. The parents were apparently equally competent to be parents (at whatever level that was), and it was not at all clear which parent should get custody. The referee painfully decided that the mother should receive custody. The mother promptly turned the custody over to the father indicating that she had never really wanted custody, but wanted to prove to the father that she could win over him!

2.   One parent is afraid that the children would interpret a willingness to let the other parent have custody as an indication that the children are unloved or are willingly abandoned. ("I fought for you, but the judge wouldn't let me have you.") This communication allows the noncustodial parent to reassure the children that he or she is not abandoning them.

3.   Sometimes custody battles are used as bargaining tools in the divorce. ("I will drop my request for custody if you will be willing to accept lower child support payments.") Fearful that they might not win, parents have accepted such blackmail to avoid the possibility of losing the children.

4.   The parent has unresolved feelings from childhood. ("I don't want to do to them what was done to me.") These custody battles are often attempts to avoid imposing on the children an unresolved anger or hurt from childhood.

Mental health professionals should recognize that requests for custody can be quite complex. While such requests can come out of a genuine feeling of affection and belief of superior parenting, they can also originate from anger, fear, and manipulation. Careful evaluation of explicit and inferred reasons as to why each parent wants custody is needed.

Inappropriate Custody Wishes; True Custody Battles

There is a variety of inappropriate justifications for custody battles that are not false battles, that is, the parent truly wants custody, but does not have any particular bonding to children or any sense of what is better for their welfare.

Some parents request custody as a continuation of a control battle in the marriage. This reason is similar to the first reason given for false custody battles, but here the parent will want custody and will keep it.

Some parents seek custody as a means of revenge. The parent wants custody in order to hurt the other parent.

Parentification of the child (Musetto, 1980) is yet another motive for requesting custody. When a parent has become dependent on the child, a request for custody may be a wish to continue that dependency relationship. Loss of the child may evoke memories on the part of the parent of his or her own earlier deprivation, exploitation, or neglect.

Parents preoccupied with control or revenge or who are dependent on the child will often make desperate and dramatic attempts at custody.

Professional Judgment Versus Bias

One reason why custody evaluation is so difficult to do well is that all professionals carry unexamined assumptions about mother-child relationships and father-child relationships that are a function of their own childhoods. Woody (1977) asked a large number of lawyers, psychiatrists, psychologists, and social workers (half male and half female) how they made custody decisions. He found that expert witnesses often make judgments that may be unrelated to the merits of the case. Older professionals tend to show more preference to the mother and are more likely to be influenced by a traditional morality. Never married professionals give greater weight to emotional ties and less support to the mother. Women psychiatrists and psychologists are more likely than women social workers or lawyers to favor the mother over the father for custody.

Girdner (1985a) suggested that preconceptions on the part of the court and of mental health professionals concerning "appropriate behavior" for men and women presents problems for both sexes. Women have fought against sexual discrimination in the work place and other public areas and men are starting to fight in the private domain of family life. Fathers' rights groups have claimed that the 90 percent mother custody rates and the tender years doctrine have unfairly discriminated against father custody. Polikoff (1982) argued that the reverse is true. Fathers have not wanted custody. When they do want it, they have substantial chances of winning. Of course, such statistics ignore fathers who do not try for custody because they believe that they cannot win.

Polikoff cited studies that found that from 45 percent to 63 percent of fathers who request custody obtained it. Polikoff noted that courts have supported father custody because (1) the father is financially better off than the mother, (2) mothers and not fathers are criticized for being employed, and (3) remarriage of the father and not the mother is seen as providing a supportive stepparent. Specific court cases were cited to support these views.

Mental health professionals have a great deal of difficulty being objective when they use different criteria for assessing normality in men and women. Girdner (1985a) noted that Gardner's (1974) evaluation of parental capacity examined maternal capacity in women and paternal capacity in men. Girdner noted that feminists have criticized Gardner's approach as requiring that maternal capacity be evaluated by conformity to traditional sex roles. The view that fathers are marginal and replaceable is also a stereotype. In an 18-month ethnographic analysis of court behavior in child custody decisions, Girdner found that fathers had to justify lower levels of past involvement with the children. The father had to show that the mother did not perform the role of mother adequately or that he had excelled beyond that normally required of a father. If the father deviated too much in the direction of parenting, the role violation might work against him in the custody process. When a father takes over household tasks, for example the tasks are seen as unnatural and done for instrumental reasons rather than as acts of love (which are motherly). For mothers, the problem was that role expectations were so high that it was not difficult to find occasions where the mother deviated from them. In fact, sex acts by a mother were seen as "self-gratifying animal acts," while the father's sexual behavior tended to be overlooked. The mother's attorney attempted to show that she was an excellent mother and the father's attorney tried to show that she had fallen below standards.

Thus, the mental health professional needs to be particularly sensitive to attitudes about sex role and psychological health. It is useful to ask the question as to whether a particular evaluation would change if the behavior were by the opposite gender parent.

Hare-Mustin (1976) felt that mental health professionals may place more emphasis on exhaustively evaluating the degree to which the mother meets traditional sexual role stereotypes rather than evaluating the father. If the mother fails to meet these characteristics, the mental health professional may recommend that the child go to the father. Mental health professionals were criticized for bias in what constitutes parental capacity, given that there is almost no research on what parent capacity is. Hare-Mustin indicated that even though Gardner's (1974) language indicated bias against nontraditional attitudes and against women in particular, Gardner had many useful ideas.

The Hired Gun: The Professional as Advocate of One Parent

There are additional problems of potential bias when the mental health professional has been hired by one particular parent. As Derdeyn (1975) pointed out, two major problems exist when the evaluator is hired by one parent: (1) the opposing parent will likely refuse to be interviewed (and properly, this author feels); and (2) the recommendations will not be used by the lawyer if the advice is not beneficial to the client. Finally, the clinician can lose objectivity by becoming emotionally invested in the parent who hires the evaluation.

The mental health professional is on safer ground if representing the child or both parents rather than one parent. In situations where one parent is unavailable due to geographic distance, severe pathology, or refusal to participate, the mental health professional should proceed with great caution, remembering much of the evidence against the absent parent may be hearsay. While a mental health professional can assess the quality of parenting of the parent available, no comparison can be made in terms of which parent is better. Without access to the other parent, there is also no opportunity to hear concerns that the other parent might have, concerns that are unlikely to be provided by the accessible parent.

A child custody team of at least two professionals (for example, a psychologist and a social worker), preferably of different ages, sex and/or professional background is likely to be an improvement over a single individual. A man and woman team may be particularly helpful in that each might tend to elicit different responses from each parent. A team can provide emotional support for each other to reduce burn-out. In addition, assumptions about child development, parent-child relationships, and the quality of evidence for conclusions can be checked out with another viewpoint.

Under normal circumstances, the mental health professional team can provide better evaluations of child custody than can a single individual. Under conditions where there are a limited number of mental health professionals that are trained for child custody, such as in rural areas, consultation with a colleague can be helpful in reviewing potential biases.

CRITERIA FOR CUSTODY EVALUATION

Charnas (1981) noted that there is a lack of guidelines or criteria in the law and in social science literature concerning the decision-making process. In the absence of criteria, parent-child bonding or the "psychological parent" has been used. The term "psychological parent" refers to the parent who fulfills the child's psychological and physical needs (Goldstein, Freud, and Solnit, 1973). Judges and lawyers have difficulty with accepting the bond as a criteria since they prefer to make decisions on objective data rather than subjective evidence (Charnas, 1981). In Charnas' study of judges and mental health professionals that were members of the Association of Family Conciliation Courts, the parent assigned custody in a simulation study was overwhelmingly the one with a more positive and consistent emotional bond with the children.

Benedek (1972) summarized Michigan law concerning custody evaluation. Best interests of the child were defined as requiring the following:

1. Love, affection, and other emotional ties between the child and each parent.
2. The capacity and disposition to give the child love, affection, and guidance, and to continue to raise the child in the present religion or creed.
3. The capacity to provide the child with food, clothing, medical, and other remedial care.
4. The length of time the child has lived in a stable, satisfactory environment and the desire of maintaining continuity.
5. The permanence of the home as a family unit.

6. The moral fitness of the parents.
7. The mental and physical health of the parents.
8. The home, school, and community record of the child.
9. The reasonable preference of the child, if the court thinks that the child is of sufficient age to express a preference.

These guidelines are remarkably similar to what mental health professionals use as guidelines for determining custody. Woody (1977) found that mental health professionals used the following criteria to make custody determinations:

1. Love and affection between each parent and the child.
2. Other emotional ties.
3. Length of time in an emotionally or psychologically stable environment and the importance of continuity for the child.
4. Mental health of each parent.

If there is a conflict in the aforementioned values, so that a decision cannot be made from those principles, mental health professionals also use the following criteria:

5. Support for the parent that will provide geographic stability.
6. Support for the parent with a good health history.
7. Support for the parent with traditional morality.

The Group For the Advancement of Psychiatry's (1981) report proposed five major principles of custody determination:

1. Custody decisions should be a part of the process of the developmental change in a family.
2. Family ties and family continuity have an importance that transcends divorce.
3. The history of mental illness in a parent does not in itself preclude effective parenting.
4. Prevailing values regarding family styles do not necessarily correlate with parenting capabilities.
5. A child's opinion in custody disputes has relevance, but it is only one part of the evaluations and should not alone determine custody (more on this issue in Chapter 6).

Dr. Lanning Schiller of Boulder, Colorado (personal communication, 1985) also recommended the following criteria: the capacity of each parent to facilitate child growth; awareness of child development; avoidance on the part of the parent of role reversal; identification with the child; and satisfying the parent's own needs from the child.

RESEARCH ON CUSTODY ARRANGEMENTS

There has been some research on how court officers and mental health professionals who work with divorce cases go about making decisions concerning custody. McDermott, Tseng, Char, and Fukunaga (1978) analyzed the custody evaluation reports and recommendations for 64 consecutive contested divorce cases in family court in Honolulu in 1974. They found eight major categories that were used to make recommendations for custody:

1. Caretaking arrangements (100 percent of the cases)
2. Parenting skills and commitment (95 percent)
3. Child's wishes (94 percent)
4. Child's adjustment (92 percent)
5. Parent's own interpersonal relationships (91 percent)
6. Parent's motivation for custody (89 percent)
7. Parent as a functioning adult (69 percent)
8. Assessment of alternate caretakers (68 percent)

Only the first four categories were clearly emphasized in the final evaluation and custody recommendations. The authors noted that evaluation workers (mental health professionals who do custody evaluations) did not try to project the possible future adult-child psychological adjustment, but were more focussed on present ability to care for the child.

When McDermott, et al. (1978) looked at difficulties in evaluation, four major problems in doing a custody evaluation were identified by the workers:

1. *Obtaining evidence on the natural parent-child relationship or natural home environment.* The custody investigation often triggered abnormally high anxiety or unusually tolerant behavior in families. It should be remembered that women look less well adjusted at the time of the decision to separate and men look worse some time after the separation. Discovering a child's real preferences for either parent was difficult. Older children were often under pressure from loyalty conflicts or direct bribery.

2. *Assessing the data.* Data were often conflicting or inconclusive. It was difficult to determine, for example, if a close relationship between a parent and a child was healthy, supportive, and helpful for the child's psychological growth.

3. *Predicting the effects of certain factors on child development.* Examples were custody awards of infants to fathers, conflict between parents, cross-sex parent-child combinations, alcoholism, and religious fervor.

4. *Difficulty in choosing between "poisons."* In 11 of the 64 cases the parent most available did not have the best parenting skills. In 8 of the 64 cases, the parents had difficult types of parenting skills that worked together, but not alone, sometimes with extreme, opposite styles.

Lowery (1985) looked at 80 court offices and 104 mental health professionals (psychologists and social workers) in Kentucky and asked how they saw themselves in terms of how they made custody decisions. Each group rated 19 different criteria. The top 10 ranked order of criteria for court officers from most common to less common were:

Mental stability
Sense of responsibility to the child
Biological relationship when one parent is a stepparent
Moral character
Stability in the community
Affection for the child
Keeping siblings together
Access to schools
Keeping a young child with the mother
Physical health

For mental health professionals, the top 10 in order were:

Sense of responsibility to the child
Mental stability
Affection for the child
Keeping siblings together
Moral character
Stability in the community
The child's wishes
Access to schools
Professional recommendations
Physical health

Both groups gave substantial weight to items that involved evaluating the prospective custodians and stable, mature adults.

When 84 judges and 32 trial commissioners in Kentucky (Settle and Lowery, 1982) were evaluated, the following criteria were rated as important in assigning custody: mental stability of each parent (9.96 on an 11 point scale); each parent's responsibility to the child (9.95); biological relationship to the child (9.46); each parent's moral character (9.37); each parent's ability to provide stable involvement in the community (9.09); each parent's affection for the child (9.01); keeping the child with brothers/sisters (8.89); each parent's ability to provide access to schools (8.13); keeping a young child with the mother (8.13); and physical health of each parent (7.95). An additional 10 criteria were given lower ratings.

In another study by Lowery (1984), with 100 clinical and counseling psychologists and 100 social workers, the top-rated criteria were: quality of the parent-child relationship; parent's mental stability; parenting skills; amount of contact with the child by the custodial parent; and the parent's affection of the child. Least important were the availability of a two parent home and keeping the child with the parent of the same sex. When the data was subjected to factor analysis, 44 percent of the variance was accounted for by a factor involving which parent was a mature, responsible person who had a loving relationship with the child. There were no differences between the two professional groups concerning rated criteria.

In a study just on judges (Lowery, 1981), the major cluster accounting for a comparable 47 percent of the variance in judges' decisions, included: the parents sense of responsibility to the child; each parent's mental stability; each parent's ability to provide access to schools; each parents's moral character; each parent's ability to provide continuing involvement in the community; and each parent's financial sufficiency. Less important was a second factor (16 percent of the variance) involving parent's ability to provide access to the other parent; the length of time each parent has had custody of the child; the physical health of the parents; and each parents's ability to provide a two-parent home. A third factor of (15 percent of the variance) included the advice of professionals (it is clear how much professionals advice makes a difference!) and the wishes of the child.

Felner, Terre, Farber, Primavera and Bishop (1985) found that 74 attorneys and 43 judges from an unnamed northeastern state gave greatest value for custody to (1) emotional stability and ability to care for the child and (2) time availability of each parent, stability of living arrangements, child care arrangements, and financial resources. One-half felt the child's wishes were important and one-third felt that the child's gender and emotional maturity were important.

THE EFFECTIVENESS OF CUSTODY DECISIONS

There has been remarkably little research on the effectiveness of custody decisions. While mental health professionals advise the court about attachment bonds, parenting skills, mental and physical health, stability, and continuity of care, there is no research to indicate whether such predictions are correct in terms of subsequent parent-child relationships.

In the 1979 movie *Kramer Versus Kramer,* which was one of the first popular movies to explore father custody, the mother left the home in order to explore alternatives for herself. The father, who had previously been little involved in the child's upbringing, made significant changes in his life to accommodate to the demands of single-parent fathering. My first response to this touching movie was that the father's dramatic change into an involved, caring father was unrealistic. Subsequent clinical experience and research, however, demonstrated that such changes do happen and are not unusual. Dramatic changes occur in the relationship between the father and the children in mother custody homes as well. What is surprising is that the direction of the change is presently impossible to predict. Wallerstein and Kelly (1980b) noted that 18 months after the separation, one-half of the father-child relationships had significantly changed from the pattern that was present during the marriage; 25 percent were closer and 25 percent were strikingly deteriorated. Mental health professionals were warned about making predictions about the postdivorce relationship between the father and child based on predivorce findings. They noted that the visitation relationship is unique and not related to any experience in the predivorce, intact marriage.

Since postdivorce visitation relationships for father and the child cannot be predicted from predivorce father-child patterns, some mental health professionals have assumed that it is almost impossible to determine custody that is in the best interest of the child. The lack of a relationship between predivorce father-child relationship and father visitation should not be used to indicate that father custody cannot be recommended based on predivorce father-child relationships.

Visitation has a completely different set of predictor problems than custody. It very well may be that the responsibilities of custody insure that continuation of high quality parenting is likely to continue, although admittedly the data have not yet been collected.

Father Custody

Because the nurturant role has traditionally been assigned to mothers, fathers who sought custody were, in the past, suspect. With a move toward androgynous parenting, fathers are increasingly interested in having custody of their children even in the absence of evidence that the mother is a poor parent.

Fathers do have different patterns of parenting as compared to mothers (Lewis, Feiring, and Weinraub, 1981). As a group, fathers in intact families spend much less time in one-to-one interactions with the children. They are more concerned than mothers with sex role development. They spend less time with caregiving activities, but more time in play. In observational studies, there have been few differences observed between the behaviors of mothers versus fathers. Lewis et al. (1981) concluded that fathers appear to be as sensitive and as concerned with childrearing as mothers.

Lamb (1981) in his naturalistic home observations of 7-, 8-, 12-, and 13-

month-old infants found that they showed no preference for mother or father in terms of attachment, but preferred either parent to an unfamiliar visitor. By 2 years of age, boys showed preference to fathers but girls still showed no preference.

Turner (1984) evaluated 26 divorced fathers who had won a contested divorce and found that they fell into two categories: (1) fathers who had been actively involved with their children throughout the marriage and wanted to continue that relationship (9 fathers); and (2) fathers who had not been actively involved in parenting prior to divorce and who waited until two years after the divorce to seek custody (17 fathers). Interestingly, the second group accounted for almost two-thirds of the sample. The small sample size, however, limits generalization of the findings.

Fathers who sought custody immediately were characterized as having had a close father-child relationship during the marriage, pleased with the pregnancy, were involved in birthing and infant care, were involved in at least half of child care activities during marriage and wanted to continue their close relationship with the child. Fathers who sought custody some time later did not have these characteristics and wanted custody either because of anger at the ex-wife, because of restrictions or denial of visitation, or because they felt that the ex-wife was a poor parent (for example, due to alcoholism, neglect, or abusive behavior). Fathers who sought custody immediately also were more positive about the beginning of the marriage, felt the separation and divorce were a tremendous loss, wanted reconciliation, and had a more friendly relationship with the mother postdivorce than did fathers who sought custody later.

The most extensive research on father custody has been done by Warshak and Santrock (Santrock and Warshak, 1970; Warshak and Santrock, 1983a; 1983b). They studied 64 white, middle-class families with children from 6 to 11 years of age, half boys and half girls. One-third came from father custody homes, one-third from mother custody homes, and the remainder from intact homes. (The 1979 report was based on a slightly different number of children). In spite of the relatively small number of children in each category, this study is extremely important because it is one of the few systematic, carefully measured studies comparing the type of custody. Children were an average of 8.3 years old and about three years postseparation. Recognizing that previous articles on father custody were based on case histories and parent report and seldom on direct measurement of the children, they developed a multimethod evaluation approach that included observation of a structured parent-child interaction, a parent interview, and a child interview.

In terms of the results for the parent-child interview, there was a clear relationship between type of custody and adjustment in the child. Children living with the same-sexed parent were better adjusted than children living with the opposite-sexed parent. Boys in father custody homes were less demanding than were girls in father custody homes and were more mature, sociable, and independent. Girls in mother custody homes were better adjusted than boys in mother custody homes. Boys in father custody homes performed more competently socially than did boys in intact homes. Girls in father custody homes did poorer than girls in intact homes. For mother custody, there was little difference from children in intact homes.

When the interviewer ratings were examined, similar results were obtained. Children in same-sex parent custody arrangements were rated as more socially competent than children living with opposite sex parents. Boys in father custody were also rated as more honest, more appealing, and having higher levels of self-esteem. Girls in father custody homes were rated as low on these dimensions.

There is no evidence that fathers who want custody and obtain it are in general inferior to mothers who obtain custody. Since the father who wants custody and obtains it is relatively uncommon, such results should not be interpreted to indicate that there is no difference in the quality of parenting because of the gender of the parent. The father who wants custody and obtains it is probably as competent on the average as the typical mother. In general, fathers would seem to do better with boys and mothers would seem to do better with girls. Specific individuals may not follow this pattern. Fathers and mothers may be differentially beneficial to each gender child as a function of the age of the child. The age by gender of child by gender of parent is a research question that has not yet been tested.

When the recollection of parents about the divorce and the children's response to the divorce was evaluated, type of custody was not related to the children's response to the divorce. Postdivorce relationships may have been affected. Custodial mothers reported that the father-child relationship deteriorated, particularly for daughters, following the divorce while custodial fathers indicate that half of the time the mother-child relationship improved. In terms of the children's perception of the postdivorce relationship, most children were quite positive about their visits with the noncustodial parent and 62 percent wanted more frequent visits. Although not statistically significant (and therefore a finding that may be due to chance), more children living with the opposite sex parent wanted more visitation (75 percent), than children living with the same sex parent (50 percent).

Support systems were being used by fathers with custody more than mothers with custody. Fathers used additional babysitters, day care, and visitation with the noncustodial parent an average of 24 hours per week while the custodial mother used such alternatives 11 hours per week (Santrock et al. 1979). These differences were not due to the greater likelihood of employment of the father. Fathers with custody were also much more likely to have the children in contact with the noncustodial mother than were custodial mothers to have children in contact with the noncustodial father. The children in contact with other caregivers were rated as warmer, more sociable, and more conforming than child with less contact with other adults. These results were interpreted to mean that the child obtained higher quality care from the other adults and had a custodial parent with less depleted resources.

Hodges, Wechsler, and Ballantine (1979) also found similar results for younger, preschool children. Children with more contact with nonparent caregivers were found to be less anxious in terms of parent ratings. The data were interpreted to indicate that children may benefit from being away from a parent in stress and having contact with an adult who may be functioning under less stressful life situations. Obviously, both the child and the parent may benefit.

It is interesting to note that parenting style was important in the personality development of the child, regardless of the type of custody. An authoritative parenting style, which involves parental warmth, clear rules, and extensive verbal interaction, was related to higher levels of social competence in the child than was a laissez-faire or authoritarian parent style. The authoritative parenting style also resulted in lower levels of anger and demanding behavior (Santrock et al. 1979). The parenting styles of high levels of permissiveness (laissez-faire) and high levels of power-oriented strictness (authoritarian) interacted with type of custody. Other research has shown that when parents make errors in parenting, mothers tend to err in the direction of excessive permissiveness and fathers err in the direction of excessive strictness. This pattern has implications for what happens in mother custody, father custody, and remarried families.

In this study, mothers using authoritarian child rearing did not seem to affect social competence, but mothers using laissez-faire styles had children with little warmth, high anger, high demanding behavior, and little conformity. Fathers using a laissez-faire style had no apparent effect on social behavior as compared to other styles, but fathers with authoritarian parenting had children who were high on anger and low on independence as compared to other parenting styles.

Regardless of whether the mother or father obtain custody, an authoritative parenting style with warmth, clear rules, and open verbal interchange serve the child best. Custodial mothers with laissez-faire parenting styles and custodial fathers with authoritarian parenting style are particularly likely to put the child at risk for less mature social behavior. Consultation with parents is particularly recommended under such circumstances.

The magnitude of differences in terms of benefits of same-sex parent custody were not sufficiently strong to lead to the conclusion that it should be used as a guide to custody arrangements. At the same time, the old folklore that the mother is always better for the child is clearly disproved. Warshak and Santrock (1983a) also noted that such data cannot be used to support reversal of previous custody arrangements. In addition, they noted that these results were obtained only three years after the separation and little is known about long-term effects of different custody arrangements.

Another major study of different custody arrangements was done by Luepnitz (1982). The data collected for this study predated the Warshak and Santrock study, and information on differential responses by sex of the child was not collected. The study compared 16 mother custody families, 16 father custody families, and 18 joint custody families, with 91 children. As for the Warshak and Santrock study, (1983a) the children were about 3.5 years from the final separation. Children were evaluated for self-concept and the family was evaluated for home atmosphere, parental adjustment, and family functioning. Luepnitz found no advantage to mother custody homes. The emotional climate of father custody homes was just as positive as homes headed by a mother. The only variable that predicted poorer adjustment in children was parental conflict, results consistent with other studies on the effect of continued parental conflict on child development (see Chapter 3).

Mother and father custody each had its advantages and disadvantages. For advantages for the mother, the Luepnitz study found that (1) mother custody led to fewer custody fights than the other forms of custody and (2) the mother was free to take children and leave town. The disadvantages of mother custody for the mother were (1) feelings of being overwhelmed by the constant responsibility of parenting, (2) feeling less support from the former spouse than did the mother with joint custody, (3) needing more substitute care and having trouble affording it, and (4) missing the perspective of a second adult. For father custody, the advantages for the father were seen as feeling less discrimination in housing and credit and feeling free to take the children and leave town. The disadvantages for the fathers with custody included two of the disadvantages for mother custody, that is, needing substitute care and missing the perspective of another adult.

Parents were able to develop cross-gender skills. Mothers became more involved in work, money management, and care maintenance. Fathers became less involved with work, spent more time with children, and learned to cook, sew, and do laundry.

Only one study has been found that looked at the characteristics of fathers who obtain custody and fathers who did not seek custody (Gersick, 1979). In that study, 20 custodial fathers were compared to 20 noncustodial fathers in terms of demographic variables, families of origin, participation in child rearing, sex-role orientation, and characteristics of the divorce. Men with custody were more likely to be closer to their own mothers than their fathers and more likely to be later-born children with both brothers and sisters. The relationship with the father was respectful, but relatively unemotional. Perhaps stereotyped sex role training was reduced, leading the father to be more androgynous in orientation. The family of origin was seen as competent, the father was a provider and protector, and the mother was able to give great warmth and intimacy. Most of the custodial fathers wanted more closeness to their fathers as children and may have given greater importance to the father-child bond because of that lack.

Also, men who felt that they were wronged, betrayed, or victimized were more likely than others to seek custody. Involvement of the ex-wife in a relationship with another man was a common description of fathers with custody and rare in noncustodial fathers. In 18 of the 20 cases where the father obtained custody, it was with the pretrial consent of the mother.

Fathers who seek and obtain custody are likely to be more androgynous in terms of training from family of origin. They are also more likely to be angry and resentful of the ex-spouse. Seeking custody, regardless of which parent seeks it, can be an expression of affection and bonding and/or an expression of rage and revenge.

When joint custody was rare, this author was consulted several times about the appropriateness of a family deciding that the father should obtain custody. In some cases, the mother wanted to develop a career and the father was already established and had more time to devote to the children. In other cases, there was agreement between the parents that the father was a better parent. In essence, the question was whether such an arrangement was in the best interests of the child. Such requests were always taken seriously. However, since there may be hidden agendas, I never assumed that the parents have told the entire story. I always interviewed each parent separately and evaluated each child. In every case (admittedly a limited sample), the results were the same. Each parent was basically a decent, warm, caring parent. The children were relatively equally bonded to each parent. The children were generally receptive to the idea of father custody. In each case, the parents' decision was sound.

It would have been more difficult to decide which parent should get custody based on the best interests of the child. Indeed, joint legal custody with primary physical custody with the father would likely be a recommendation that I would make now.

There is so much social pressure for the mother getting custody that the mother may have been afraid of being harshly judged even if the decision is made with warmth and caring for the children. This author suspects that those mothers felt that there was less stigma in having a mental health professional recommend father custody than voluntarily relinquishing custody without professional advice.

Joint Custody

In the last 5 to 10 years, joint custody has been offered as the optimum solution to the custody problem where both parents are relatively equal in terms of quality of parenting—and therefore in terms of the best interests of the child. Continued contact with both parents is helpful for psychological development, so split responsibility (and usually time) between each parent should work well. As previously mentioned, joint legal custody refers to joint responsibility for the welfare of the child. In practice, however, most joint legal custody involves a more equal distribution of time between the parents. Some children switch homes every six months (with visitation with the other parent during that time) and some children switch every day.

Galper (1978) developed the term "coparenting" to refer to the equal involvement of both parents in the caring for the child. Coparenting requires mutual respect and some harmony between parents. It is an agreement that both parents are intimately involved in rearing the children. One parent does not have the right to move to another city and automatically take the children along. If such a change were to occur, it would be a decision that was mutually agreed on.

Ahrons (1979) identified three patterns of joint legal custody families (which were referred to as "binuclear families"):

1. Parents as very good friends. These parents choose to live in the same neighborhood so that the child can attend the same school and have the same playmates. Shared time with both parents and children occur.
2. Parents cordial with each other. These parents share responsibility fairly equally, but seldom spend time together. The families rely heavily on the telephone for communication. This pattern has more unresolved anger.
3. Parents disengaged with each other except in a formal manner. These parents tend to be bitter enemies. The nonresidential parent is the most displeased with the arrangement and has less involvement with the child.

Four primary patterns of shared physical custody have been described in the literature (Atwell, Moore, Nielsen, and Levite, 1984). The first such pattern is long-term block time. This arrangement describes shared residential custody with joint legal custody. Children spend long periods of time with each parent (for example, summer with one parent and winter with the other, school year with one parent and vacations with the other, or alternating years). The second pattern is alternating short-term block times. This arrangement includes patterns such as alternate months, alternate weeks, split week, every other day, and split day. "Bird's nest" describes the third situation. Here, the children stay in one home and the parents move in and out. In the fourth pattern, free access, the children go back and forth at will. What is strongly needed is research on the relative effectiveness of these arrangements for child adjustment.

Reppucci (1984) suggested that joint custody may only be in the child's best interests if conflict level is low, since there is substantial evidence that continued conflict is harmful to the child (Emery, 1982). Reppucci also noted that where conflict levels are high, sole custody may be better for the child.

Joint custody invites continued high involvement in the child's life by both parents. Thus, continued conflict may occur where parents cannot agree on how to raise the child. A 1980 California law established joint custody or sole custody as the preferred legal arrangement. Judges must consider joint custody if either parent requests joint custody, even after custody has already been awarded (Clingempeel and Reppucci, 1982). Interestingly, the California law requires that if joint custody is not awarded, sole custody should be considered for the parent that is most willing to support the child's continuing relationship with the other parent.

One additional hope for joint custody is that the economic well-being of children would be better protected. If postdivorce anger is reduced and both parents continue in the day-to-day decision making for the child, increased involvement should lead to better child support. Folberg and Graham (1979) noted that noncompliance with the child support order only one year after divorce ranged from 62 percent to 47 percent. In Wisconsin, 10 years after the divorce 79 percent of fathers had ceased paying *any* support and in Illinois 59 percent had quit. Given the information in Chapter 3 of the importance of economics for the adjustment of the child, any move which financially supports the child should be seriously considered. However, financial blackmail should not be a basis for awarding either joint legal or shared physical custody.

Just as there are wrong reasons for seeking custody, there are destructive reasons for seeking joint custody. When a parent feels that winning or losing is the issue in the custody battle, rather than the mutual attachment to the children and concern for their happiness and well-being, joint custody may be a compromise that is not in the child's best interests. Ramos (1979) noted that some fathers may feel that the wife has won all that she should and that winning custody of the children is too much. In this situation, the children are treated as part of the property settlement.

Joint custody would seem to work under the following conditions:

1.   *Parents are able to maintain a relatively cordial postseparation relationship with one another.* Such parents can communicate without stirring up old unresolved issues. Hetherington, Cox, and Cox (1978) noted that if there are high levels of conflict between the parents, the benefits of frequent visitation with noncustodial fathers disappeared. The study argued that the mother's continued positive relationship with the father was the best support system for the mother being effective with the children. It should be noted that the children involved were preschool age and that age may require greater levels of support from the noncustodial parent than at other ages. Derdeyn and Scott (1984) concluded that when substantial conflict exists, sole custody may be better for the child. Consistent with this view, in a study of lawyers and judges from a northeastern state (Felner, Terre, Barber, Primavera and Bishop, 1985), the following were mentioned as standards for joint custody: a good relationship between parents with cooperating positive communication; shared goals; and a low level of conflict.

Greif (1979), in a study of 10 joint custody families, noted that several joint custody fathers reported angry, hostile relationships with their exwives. Some of these families avoided contact by using school as the transition place to change residential custody.

While joint custody ordinarily requires increased communication between parents and requires some basis for communication, such an arrangement can work even under conditions of significant anger—if the parents can develop procedures that avoid conflict.

2. *The cause of the divorce was not parenting.* This requirement is not too demanding. Relatively few parents list parenting as a primary cause of divorce. It is seventh or eighth in lists of why the divorce occurred. Incidently, parenting is one of the most serious sources of conflict in second marriages (Messinger, 1976).

3. *If coparenting is the goal of the joint custody, parents needs to make a commitment to maintain geographic proximity to each other.* Children seem happiest when they have relatively equal access to both parents. Children who are switching households are best served when both houses are in the same schools catchment area and they have the same access to peer groups in both houses. Ricks (1984) argued that lack of geographic proximity creates difficulties for joint physical custody. Ricks felt that some children resent travel time and separation from friends, particularly for alternate year switches.

Since one thing that divorced couples do is move, this requirement is not trivial. For families in which joint decision making rather than shared time was the goal, Folberg and Graham (1979) found that not even geographic proximity was needed. They noted a magazine article in which one family was reported to adjust to joint legal custody over a 10,000 mile move from California to England.

4. *Joint custody involving coparenting may work best if the age spread of the children in the family is not great.* Abarbanel (1979) noted that joint custody families with a wide age spread between children may have more adjustment problems than those families with a narrow age spread. Older children often prefer more control and may resent being tied to younger children's schedules. Given that visitation needs may differ widely by age, and most families do not provide individualized changes in residence, it is understandable why wide age ranges are difficult. One possible solution to this problem is splitting the residential changes by subgroups so that the older children change once a week and the younger children change less often.

If all of these conditions can be met, why did the couple get divorced in the first place! In actuality, many couples who are willing to give a high priority to their children and who recognize the importance of the bond between the children and each parent are willing to make this commitment.

As Derdeyn and Scott (1984) have noted, concern for what criteria should be used to determine successful joint custody has been given less weight as the enthusiasm for joint custody has increased. Part of that enthusiasm comes from the courts who are freed from the painful decision of having to decide which parent is best for the child.

Irving, Benjamin, and Trocme (1984) noted that good predictors of outcome success included commitment to parenting, good communication skills, flexibility, the ability to circumscribe marital conflict from the children, and good faith with following the arrangements. When remarriage occurs (without a long distance move), Grief and Simring (1982) felt that joint custody worked better than sole custody. Feelings of loss were reduced. Joint custody permitted the remarried couple significant time together without parenting. "Instant" parenting needs were reduced.

That enthusiasm would seem to come more from California in which joint custody is presumptive than from states where it is not. In a previously mentioned study of lawyers and Superior Court judges in a northeastern state (Felner et al., 1985), most felt that maternal custody was the most viable and paternal custody the next best alternative. Lawyers were equally divided on preference for paternal versus joint custody. Judges approved of joint custody in only 11 percent of the cases.

Problems in Joint Custody

Problems in joint custody may arise when one parent remarries and job opportunities in another area for that parent or parent's new spouse develop. How do the parents now handle the wish to have shared residential time? Suits for sole custody (or primary geographic custody) occur. The judge then has a choice of deciding what is best for the child or ruling that the parent that is changing the agreement is at risk. Even long distance families can consult over important decisions that affect the children's lives.

A variety of mental health professionals have made statements that would indicate that they would not approve of shared residential custody. Lewis (1974) said that for children from six months to six years, "continuity of care and affection is paramount and overriding." Psychological discontinuity if reaching a critical point would lead to damage to the child's development.

Ramos (1979) listed several problems that have developed in shared residential custody:

1. One parent was not able to stay sufficiently involved. After a period of time some parents withdraw from either making joint decisions about the child's welfare or provide less and less joint residential time due to competing interests or job demands.

2. The constant shifting has led some children to feel that they have a transient life with no home base anywhere. Indeed, the concern that there will be a sense of homelessness has led some mental health professionals to recommend against joint residential custody for any child. Experience with joint residential custody has clearly not confirmed this outcome as a common consequence, but some children do have trouble with the constant changes. There is no research as yet to predict which children will cope well or poorly to a joint residential custody arrangement.

3.   Joint residential custody tends to cost more. Because the child may spend a significant amount of time in two homes, a greater amount of space for the child is needed in two settings.
4.   Changes in needs over time may require different arrangements.

Irving et al. (1984) also mentions several contraindications for shared physical custody:

1.   Very young children.
2.   Children with emotional problems for whom the arrangement is confusing and anxiety-provoking.
3.   Parents who use their children as a weapon or whose anger toward their former spouse persists.
4.   If the joint custody has to be court-ordered, it will likely be less satisfactory.

According to Irving et al. (1984) predictors of successful outcome for joint custody were: commitment to parenting; reasonable communication skills; flexibility; the ability to circumscribe or separate marital conflict from the children; and good faith with regard to the arrangements. Poor success occurred when the cause of the divorce was a break of trust (such as an affair), guilt, or feelings of being coerced by the mediator.

Evaluating Joint Custody

There are few evaluations of joint custody, but the increased use of this arrangement is likely to result in significant increases in research in the next few years. Ahrons (1979) reported data from 41 divorced parents who had court-awarded joint custody in California. The marriages were an average of 11.6 years at divorce. The children ranged from 1 to 17 years of age with an average of 11.7 years. Obviously, there was not a simple ratio of length of marriage to number and age of children.

These families involved joint legal responsibility, not necessarily joint time. The minimum time in the secondary household ranged from a couple of hours per week to 50–50. Most of the sample (71 percent) spent some time with both parents and the children.

The greater the amount of conflict between the two parents, the lower the amount of nonresidential parent-child involvement ($r = .43, p < .01$). The more supportive the relationship between the two parents, the more parent-child involvement there was likely to be ($r = .53, p < .001$). The few divorced spouses who had bitter conflict had little or no postdivorce involvement with each other.

The "best friend" relationship involved continued coparental relationships. As might be expected, anger tended to be moderate to low. These parents were strong supporters of joint custody. The coparenting relationship which characterized all but a few of the parents remained child centered.

Abarbanel (1979) reported on a case history evaluation for four joint custody, coparenting (joint residential custody) families. Children lived with one parent no longer than two weeks at a time. The children appeared well-adjusted and had no severe behavioral problems. They felt at home in both settings. For two of the three only children in the study (4 and 5 years old) joint custody was accepted as a way of life. The children tended to do well when the discrepancy between the two homes was minimal. Abarbanel hypothesized that if a child had a "difficult" temperament, frequent moving back and forth might be unsettling.

Children with difficult temperaments may have a particularly difficult time handling frequent changes in joint physical custody.

Abarbanel proposed the following requirements for joint custody to work: commitment to joint custody by both parents; support of the other parent; flexible sharing of responsibility; and agreement on the implicit rules. Even with these conditions, the age, sex, number, and age range of the children may affect the success of joint custody. Geographical proximity was crucial for the success of the four families evaluated in this study. The effect of cohabitation and remarriage on the success of joint custody was unknown.

Greif (1979) reported on the father-child relationship of 40 fathers of 63 children ranging in age from 5 to 12. Of these 63 children, 10 were in joint legal custody (generally including shared physical custody). Although the small sample size precludes data analysis on joint custody, the fathers did not perceive a change in paternal influence after the separation. Those fathers who had less contact with their children perceived significant decrease in four areas of paternal influence (emotional development, moral development, teaching the child how to behave, and financial decision making).

In contrast, fathers with shared custody perceived no loss in influence in any of 10 areas of fathering, but did perceive significant increase in recreational activities. Joint legal custody fathers also described relationships with more open expression of emotion. The fathers with joint custody felt that it worked well and were the most satisfied with their postdivorce relationships.

All the father-child relationships with joint custody had high satisfaction scores while father-child relationships in which the children were in sole mother custody accounted for all the low satisfaction group (58 percent of the mother custody families had low satisfaction for the father-child relationship). For joint custody, separations were less painful since the father and child knew that there would soon be a long period again together. The concern for severe adjustment to two households was not justified. Children were reported as needing only a short initial adjustment period. While encouraging, the study was limited to 10 children in joint custody and that small sample severely limits the ability to generalize.

Steinman (1981) evaluated 24 couples who voluntarily chose coparenting. The residential time arrangements ranged from 50–50 to 67–33. In half of the homes, the children split residences every three to four days. Twenty-five percent arranged a week-to-week schedule. The others had varied arrangements, alternating every day (!), every two weeks, every three months, and, in one case, every year. The arrangements had continued for a minimum of six months before the study.

Parents were described as maintaining a strong ideological commitment to joint legal custody and open access. They actively valued each other as parents. Finally, the other parent was actively valued on behalf of the child. Many of the couples had had lengthy separations. Of the 21 legally married couples, 18 had been separated for 2 to 4 years without getting a final divorce. The educational level of the parents were similar, and all but one of the women were employed. Indeed, one of the motivations for joint custody on the part of the mothers was a desire for relief from child-rearing responsibilities. The children felt that they had two "psychological parents." They expected and received nurturing, discipline, and guidance from both parents. Parents did not split parenting functions along traditional gender lines.

While the parents liked the arrangement, one-third of the children felt overburdened by the demands of maintaining two households. The children were troubled when parents were in major conflict over childrearing values. They worried about the parent who was alone. Children typically knew when switches in households would occur. About 25 percent experienced confusion and anxiety about their schedules and switching. Of those, half were in the youngest group (4- and 5-year-old girls). Four 7- to 9-year-old boys also struggled to keep up with the schedule. "The big problem with joint custody is that you have to remember where the spoons are." For one child, the 120 miles between parental homes produced major disruption. Two adolescent girls wanted to spend more time with peers and school-based social activities and wanted to be in one home.

It is clear that some children, particularly younger ones, have difficulty with joint physical custody.

On the positive side, the children did not get caught up in loyalty conflicts and valued the joint custody arrangement. Most were able to master the practical problems. This mastery plus the feeling of being loved and wanted by both parents led to heightened self-esteem.

Ilfeld, Ilfeld, and Alexander (1982) looked at 414 consecutive custody cases in Los Angeles court over a two-year period. They compared the relitigation rate for joint custody cases (138) versus sole custody cases (276). Both sole custody and joint custody cases were based primarily (91 percent of sole custody and 86 percent of joint custody) on agreement between parents. Their data also included a small number of cases (18) in which families were given joint custody without the consent of both parents. Relitigation rate for the joint custody families was 16 percent at the end of two years. There were half as many relitigations involving joint custody as sole custody cases ($p < .001$). When the small group of nonagreeing joint custody cases were evaluated, only six (33 percent), had been involved in relitigation, which was almost the same as for the sole custody sample (32 percent). Thus, the authors concluded that the belief that both parents must have a commitment to joint custody for it to work was not supported by the data.

Joint custody would seem to reduce relitigation and equalize contact with both parents.

Ilfeld et al. (1982) cited Pojman's (1982) dissertation on four groups of 20 boys from 5 to 13 years of age, living in joint custody, sole custody, intact happy marriage families, and intact unhappy marriage families. Pojman found that boys from joint custody families were better adjusted than boys of sole custody and unhappy marriage families as measured by the security scale of the Louisville Behavior Checklist and Inferred Self-concept Scale. There was no differences in adjustment between boys from sole custody and unhappy marriage families.

None of these studies are able to assess the question of cause and effect. Does joint custody produce better adjustment or do parents with better child rearing and greater parental involvement, which in turn predicts better child adjustment, want joint custody? When children are better adjusted, parents may be less likely to see the other parent as a "bad" parent, and be more willing to consider joint custody. Thus, the alternative that good adjustment in children "causes" joint custody must also be considered.

Luepnitz's (1982) study, previously discussed, is one of the few that evaluated joint custody as compared to sole custody. The study had only 11 families with joint custody. There was no benefit to the adjustment of the children for any custody arrangement. The amount of visitation also did not predict poor adjustment. Most children in sole custody arrangement were dissatisfied with the amount of visitation that they had with the noncustodial parent. For joint custody children, most were satisfied with the amount of contact that they had with each parent. In joint custody, the child maintained an appropriate parent-child relationship with both parents, while in sole custody, the child developed an "avuncular" relationship with the noncustodial parent.

Joint physical custody would seem to increase the children's satisfaction with access to both parents and maintain both parents in a parental roles.

While the question of increased conflict was raised early as a possible outcome of joint custody, Luepnitz did not find conflict to be a problem in joint custody families. Half of the sole custody families had returned to court to fight about money, while none of the joint custody families had.

As previously mentioned, Luepnitz (1982) also reported that joint custody presented several advantages to the parents: there were fewer court battles over money than sole custody families; child support payments were more likely to be paid to the single mother; the father found less discrimination in housing and credit; both parents had a built-in break from parenting; both parents felt that it was useful to have the perspective of two parents in disciplining; and both parents felt that they could rely on each other for child care.

The disadvantages were self-apparent. Parents felt that they were tied to their exspouse in a way that did not occur in sole custody arrangements and that they could not easily move out of town. In addition, the movement of children between households was a hassle.

The study concluded that joint custody at its best was superior to sole custody at its best. Luepnitz predicted that as parents understand the option of joint custody, it will increase in popularity.

D'Andrea (1983) compared 24 fathers in joint custody with 22 noncustodial fathers with visitation. Fathers with joint legal custody spent much more substantial time with their children. Joint custody, as compared to noncustodial sole custody, was related to statistically significantly higher paternal involvement in terms of self-perceived knowledge of and influence on the child. Paternal involvement and paternal self-esteem were related to one another, and paternal self-esteem was significantly higher for joint custody fathers as compared to noncustodial fathers.

Irving et al. (1984) presented preliminary results of a large scale study involving questionnaire results for 201 parents (involving 75 couples and 51 individual parents) all of whom where involved in a shared parenting arrangement. The Joint Custody Project was initiated in Toronto, Canada in 1982. The questionnaire involve 114 items that took from one-and-a-half to two hours to complete. With an extensive interview, there were 268 variables available for each participant.

Of the sample, most have at least some university or postgraduate education. The majority were only married once, the marriage lasting an average of nine years or more. Typically, the parents had two children, the first from 7 to 13 years old and the second 5 to 10 years old. At the time of the study, the majority had been separated two to four years. While they reported a high level of conflict at the time of the separation, at the time of the study feelings were generally more positive. About 10 percent had remarried and 25 percent were living in a common-law relationship. Many of the former spouses continued to live with a short ride (46 percent) or walking distance (32 percent) and 75 percent were within five miles. Joint legal custody with shared access may encourage less geographic mobility. Of course, those who choose joint legal custody may be less distressed and feel less the need to move.

The decision to have shared parenting was almost always initially suggested by one or the other spouse (85.3 percent), seldom by lawyers or mediators. In most cases, the agreement was in writing. About 50 percent of the parents spend an equal amount of time with the children. The most frequent pattern was a one-week rotation and an equal division of holidays and vacations. The next largest group (30 percent) had a 75/25 split.

Some parents indicated that it worked from the beginning, but these were a minority (36 percent). The ironing out process took up to a year (32 percent), even though some reported fairly early success (41.8 percent). Some 23 percent of the children were upset for a time following a shift in residence, an issue not addressed in other studies.

Potential difficulties in the coparenting relationship did not arise. Most reported that their relationships with the former spouse was moderately friendly and over time it had remained the same or become more positive. Parents seldom talked about anything other than the children. New partners were seen as having a positive effect on the children. This finding is very different from the research on remarriage with more traditional sole custody discussed in Chapter .

Satisfaction with the coparenting was high, with 77.4 percent overall satisfaction and 86.2 percent satisfaction with the schedule. There was no association between the physical arrangements of schedules and satisfaction. Social class was not related to satisfaction. Satisfaction was greater if the arrangement was arrived at without court involvement, if guilt was low, if preseparation conflict was low, if a longer time had past, and if the duration of shared parenting was longer. Those who had court ordered shared custody were not satisfied.

Derdeyn et al. (1984) in reviewing the studies on the effectiveness of joint custody noted that small sample size and lack of direct assessment of the adjustment of the children limit the implications of the research. They also noted that the research forms an insubstantial basis for public policy. The enthusiasm for joint custody has outdistanced any empirical basis for justifying it!

What is also unfortunate is that the small amount of research on joint residential custody has not permitted judgments of the most appropriate residential time arrangements by age of child. It is simply not known whether a particular pattern facilitates or interferes with good adjustment. In addition, mediating factors such as age, sex of child, parental conflict, the child's cognitive abilities, and temperament have not been evaluated.

In a study of 133 children within 30 months of the separation of their parents, the impact of joint legal custody for one-third of the sample was evaluated (Wolchick, Braver and Sandler, 1985). Children were an average of 11.1 years old in the joint custody group and 11.7 years old in the maternal custody group. In three-fourths of the joint legal custody group, there was a primary residential parent, suggesting that less shared residential custody occurred with this sample than might usually be the case.

Self-esteem was significantly higher for children in the joint custody families than for children in maternal custody. Both boys and girls of joint custody families reported more positive experiences in the last three months than did children in maternal custody. Boys in joint custody reported fewer negative experiences than boys in maternal custody.

Symptomatology as rated by parents and by children did not vary by group or gender of child. In this study, the participants were from a state without presumptive joint custody, and parents were self-selected into the group to which they belonged. Therefore, it is not possible to tell whether joint custody per se was responsible for the differences between group or whether the parents who approve of joint custody are different on other dimensions (for example, parents who are fighting less).

Age of the Child and Joint Residential Custody

The recommendations concerning visitation patterns given in Chapter 7 are appropriate for consideration for joint custody. As Clingempeel and Reppucci (1982) noted, evidence of multiple attachments and the lack of evidence for harm to social-emotional development of day care does raise questions about what coparenting arrangements would be appropriate for young children. Rarely do parents request joint residential custody for infants. If they do, the mental health professional must be prepared to decide the best pattern of residential changes for a young infant. As discussed in some detail in Chapter 7 concerning the length and frequency of visitation in young children, there is some reason to believe that infants can easily tolerate frequent contact with two parents if each parent has daily or almost daily contact with the child. Under such conditions, the child will bond to both parents.

No one has looked at the effect of daily changes in where the child sleeps, but intuitively it would seem that such frequent changes would be unnecessarily confusing to the child. Clingempeel and Reppucci (1982) noted that such frequent contact with each parent might reduce fears of abandonment, but might also increase wishes of reconciliation. They concluded that one generalization that could be made from such data is that children under three might require greater stability of single-parent residential custody. They also noted, however, that continued relationship with both parents is highly useful to young preschool age children.

It is not known whether repeated separations in very young children due to alternating residential care would lead to adjustment problems. It is interesting to note that while there are no studies evaluating the effect of joint residential custody for very young children, the case histories described by Atwell et al. (1984) indicated that there were problems with joint custody: An alternating three-month block created problems for a 2 year old, and a split week pattern was related to provocative and oppositional behavior for a 3 1/2 year old, anxiety for a 5 year old, and dependency in a 2 1/2 year old. In contrast, a 4 1/2 year old was doing well with a split week pattern and a 4 year old was having good adjustment with an alternating daily schedule. The only other cases discussed in some detail were a 10 year old having trouble with an inconsistent split week and three children, ages 11, 8, and 6 1/2 having trouble in a bird's nest pattern. Obviously, how the parents handle the children and each other may have more to do with the success or failure of joint residential custody than the particular pattern.

Thus, while there are theoretical positions and some case histories, concerning the effect of alternating residences on young children, there is almost no empirical data to guide clinicians. If both parents are having almost daily contact with the child, the child can probably handle physical joint custody, as long as he or she sleeps in the same house. If daily contact is not likely (and few divorced parents are on such good terms as to permit that frequent a contact), joint residential custody may be a goal to develop as the child becomes older.

For infants and toddlers, joint residential custody is probably inappropriate although the question has not been researched. For preschool aged children, joint residential custody should be considered only if both parents have frequent, almost daily, contact with the children. If such frequent contact is not feasible, it may be more appropriate to have residential custody initially with one parent with frequent visitation for the other (see Chapter 7). Under such conditions, parents can slowly increase the amount of time that the child spends with the less frequently seen parent until by age 6 or 7, equal time with each parent has been developed.

Basically, there are no guidelines about what pattern of change is best for joint residential custody. Part of the decision depends on the ease with which the child has access to the other parent and to friends. For school age children, changes of less than one week seem to be very confusing. This author had one 12-year-old in therapy who changed every three or four days depending on the job responsibilities of one of the parents. While she complained that packing was tiresome, she still indicated a strong preference for equal access to both parents. California law provides nine patterns of alternation of residential custody that take into account the age of the child and the proximity of the parents to one another (Clingempeel and Reppucci, 1982).

If the change in residence is infrequent, with long periods between changes, bonding with each parent is best supported by providing visitation contact with the nonresidential custodial parent.

Clingempeel and Reppucci (1982) reported on a joint residential arrangement in which the child changed residences and schools every two weeks. Supposedly, the child adjusted well to this situation, but given the incredible complexity of that life, it is reasonable to propose that the child adjusted well in spite of, rather than because of, that residential arrangement. It is important to note that the courts are charged to come up with plans that are in the best interests of the child, not plans that can just be tolerated. The failure to see symptoms in the child does not prove that no harm is occurring or will become apparent sometime in the future. The fact that a child can survive such a program does not mean that optimal adjustment will occur. Irving et al. (1984) noted that joint residential custody is not appropriate for very young children or those children with emotional problems who experience the frequent changes as confusing and anxiety provoking. There is no discussion as to the lower age for joint residential custody and how frequent changes can occur.

The Association of Family Conciliation Courts has compiled a useful handbook that includes some of the aforementioned references in addition to others (Milne, 1979). Articles on the psychological impact of joint custody, case law, a sample joint custody agreement, and an annotated bibliography current to the 1979 publication date are included.

SUMMARY

Custody evaluations require specification of the criteria for custody and awareness of child development. It is important to monitor sensitivity to potential biases in the assessor. Proper custody evaluation requires an understanding of the effects of mother custody, father custody, and joint custody on child development. Joint custody has been surprisingly effective, even when there is a significant level of parental conflict.

In the next chapter, specific guidelines for conducting the custody assessment are reviewed. In addition, report and courtroom testimony are covered.

CHAPTER 6

Custody Evaluations: Models of Assessment

Custody evaluations refer to the process of gathering information, interpreting data, and forming and communicating a recommendation concerning child custody.

There is no national standard for custody evaluations. In private practice settings, custody evaluation often uses the guideline that "more is better."

Given the complexity of family relationships, the problem of predicting future stability in the midst of upset over the divorce, and the problem of changing developmental needs over time, the judge or referee needs the wisdom of Solomon. Remember, however, Solomon was wise only because his strategy worked! What would he have done if both mothers had agreed to split the baby in half?

PRECUSTODY EVALUATION NEGOTIATIONS

Who is the Client?

Unless the child's welfare is at stake, mental health professionals should avoid representing one party against the other in a custody battle. The first responsibility of the mental health professional is the welfare of the child—not representing one side of the parent's arguments. If the mental health professional represents one parent, the other parent will see the professional as an adversary and will be reluctant and/or less than truthful about providing information. In order to best evaluate which parent is more appropriate (or if joint custody is reasonable), the mental health professional needs to be in an equal relationship with each parent (Chasin and Grunebaum, 1981).

Avoid representing one parent against the other in a child custody dispute. The position of guardian ad litem for lawyers is best for the mental health professional. The position should be that the mental health professional is the representative of the best interests of the child, not of either parent, regardless of who is paying for the service.

Negotiations

At the beginning of negotiations and prior to contact with the parents, it is useful to establish a working relationship with the attorneys involved (Goldzband, 1982).

The mental health professional should not get in the position of allowing only one lawyer to read a report and decide at that point whether the report would be useful in court. If the assumption is that the report is focussed on the child's best interests, legal strategy should not be the basis for deciding whether the report is used by the court. If the assessment is being done in response to a court order, the court should stipulate that the report should go to both sides.

If the evaluation is being done at the request of one lawyer, get a written agreement prior to the evaluation that the report will be submitted to both lawyers and the court. Without such a stipulation, obtain a court order signed by the judge. If the court orders the evaluation, such an agreement is not necessary.

Each parent should have a written explanation of the evaluation process, the limits of confidentiality (there are none), and the procedure for billing. Nothing said in the assessment can be kept secret. Chasin and Grunebaum (1981) provided a copy of such a basic contract. This explanation should be obtained prior to starting the evaluation. As an added safety measure, the parties should be required to sign it.

Suarez, Weston, and Hartstein (1978) and Shafte (1985) suggested that a stipulation of the ground rules be signed in court. The ground rules should indicate that evaluation can include the parents, the children, and any other person (including grandparents, new spouses, live-in partners, housekeepers, child care workers, teachers, and so forth) deemed necessary by the evaluator. Suarez et al. (1978) also suggested that the stipulation include the requirement that the parents provide any pertinent records or files including previous psychiatric evaluations, medical files, and school records. The request should also include police records, medication, and the fact of psychotherapy. The content of psychotherapy should be protected from evaluation (see the discussion as to why later in this chapter).

The stipulation should include information about fees and who pays them. Note that fees for expert testimony may be different and extra from fees for evaluation. Suarez et al. (1978) additionally indicated that the evaluator should have at least one week's notice prior to a court appearance. Some states require that the report be available a minimum number of days prior to court. Skafte (1985) noted that without the court order, the mental health professional could be vulnerable to lawsuit if either parent claimed at a later time that the evaluation was not done with their permission. Both parties should stipulate as to the assessment if a court order is not available.

Fees

This author recommends that payment be made in advance as does Goldzband (1982). However, it is extremely important that concern over payment not be an issue for the mental health professional in deciding which parent is best suited for custody. Concern over payment or anger at nonpayment could affect the decision making process even for the mental health professional who makes conscientious efforts at avoiding being influenced by that problem. In addition, one parent is likely to be dissatisfied with the report. It is very difficult to get an angry parent to pay for those services.

Collect the anticipated fees in an escrow account prior to beginning the evaluation. Do not complete the report if additional fees have not been paid.

MODELS OF CUSTODY EVALUATIONS

Custody evaluations done by the court, probation department, or a social services agency are likely to be considerably shorter than those done by a private practicing mental health professional. For example, in Denver District Court the following information is gathered (Watson, 1979):

1. An interview with each parent including questions concerning education, number of marriages, number of children, and military service.
2. Employment check and police check.
3. Physical and emotional health of each party including physician and therapist reports.
4. Neighbor or other witness interviews, if appropriate.
5. Background information from school principal, teachers, social workers, nurses or other school personnel. Children are interviewed at school.

As is not surprising, institutionally based custody evaluation teams, are likely to use institutionally based information. Private practicing professionals are less likely to use such sources as employment and police record checks. In addition, private evaluation teams are likely to prefer an office setting as an interview site.

A private evaluation is likely to include the following:

1. Several interviews with each parent alone. Parents need to be reminded that nothing in the interview is confidential. The parent must be made aware that nothing is allowed to be "off the record." Skafte (1985) indicated that there are advantages to seeing the parents together for the first interview, even though the level of tension in the interview tends to be high.

2. Several interviews with each child alone. Gardner (1976) recommended observing preschool age children two or three times and older children three or more times. Children also need to be informed that the interview is not confidential. The evaluator should, however, try to protect the children in terms of the relationship with each parent whenever possible.

3. Interviewing the parent and children together.

4. Interviewing teachers, babysitters, and other significant people in the children's lives. If grandparents play a significant role, they should be interviewed as well. If one or both parents are in a new relationship to which the children will be exposed, that person should be seen. Chasin et al. (1981) also seek out conversation with significant others, including grandparents, housekeepers, friends, teachers, physicians, neighbors, and psychotherapists.

5. Home visit. This visit allows determination of the safety of the home setting and provides additional information about the sensitivity of the parents to the children's needs.

6. Chasin and Grunebaum (1981) tell parents that not only will the evaluation team speak with them, but that they would also be willing to read any material that the parent might want to submit and to talk with anyone whom they feel has information that would help the court make a decision about custody.

In a home with two children, the above model could take 20 to 40 or so staff hours, not including team meetings to pull the information together and writing of the report. In a more complex or difficult evaluation (i.e., where there are serious accusations that require investigation or where more children are involved) the staff time may be considerably longer. In addition, the custody team can expect to be required to testify in court, permitting cross-examination of the report and its implications.

It is not surprising that private custody evaluation can cost anywhere from $1000 to $5000 for a simple evaluation. Complex battles cost much more. This cost puts private custody evaluations out of the reach of most families, who may already be paying substantial legal fees for a contested divorce. Given that income is already being stretched by now serving two households, it is understandable that 90 percent of divorces do not have contested court battles.

The British Columbia, Canada Service Delivery Standards

In a rare move in the area of child custody assessment, the British Columbia Corrections Branch developed a set of standards for custody and access assessment in 1985. These standards defined mediation, conciliation, and the procedures for assessment of custody. The law provides a specially trained

Family Court Counselor to perform the assessment, but private evaluations are permitted as an alternative.

The best interests of the child is the primary consideration for custody determination. The British Columbia law specifically excludes from consideration behavior of a parent that does not affect the child.

All parties to the assessment, including the children, are notified that nothing is confidential and they have the right to withhold information. This limit to disclosure protects people from self-incrimination. Other people contacted as part of the investigation however, such as teachers or neighbors, do not have that right.

In the first interview, the Family Court Counselor tries to see both parents together in one of their homes, if possible. The names of other people who can provide information are requested. If the parents live in the same area as the counselor, the counselor shall observe the child in the presence of both parents, jointly or separately. The observation should be done in the environment in which the child might be placed, if possible. This requirement applies regardless of the age of the child.

The child's views shall be obtained in a manner appropriate to the age of the child. The child is not asked to make a choice. It is recognized in the standards that such a choice might be damaging to the child. The child is given an opportunity to express feelings.

The report, which must be provided to every party at least five days before the hearing, is prepared by the Family Court Counselor. Sources of information are identified, provided that such sources do not damage constructive or essential relationships. The parties are informed that they have the right to ask any questions to clarify the contents of the report prior to hearing, but dispute of the content must occur in court.

The development of assessment standards is a very exciting innovation for a jurisdiction. While the evaluators still have wide discretion about how to collect information, some information is required for all evaluations. Such a data base provides a common set of criteria for all assessment and an opportunity to research the effectiveness of the process.

Additional Evaluation Procedures

There are additional evaluation procedures that some teams use, based in part on the professional roles of the members of the team. Dr. Lanning Schiller (personal communication, 1985) has found it expedient to obtain most factual information through a long written questionnaire rather than an interview. Interviewing is only used for more probing questions.

Psychological testing is most commonly done as part of the evaluation of the children and parents. Bonding with each parent can be evaluated with projective techniques. Thematic Apperception Test evaluations, whether using the adult, children, or individual cards, can be helpful. For example, when a child sees all adult women as angry and controlling, the examiner can combine that information with other obtained information to fill out the picture of parent perception. Use of the Minnesota Multiphasic Personality Inventory can catch some false negatives that were not apparent in interviews and projective testing can be helpful in picking up borderline pathology (a type person that can look quite healthy on interview).

No custody evaluation should be based solely on test results. The implications of test materials are given meaning only in the context of other information.

While both lawyers have the right to see the test materials, the psychologist should not make the mistake of explaining the process by which recommendations based on the test materials were obtained. Learning to interpret test materials takes years. The well-meaning psychologist who tries to draw an inference from a single, out-of-context piece of information is setting himself or herself up for a cruel and effective cross-examination that can discredit the testimony. Since it is clearly true that idiosyncratic experiences may lead to particular perceptions (although why the child chose to remember that particular perception is another matter), it is always possible that one perception has limited meaning.

It is the pattern of perceptions on projectives that permit valid inferences about the functioning of the child. The psychologist should refuse to answer questions concerning the interpretation of individual responses, since the original evaluation looked at patterns.

Family Interview

Relatively few evaluators start with family interviews. Musetto (1980), however, recommends beginning an evaluation by seeing the parents and children together unless the level of anxiety is too strong. The advantage of a joint meeting is to emphasize the fact that custody and visitation evaluation is a family problem and the family needs to be responsible for solving it. The interviewer talks to the family about the joint responsibility for the problem, rather than focussing the blame on one particular person. "Psychological" parents should be willing to acknowledge their own contribution to the family problem.

Following Bowen (1976), Musetto discussed a systems analysis of families. He noted that families tend to form triangles. In order to maintain a relationship, parents may divert attention to children or to issues. Since the family is a system, the whole family contributes to maintain the status quo. When there is a problem between two family members, the question must be raised as to the role of other family members in maintaining that problem. Family interviews gives the evaluator an opportunity to understand those dynamics and to help the family accept responsibility for the problem and the solution.

Bentovim and Gilmour (1981) used a family therapy model of assessment and intervention. They proposed a model in which a focal hypothesis that is, a primary theme that explains how the family operates, was generated to understand family functioning. The surface action described ways in which the family normally nurtured and socialized each other. If the surface action is pathological, it may reflect a rigid repetitious behavior that overrides individual needs. Depth structure, refers to more enduring family scripts from historical child rearing, and is analyzed in terms of family system issues from the family of origin or family of procreation.

To evaluate surface action and depth structure, Bentovim and Gilmour proposed seeing together all significant family members and professionals and seeing them in various combinations. During these interviews, interactional tasks may be used to avoid parental attempts at convincing the evaluators of a point of view. Such tasks might include: caretaking (infants); play, setting limits, separations, or reunions (toddlers); and talking about the divorce situation while eliciting the child's wishes and opinions (older children). Genograms, that is, diagrams of family history including major events, were used to collect information.

Parent Interview

There are a variety of questions that are useful in evaluating parenting. The GAP report (1981) suggested the following criteria for parent evaluations: "(1) Basic mental health status; (2) personality functioning; (3) past personal history with particular reference to their own childhoods; (4) degree of flexibility in accepting feedback to their parenting responsibilities; (5) probable method of restoring missing mate (cooperative or noncooperative); and (6) ability to form treatment alliance where their children are concerned." Parents should be questioned about suicide and homicide attempts as well as their own childhoods, especially concerning divorce and how it was handled, abuse, alcohol, drugs, discipline, and affection. Evaluation of parental scripts may provide information on areas to explore about present parenting. Gardner (1976) suggested starting the interview by giving the parent the opportunity to tell the interviewer anything on his or her mind.

Other suggestions for useful questions are:

1. Why do you want custody of the children? (This question is an obvious one, but it may produce some surprising answers.) A common set of answers include the affectionate bonds with the children and a wish to protect the children from the inadequate parenting of the other parent.
2. Every family has different ways of expressing their love for each other. Some touch a lot. Some say that they love each other. Others just know it. How do you express affection for the children? How do they express affection for you. (This is essentially the same question that the children should be asked.) What do you see as true for the children's other parent in terms of affection.
3. How do you provide for discipline for the children. What do you think

about spanking, yelling, taking away privileges, grounding? How often do these punishments occur? For what behaviors? What do you see as true for the children's other parent in terms of discipline?

4. Do you consider yourself to have deficiencies with regard to handling the children (Gardner, 1976)?

5. What is the history of the child? Was the pregnancy wanted? Was birth control being used? How was the pregnancy? What was the labor and delivery like? Before the birth, did you have any preference for the sex of the child? How did you feel about the baby? How was the infancy? Did the mother breast feed or bottle feed? Why? What was the temperament of the child (i.e., biological rhythms, eating regularity, eating ease, sleep patterns, and attachment)? What is the history of childhood diseases? Childhood accidents? When were the milestones for sitting up, walking, talking, and toilet training (these answers are notoriously inaccurate)?

6. What complaints does your spouse make about the way you handle the children (Gardner, 1976)?

7. What activities do you enjoy doing with the children? What activities bore you or irritate you?

8. What do you hope for the children in terms of your dreams for them (an adaptation of one of Gardner's questions).

9. What do you see as the needs of children in general at this age (i.e., the age of each child)? How do you think things are going to change in terms of the children's needs?

The following set of questions was suggested by Chasin and Grunebaum (1981):

1. What is the ideal custody arrangement for your family? Why?

2. How would it affect you if the other parent got custody?

3. Joint custody involves equally shared decision-making and may or may not involve equally shared child care. What would be its benefits and drawbacks for your family?

4. What aspect of your ideal arrangement would you be willing to negotiate?

5. Describe each child's daily routine, friends, teachers, likes, dislikes, interests, fears, skills, and problems. For each problems, describe the remedy you feel would be most effective.

6. What are your strongest assets as a parent? What are your weaknesses?

7. What are the strengths and weaknesses of the other parent?

8. "If you had custody of the children, how often would you like them to see the other parent?" (Skafte 1985)

The last question is particularly good. It is important to assess the understanding that each parent has concerning the needs of children to have contact with both parents. Indeed, California law requires some preference be given to the parent who is most willing to support access to the other parent.

Skafte (1985) proposed that the parents be interviewed in a joint session. Skafte felt that information obtained by such an interview outweighed the tension produced. Joint assessment might provide useful information on the likelihood that joint legal custody would work. Such an interview should begin with questions concerning the history of the relationship, the effect of having children, parenting, child care responsibilities, changes in relationships with the children, the decision to separate, the change in the children's lives after separation, desire for custody, plans for the children, and access to the other parent if you had custody, according to Skafte.

Skafte then provided an additional set of questions for interviewing each parent separately. Those questions focused on the parent's own childhood, young adulthood, marriage, separation, feelings about the children, feelings about custody and how the parent expects to handle it, expected allegations from the other parent, and thoughts about visitation.

D'Andrea (1983) used a measure of "fathering" developed from Greif (1979) and Roman (1977 cited in Abarbanel, 1979) that could be used for evaluation of parents of either gender:

1. Routine daily care and safety of the child;
2. Intellectual development;
3. Physical development;
4. Teaching the child how to behave;
5. Recreational activities;
6. Emotional development;
7. Religious development;
8. Moral development;
9. Giving the child a sense of being a part of the family; and
10. Financial decisions making affecting the child.

A measure of perceived knowledge of the child was obtained by the number of "I don't know" responses to the questionnaire.

Child Interview

The GAP report (1981) proposed the following areas to be included in the child evaluation: basic mental health status, previous developmental course, coping with particular attention to restoring the missing parent and grief, attachment to parents, phase of development, degrees and severity of psychological impairment and treatment if any, and ability to use substitute objects as resource in lieu of missing parent.

Lewis (1974) raised some difficult questions concerning information given to the primary school age child concerning the purpose of the interview and testing. If it is clear to the child that confidentiality is not present, will the data be limited because of the defensiveness of the child? Will the child feel betrayed when learning of the information given the court? Should the child be encouraged to open up old wounds, when a therapeutic relationship does not exist and follow up is not going to be possible.

Even though the child may be more defensive or try to distort information to fit wishes, providing a child with the information concerning the purpose of the interviews and with the limits of confidentiality is likely to produce less harm to the child later than concealing such information. The mental health professional has an obligation to protect the best interests of the child not only in terms of the custody decision, but also the custody evaluation process. The evaluator should discourage the child from opening up unresolved areas to a greater degree than can be easily handled and should request more time with the child if inadvertent stress occurs as a function of the process.

Chasin and Grunebaum (1981) proposed telling the parents exactly what the evaluator wants the parents to say to the child about the interview. They suggested saying something like, "You are going to see someone who will help us decide the best way for us to take care of you after the divorce. He won't hurt you or give you tests (This latter comment should be changed, of course, if tests are to be administered). He wants to play with you. He wants to understand you." They then suggested telling the parent that the first question to the child would be, "What did your parent tell you about your visit to me." If the child does not or cannot answer, the assessor should provide some structure and then proceed.

In meeting with the child alone, the type of questions and the wording of the questions must be altered to take into account the vocabulary and developmental needs of the child. Gardner (1976) has a list of useful questions that might be asked the child. Some of the questions are indirect, others ask the child directly feelings about the family. Examples are:

A child is ashamed to tell his father about something. What is it?

Act out what you would do if you found that you had magic powers.

Tell about a time when your feelings were hurt.

If you had three wishes, what would they be (a standard child interview question)?

Tell something about your father that gets you angry.

What are the worst things a child can say to his mother?

Remember that attachments and conflict change over time and the overall pattern is more important than single responses.

If the child is over 8, I find it useful to ask the same questions to the child that I asked of each parent, rephrasing the questions to make them appropriate.

Skafte (1985) proposed merely observing children under 3. Play evaluation was suggested for children from 3 to 5:

1. "Mommy's house, Daddy's house." This place uses stuffed animals, dolls, puppets, or small figures. The stuffed animals have parents in two locations and the evaluator develops a fantasy to tap relationship with each parents. Skafte gave several examples of questions that would be helpful in developing the fantasy.

2. "Calling Mom, Calling Dad." The evaluator develops a fantasy of a telephone conversation with each parent. The child is then encouraged to play the role of the parent while the evaluator plays the child.

3. "If you could change yourself into an animal, what animal would you be? Why?" This game is a standard projective device for young children. It is also useful to get the child to imagine each member of the family as an animal and report which animal and why.

4. "If you could have three wishes, what would they be?"

5. "Island Game." Skafte recommended developing the fantasy in some detail. The child is on an island and has everything she needs. She was lonely because no one lived there with her. A magic fairy gave her the chance to have someone with her. Who did she choose? Then give the child the chance to add another person. (Skafte recommended drawing the island and people to increase involvement.) The child is then given the chance to have anyone on the island. Skafte ended the fantasy by having everyone go back to the land where they lived and live happily ever after. (I like very much Skafte's variation of this common assessment technique. The child's order of preference is assessed, but the child is not left with a fantasy of isolation from either parent.)

For 5- to 8-year-olds, Skafte included:

1. Three wishes.

2. In whom can you confide: This game gives the child a moral dilemma and asks how the child solves the problem and to whom the child would go to for help in solving the problem.

3. Best and worst features of living with each parent.

4. Draw your family.

5. Complete the sentences.

For children 10 years of age and older, Skafte proposed:

1. Draw your family.
2. Complete the sentences.
3. The worst and best things about being with each parent.

Should the Child Be Asked with Whom He or She Wants to Live?

The GAP (1981) report indicated that a child's opinion in custody should have relevance, but only as one aspect of the evaluation. It should not determine custody. The Michigan statutes (Benedek, 1972) mentioned above required that the child's opinion concerning with which parent that child wants to live be assessed. As many as 20 states have statutes that require taking into account the child's preference if the child is over 10 years of age (Reppucci, 1984). Older children are more likely to be asked for their preference (Felner, Terre, Goldfarb, Farber, Primavera, Bishop, and Aber, 1985), but judges and lawyers reported difficulty in knowing how to weigh the child's preference. Some states require that older children's preference be honored unless there is strong reason not to do so (Weiss, 1979, p. 331). This requirement is most unfortunate given the evidence that children may be placed under significant stress by that evaluation. Franklin and Hibbs (1980) noted that depression may result as a reaction to expressing a preference for one parent. The child could feel even more divided in terms of loyalties by expressing a preference.

Mental health professionals should not ask the child with whom they want to live and should advise the court to avoid asking the child that question. If the judge or referee insists that such a question will be asked, request that it be given in chambers without the presence of the parents. There are a variety of ways to assess how the child feels without a direct question. If the child feels compelled to indicate a preference without being asked, the opportunity to talk should be given. The interpretation of the meaning of that communication should be based on the context.

Weiss (1979) noted that the advice given above to have the child asked about preference for custody in chamber creates its own set of problems. What may be the most critical testimony in the hearing would be inaccessible to the lawyer and not subject to examination.

There are a variety of cogent reasons why it is advisable to avoid asking the child which parent they want. First, the child will answer this question for many wrong reasons. Regardless of the logic of the answer, the choice places the child in the position of having to accept one parent and reject the other. Even if the parents can accept that choice (and many parents are hurt and angry at the choice), the child is at risk for carrying the guilt for that rejection.

Second, some children will make a request based on their view of the best deal that they can make for the quality of life: which parent has the latest bedtime; which parent does not censor television watching; which parent is most permissive or seldom punishes. Although this strategy may seem perfectly reasonable from the child's point of view, it may not be in the child's best interests.

Third, some children (particularly those between 10 to 12) will try to decide which parent needs them the most. One girl told me that she was picking her mother because her mother was emotionally upset and would have trouble getting along without the daughter. The girl was closer to her father, but saw her father as stronger and able to survive without her help. The girl was petrified that the choice would invite rejection from the father, but felt it was the only decision she could make. It would be far better for the court to decide that the child's best interests was not to take care of the mother. Often, children will not tell the judge why a particular choice was made because they recognize that the truth would undermine their strategy. In addition, the child may have little insight as to why a particular choice seems correct.

Fourth, the child may feel compelled to punish the parent that he or she sees as responsible for the divorce (Weiss, 1979). Out of anger (and limited cognitive ability to understand empathetically why a parent might decide that a relationship is harmful), the child may reject a parent who might be of more benefit to the long-term development of him or her.

Chasin et al. (1981) reported a case in which the child felt so much guilt at testifying against one of the parents, that the child was never able to reestablish a relationship. They also noted that another problem with asking for a child's participation in the decision is that indelicate or dishonest handling of the child by any of the professionals involved may lead the child to distrust the legal and therapeutic process.

Clearly, some parents coach the children as to what to say to the judge when this question is asked (Reppucci, 1984). It is difficult, if not impossible, for the court to ensure that such pressure does not occur.

Finally, there is an ebb and flow of attachments that children have with parents. Sometimes they are more attached to one parent and other times they are more attached to the other parent. It is unfortunate that a relatively irreversible decision is made, based on the timing of that varying attachment.

Mental health professionals may recommend that custody be given to one parent, not because the child needs the particular parent at the moment, but because the next developmental stage that is pending would make one parent better. No child has that perspective.

If the mental health professional does not ask the child for parental preference, what choices are there? The nature of the child's bond with each parent can be evaluated without ever asking the child for a preference. The following questions can be useful in determining that issue:

1.   When you have a problem, to whom do you go?
2.   When you are sick, who do you ask for help?

3. When you wake up in the middle of the night with a nightmare who do you ask for help? Why?

4. Which parent do you play games with? Which games?

5. Do you have any hobbies? Does either parent help you?

6. How is anger expressed in the house?

7. How are you punished? Who does the punishing? How do you feel about it? What are you punished for?

8. If you are happy (had fun at school, got a good grade), which parent would you tell?

9. What do you imagine it would be like if you spent weekdays with mother and weekends with father (Chasin et al., 1981)?

10. In which home would you like to spend school nights and why? In which home would you like to spend weekends and why?

Data from Pearson, Munson, and Thoennes (1983) on how often children are interviewed by judges or by investigation teams indicated that such interviews are surprisingly rare. In Denver, Colorado, judges were reluctant to interview children of any age. (It would not be surprising, however, to find regional differences on this issue.) In their data of 100 cases from 1972 to 1976, the judge only interviewed the child in eight cases. Judges found it difficult to talk to young children. One judge indicated that younger children only cried that they wanted both parents. The mean age of the few children that were interviewed was 11.1 years. In no case was a child interviewed by a judge prior to setting temporary custody orders; which is an important issue because temporary orders often become permanent.

An investigation was conducted in only 47 percent of the 100 cases that were assigned to the Probation Department. In those investigations, children were seen only in about half of the cases. Thus, children were consulted or observed in only 26 percent of the contested cases! While the present argument is to avoid asking the child for preference, there is a strong assumption that evaluating the child is important for custody recommendations, an evaluation that appears to be relatively uncommon in court ordered evaluations. (See the later section on the evaluation process).

Parent-Child Interview

While there are no guidelines about what questions might be asked during the joint parent-child interview, the important issue is the evaluation of how the parent and child interact. When they are asked to think about a question, does the parent listen to the child's opinion? Does the child listen to the parent's opinion? Do either interrupt the other? How does the parent handle inappropriate behavior on the part of the child? Misbehavior on the part of the child during the interview puts the parent at considerable stress, since the parent knows that an evaluation is occurring. Some parents let the child have more freedom than they would in private on the incorrect assumption that mental health professionals value permissiveness above all. If the parent puts no limits on the child, the professional should request that limits be set, and see how well the parent can accomplish that goal. Remember that boys from 4 to 6 years old do not tend to obey mothers.

Another important dimension to evaluate in the parent-child interview is the nonverbal behavior. Where do the participants sit? Does the child cling to the parent or show indifference? Is there evidence of bonding? Does the parent show a wish to protect the relationship between the child and the other parent? Suarez, Weston, and Hartstein (1978) encouraged the use of a one-way window whenever possible, observation of the parent and child during unstructured play activity and the more structured story telling activities of the Thematic Apperception Test (TAT) or Children's Apperception Test (CAT). Chasin and Grunebaum (1981) observed parent-child interactions around a structured task. A parent might be asked to guide a 3-year-old child in building a structure of blocks or make a puppet play. For older children the task might be to jointly plan a vacation.

The GAP (1981) report suggested the following dimension of evaluations for parent-child interactions: What is the spontaneous response of the child to the parent. Is the parent viewed as an asset—and if not, why not? How in tune with the child is the parent? Is the parent "listening" or "telling?" How psychologically nurturing is the parent?

Keep careful notes about all interactions, observations, and testing information. Never depend on memory on the assumption that you can recall an interaction later. It is the nature, particularly for more complex and angry cases, that there is significant delay before reaching court. You may have to wait months and perhaps even years before testifying.

A Measure of Parent-Child Behavior

McDermott, Tseng, Char, and Fukunaga (1978) developed a measure of parent-child behavior, the Parent-Child Interaction Test. Each parent was asked to work together with his or her children to tell stories about a modified set of the Children's Apperception Test cards and to build together a wooden block tower. The interaction of the child with each parent was videotaped. The child's behavior was evaluated on degree of comfort, initiative, spontaneity, fantasy expression, range of feelings, and separation behavior. The parent was evaluated on attachment, empathy with and sensitivity to the child's own level, monitoring the child's needs, discipline, guidance, consistency, patience, intellectual stimulations, emotional expression, spontaneity, physical closeness, encouragement, and acceptance.

While no data were presented to indicate whether such a systematic approach improved the quality of custody decisions, the impression of the authors was that the test was of significant help. A two-year follow-up of child adjustment was of limited usefulness, however, because the data were used originally to make the decisions of custody. Thus, it was impossible to determine whether the test improved the decision-making process. The authors indicated that the test provided dramatic information about the effects of particular custody arrangements. (However, they did not present the means of the scales or the analyses, so it is impossible to determine if anyone else would come to the same conclusion.) They indicated that their data supported terminating visitation rights in cases in which the custodial parent strongly opposes visitation or strongly dislikes the former spouse and pressures the children to have similar attitudes. Again, there is no data on the adjustment of children when such visitation is eliminated. They also noted that for two cases, strong religious orientation masked an inability to tolerate spontaneity and autonomous thinking.

Criteria for Custody

Chasin and Grunebaum (1981) recommended using the following criteria for custody. They recommended favoring the parent who:

1. Is most likely to foster visitation and who shows the most objective and respectful attitude toward the other parent. It should be noted that the law in some states requires greater weight to be given to the parent who is willing to support visitation with the other parent.
2. Will maintain the greater continuity of child contact with relatives, friends, neighborhood, schools, and so forth.
3. Has the best child rearing skills.
4. Shows the greater humanity, consistency, and flexibility in handling the child.
5. Is one to whom the child is most deeply attached.

Awad (1978) noted that "mental fitness" (implying degree of adjustment) is rarely relevant. However, Awad suggested that if psychological adjustment is an issue, the questions as to whether the psychiatric problems interferes with parenting capacity, whether a psychosis is "involving" or "noninvolving," and whether the symptoms and psychosocial adjustment affect the child should be addressed. Awad noted that diagnosis tends not to be a useful criteria.

Musetto (1980) proposed that custody be awarded to the psychological parent (a term used in Goldstein, Freud, and Solnit, 1973). Musetto defined the psychological parent as one who (1) acknowledges their own contribution to the family problems, (2) allows their children to express genuine feelings, (3) accepts the responsibility for being a parent, (4) expects some fair consideration from the children for the efforts, and (5) neither infantilizes nor parentifies the children. Psychological parents do not want custody to force reconciliation, secure financial aid, or replace a lost child. Psychological parents want their children and are able to care for their needs. They provide support, stimulation, guidance, and limits. They care for the child's physical needs.

They help the child control instinctual urges, support moral development, and empathy. They provide good models for identification. The psychological parent supports the loyalty of children with both parents and encourage positive contact with both parents. Psychological parents support their children's relationships with grandparents and extended family on both sides. Such recommendations should be tempered with an evaluation of the overriding welfare of the child, so that damaging relationships are not ignored in the name of maintaining ties.

It is interesting to note that when parents are asked what the most important criteria for custody (Lowrey, 1985b) should be, three factors emerge:

1. Concern for selecting a parent who was both in a position for and would give a high priority to child rearing;
2. Concern for maintaining the child's social network, including relatives and the noncustodial parent; and
3. Concern for conventional cultural values such as a good education and religious and moral training.

Both mothers and fathers tended to see almost all of the 20 items that were provided for ratings as differentially favoring one parent over the other. Mothers rated all items as more likely favoring the mother. The father saw about half of the items as neutral or slightly favoring him. Finances, continuity of the child's environment, and time for the child was not high on either parents list. Lowrey suggested that parents did not pay as much attention to items that may have been disadvantageous to themselves.

Making an "Impossible" Custody Decision

If the previously discussed recommendations were all that were involved, many mental health professionals would be willing to participate in custody evaluations. However, often the trade-off is in terms of values. One parent is loving, but chaotic. The other parent is more distant, but stable. Which value is more important, affection or stability? Generally, the negative impact of the less desirable characteristics has to be weighed in the trade-off with the more desirable.

An additional problem that makes custody evaluation difficult is the problem raised when one parent is better at providing for needs at one age, but the next stage is probably more easily handled by the other parent. One advantage of joint residential custody is that the child can get a different set of needs met from each parent. If the home environment of the parent which is not appropriate for that age child is severely detrimental, the child may not be able to wait until residential custody switches to get those needs met.

It is not unusual for a mental health professional to conclude that the problem is not which parent is in the best interests of the child, but which parent provides the least harm. If additional protections need to be built in, recommendations for such protections should be included in the evaluation.

Fine (1980) recommended five criteria for the least detrimental available alternative:

1. The custodial parent should enjoy a nurturing and psychologically appropriate relationship with the child.
2. The custodial parent should have the capacity to be a nurturing and mature parent.
3. The custodial home should be able to provide for the needs of the child: food, shelter, education, medical care, and special needs.
4. Siblings should not be separated in the custody disposition. (See the discussion on this issue in Chapter 5).

Evaluation of Homosexual Parents

Prior to recent changes by the American Psychiatric Association on whether homosexuality was a criteria for maladjustment, homosexuality would have been grounds for denying custody. Indeed, in many court jurisdictions it would continue to be a decisive factor. There is no evidence, however, that homosexual parents have any particular deficit in parenting ability (Waters and Dimock, 1983). Kirkpatrick, Smith, and Roy (1981) did a careful study of 40 children, 20 boys and 20 girls, half of whom lived in homes with lesbian mothers and half with heterosexual mothers. They used an extensive mother interview and tested the children on the Wechsler Intelligence Scale for Children, the Holtzman Inkblot Test, the Human Figure Drawing, and a 45-minute semistructured interview. The testers were blind as to the type of family to which the child belonged.

The maternal interest of the two types of mothers were the same. Lesbian mothers were more interested in breast feeding than heterosexual mothers. The marriage had been the same length for the two types of families. The lesbian mothers did not cite sexual dissatisfaction as the reason for the divorce (as might be expected), but indicated that the absence of psychological intimacy was the basis of their decision to leave the relationship. Heterosexual mothers listed drug use, alcohol, other women, psychotic behavior, and physical abuse as reasons for leaving the relationship. Visitation patterns were the same for the two families. There were no differences in gender development in the two groups of families. The lesbian mothers were more concerned about providing adult male figures for their children than were the heterosexual mothers. In addition, they found that children of lesbian mothers were just as well adjusted as children in the custody of heterosexual mothers.

Hoeffer's (1981) study of 20 lesbian and 20 heterosexual single mothers and their only or oldest child (age 6 to 9) found few differences on measures of sex-role behavior. The mothers had little impact on the boys' behaviors because the mothers were infrequently involved in encouraging particular play. Boys were just as sex typed regardless of which type of family they lived in and were more sex typed than the girls.

There were no studies found that looked at the adequacy of parenting for homosexual fathers. Clinical experience has suggested that gay fathers can be just as caring and concerned for the child's welfare as lesbian mothers. Higher levels of homophobia for males may lead to fewer cases of custodial homosexual fathers than custodial heterosexual fathers, but this author has seen no data on the frequency of custodial homosexual fathers or mothers.

It should be remembered that there is no evidence that homosexuality is contagious from one generation to the next (an issue that is important only if the task is to reassure the court that homosexuality is an unlikely outcome). One could argue that there is nothing wrong with a parent deciding to rear a child with a homosexual orientation, but the courts and many mental health professionals (who are willing to accept the adult decision to be homosexual, but not the imposition of that decision on a child) are likely to disagree.

It is important to evaluate a family with a homosexual parent in the same manner as one with a heterosexual parent. The most important rule for both is that the child is not being exposed to sexually explicit material or to sexual behavior of adults. The question may need to be more explicit in an evaluation with a homosexual parent because norms concerning parenting behavior are less well defined and the "coming out" behavior (and concomitant increase in self esteem) may feel at odds with "hiding" something about the homosexuality from the children.

THE CUSTODY EVALUATION REPORT

The report should be written by the custody evaluator. It should be provided to lawyers on both sides and to the court. The report should begin with the question being asked by the court. This is usually, "what custody decision is in the child's best interest?" A summary of the data used to come to a recommendation should be listed next. The total amount of contact with each person involved and the types of interviews, tests, and other spoken and written data should then be listed (Lewis, 1974). Finally, the bases for the findings of fact that led to the conclusion should be given. Do not include comments that require professional training for a reader to understand. If possible, the report should give positive support to both parents in terms of each one's strength. The report should not be biased to support its conclusion: Give the facts, the opinions formed from those facts, and the conclusions.

Awad (1978) noted that it is useful to give each party's version of the history of the marriage, separation, and how the current arrangements are working. As in court testimony, jargon should be avoided. Awad also recommended that for situations where there is no clear-cut recommendation, it is useful to report the situation as precisely as possible and to list the advantages and disadvantages of each alternative.

Skafte (1985) gave an excellent example of report writing, including common mistakes that therapists-turned-custody-evaluators are likely to make. For example, therapists will often pad reports with irrelevant information, give "short story" examples, and use too technical language. Skafte particularly stressed keeping the report as short as possible (e.g., 7 to 10 single-spaced, typed pages) by eliminating irrelevant details.

Feedback to the Contesting Parents

Some evaluators prefer to have joint meetings with the parents to provide feedback on the report. Others prefer to meet separately with each parent (and the lawyer for that parent) to provide information concerning the findings and to explore with the parent feelings about the report. Careful feedback can increase acceptance of the report by both parents. Suarez, Weston, and Hartstein (1978) recommended that the initial stipulation indicate that the feedback should be given to the two lawyers (without parents present). They suggested that the feedback session be used to explore with the lawyers constructive alternatives and the role that the lawyers might play in facilitating those alternatives. The purpose of the meeting is also to find alternatives to litigation. While the meeting with lawyers provides information about how the evaluation was done, findings of the evaluation and recommendations, Suarez, et. al. (1978) indicated that the evaluators must be firm in discouraging claims and counterclaims that reinstate a courtroom battle.

Evaluation of Custody Reports

Clawar (1984) proposed criteria for evaluating the scientific respectability of a custody report. Those criteria serve as useful reminders to custody evaluators to take care in evaluation and writing.

1. A full history. Have appropriate data been collected?
2. Credentials of the author of the report or expert testifying on the report. Experts should limit their testimony to their area of expertise.
3. The ability to duplicate or replicate the findings. Are procedures and findings sufficiently detailed to permit replication of the process?
4. The amount of time involved in evaluation.
5. One fact a case does not make. The report should focus on patterns or themes.
6. Consulting or supportive opinions. Was collaboration used?
7. Relevancy of material. Were tests used appropriately for the questions asked? How recent is the material on which opinions were based?

8. Source of referral. Was this report potentially biased based on the source of contact for hiring the professional?

9. Clarity of report. How clear is the report?

10. Language usage. Is it neutral or adversarial? Are the technical terms vague?

11. Reporting office behavior and testing versus behavioral observation outside of the office. What is the context in which observations were made and can the conclusions be generalized to other contexts?

12. Self-critical. Does the report indicate its own limitations.

13. Conclusions. Were the conclusions based on the material used for the evaluation?

TESTIMONY IN COURT

Testimony in court depends on the presentation by lawyers and the testimony by witnesses, which might include the parents, the child, neighbors, and mental health professionals. Expert witnesses are those that are recognized by the court as having special training and experience that enables them to draw conclusions from findings of fact and hypothetical situations. Lay witnesses, including the parents, children, relatives, neighbors, teachers, and friends, are considered incapable of such interpretation. Their testimony is restricted to things that they have observed. They may not comment on or draw conclusions about what they have observed.

One problem with expert testimony in the area of mental health is that there is a variety of folk wisdom in the culture about what is best for children. Judges have strong opinions about how children should be raised. A judge would not presume to contradict a medical pathologist concerning evidence and opinion as to the cause of death, but may feel quite comfortable telling mental health professionals that their opinions about children are wrong.

Should a Psychotherapist Testify?

Mental health professionals who have had a therapeutic relationship with a client who is involved in a custody dispute should have second thoughts about how useful their testimony would be to the court. Girdner (1979) noted that judges and lawyers have difficulty with the testimony of expert witnesses who are therapists for a variety of reasons:

1. Judges and lawyers see therapists as too influenced by "unreliable" verbal behavior. Often, legally trained people feel that mental health professionals draw opinions based on seemingly hearsay evidence.

2. The client's feelings, emotional needs, and perceptions are not directly observable and are considered irrelevant.

3. There is a major value difference between judges and mental health professionals. Mental health professionals work hard at avoiding value judgments about behavior. Judges can come to the conclusion that therapists have no values at all.

Awad (1978) strongly recommended that therapists refrain from giving any report to the evaluation team if such a report would interfere with the therapeutic relationship. A clinician seeing a client particularly if it is a parent, should not volunteer an opinion on the custody of a child. The therapist knows little about the capacities of the other parent or the attachment and choice of the child.

Therapists should be reluctant to participate in a custody evaluation by providing expert testimony on behalf of their client. First, the therapist has not had equal access to both parents. The view of the other parent is based entirely on hearsay evidence that would be vulnerable to aggressive cross examination. Second, the therapist is not in a position of making a judgment of the relative merits of the two parents. Finally, the therapist is an advocate of the client and expert testimony should be given in the position of being an advocate of the child.

When the child is the client of the therapist, the therapist should be cautious in extrapolating from therapy information to assumptions about the adequacy of parenting. The therapist may see the parents through the child's eyes, and that perception can be distorted through needs and developmental stage.

In general, however, a therapist who is asked to participate should decline, informing the client and/or the lawyer why the information would not hold up in court and why such information might be harmful to the client. Clients may not anticipate the questions that a therapist may be asked, and the answers could be painful or embarrassing. In addition, if the testimony does not result in help to the client, the previously terminated therapy can be seriously damaged.

It is not unusual for the client to want to use the therapist in court when the client has the therapist's support of that person's position: "If indeed your husband is doing that behavior with the children, it could be substantially harmful to the children." The client focuses in on the single statement, without considering the other testimony that might come out in court. Confidentiality usually cannot be partially released. Either the therapist can say nothing in court (note that not every state may provide confidentiality rights to the client) or must answer all questions.

Even making referrals for parents to mental health professionals for custody evaluations is risky. Therapists should avoid giving referrals to other mental health professionals for custody evaluation. The outcome of that evaluation could contaminate the therapy. The same is true for providing referrals for lawyers.

Testifying Under Protest

Mental health professionals as a group hate to testify in court. They tend not to understand the rules for evidence. They dislike the strategy of a hostile attorney trying to discredit their credentials. Such attacks can tap vulnerabilities that most of us have concerning our competence.

Any therapist who had any association with a case can be subpoenaed to testify. Some mental health professionals become involved because a parent requested consultation concerning a separation or divorce, liked (or misconstrued) the comments made by the professional, and then informed the lawyer.

Therapists, particularly child therapists, often do not want to get involved in the custody battle. Since confidentially is controlled by the parents and not the child, the therapist may be in a painful position if either parent decides that the therapist's testimony could be useful. The therapist can request the judge to keep the child's welfare protected by avoiding testimony from the therapy. If that request is denied, the therapist can request that such evidence be given in chambers so that the parents would not be informed about the child's concerns.

Courtroom Dynamics

Most mental health professionals do not know the rules of courtroom performance. It may be useful to review them.

Girdner's (in press) analysis of court behavior notes that the discourse of a custody hearing is structured by legal categories which were derived from procedural and substantive law. Such rules cover who can be spoken to, by whom, when, and how. The rules also structure what can and what cannot be said. These requirements for lawyers lead them to manipulate the rules of evidence to present evidence to support their case, to discredit the evidence of the other side, and to prevent the other attorney from doing the same.

A fair trial in adversarial proceedings assumes that each lawyer is of equal competence, an assumption that is seldom fulfilled. Girdner (1985b) found that style of the lawyers also made a difference. Lawyers were classified into three styles for divorce litigation: soft bargainer, hard bargainers, and principled bargainers. Soft bargainers are avoiders of risk and dislike conflict. Soft bargainers obtain fair bargains with other soft bargainer lawyers and with principled bargainers. They accept poor bargains with hard bargainers. Hard bargainer lawyers have winning as their primary goal and rarely negotiate except in an aggressive manner. Part of their strategy is to emotionally destroy the other party. If both lawyers are hard bargainers, the case is likely to end up in court. Principled bargainers attempt to negotiate a fair agreement. They see the task as problem solving rather than winning or losing.

According to Girdner, judges give less credence to relatives and friends because they see the testimony as biased. However, parents are often profoundly influenced by what a friend or relative says in court and may hold grudges for years in retaliation for unkind testimony.

Professional Witness Behavior

1. *Be prepared to present your name, address, and professional qualifications.* Expect to have those qualifications challenged if the opposing lawyer expects your testimony to be unsympathetic to that lawyer's point of view. Do not be defensive about those qualifications. It is up to the judge to decide if your experience qualifies you as an expert witness. Nothing but credibility problems are gained by questioning the right of a lawyer to examine your training or experience.

2. *Dress professionally.* Judges are offended by dress that does not reflect proper respect for the court. Credibility can be lost if dress is too casual.

3. *Be polite.* Address the judge as "your honor." Speak slowly and clearly, particularly if there is a court recorder. Avoid jargon. Assume that the court will know words in general use, but not technical words. It is better to avoid the words altogether rather than constantly explain their meaning.

4. *Do not joke or wisecrack (Gardner, 1976).* While you may want to communicate that you are not intimidated and are relaxed on the stand, joking may communicate that you are not taking your role seriously.

5. *Use direct quotes whenever possible.* Do not quote one parent about the other (Gardner, 1976). If allegations are referred to, be careful to call them allegations. Credibility can be lost if you make the mistake of accepting as fact something told to you by one parent. It is acceptable to say the following: "I was given the following information from Mrs. X. I do not have direct knowledge of the veracity of this information. I can state, however, that if such behavior occurred, it would have the following effect on children."

It is also acceptable to present such testimony in the form of hypothetical situations, if requested to do so by one of the lawyers. If a hypothetical situation presented by a lawyer differs in important ways from the case at hand, indicate that your answer is limited to those conditions and that other conditions would potentially lead you to different conclusions.

6. *Do not state cause and effect in absolutes.* Given the nature of prediction in mental health, it is seldom the case that A always causes B. It is acceptable to talk of high risk behaviors or evidence that such behavior has already adversely affected the child. Be ready to admit that there is no certainty as to outcomes.

7. *Do not use diagnoses (Gardner, 1976).* It is not your role to provide a diagnosis, so avoid diagnostic terms altogether. You do not want to get into an argument over the meaning of technical terms. A lawyer is likely to pull out a dictionary and read you the definition in there.

8. *You may take notes and refer to them.* It is useful to refer to notes to

provide the exact time and length of contacts for the evaluation. *Never* take any notes to court that you would feel uncomfortable having the entire court review. Either lawyer can ask to see your notes and can read them to the court. Never keep notes that would be embarrassing to have read in court. You may be required to bring all notes and all files you have on a case.

9.   The lawyer who expects you to be sympathetic will tend to ask you open-ended questions that allow you to develop answers in some detail. The lawyer who sees you as antagonistic will ask questions to be answered "yes" or "no." Do not be upset if you are not allowed to develop an answer, and do not worry about refusing to answer such a question if it cannot be answered simply.

10.   If you are not given an opportunity to say something that you think is important to the judge's decision, do not try to squeeze it in your testimony. Rules of evidence will generate an objection and you may be prohibited from speaking. Instead, at the end of your testimony tell the judge that you have further testimony that may be of use to the court in arriving at its decision. In most family relations courts, you will be permitted to give your testimony.

11.   *Do not bias your report.* Give a full report of the findings of fact, including information both favorable and nonfavorable to your conclusion. Admit freely valid points that are at odds with your point of view.

12.   If you are asked about your fee, do not be apologetic. Remember, you are charging for your time, not your support.

13.   If you are treated rudely by a lawyer, respond with marked courtesy. It is often useful to deliberately slow down and relax and answer the question when vigorously attacked on the stand (not really as common as people imagine from television watching).

14.   Watch out for distortions of previous testimony. If you are incorrectly quoted, point out the error.

15.   Be prepared to lose. While your investment in the child may lead you to be indignant if the court chooses to ignore your recommendations, be glad the final decision is not your responsibility. On one occasion, I have had my advice followed, only to learn later that the parent I recommended ended up being an abusing parent! Remember that your opinion may be limited and your ability to predict the future may be flawed.

The Effect of Expert Testimony on Court Decisions

Ash and Guyer (1984) studied 119 consecutive cases beginning in October 1978 in which a child custody evaluation was completed by the child psychiatry service at the University of Michigan. Most of the cases could be characterized as having intense conflict between parents, allegations of child abuse, and allegations of severe mental impairment. Most of the referrals came from the community in which the university was located and most were ordered at the judge's initiative or by agreement of the attorneys or by an agency of the court. Of the cases, 59 percent were during the original custody battle and 41 percent were postdivorce.

Since the evaluations were part of a training program, there were 43 different evaluators and many different approaches to doing evaluations. The average evaluation took 8 to 12 interviews and always included individual interviews with each parent and each child over 3 years of age, joint interviews of parents with children, and a final interpretative interview. Evaluators were available for court testimony, but only 5 percent were asked to do so.

Of the 92 custody cases, sole custody was the recommendation in 83. The court followed the evaluators recommendations in 90 percent of these 83 cases. There was no clear pattern for cases in which the recommendations were not followed, except that trainees were less likely to have their advice followed than were staff evaluators (however, this difference was not statistically significant). In the nine cases of joint custody recommendations, seven were followed by the courts.

AVOIDING RELITIGATION

According to Westman, Cline, Swift, and Kramer (1970) in a study of 148 consecutive divorces not involving mediation, 53 percent of the 105 families with children were involved in relitigation after the divorce. Of the 43 families with no children, only 2 percent had relitigation. Any move that mental health professionals make that reduces anger and the likelihood of relitigation is likely to benefit the child.

Recommendations to reduce relitigation include:

1. Careful interpretation of the recommendation that supports the integrity and self-esteem of each parent.
2. Avoidance of "loaded" evaluations that agree with the description of one of the complaining parents. If the report would seem to agree with the complaints of one of the parents, using a vocabulary that is different from that used by the accusing parent is more likely to avoid feeding the conflict between parents.
3. Spell out possible solutions to as many anticipated problems as possible. For example, avoid the phrase "liberal visitation" if it seems likely that in the future parents would have difficulty negotiating. Permit changes in the agreement, if it is with the mutual consent of both parties. Consider visitation schedules as a function of the developmental stage of the child (see the next chapter) and how moves out-of-state should be handled. Consider mediation or arbitration as required alternatives to relitigation.
4. Consider supporting joint custody. Ilfeld, Ilfeld, and Alexander (1982) found that relitigation rate was one half in joint custody arrangements than in sole custody arrangements.

SUMMARY

Careful evaluation, balanced and fair approaches to both parents, extended interpretation, and professional presentation of information are all needed to do an effective evaluation. These procedures do not insure that "the best interests of the child" are served. However, failure to provide such standards do ensure that the child's interests are not served.

CHAPTER 7

Visitation and Access

Husband Disputes Ex-Wife's Visitation Rights to Two Cats

St. Paul, Minn. (AP) A 24-year-old man is going to court in an effort to end his ex-wife's visitation rights to their two cats.

A hearing has been scheduled for Dec. 10 before a court referee on the documents filed by M. B. in Ramsey County Family Court.

In the documents, B. claims his ex-wife, M. B., talked of having the pets "put to sleep," "has visited the cats approximately 12 times since February," and didn't visit them at all last summer.

When she does visit, he said, she favors one cat, he claimed. (Boulder Daily Camera, November 17, 1984, p. 3A)*

This news article demonstrates the intensity of emotions around visitation even with animals. In spite of this intensity, there has been relatively little research on frequency of visitation and even less on the effects of visitation patterns on child adjustment. Given that judges, lawyers, and parents make daily decisions that affect children's lives in unknown ways when it comes to visitation, it is distressing to learn that no one really knows what is best for the child. To what degree is the best interests of the child served by visitation patterns that include alternate weekends, alternate holidays, and six weeks in the summer? What is the most appropriate visitation pattern for an 8 month old? While an answer can be given from a theoretical point of view, there are enough times when the theory is not supported by the empirical research for caution to be recommended. The research has not been done.

As Kelly (1981) pointed out, attempts on the part of parents to alter patterns of visitations based on the quality of bonding or needs of the child were met by strong resistance by the noncustodial parent's own attorney. Attorneys (and judges) have been excessively influenced by case law, where the past determines the future. Thus, every other weekend is the best pattern because there is ample precedence, that is, "that is the way it has always been done." Deviations in visitation have required written advanced notice, so that even when the unusual visitation requires no inconvenience for anyone, parents rigidly hold to the written agreement as a bludgeon over the other parent. When parents

*Reprinted with permission from Associated Press.

are able to peacefully negotiate their visitation patterns, lawyers should not provide impedeiments to that process.

VISITATION AS A SOURCE OF CONFLICT

Visitation provides a chronic problem in requiring parents who were not able to maintain a marriage with each other to negotiate times, places, and activities, thus forcing continued contact and encouraging continued conflict. Visitation (and money) serve as the most common causes of conflict. As has already been demonstrated in Chapter 3, chronic conflict serves to increase the likelihood of poor adjustment in the children.

Visitation can be a major source of conflict between parents because it is a constant reminder of the marriage and its failure (Benedek and Benedek, 1977). Benedek and Benedek also noted that visitation may be a source of spying on the other family, of conflict of loyalties for the child, and of denial of flexibility in permitting normal childhood activities.

THE COURTS' DILEMMA

Courts have short patience with parents who continue to come back to litigation as a way of solving chronic disagreements. The courts have difficulty in establishing an objective view in determining which story to believe and have limited resources for dealing with a chronically irresponsible parent. Contempt of court is available for a parent who does not follow instructions, but most judges are reluctant to use it against parents. However, while it might be possible to limit the contact an irresponsible parent has with the child, visitation is looked on by most judges as a right of the child as well as the parent. To punish the child for the parent's irresponsibility seems inappropriate. In addition, there is general agreement that visitation with the noncustodial parent is good for the child (with the possible exception of an abusing or severely pathological parent). Therefore, limiting visitation to punish the irresponsible parent is damaging to the child.

There are paradoxes in recommendations for visitation patterns. "Liberal visitation" with permission of both parents is a common phrase in divorce agreements. Yet such a phrase invites additional litigation when parents cannot agree on a reasonable pattern. Frequent visitation would seem to be in the child's best interest, but the increase in conflict that frequent visitation might create could be harmful to the child. Visitation agreements that are jointly obtained or court ordered seldom suggest changes as a function of the age of the child, yet it is clear that the most desirable pattern is likely to change over time. Even the child's wish to visit is likely to decrease and increase as a function of stage-specific issues or the changes in attachment that normally occur for children. Intact families tend to tolerate well the ebb and flow of attachment that children show toward parents. At one time, a child might prefer to walk with the mother, later that year with the father, followed even later by a return to the mother. If the parents are comfortable with their relationships with the child and each other and are not competitive for affection, these changes cause little or no anxiety on the part of the parent. Parents from divorced families do not easily tolerate this cycle of change in affectional ties. The competition is often quite marked and a period of time in which a child prefers the other parent may be seen as alienation intentionally caused by the other parent.

Divorced parents have difficulty tolerating the ebb and flow of attachment in children. Help them understand that it is normal for children to have more intense or less intense affectional ties over time.

It is important that even if the parent decides to accommodate a child's wishes for less contact, *some* contact must be required so that increased affection can occur later in time. If there is reason to believe that the reluctance is covering anxiety from dangerous dynamics (such as child abuse or sexual abuse), continued contact may still be desirable, but under supervision.

As Weiss (1979) has pointed out, visitation is a limitation on the authority of the custodial parent. While the custodial parent is given the power to make the crucial decisions that affect the child's life, the noncustodial parent is given some control over the child during visitation. Goldstein, Freud, and Solnit (1973) proposed an extremely controversial policy to give the custodial parent absolute control over visitation. They suggested that the noncustodial parent should see the child at the discretion of the custodial parent and have no legal rights to visitation beyond the wishes of the custodial parent. This recommendation generated so much controversy in the courts that one lawyer recommended avoiding quoting anything from that book in a particular court. Weiss (1979) believed that the most useful aspect of this recommendation is the increased power and elimination of helplessness that custodial parents feel about the disruptive nature of visitations from the noncustodial parent. Certainly a parent who feels that a visitation is harmful to the child would feel less upset by being able to limit or eliminate such visitation. Weiss felt that the major disadvantage of such a proposal would be the reduction in contact between the child and the noncustodial parent. Most children benefit from frequent visitation. Since limitation of visitation might occur because of retaliation against the noncustodial parent rather than because of potential harm to the child, in most cases (but not all) the child would seem to be potentially harmed by a policy that gives too much control to the custodial parent.

Benedek and Benedek (1977) noted that enforced visitation can provide a face saving device for the custodial parent. Hoorwitz (1983) felt that giving too much power to one parent increased the need for competition and revenge for the parent out of power. Hoorwitz also noted that while eliminating visitation might reduce conflict on a temporary basis, the child needs to learn that conflict is inevitable in life.

The Uniform Marriage and Divorce Act (Foster, 1973) provided the following visitation provisions:

(a) A parent not granted custody of the child is entitled to reasonable visitation rights unless the court finds, after a hearing, that visitation would endanger the child's physical health or significantly impair his emotional development.

(b) The court may modify an order granting or denying visitation rights whenever modification would serve the best interests of the child; but the court shall not restrict a parent's visitation rights unless it finds that the visitation would endanger the child's physical health or significantly impair his emotional development.

It is interesting to note that the aforementioned criteria place visitation as a right of the noncustodial parent, not the child. Thus, when a parent behaves irresponsibly, the question is raised about whether that parent's rights can be changed. The rules indicate that restriction cannot occur as a function of irresponsibility, but only for the child's benefit.

Does the Court Follow Professional Recommendations for Visitation?

In the study of custody and visitation evaluations by Ash and Guyer (1984), visitation recommendations were made in 106 of the 119 cases that were evaluated by the University of Michigan. Liberal and reasonable visitation was recommended in 74 percent of the cases, and the court followed this recommendation 97 percent of the time. Limited, unsupervised visitation was recommended in 11 percent of the cases, and the court followed this recommendation only 50 percent of the time. Generally, the court was more permissive than was recommended. Supervised visitation was recommended in 7 percent of the cases, and these recommendations were followed 100 percent of the time by the court. Visitation at the custodian's discretion was made in 7 percent of the cases, and that recommendation was followed 88 percent of the time by the court. The high percentage of recommendations that were followed by the court may reflect the high respect that the Michigan courts had for University of Michigan Custody Evaluation program. In no case was it the practice of these evaluators to specify particular visitation patterns. This lack was surprising because it is a more common characteristic in other jurisdictions and one that has some benefits in terms of reduced relitigation.

THE FUNCTIONS OF VISITATION

There are a variety of important psychological functions for visitation. It is important to keep these functions in mind when evaluating particular visitation patterns or determining if an ongoing visitation pattern has been successful (Hodges, in press).

1.   *Visitation agreements must protect the rights of the child for access to the noncustodial parent.* Courts have typically determined that frequent visitation is generally "in the best interests of the child." Except in cases with child abuse and severe pathology, courts are reluctant to block visitation entirely.

The custodial parent is often hurt and angry at the noncustodial parent. If the child is attached to the custodial parent, the wish to please that parent may place the child in a very rough position. Expression of a wish to see the other parent may invite upset and rejection. Clear visitation rules free the child from some of the psychological pressures of pleasing each parent.

While visitation agreements that permit liberal and frequent visitation may seem helpful to the child, failure to designate some pattern of visitation may place the child in the position of having to request visitation. Such requests may jeopardize the child's relationship with the custodial parent.

2.   *Visitation agreements must protect the rights of the noncustodial parent.* Less discussion has been focused on the degree to which the custodial mother controls the access of the noncustodial father to the children. Indignation over the harm to the children, and anger over the increased financial issues, jealousy, and competition between parents may all keep the anger alive.

Even when the separating parents are cordial at the time of separation, recommend to the parents that they each consult a lawyer and work out a written agreement for visitation that would assume that they are no longer cordial. To avoid relitigation, the stipulated agreement should include procedures for conflict resolution when parents cannot agree. The use of mediation or arbitration are examples of such procedures.

The point in time when control of visitation becomes an issue for two parents who are cordial at the time of divorce is when one of the separated parents enters into a romantic relationship with someone else. Failure to pay child support often leads to battles over visitation.

3.   *Visitation agreements must insure that the emotional bond of the child with both parents is protected.* There is substantial research that indicates that children need contact with adults of both sexes for balanced development (see Chapter 8 on single parenting). Assuming that neither parent is grossly pathological, it is important to maintain the affectional bond with both parents. Basic trust and self-esteem are maintained in the child by having predictable parents who care. The child's primary means of understanding what it is like to be an adult of a particular sex is established by having continued affectionate contact with the parent of that sex. It is clear that children can resolve these issues with one understanding parent and without any contact with the

other parent, but the task is certainly easier with continued affectionate contact with both parents where possible.

Because of the child's need to have contact with adults of both sexes in order to be able to understand what it means to be an adult of either sex, mental health professionals should encourage some visitation with the noncustodial parent even under difficult circumstances. If the noncustodial parent is abandoning, Big Brothers, Big Sisters, or a relative or friend of the family can be used to partially satisfy that need.

In addition, the child's origin of "who am I" is based partly on his or her understanding of who the parents are. The child needs to integrate those origins into the self-concept.

4. *Visitation provides the custodial parent with relief from the parenting role.* While the courts are unlikely to ever use this criterion for deciding visitation, custodial parents have often mentioned to me the need for some relief from the parenting role. I grew up in a single parent family because of the early death of my father. While single parenting produced some problems, the most negative from my point of view was exhaustion. Single parenting is an unrelenting, demanding job. Work, meals, housecleaning, and parenting all give little time for oneself and no time to be sick or to have a sick child. Even when a spouse was of little help in parenting, that spouse could watch an infant while the parent went to the store (or even the bathroom!). Visitation provides some relief from that responsibility and many custodial parents look forward to the weekend with no children to care for.

5. *Visitation provides alternative role models for the child.* One disadvantage of single parenting is that the number of ways to solve problems is limited by that parent's repertoire. With visitation contact, children can learn to use the problem solving skills of both parents. In addition, role limitations of each parent, whether sex role defined or simply a function of experience, limit the child's ability to solve problems of living, such as how to cook, sew, fix cars, or repair household articles.

VISITATION FREQUENCY

Visitation Frequency and Age of the Child

No one has reported on visitation patterns with infants. Tierney (1983) collected the first systematic data on preschool children. This study evaluated 67 children of divorce, 64 of whom were in mother custody homes. Data was obtained from 67 mothers on 32 boys and 35 girls. The decision for the visitation pattern was made jointly by the parents; only in eight cases was the visitation pattern determined by the courts.

In 52 percent of the cases, only reasonable and liberal visitation was indicated. The failure to designate a particular visitation plan is a common source of additional litigation later.

For the preschool children in Tierney's study, the range of visitation ranged from no contact to daily contact. The typical frequency of visitations was bimodal with 24 percent having no contact with fathers and 24 percent having contact every two weeks. Duration of visitation ranged from an hour or less to two to five months. Most typical was several days (40 percent). Age of the child was significantly related to length of visitation, although at a low level ($r = .29$, $df = 47$, $p < .05$) with younger children receiving shorter visits. While this correlation is low, the range of 3 to 5 years is very narrow and any relationship is surprising. There was no relationship between age of the child and frequency or consistency. Sex of the child was unrelated to frequency, duration, or consistency of visitation as reported by the mother or the father.

In their study of children from 2 to 18 years of age, Kelly and Wallerstein (1977b) and Kelly (1981) reported that at the time of the divorce, about two-thirds of the children were visited about two times a month. About one half were as high as one to three times a week, but only about one-fourth had overnight visits, usually the 6 to 12 year olds. One-fourth of the children had almost no contact with the noncustodial parent and 5 percent had no contact. Only 20 percent of the children were satisfied with the amount of visitation. Those most satisfied were boys from 11 to 18 years of age. Most satisfied of all were 7 to 8 year old children with (1) visitation two to three times a week (2) living within biking distance of the noncustodial parent, and (3) with free access to each parent. Children only liked brief contacts if they were combined with overnight visits and if the contacts were frequent. Resistance to visitation occurred in 11 percent of their sample, usually in children over 9 years of age. Even these children continued to visit.

By 18 months postdivorce, 60 percent of the children in the Kelly (1981) and Kelly and Wallerstein (1977b) studies were seeing the noncustodial parent at least twice a month. The amount of overnight and weekend visits had doubled during that year. While duration of visits had gone up, frequency of visits had decreased. Now, 29 percent continued to visit once a week as compared to 42 percent at six months. Boys between 2 to 8 were more likely to visit with the father. From 9 to 18 years of age, however, girls had more frequent visits. The younger children had more frequent visitation averaging about once per week, which peaked at 7 to 8 years of age. These children were reported as longing for more visits. Adolescents visited more often than 9 to 12 year olds, a finding that is at odds with the view of adolescents as more withdrawn from parents. Kelly and Wallerstein (1977b) wondered if the relatively low frequency of visitation in 9 to 12 year olds was not due to anger on the part of the child.

Adolescents demonstrated a sharp drop in visitation frequency in the year following the six month interview. The most common pattern was an occasional visit, lasting several hours. Weekend and overnight visits were rare. Adolescents seemed content with this visitation arrangement. Girls visited fathers much more frequently than did boys, often once or twice a week, a pattern rare among boys. Infrequent and no visitation was occurring for 25 percent of the children and this pattern was most typical for the 9 to 18 year age group. By 18 months postdivorce, the amount of abandonment (i.e., no visitation at all) was 8 percent, a small amount compared to Tierney's (1983) 24 percent, obtained in the previously discussed study of preschool children.

At the five year follow-up (Kelly, 1981), visitation frequency had been maintained at a fairly high level, suggesting that the drop from the initial interview to the 18-month interview did not continue so drastically. One third of the children had not changed in their visitation pattern since the 18-month interview and 20 percent had increased the frequency of visitation. Weekly visits were common for 25 percent of the sample. Kelly noted that mothers who were committed to supporting the father-child relationship played a major role in facilitating the high rate of visitation. About 20 percent of the children visited two or three times a month, usually alternating weekends. Another 20 percent visited monthly. Vacation and holiday visits only increased due to the greater number of children who lived geographically distant from the noncustodial parent. The percentage of such children was not reported. Erratic, infrequent visitation was occurring for about 17 percent of the children, the same number as at 18 months. The statistics for children with no contact was also the same as at 18 months.

One-fifth of the children did not like visitation at the five-year follow-up. Hurt was common if the father was self-absorbed or intensely involved in other activities or people. Infrequent visitation routinely caused hurt. Younger children interpreted such infrequent contact as evidence of their unlovability.

Warshak and Santrock (1983a) looked at child's feelings about visitation as a function of the sex of the custodial parent (the only study that has looked at visitation with noncustodial mothers). More that two-thirds of the children felt that the frequency of visitation was inadequate to meet their needs. Three of the 64 6 to 11 years olds wanted less visitation. Sixty-two percent wanted more visitation.

The children expressed a great deal of satisfaction with the visits. Half of the children rated the noncustodial parent as nicer to be with since the divorce. Not one child in the study had reported not enjoying the most recent visit, and 87 percent said they had enjoyed it a lot.

In a study that did not specify the age of the children, Koch and Lowery (1984) obtained questionnaire data from 30 fathers out of a sample of 132 noncustodial fathers invited to participate. It is not surprising that given the high geographic mobility of postdivorce adults, 55 percent of the sample were unreachable, including 27 percent with no forwarding address.

The participants were middle income, white, and very involved with their children. The fathers were 8 months postdivorce and 33 months postseparation. Of this specialized population, 73 percent of the fathers reported paying child support. Visits took place at the father's home. Fifteen fathers (50 percent) had visitation on a weekly basis, six on an every other week basis, and six on a less than monthly basis. Only two of the fathers reported irregular visitation. The length of visits ranged from four hours to two months. Weekend visits were the most common pattern. Age of the children was not mentioned in the study.

More than half of the fathers were not satisfied with the amount of visitation and wanted more. More than half the fathers were satisfied with the regularity of the visits. The average distance between father and children was 301 miles and, as might be expected, geographic distance was correlated with frequency of visitation ($r(28) = -.64$, p $<.005$).

The correlation of relations with former spouse and frequency of visitation was not statistically significant, although the total amount of visitation was correlated with relationship with former spouse ($r(28) = .64$, $p <.005$). Amount of visitation was correlated with father-child relationship, as might be expected ($r(28) = .39, p < .025$). The fathers' marital status and the fathers' social life was not correlated with frequency of visitation.

Hirst and Smiley (1984) studied the access pattern for 147 (out of 200 invited) families in the Brisbane, Australia area. The families were picked from court records for January to September 1977. Mother custody was characteristic of 88 percent of the families and father custody in 12 percent. On the average, there were two children per family, ranging in age from 1 to 17 and averaging 9.8. The modal time since separation was three to four years. They found that noncustodial parents were more likely to have formed new domestic relationships than were custodial parents.

The study reviewed the frequency of five visitation patterns that were occurring at the time of the interview: free access (9 percent); flexible regular access (13 percent); rigid regular access (13 percent); irregular access (33 percent); and no access (32 percent). Of interest was the finding that only 17 percent of the cases had fortnightly arrangements, a finding particularly significant since every other weekend was a common guideline in that jurisdiction.

As others have found, there was a general decrease in visitation over time, with 50 percent showing a decrease in the one year following separation and only 9 percent showing an increase. Where free access was occurring, the family tended to be quite happy with the arrangement. Surprisingly, where visitation had ceased, 83 percent of the custodial parents were also happy with that arrangement. Regular but rigid visitation was viewed negatively by most parents, a finding that is important for considering how specific court-ordered visitation should be. If there is not some flexibility and cooperation between parents, future visitation is limited. When parents decided the visitation plan, free and flexible visitation was more common (25 percent) than when the court ordered the visitation (6 percent).

Hirst and Smiley (1984) felt that when conflict is high, regular rigid arrangements may be necessary to help the parents through the transition period.

They felt, however, that if the parents were unable to reduce the level of conflict, enforced rigid visitation was not helpful beyond 18 months.

The Prediction of Visitation Frequency

In the follow-up study at five years postdivorce, Wallerstein and Kelly (1980c) provided additional information about visitation. Even from the onset fathers had practical problems in visitation, such as what to do and where to go. About 20 percent of custodial mothers saw no use for the visitation and actively tried to prevent it. Fathers who were depressed after the separation often found it extremely painful to visit with the child and avoided the visitation. If the father was the initiator of the divorce, he often felt guilt at leaving an affectionate parent-child relationship. Guilt led either to a reduction in visitation or an initial upsurge which was not maintained. The intense anger of the parents also played a role in determining visitation patterns (Kelly, 1981). Bitter custodial parents often tried to severely limit visitation or to sabotage those that were legally permitted. One strategy was to entice children from wanting visitation by providing more attractive alternatives. Setting up medical appointments, parties, or lessons were other strategies used by custodial mothers to prevent the noncustodial father from having access to the children.

A study by Bloom and Hodges (unpublished data) showed that visitation increased if the custodial parent participated in the intervention program as compared to the nontreated control. The six month long intervention program was designed to help newly separated adults with crisis intervention and information. When the noncustodial parent participated in the program, there was no effect on visitation. This result suggests that the custodial parent maintains much control over the access of the noncustodial parent to the children. Since the intervention program has been demonstrated to be of significant help to those who participated in it (Hodges and Bloom, in press; Bloom, Hodges, Kern, and McFaddin, 1985), participation may have increased awareness of the importance of contact of the children with the other parent. While it is surprising that participation in the study by noncustodial parents did not change visiting behavior, it may be that participation in the study reflected an already high level of concern about the children.

In the Wallerstein and Kelly (Kelly, 1981; Kelly and Wallerstein, 1977b; Wallerstein and Kelly, 1980b, 1980c) studies, a variety of factors were found to increase the frequency of visitation; open yearning for visitation by children, especially those under nine; strong commitment by many fathers; the open support of half of the mothers for visitation; children who expressed pleasure in visitation; children who were not angry at the father for the separation; fathers who were lonely, psychologically intact, and not depressed; fathers who were economically secure and better educated (not a strong predictor of frequent visitation); and low conflict between parents.

Tierney's (1983) study of preschool children and visitation looked at predictors of visitation, such as conflict and quality of parenting. Total amount of conflict between parents correlated significantly with frequency and consistency of visitation. The greater amount of conflict was associated with less frequent and less consistent visitation. These relationships were found for general conflict (r's ranged from .41 to .61) and for conflict associated with visitation (r's ranged from .34 to .79). Conflict was generally not related to duration of visits. The exception was a .25 correlation for duration and conflict as reported by the mother, $df = 46$, $p < .05$, with the greater the conflict, the longer the duration of the visits. Also the more the parents disagreed on parenting, the longer the duration of the visits ($r = .34$, $df = 28$, $p < .05$).

Finally, Tierney looked at behavior of the child during the visitation and visitation patterns. The more withdrawn the child was during visitation, the less frequent was visitation ($r = .44$, $df = 26$, $p < .01$) and the more regressive the child, the less frequent the visitation ($r = .34$, $df = 26$, $p < .05$). Surprisingly, there was no correlation between aggression levels and visitation pattern. It should be remembered that correlations do not imply causation.

A research study on separation and divorce (Bloom et al., 1982, 1983, 1985; Hodges, Tierney, and Buchsbaum; Hodges and Bloom, in press) provided information concerning the prediction of visitation patterns.*

The study looked at five domains of variable that might be related to frequency of visitation: (1) demographic variables; (2) parental discord variables; (3) stress variables; (4) decision to separate variables; and (5) visitation pattern variables. The following are preliminary analyses of those data:

1. *Demographic variables.* Noncustodial parents were found to do less frequent visitation if their own parents were ever separated. The fewer the adults with whom the noncustodial parent was now living, the more frequent the visitation. The fewer times that the custodial parent had moved since separation, the more frequent was visitation.

2. *Discord.* The higher the postdivorce discord, the less frequent the visitation. The reason for the decision to separate also contributed to amount of visitation. Low visitation frequency was related to high frequency of spouse's neglect of the home, predivorce physical abuse, verbal abuse, high levels of predivorce money problems, high levels of seeing the spouse's nagging as a contributing factor to the divorce, and high levels of drug and alcohol use. Higher levels of visitation were related to seeing infidelity as a contributing factor in the divorce.

3. *Stress since separation.* Stress levels were not found to be related to visitation patterns.

4. *Decision to separate.* If the noncustodial parent made the decision to separate, the visitation tended to be more frequent. The same was true if the

---

*David Stevens, one of my doctoral students, had primary responsibility for the analysis of this unpublished data.

noncustodial parent was in favor of the decision to separate. Perhaps the non-custodial parent's guilt or lack of anger made visitation more frequent.

5.   *Visitation variables.* When the noncustodial parent saw the visitation arrangement as being satisfactory to the child, visitation was more frequent. Among noncustodial parents, the more frequent visitation was correlated with taking greater levels of responsibility in parenting the child.

When all the statistically significant variables were entered into a multiple regression equation to see how well the frequency of visitation could be estimated, the following variables were predictive independently.

1.   For noncustodial parents, higher visitation frequency as compared to lower frequency was related to fewer adults in the noncustodial household, fewer problems with friendships, and sexual problems being a major complaint prior to separation:
2.   For custodial parents, higher visitation frequency was related to money problem as a contributor to the separation, geographic proximity of the noncustodial parent, sexual problem as a major complaint prior to separation, and low levels of neglect of the home as a major problem prior to separation.

Abandonment

Awad and Parry (1980) noted that anytime a parent is alive, but not available, the child will fantasize about that parent. According to Awad et al., the fantasy is a combination of the memory of the parent, the projection of the child, and the often negative projection of the custodial parent. The child will, of necessity, develop an egocentric and usually negative explanation as to why the noncustodial parent is abandoning. Loss of self-esteem is a common outcome. Abandonment can also lead to concerns about having to depend on a single parent for survival, thus causing increases in anxiety.

PATTERNS OF VISITATION AND CHILD DEVELOPMENT

Time Perspective and Child Development

While personality theorists have not developed recommendations for visitation that cover the entire developmental span from birth to 18 years, theorists have focused on the visitation patterns of young children. Numerous theorists have recommended that the visitation pattern should take into account the child's time perspective, thus ensuring a sense of continuity of care and affection. For example:

1. Visitation should provide for the child's sense of time and continuity (Tulloch, 1976).
2. "[T]he need of every child for unbroken continuity of affectionate and stimulating relationships with an adult." (Goldstein, Freud, and Solnit, 1973, p. 6).
3. "Criteria for the needs of the child are clearest between the ages of 6 months and 5 to 6 years, *particularly in the first two or three years.* Here, the general and stage specific needs coincide; *continuity of care and affection is paramount and overriding.*" (Lewis, 1974, emphasis added).

The increase in time perspective has a predictable path during the preschool years. The child slowly understands that "wait a minute" and "wait an hour" have different meanings. "After nap time" or "this afternoon" are more difficult. For the young child, "tomorrow" is an undefined, infinite time away, yet the child slowly learns the meaning of tomorrow. "The day after tomorrow" is a far more complex concept (thus making weekend visitations a potentially confusing pattern for the young child). One of the author's children used "the day after yesterday" for some months while straightening out time perspective. The author's children also used commercials and a favorite children's show as a time marker. "We will go in two "Gilligan's Islands."

The concept of tomorrow is seldom understood by 3 year olds, but 4 year olds understood the idea. By age 5, "the day after tomorrow" is conceptually understood, but a "week" may be a vaguely conceived time period. By age 6 or 7, the child can count and can understand the concept of "a week" or "a month." By age 7 or 8 an infinite time sense develops so that the child understands the concept of "forever."

Since the time perspective of children is variable and changeable before the age of 7, these recommendations imply that visitation agreements of children under 7 should take into account the changing stages of the child. Longer and longer visitations could occur during the ages from birth to 7, from brief hour-long visits to full weekends, to weeks. If the visitation pattern violates the short time perspective of the child, the child may have difficulty remembering the absent parent and will not be able to understand intuitively when he or she will return to the custodial parent. The results will be insecurity, anxiety, and difficulty in establishing a firm identification with either parent. Keep in mind, however, that basing the visitation patterns on chronological age could be a mistake, since each child has a unique age pattern for learning time concepts. Whether these time perspectives make a difference to the young child will be discussed in the next section.

Almost no theorist has discussed visitation pattern implications for older children, although supporting the affectional ties with the noncustodial parent is often discussed. Problems around the content of visitation will be discussed later in this chapter.

VISITATION PATTERNS AND CHILD ADJUSTMENT

Only one study has looked extensively at the variables that predict children's reaction to the visitation itself. Johnston, Campbell, and Mayes (1985) studied the distress and symptomatic behavior of 44 children aged 6 to 12. All of the children were involved in severe postseparation disputes over custody and care. The children were evaluated an average of three years and three months postseparation.

Only three children were able to make the transition between parents without stress. These children were given clear permission to be with and enjoy the other parent in spite of the ongoing conflict between the parents. All of the other children were typically symptomatic at the time of transition. Since the children were making an average of two transitions a week, they were frequently stressed. When the conflict was long standing or if there had been violence, the child was quite apprehensive and vigilant.

The mildest reactions reported by Johnston et al. was quieting and withdrawal at transition. Parents reported "spaced out" behavior and unresponsive reactions. More distressed reactions included high anxiety, apprehension, tension, and restlessness. They reported that almost three-fifths of the children resisted going on visit and returning. Two-fifths of the children demonstrated some kind of somatic symptom at the time of transition. Parents used the problems of the child as proof that the visitation was harmful. These children were quite upset by a chaotic schedule. The most distressed were those where the access pattern was never made clear and plans kept changing. Flexibility meant more fighting.

Children reported being highly distressed at meeting the other parent accidentally during a nonvisitation time. They did not know how to respond.

Children whose parents are in severe conflict will show a high frequency of symptomatology at times of transition. Unpredictable visitation times increased stress.

Preschool Age Children

Tierney's (1983) study looked at the effect of frequency, duration, and consistency of visitation patterns for mother-custody families and adjustment in 67 preschool children ranging from 3 to 5 years of age. In addition, Tierney looked at whether the child's time perspective facilitated adjustment to visitation. Other variables investigated in this study were quality of parenting and parental conflict.

Given that there was ample evidence in the literature that (1) conflict between parents was harmful to the children and (2) conflict and visitation might interact, Tierney looked at the effect of visitation patterns for children with parents who had low levels of conflict. Low frequency of visitation was negatively correlated with the father's ratings of the child's adjustment, with infrequent visitation related to high levels of father rated levels of maladjustment in the child ($r = -.36$, $df = 23$, $p < .05$). Frequency was unrelated to mother or teacher ratings of the child. Duration of visitation was also unrelated to mother, teacher, and father ratings. Consistency of visitation as reported by the mother and the father was correlated with the Louisville Behavior Checklist total maladjustment scores as reported by the mother ($r = .37$, $df = 39$, $p < .01$ for the mother; $r = .37$, $df = 25$, $p < .05$ for the father). When correlated with the subscales of the measures of adjustment of the Louisville Behavior Checklist, inconsistency of visitation correlated significantly with school disturbance problems, neurotic behavior, normal irritability, fear, aggression and inhibition. Thus, for preschool children, the findings are similar to those reported by Johnston et al. (1985).

The next part of Tierney's study, looked at whether visitation patterns would predict adjustment when quality of parenting by the mother was high. Under these conditions, low frequency of visitation was correlated with total mother report of behavior problems in the child ($r = -.31$, $df = 30$, $p < .05$) with low frequency related to more problems. In this case, duration and consistency was unrelated to ratings of adjustment. Low frequency of visitation for this group was correlated with schools disturbance problems, hyperactivity, and dependency.

When Tierney looked at time perspective, most parents kept duration and frequency within an appropriate range. With this limited sample, time perspective is unrelated to adjustment.

As previously mentioned, the problem with making inferences from this research is that correlations do not establish cause. While it is reasonable to assume no causal relationship between two variables when the correlation is zero, the presence of a correlation does not permit as inference of causation. For example, the correlation demonstrating a relationship between low frequency of visitation and maladjustment in the child as seen by the father would tempt a conclusion that low frequency of visitation causes poor maladjustment. It is just as likely that a father spending time with a child who he sees as maladjusted would find those visits as less rewarding and the maladjustment could cause the infrequent visitations. Most probably, both are true and the relationship is interactive.

Professionals should remember that while parent behavior can cause specific adjustment levels in the child, children's adjustment problems can lead to that same behavior in the parent. Professionals should be cautious about assigning blame for particular family interaction patterns. If noxious behavior on the part of the child is the cause of the behavior in the parent that causes concern, simple recommendations for change in parental behavior are likely to be ineffective. Family therapy approaches may be needed to affect the interactive process.

Hetherington, Cox, and Cox (1979) reported that except where there was conflict and ill-will between parents or severe disturbance in the father, frequency of the father's contact with the child was associated with a more positive adjustment in the child and better functioning in the mother.

School Age Children

Kelly and Wallerstein's (1977b) study, where most of the children were school age, did not report systematic analysis of the relationship between visitation frequency, duration, or consistency and adjustment. It did report that infrequent visitation correlated highly and significantly (though the levels were not reported) with a destructive visiting pattern. There were few reported instances where frequent visitation was harmful to the child. In those instances, severe pathology in the noncustodial parent was being manifested during visitation. Examples included sexual abuse and a case where the child was being exploited as a servant for the visits. Kelly and Wallerstein did not feel that pathology alone was grounds for eliminating visitation altogether.

A more extensive analysis of visitation on their project at the five-year follow-up provided more information (Wallerstein and Kelly, 1980c). This report did not note any correlation of the relationship between the noncustodial father and child and the predivorce father-child relationship at 18 months postseparation. About 25 percent were closer to their children after the divorce than before and 25 percent had markedly deteriorated in their relationship.

Professionals should be cautious in predicting postdivorce relationships for a noncustodial parent based on predivorce relationships between that parent and the child. At least for the noncustodial father, the ability to predict is quite limited. This recommendation does not apply to custody recommendations.

Jacobson (1978) reported the adjustment of 51 children who had experienced parental separation within 12 months of the interview to visitation time. The children ranged from 3 to 17 years of age. The mean time since separation was 140 days. Children had typically lost an average of 21 hours of time for a two-week period with the mother from before the separation until the interview, dropping to about 73 hours. Time lost with the father was about 33 hours per two-week period, dropping to about 20 hours. Generally, the more time lost with the parent, the greater the maladjustment. Greater time lost with the father was related to a high level of problems in the areas of aggression, inhibition, cognitive disability, and overall severity of maladjustment. For the mother, only the sensitivity scale was significant in time lost with the mother. Jacobson then separately analyzed the data by age groups 3 to 6 and 7 to 13. While each group showed time lost with the father to be inversely related to adjustment (i.e., the more time lost, the poorer the adjustment), the relationship was stronger for the older children.

Lowenstein and Koopman (1978) looked at the relationship of visitation pattern and adjustment in boys 9 to 14. This study evaluated 20 boys and their mothers and 20 boys and their fathers. No relationship was obtained for self-esteem levels and gender of custodial parent. Also, no relationship was found for self-esteem and time in a single-parent home, and quality of parental relationship. Self-esteem was related to whether the boys saw the noncustodial parent once a month or more or less than once a month (This frequency of visitation was selected for analysis and should not imply that data supported once a month as the critical cut-off). Boys who saw the noncustodial parent more than once a month had higher self-esteem. While the small sample size would probably not permit a breakdown by gender of custodial parent, it is unlikely that significance could have been obtained without both groups being involved in the results.

Regardless of the sex of the custodial parent, when the level of conflict is low and pathology in the noncustodial parent is low, data seems to suggest that frequent contact with the noncustodial parent is important for self-esteem.

Hess and Camara (1979) evaluated 16 families of divorce and 16 intact families with children. In this study, the children were between 9 and 11 years of age. When visitation was specifically addressed, the study found that boys saw their fathers more frequently for longer periods of time and were in touch more often between visits than were girls. For boys and girls, the quality of the relationship with the father was related positively to duration of visitation, but not frequency. Neither frequency of visitation or duration was significantly correlated with adjustment, while quality of the father-child relationship (for both intact and divorced families combined) was strongly related to aggression ($r = -.41$, $p < .01$), social relations ($r = .54$, $p < .001$), and work effectiveness in school ($r = .40$, $p < .01$).

Kurdeck and Berg (1983) evaluated the adjustment of 34 boys and 34 girls, averaging about 10 years old, in terms of the children's attitudes toward the separation, understanding the divorce, locus of control, and interpersonal understanding. In addition, the mother's description of the child's attitudes, emotional reactions to the divorce, environmental change, social support system, divorce adjustment, current stress levels, and interparental conflict were evaluated. Teachers also provided a description of the children's personal and social competence. The results were similar to those found by Hess and Camara (1979). Adjustment in the child was unrelated to frequency of visitation, regularity of visitation (not mentioned in Hess and Camara), or phone contact with the noncustodial parent. Children's divorce adjustment was related to a variety of variables including time spent alone with the noncustodial parent. Visitation duration that is shared with dates or cohabiting partners may not be the important variable, but exclusive visitation time may be more important. Given the tendency for noncustodial parents to share visitation with live-in boyfriends or girlfriends, it is important to share this information with parents.

Noncustodial parents should insure that significant visitation time be spent with the child alone, without the inclusion of significant others.

Adolescents

No research has been found that studied visitation frequency, duration, and predictability in adolescents. Perhaps the degree of control that adolescents have on the visitation pattern accounts for this lack. In addition, as indicated in the previous section, visitation tends to be shorter and less regular at this age. While not studying visitation and adjustment issues, Springer and Wallerstein (1983) did evaluate the adjustment of 14 adolescents in the larger Wallerstein and Kelly (1980c) study. They reported that the adolescents experienced significant conflict around visitation. The wish to spend time with friends conflicted with concern about hurting their parent's feelings. Anger about the failure for parents to include them in the planning around visitation was frequently expressed. Teenage girls had particular problems around spending extended times with their fathers. Perceiving their fathers as adult men created anxiety in some of the adolescent girls. Often, the father shared their anxiety. If there was a good relationship between the daughter and father, this anxiety was overcome. If, however, this anxiety occurred in the context of a poor daughter-father relationship, the daughter rejected continued contact. The young adolescent boys did not generally experience as much anxiety in visiting with fathers.

RECOMMENDED VISITATION PATTERNS BY AGE OF CHILD

This author has received numerous requests from lawyers to suggest particular visitation patterns as a function of the age of the child. This section is an attempt to provide that guidance. Since the research is meager, it is likely that the recommendations provided below will undergo extensive revision over the next few years. There are certain assumptions that underlie the recommendations: (1) the child has a reasonably strong affectionate bond with both parents; (2) both parents have a basic understanding of children's needs; (3) both parents can adjust to the changing needs of the children as a function of developmental changes, and (4) Both parents can provide for the physical safety, nurturance needs, emotional support, interest, and ability to interact regularly with the child. Violation of these assumptions might lead to a recommendation to increase or restrict visitation (depending on which parent had the problem).

Factors that Might Limit Visitation Recommendations

Several factors should be taken into account in reducing the frequency and duration of visitation. The amount of reduction would be based on the assessment of the resilience of the child, the social buffers that protect the child, and the severity of the problem. Specific suggestions for handling each of the problem areas in terms of visitation and protection of the child are discussed later in the chapter.

Factors that limit the maximum amount of time for visitation are:

1. Conflict between parents
2. Irresponsible parent
3. Long distance between parents
4. Severely maladjusted parent
5. Sexually or physically abusing parent

Factors that Might Increase Visitation Recommendations

Other factors may lead the mental health professional to recommend longer visitations than are listed below. For example, when long distance requires some compromise between the child's need for stability and the need for the child and parent to be bonded to one another. Such an increase in visitation time would be minor, however, rather than serving as an excuse for extended visits for very young children.

The following recommendations are based on minimizing the risk to the child. Provided that the parents are "good enough," visits occur without stress, and other basic needs are provided for, the visitation patterns described below are designed to produce no additional stress.

It is the responsibility of mental health professionals who use the following guidelines to balance the needs for stability and predictability of the child against other needs of the family, for example needs created by long distance between child and parent, need for bonding between parent and child, frequency of contact, quality of parenting (particularly awareness of the needs of young children) and quality of the custodial home.

Infancy

Birth to Six Months of Age

As a result of research in the 1960s and 1970s, it has become clear that infants do not just develop attachment bonds to one person, but can become securely attached to several parental figures. Attachment is not related to who the primary caregiver is from the point of view of feeding and changing diapers, but rather who provides talk, play, cuddling, and rocking. Attachment is determined by the quality of the interaction between the adult and infant.

According to Sroufe (1979) the primary issue of development at this age is physiological regulation and the primary need of the infant is smooth routines. From 3 to 6 months, the need is for the reduction of tension with sensitive, cooperative interaction between the infant and caregiver. Visitation should not interrupt the ability of the two families to provide those routines.

An important function of visitation during this period is to facilitate sufficient contact that the child will develop affectionate bonds with the noncustodial parent and the noncustodial parent will also develop feelings of attachment. While it is clear that such bonds can develop later, it is much more difficult to do so.

While there is no research on noncustodial father-infant visitation (and for the mother to be noncustodian is very rare for infants), some inferences about multiple attachment and infant needs can be drawn from several studies. According to the U.S. Department of Labor, in 1979, 40 percent of all United States mothers with children under the age of 3 were employed. Thus, a large percentage of children are separated from their mothers from a very early age regardless of the family marital status. Research on families with two wage earners demonstrated that fathers were more active in child care (Pedersen, 1981). In observations of 5-month-old children that were from either one or two wage earner families (Pedersen, Cain, Saslow, & Anderson, in press, cited in Pedersen, 1981), there was no differences in the quality of either parents' caregiving behaviors. Mothers in both types of families spent more time than fathers in feeding. Mothers who worked spent more time in verbal interaction with their babies compared to nonworking mothers. Fathers in two wage earner families actually interacted less with the infants than fathers in one wage earner families, perhaps because the mothers' need to interact with the infant after work crowded out the father.

Bowlby (1969) proposed that from birth to 2 months of age, the infant is at a preattachment stage, with undiscriminating social responsiveness. The infant needs social stimulation, but will respond to any adult that provides that stimulation. At the same time, the child is slowly learning to recognize parenting or caregiving figures. From 2 to 6 months of age, the child shows greater responsivity to familiar figures, and will smile more and vocalize more to familiar adults (Bowlby, 1969). At 4 to 6 months of age, the infant will be wary of unfamiliar people (Bronson, 1972). The infant will frown, breathe heavier, and perhaps cry when a stranger approaches.

From day care research, it is clear that very young infants can tolerate contact with adults other than mothers. Kagan, Kearsley, and Zelazo (1978) compared day care versus home care children from 3½ to 29 months and found that high quality day care had no effect on language, cognitive functioning, or attachment with parents or other adults. High quality day care means warm consistent care in a day care center with a ratio of no greater than four infants for each adult caregiver. If very young infants can handle such intensive daycare without harm, obviously they can handle visitation also without harm, provided that the visitation is both frequent and predictable.

Skafte (1985) also noted that for infants, short, frequent visits are much better than longer visits spaced far apart. Skafte recommended daily contact of a few hours as ideal, however practical considerations may prevent such an arrangement. If both parents are employed, it would be difficult for a custodial and noncustodial parent to find enough waking hours in the day for both to have quality time with the child. Skafte recommended that no more than two days in a row go by without time with the noncustodial parent.

Bentovim and Gilmour (1981) raised concerns about long-term reactions to separation from the primary caregiver to whom an infant is attached. They also emphasized the importance of continuity.

Thus, the recommendation for visitation for infants is the opposite of what often occurs in the thinking about frequency versus duration. Parents whose schedule or preferences lead to less frequent visitation want to compensate for that reduced frequency by increasing the duration. While such a compensation is appropriate for school age children (and perhaps preferable), it is not recommended for infants.

For infants from birth to 6 months, a frequent and predictable visitation pattern is recommended. The more frequent the noncustodial parent can be available, the longer the duration should be. For infants who can only be visited once or twice a week, visitation should not exceed one or two hours. Infants visited every day or every other day can develop attachments to the noncustodial parents that can maintain their security. Infants should spend more waking hours with the custodial parent than the noncustodial parent. Stability of child care location should be maintained. Subject to the needs and abilities of the custodial and noncustodial parents, such visitation could be for one hour or part of a day. Overnight visits are likely to not be in the child's best interests. Infants should have eating and sleeping arrangements as stable as possible.

No research indicates the upper limit of child care for infants that can occur without harm. Extensive time away from the custodial parent leaves little waking time for interaction. While working time of eight hours per working day may be tolerated, a mother who can visit during lunch time and who can support significant waking hour time would be better for the child.

Dishon (1985) noted that professionals concerned with object constancy in the bonding of parent and child would be concerned about separating the child from the primary parent (usually the mother) for more than brief periods prior to 30 to 36 months of age.

Six to 18 Months of Age

True attachment to parental figures begins around 6 months of age. Sroufe (1979) noted that the issue for development at this age is the establishment of an effective attachment relationship and the role for the caregiver is to provide responsive availability. Stranger anxiety often begins at 6 or 7 months and peaks at 8 to 12 months. Children will show apprehension and possibly cry when picked up by a stranger and will calm down when held by a consistent parental figure. Attachment is not limited to the mother. The child can attach as well to the father and to a child caregiver. Children with multiple caregivers will be more comfortable with strangers and will show less intense responses. Also, the stranger anxiety response will show a delay if there are multiple caregivers. The response to strangers would seem to be related to the ability of the infant at this age to recognize that the situation is strange and recognize the inability to do anything about it.

For the same reason, separation anxiety becomes more common during this time. Infants that previously showed no distress at a parent leaving, now cry when parents leave the house. Separation anxiety typically develops at about 8 months of age and peaks from 1 to 1½ years of age. It can be still quite strong at 2 years of age. For infants 12 to 18 months of age, if the father is present, the separation response to the mother may not occur, even in the presence of a stranger. However, if both parents leave, the child would cry (Kotelchuck, 1972). Children are less likely to cry if they have some coping skill for handling the separation. For example, children who can crawl after the departing parent are less likely to cry (Rheingold, 1970). Children are much more likely to cry when left alone in an unfamiliar room than a familiar room (Ross, Kagan, Zelazo, & Kotelchuck, 1975).

Given the reactions of infants 6 to 12 months of age to strangers and to separation, the frequency and duration of visitation depends in part on the prior contact of the infant with the noncustodial parent. If that parent has participated frequently in child care, the frequency and duration of visitation can be greater.

If a child 6 to 12 months of age has had little prior contact with the noncustodial parent, visitation should be initially short and frequent to provide familiarity and comfort to the infant.

In the latter part of this period, the child has as a primary issue exploration and mastery of the environment (Sroufe, 1979). The parent or caregiver must provide a secure basis for this exploration. Since the child is now capable of walking and beginning speech, both the custodial and noncustodial parent must provide a safe environment. Safety in the environment is a requirement at all times, but it becomes a more crucial issue as soon as crawling begins.

Goldstein and Solnit (1984), in giving advice to noncustodial parents, noted that children under 3 quickly lose feelings of attachment to people that they do not frequently see. For example, a young child may show stranger anxiety to a parent not seen for several days. Skafte (1985) also recommended that no more than two or three days go without time with the noncustodial parent. Skafte recommended against overnight visits at this age.

As for younger infants, short visits of one to three hours are recommended if frequency of visits is low. If contact is regular and frequent, the child can handle visitation that are daily or every other day. The length of such visitations can be adjusted to the needs and wants of both parents. The noncustodial parent should recognize that the infant of this age needs predictability and familiarity. Visitation will work best when visitation occurs in the same location every time. The infant should not be left with another caregiver during visitation unless the infant has had frequent opportunity to interact with that caregiver. Overnight visits are probably still not in the child's best interest. However, overnight visits might be considered when bonding between the child and noncustodial parent needs to be supported or long distance makes short visits impractical. Overnight visits should be considered less than desirable and used only when other considerations are more important and some instability to the child is worth the trade-off.

Frequency of visitation for infants should vary according to the noncustodial parent's sensitivity to the infant's physiological and psychological needs. The infant needs to be fed, warm, and comfortable. Almost all parents recognize those needs. The fact that the infant needs to be held, talked to, stroked, and played with are psychological needs to which some parents are less sensitive.

The temperament of the child may also help determine frequency and duration of visits. An easy child will handle liberal visitation. A slow-to-warm-up child may need a slower transition to more frequent and longer visitations. A difficult infant may require less frequent and shorter visitation. Noncustodial parents will find a difficult infant less rewarding to have around and may request less time. However, the needs of the custodial parent for relief from a classically difficult infant can be profound.

For infants, temperaments should be taken into account in setting the visitation pattern.

Finally, the desire of the noncustodial parent to have contact with the infant and to provide comfort for the infant should be taken into account. Noncustodial mothers or fathers who want frequent contact and bonding with the infant can be granted that contact and it will benefit all concerned, infants and both parents.

Toddlers

Children aged 18 months to 3 years are considered toddlers. The task of children during this period is individuation (Sroufe, 1979), that is, the child works at being an individual separate from the parents. The child needs firm support both in terms of limit setting and freedom to explore. The "terrible two's" is an important developmental stage. The child must be given permission to resist the parent on unimportant issues, but required to obey in areas of safety, self control, and social interaction. The child who is too resistive may have too many pressures for new skills or obedience to handle. Since time perspective is increasing and children can remember people whom they have not seen for several days (but not weeks or months), children can tolerate longer times between visits and longer visits.

Skafte (1985) recommended entire days and overnights by the time the child is three. Skafte also felt that entire weekends are too long for such young children. This author agrees with both of those recommendations.

Children from 18 months to 3 years of age can handle visitations that are less frequent than for infants, but consistency and frequency are still important. An 18 month old child who is visiting only on weekends can handle parts of a day. By three years, the child can spend an overnight without harm. Weekend visits are still not recommended. (Several times a week rather than a long weekend is more helpful to the child.) Long visitations during the summer vacations are not recommended. While the exact length of a long visitation during the summer for this age child is not known, a child familiar with and bonded to the noncustodial parent can handle three to four days. A child who has not had frequent contact with the noncustodial parent due to geographic distance, for example, should not be separated from the custodial parent for more than a day or two. Of course this advice is the opposite of what such a parent desires.

Children of this age should not be required to travel to a distant geographic location for an extensive visit with the noncustodial parent. If the parent has not had regular visitation, that parent should travel to the custodial parent's locations and have short, regular visits for part of a day.

Preschool Age Children

Preschool children (i.e., those aged 3 to 5) are learning to manage their impulses, develop sex role identification, and develop peer relations. The parents need to provide clear roles and values and flexible self-control for the child (Sroufe, 1979). For this age group, Awad and Parry (1980) recommended frequent brief visits rather than day long or overnight visits. Other clinicians have indicated that children of these age can tolerate day long visits and overnight visits quite well. According to Tierney's (1983) study, low conflict and high quality parenting may be very important. This data also indicated that children of this age are more affected by predictability than by frequency and duration of visits. Parents in this study were generally using reasonable levels of frequency and duration.

For preschool children, professionals should take into account that conflict between parents and high quality parenting may be more important than pattern of visitation. Given low conflict levels and high quality parenting by the mother, the professional should emphasize the importance of consistency. With low parental conflict levels, frequency is important. If quality of parenting by the mother is high, frequency of contact with the noncustodial father correlates with adjustment. Support of more frequent visitation should be the next level of priority after consistency. There is no evidence at the present time to demonstrate that time perspective is a critical variable in the adjustment of the child. These recommendations are based on correlation, and cause and effect are not established. These recommendations should be considered tentative.

One trouble with "frequent and liberal" visitation without specifying the pattern of visitation is that visitation is often set with the needs of the parents in mind rather than the needs of the child. Too often, "frequent and liberal" gets translated into "infrequent and unpredictable." Since Tierney's study is very clear that such a pattern is related to maladjustment in the child, clear statements of when visitation would occur is more useful for children of this age. Children might benefit from less frequent (not daily), but longer visits that permit the development of a relationship under conditions of normal living.

Skafte (1985) approved of long weekends, holiday time, and blocks of time for summer vacations for the 3 to 5 year-old children. This study recommended that children not go longer than one week without contact with each parent.

Preschool age children benefit from highly predictable visits. Weekend visits during the year and week long visits for holidays and summer vacations can be handled well, if limited in frequency. It is not known what the maximum long visit can be that will still benefit the child. Intuitively, visits of longer than a week may still be inappropriate without visitation with the custodial parent. If longer visitations are necessary because of distance or planning problems, the parents should be advised of methods that help these children handle such visits (see the section on long visitations for young children).

Primary School Age Children

Six to 10 Years of Age

During this stage of development the child is involving in moving from parents to teachers and peers as the primary sphere of influence. The child learns to play in a cooperative manner, to be industrious and creative, and to see the world from another's perspective. The child's time perspective permits long separations from parents while maintaining affectional bonds. The research summarized in the section on visitation and adjustment (Hess and Camara, 1979; Jacobson, 1978; Kelly and Wallerstein, 1977b; Wallerstein and Kelly, 1980c) suggests that most children do not find every other weekend, alternate holidays, and six weeks in the summer a plan that provides enough contact with the noncustodial parent. Quality of bonding and "good enough" parenting are likely to be very important in determining whether children wish for more visitation. Frequent visitation and liberal opportunity to have contact with the noncustodial parent should be permitted if the level of conflict between parents is not increased severely by that contact.

During this age period, the child is usually not ready for totally nonstructured visitation. Some visitation contact should be specified and predictable to the child. Spontaneous contact can be of enormous benefit to the child who can interpret the wish by the noncustodial parent to initiate contact beyond that required as an indication of affection and enjoyment. Such spontaneous contact will be beneficial to the parent and child only if the custodial parent is not competitive or resentful of that contact. Contact by phone or letter between visits can also increase the sense of the child as loved and enjoyed.

While predictability is important during this age, the child is also increasing contact with peers and having greater opportunities for parties, overnights with friends, and recreational sports. The noncustodial parent who insists on visitation without regard to the wishes of the 6 to 12 year old to participate in these activities may invite resentment and rejection. Beware of the custodial parent's use of these activities to block access to the child. In general, it is better to be flexible and "trade times" to take into account the child's wishes. The child's activities should not be used to reduce the frequency or duration of visitation.

Skafte (1985) felt that many families found every other weekend with some time during the week after school or in the evening for the week that did not have visitation was an appropriate schedule. Research evidence suggests that many children would find such a schedule too limited (Kelly, 1981; Kelly and Wallerstein, 1977b).

If the two parents have a reasonably cordial relationship, visitation more frequent than every other weekend may be desirable. At 7 to 8 years of age, children who have contact with the noncustodial parent several times a week were the most content with visitation. When both parents are employed, the custodial parent must have special time of (i.e., days or major parts of a day) reserved to be with the child as well. Contact once or more during the week is helpful. Children seem to benefit from more contact with the noncustodial parent rather than less, but the time of maximum benefit is not known. Flexibility within some general scheduling of visitation is helpful. When conflict between parents is high, children benefit from a more structured, predictable pattern of visitation. Long visitations during the summer are acceptable, but some contact with the custodial parent, either through visitations or phone is desirable.

Eleven to 12 Years of Age

Based on the research on visitation satisfaction, some reduction in visitation, particularly for boys, may be appropriate at this age. Skafte (1985) noted that peer involvement at this age may lead children to want less contact with the parents and a more flexible visitation schedule. As Skafte noted, sometimes spontaneous activities can enrich the relationships.

At the latter part of the primary school years (10 or 11), boys in particular seem to prefer less contact, perhaps every other week, rather than weekly. If the child prefers to maintain weekly contact, this amount of contact should be permitted.

Adolescence

Divorce creates special problems for the adolescent. Just when teenagers need to separate from their parents, their parents separate from them. Emotional upset on the part of one or more parents makes it more difficult for the teenager to separate. While visitation plans often include plans for every other weekend for teenagers, Kelly (1981) noted that teenagers usually have contacts that last several hours and seldom do overnight or weekend visits occur. A teenager required to stay home with a parent for a weekend is likely to see that requirement as being grounded, rather than an opportunity to develop a relationship. Since teenagers tend to spend more waking, nonschool hours with friends than family, long weekend visitations are likely to interfere with age-appropriate developmental needs.

Visitation with adolescents should take into account that teenagers do not need contact of long duration with either parent. Weekend long visitations may interfere with developmental needs to separate from both parents. Contact once or twice a week for one or more hours may be enough contact. Some contact should occur on a weekly or every other week basis.

HOLIDAYS AND VACATIONS

As Skafte (1985) noted, it is important to develop family traditions and strengthen family bonds through holidays. Therefore, children should have the opportunity to celebrate each holiday with each parent. Alternating which holiday is spent with which parent facilitates this goal. This author has found that when both parents live in the same community, it is possible to split important holidays such as Christmas or Hanukkah, so that the child can spend part of each holiday with both parents. For example, some families successfully split Christmas by having the child spend Christmas Eve with one family and Christmas day with the other. Other families change visitation at noon on Christmas day.

Skafte also noted that family vacations can be important time for developing relationships. Skafte recommended that children under 3 should not go on extended vacations. For children from 3 to 5, several short vacations are more beneficial than one long vacation.

VISITATION PLANS THAT RECOGNIZE THE CHANGING NEEDS OF CHILDREN

The problems of setting visitation plans are the same as those for determining custody. Children have different needs at different times of their development. Visitation agreements seldom take into account these changes over time. Tierney (1983) noted that parents of preschool children seem to adjust visitation to the age of the child even when the written visitation agreement permitted longer visitations. While the good will of parents and the awareness of child needs may permit individual negotiation that benefit the child, it is generally better to provide written plans that take the changing needs into account.

Since the ability of a child to tolerate or benefit from specific visitation patterns is not solely dependent on age, plans for evaluation (perhaps including mediation) on a regular basis may be appropriate. For parents not good at negotiating, the child's needs will be better served by approximating the changing needs in the divorce agreement. Thus, an agreement might indicate that the visitation pattern would be at a particular frequency and duration until age 3, another pattern until age 5, a third pattern until age 9, and a final pattern at age 10. The agreement might indicate that for the teen years the visitation pattern would be negotiated with the teenager involved, but would be at least two hours per week and no more than every weekend.

VISITATION PLANS WHEN THE CHILDREN IN THE FAMILY ARE IN DIFFERENT DEVELOPMENTAL STAGES

Families seldom split visitation by the age of the child. Usually, all children go together to see the noncustodial parent. Except for infants, such visitation plans make sense for the children. When the preschool age children are bonded to one another, the presence of siblings can serve to provide the stability that frequent visitation could provide and the child might be able to tolerate longer visitation than might be recommended for a child of that age without siblings. Perhaps some average of the children's ages might serve as a guideline for determining the best pattern. At the same time, infants should still not be subject to overnight visitations. While primary school age children might desire frequent visitations, the older brother or sister in high school might prefer shorter times. It is reasonable to have visitations of varying lengths taking the developmental needs into account.

Such a variable program must also take into account the needs of the custodial parent to be relieved of parenting responsibilities for some period of time. Single parenting is an exhausting job. Many custodial parents look forward to the visitation time as an opportunity to be alone for awhile.

GRANDPARENT VISITATION

The grandparent-grandchild relationship can be a special one of affection without excessive control. The pain of some grandparents about the loss of contact with their grandchildren after divorce can be profound. Typically, the parents of the noncustodial parent have little or no contact with their grandchildren. Particularly if the noncustodial parent is abandoning, the custodial parent may find contact with the grandparents painful. Most states have given grandparents the right to petition for visitation time with the child, provided the best interests of the child are protected (Derdeyn, 1985). Derdeyn made the point that such visitation laws were a departure from the more usual common law origin of laws. Vigorous lobbying by grandparents were effective in obtaining such laws. As Derdeyn noted, grandparents rarely obtain custody.

There are potential problems with such visitations, although clearly children can benefit from a healthy relationship with the grandparents. One problem is that if the custodial parent is employed, if the noncustodial parent has liberal visitation time, if both sets of grandparents want time with the child, there is little time left for the custodial parent to have with the child. Such a law also ignores the fact that grandparent-parent relationship might be strained and the children can be caught in the middle of that type of battle as well. According to Derdeyn, courts have resolved requests for visitation under such a strain in both directions, granting visitation in some cases and denying it in others.

Provided that the grandparents can be properly supportive to the parents and the grandchildren, under most conditions grandparent visitation should be encouraged. Goldstein and Solnit (1984, p. 121) did not feel that legally mandated, court-enforceable grandparent visitation rights were in the child's best interests. They felt that such an arrangement interfered with the ability of the custodial parent to be in full charge. Derdeyn (1985) also felt that giving grandparents such rights could exacerbate chronic conflict. Derdeyn went on to note that such visitation could foster competition between grandparent and parent for parenting the child and lead grandparents to try to assume a former, rewarding (and now inappropriate) role.

IMPLEMENTATION OF THESE GUIDELINES IN THE COURTS

Judges are often reluctant to overturn stipulated agreements between parents. When there is a low risk that such an agreement would be harmful to the child, even if some risk is present, judges prefer to honor such agreements. Judges can also get impatient with mental health professionals who testify with a certainty that is not justified in either clinical experience or research findings. Indeed, some children can adjust to almost any arrangement, no matter how chaotic. Since convenience to parents is obviously taken into account and best interests of the child only included around conflicted issues, the problem becomes how to facilitate the courts using the best advice that mental health professionals can give. This author feels strongly that the guidelines presented in this chapter contain sound advice. However, there are no uniform guidelines about what is best for children. The assumption is that the guidelines will change as research clarifies the unanswered questions in this area.

The following suggestions may enable professional associations or the courts to facilitate changes in their jurisdictions:

1. Provide conciliation courts, family courts, and divorce courts with the guidelines.
2. Provide lawyers and mental health professionals involved in working with families of divorce with the guidelines.
3. If judges are reluctant to overturn high risk, stipulated agreements concerning visitation, ask whether the judges would be willing to refer such cases for evaluation.
4. If the judges are reluctant to overturn high risk, stipulated agreements and are reluctant to refer such cases for evaluation, ask whether the judges would be willing to inform the parents that although the agreement would be approved, the parents should know that such an arrangement is not recommended by mental health professionals and provide parents with the guidelines.

WORKING WITH VISITATION PROBLEMS AFTER THE DIVORCE

When Can Visitation Crises Be Predicted?

Clinical experience has shown this author a variety of predivorce family dynamics that predict visitation problems later. (However, these predictors have yet to be tested more systematically.)

1. *Use of the children in marital conflict.* One parent continually complains to the children about the behavior of the other spouse. Parents try to get the children to side with their point of view.

2. *Part of the cause of the divorce is the introduction of a new relationship on the part of the spouse who is likely to be noncustodial.* There are intense conflicts and competition between a mother and the father's new relationship. Often the acting out of the anger around visitation feels justified to protect the children from exposure to the "immoral" relationship, or a strong belief that the other person is bad for the child. Even when the noncustodial parent

left the relationship, there can be significant jealousy over the other parent's new relationship. Sometimes a parent will try to exclude the other parent in an attempt to formulate a new family, a move usually intensely (and often appropriately) resisted by the other parent.

3. *When childbearing is a significant part of the conflict leading to the divorce.* This sign is particularly significant since relatively few divorces are for this reason. For first marriages, childrearing ranks fourth or fifth in reason for the divorce (for second marriages, problems with childrearing rank first). When the parents come from very different childrearing cultures, it is difficult to compromise. You can alternate vacations between the mountains and the seashore. You cannot spank today and send the child to the bedroom tomorrow or be strict about bed times today and be lenient tomorrow. If you do, you will have a very mixed up child. Problems around visitation are often generated out of anger or concern about how the children are being ruined by the other parent. Two childrearing strategies, both approximately equal in quality of parenting, can be held with intense commitment by the two parents.

4. *When the marital conflict is generated by one parents' radical change in life style.* One parent decides on extreme relation or open marriage or sudden swinging weekends. Like parenting styles, the concern for the children's welfare often is expressed in difficulties in visitation.

5. *Resentment over money.* This problem may lead to visitation conflict, particularly if there is child support. Of course, child support nonpayment leads to its own set of problems. The record for payment of child support is incredibly poor. It is common for custodial mothers to express their anger about failure to make child support payments by trying to block visitations. Since visitations are viewed by courts as a right of the child rather than the noncustodial parent, such moves are generally not supported by the courts.

6. *When one of the complaints around the marital conflict is chronic irresponsibility.* This problem is a red flag. If one spouse was chronically irresponsible prior to the divorce, why should it change later?

7. *When the level of anger is extreme.* When each person is out to get the other as much as possible during the divorce, visitation becomes a battleground. (This author counselled one couple who was still so angry at each other five years after the divorce that effective communication around negotiating visitation (when, where, and how long), as well as simple rules for parenting, could not be accomplished without the counselor's presence.)

8. *When there is a custody battle.* This author predicted that custody battles would lead to angry resentment. However, research with the Mediation Research Project (Pearson and Thoennes 1984, 1985) indicates that a *noncontested* divorce may have poorer visitation patterns. Custody battles may indicate high level of resentment, but also may indicate a high level of involvement with the children.

9. *When one or more parent has psychopathology that interacts with parenting.* Examples include parents who involve the child in role reversal where

the parent is getting primary needs met from the child, borderline parents with difficulty maintaining individuation from the child, narcissistic parents, parents who demand loyalty from the child and insist on rejection of the other parent, and parents who use the child as a pawn in the battle with the other parent.

When Is There a Low Probability of Visitation Problems?

1. When both parents agree that one parent is better as a parent.
2. When both parents agree that the other parent is also quite good as a parent.
3. When the divorce is unrelated to parenting and the parting is relatively cordial. Such partings are rare, but they do occur.
4. When the parents spend a significant amount of time with the lawyers or a mental health professional asking what is best for the children. When parents ask how they should tell the children, what concerns the children are likely to have, and how they can protect the children from hurt, the risk is low. While such concerns can still be overwhelmed by the parents' anger, such couples are generally less likely to use visitation to resolve the problems between them.

"Proof" of Poor Visitation

Beware of accepting parental reports of emotional upset on the part of the child immediately prior to or after visitation as proof of poor quality of visitation with the noncustodial parent. The child may be responding to the wishes of the custodial parent who gets upset around the time of visitation. When the child also gets upset, the custodial parent can feel justified in trying to block visitation.

Separation may be more tolerable to the child when everyone is angry. Therefore, the child may be deliberately provoking everyone so that he/she can tolerate the pain of leaving each parent.

Upset at transition times has been demonstrated to be related to chronic conflict between parents for elementary age school children (Johnston et al. 1985). Thus, children will show high levels of both psychological and physical symptoms at time of transition in response to the dispute between parents. Benedek and Benedek (1977) also noted that children act out around visitation and that such behavior did not necessarily indicate a bad visit.

Finally, anger can be a technique on the part of the child to keep the parents communicating with each other. Children who wish for reconciliation find noncommunicating parents an almost intolerable situation. Even battles are preferred to parents who do not communicate. Parents who do not talk can never reconcile. The child may set the parents up around visitation to force communication.

Mental health professionals should be cautious in interpreting the meaning of a Friday-Monday upset around visitation. While the visitation may be damaging to the child and certainly investigation of the quality of the visit is called for, there are a variety of other reasons the child may have for being upset, including trying to please the custodial parent, having difficulty with separation and forcing contact between parents.

Benedek and Benedek (1977) recommended counseling for the parents for such problems. Termination of visitation should be considered only after a thorough evaluation.

Goldstein and Solnit (1984) noted that a parent who argues that there is substantial evidence of harm because of the resistance on the part of the child toward the visits is often received by the court with little sympathy. The court may order the visitation to continue on the ground that the custodial parent influences the child's attitudes and, if the visitation is discontinued, the child will be deprived of contact with a parent to which the child is entitled. In addition, Goldstein and Solnit noted that opposition to the visitation by the custodial parent might lead to a weakening of the relationship with the custodial parent because it undermines trust.

Competition for Affection

Helping parents avoid the "Santa Claus" party atmosphere that is common of early visitation is a focus of many discussions. Sharing activities and spending time in a normal living situation is emphasized over entertaining the child. Resentment over the attractiveness of the visitation with the noncustodial parent can occur for the custodial parent who feels it impossible to compete with the excitement of a noncustodial parent into taking children out to eat, to movies, to bowling, to amusement parks, and to other nonhome-related activities. Three pieces of information can reassure that distressed parent:

1. That pattern of entertainment often occurs with a noncustodial parent who does not know how to relate to the children and uses such activities to fill up the visitation time;
2. Such a frenzied activity level tends to drop off during the first year because both the noncustodial parent and the child will tire of the constant entertainment after several months and it is expensive;
3. While children may prefer the parent who entertains, maturity often (but not always) brings the realization that a more balanced interaction with the parent is healthier.

Mental health professionals may want to reassure a custodial parent that a noncustodial parent who constantly entertains the visiting child is likely to tire of that pattern after several months. While the custodial parent is likely to experience distress at the child's obvious preference for being with the non-custodial parent, good parenting styles are likely to prevail in helping the child. The custodial parent should be warned not to try to compensate for the entertainment orientation of the other parent by becoming more strict and less entertaining. The custodial parent should try to balance the level of control and fun independent of the behavior of the other parent.

When Visitation Goes Too Well

Particularly for noncustodial fathers getting out from under a stressful marriage, the requirement to visit with the children on a regular pattern may actually improve the quality of the father-child relationship. The father may spend more time and attention with the children than ever before. The child who showed little upset at the time of the divorce may experience longing for this new warm parent. This pattern should not be used to justify stopping the visitation. The child is longing for the father because of the strong need for just this interaction. Getting too little time with a noncustodial father is far better than getting no time at all.

Irregular or Nonexistent Visitation

The problem of the noncustodial parent's irregular or nonexistent visitation is particularly difficult to deal with. Ultimately, the courts cannot force a reluctant parent to visit. Even if the coercion was successful, the argument could be made that the parent could sabotage the visit in such a way as to prevent it from being useful to the child.

Mental health professionals should try to work with a noncustodial parent to diagnose why visitation is rare or nonexistent. Even the willingness of such a parent to come in to talk may be a sign that negotiation (or therapy) could increase visitation.

The elimination of visitation often leads to low self-esteem in the child. As discussed in Chapter 3, the child may handle the disappearance of a parent as indicating to the child a sense of unlovability. Unlike the death of a parent, unexplained disappearance prevents mourning.

Chronic Irresponsibility on the Part of the Custodial Parent

Angry parents can be expert in manipulating each other. The custodial parent may schedule special activities, such as church activities or dental work (which, of course, are essential to the proper development of the child and therefore "should" take precedence over visitation) during the visitation time. In such cases, neither the parent nor the child is present when the noncustodial parent shows up.

The noncustodial parent may express anger by keeping the custodial parent waiting for hours before picking up or delivering the child, ruining the custodial parent's alternative plans. The child may be delivered hungry or tired.

Remarriage

The presence of a significant other for the noncustodial parent can create resistance to visitation from any of the parties involved. The child may resent the loss of attention from the noncustodial parent. The stepparent may have difficulties with the intrusion into the family life. Much more will be discussed about the problem of the stepfamily in Chapter 9.

PROBLEMS WITH LONG VISITATIONS

It is recognized that many families cannot provide for the kind of brief but frequent visitation that is recommended for children under 7 years of age. Long visitation for young children may increase risk because of the difficulty of the child to maintain an image and attachment for long periods of time for the absent parent. In addition the child has difficulty perceiving the return to the custodial parent at an intuitive level. Long visitation periods thus place the child in the position of being constantly separated from a parent without an awareness of when the child would return to that parent.

A 14-year-old girl who had not seen her father for five or six years was quite frightened of a two-week visit with a father 1500 miles away when contact was reestablished. The relationship would have a greater likelihood of working well if the first contact were for a long week-end or short week because the anxiety level would be lower.

There are a variety of things that parents can do for relatively long visitation that are necessitated by vacations, great geographic distance or the intractable nature of the separation conflict:

1. *Increase object constancy for the young child.* With long separations, the young child has increasing difficulty in maintaining an image of the absent parent. Photographs of the parent, cassette tapes of favorite bedtime stories, and frequent phone calls can help bridge the memory of the absent parent for the young child. Many homes have video cassette recorders and video cameras are relatively inexpensive to rent. Several video cassettes of the absent parent would be helpful to the young child. If the absent parent is in the same area, visitation with the custodial parent would be desirable even for

the "six weeks in the summer" visitation. The custodial parent must provide some ground work with the noncustodial parent, particularly if the noncustodial parent had developed a "significant other." The last thing a new wife wants around the house is a picture of the ex-spouse. The child can be a given special place to keep the material that minimizes the impact on stepparents. Phone calls can be intrusive and planning may reduce resentment generated by them. The stepparent may need counseling to understand the child's needs and reduce pressure on the entire family.

2. *Avoid or minimize long distance travel for children under 3.*

For children under 3 years of age, the long distance, noncustodial parent could come to the town of the custodial parent and visit regularly for several days. Alternately, the custodial parent could come to the town of the noncustodial parent and provide similar access.

For children 3 to 5, nonstop airline flights require an escort both ways. Usually up to 8 years of age, an escort is often required if there is a plane change. Having the parents travel rather than the child may save money and reduce stress on the child.

3. *Maintain stability of the environment in terms of familiar objects.* The child should be encouraged to bring familiar objects, toys, dolls, and transitional objects such as blankets (i.e., a "Linus blanket") as reassurance that the environment has not changed too dramatically.

4. *Maintain familiar routines.* Parents should be encouraged to maintain comparable bed times, types of rewards and punishments, and even familiar food. When a child is having a visitation in another part of the country, even the brand of the particular favorite food could be sent along. Careful preparation must be done here, since a stepmother is likely to be quite insulted if a child shows up with a suitcase full of food. It would be easy to misinterpret the behavior as an indication that the mother does not believe that the child would be adequately fed at the new home! It is enormously upsetting to young children to find that nothing is familiar, not even the taste of their macaroni and cheese.

5. *Help the child's comprehension of the passing of time.* Use visual aids on calendars to increase understanding of the time for return for the child (for 4 to 6 year olds). This technique can be helpful for young, elementary age children as well.

Newman (1981) listed numerous (101) ideas for helping a father maintain a relationship with a distant child. The ideas listed are creative ways of making letters and phone calls more fun and to maintain the relationship. Suggestions include how to stay involved with teaching the child and understanding how the child is doing at school and enjoying interactions through quizzes, stamp collecting, games, jokes, riddles, and other fun things to do over the phone.

TERMINATION OF VISITATION

Awad and Parry (1980) indicated that visitation should be completely terminated under three conditions:

1. The harm to the child outweighs the benefits. Frequently, the noncustodial parent is significantly disturbed. They found the most likely diagnosis of a noncustodial parent who is damaging to the child with any contact is paranoid/obsessional personality or narcissistic personality.
2. The custodial parent gets extremely upset at visitation which places the child in a chronic stressful situation. While Awad and Parry felt that such a problem could justify termination of visitation, overuse of this criterion is cautioned. California law requires that custody preference be given to the parent who would most likely protect the access to the other parent. A parent can use (consciously or unconsciously) increased upset as a form of blackmail to coerce the other parent out of the picture. Knowledge that such behavior would be weighed by mental health professionals would increase the frequency of such behaviors.
3. The choice of the child. Awad et al. proposed that when a child refuses visitation, whether based on neurotic or realistic reasons, visitation may be denied. To the contrary, this author proposes that in many (but not all) cases, very brief visitations can provide the opportunity for the child to develop a relationship with the noncustodial parent, should the intensity of opposition decline. The visitation should be only as long as the child can tolerate. Even a half hour a month gives some opportunity to negotiate a relationship. Clearly, if the child increases outrageous behavior to indicate opposition, visitation may have to be terminated.

Visitation should not be terminated without a formal assessment as to why the problem exists. Individual (custodial and/or noncustodial parent) consultation, couple therapy, or noncustodial parent-child therapy should be seriously considered as interventions to avoid termination of visitation.

Supervised visitation can be helpful in obtaining a diagnostic evaluation as to why the child is too adamant. See the section later in this chapter on supervised visitation for abusing parents. Awad et al. recommended supervised access with the custodial parent observing so that anxieties on the part of the parent strongly opposing visitation can be (perhaps) reduced by having fantasies disconfirmed.

Awad and Parry also cautioned the mental health professional against overuse of elimination of visitation rights. If a parent believes that the outcome of custody could block access, the battle for custody is likely to be extreme.

The anticipation of access on the part of the noncustodial parent may reduce the adamancy of the battle, since even the losing parent can continue to have a relationship with the parent.

VISITATION AND THE SEVERELY MALADJUSTED PARENT

The visitation patterns recommended earlier in this chapter were for parents having a reasonable level of cordiality and lack of severe pathology in either parent. Visitation may have to be limited when one parent: (1) has difficulty in maintaining boundaries for anger, parental role, and narcissism; (2) is psychologically abusive; (3) has borderline personality problems where there is poor separation of the parent's perspective from the child's; (4) uses the child as a pawn in the battle between the parents; and (5) pushes the child into a loyalty battle for alienation of affection from the other parent.*

If the custodial parent has such problems, the question of whether a proper custodial decision was made by the court must be raised. Several states recommend that custody be awarded to the parent who is willing to support visitation with the other parent. When held by the custodial parent, all of the aforementioned problems would make such support difficult. Suppose that the noncustodial parent is even more pathological, it is clear that visitation should be limited, because the reaction of the custodial parent to the visitation produces such stress for the child as to be potentially damaging.

When the above problems are held by the noncustodial parent, the child must be protected from the pathology by limiting the visitation to a very low level so that the strength of the custodial parent can be generally available to the child. When the pathology is quite severe, visitation may have to be eliminated. However, because of identification problems for the child and the potentially damaging effects of fantasy with visitation eliminated (see the discussion in the next section), visitation that is supervised is probably more appropriate. A discussion of supervised visitation follows in the next section.

Supervised Visitation

The Sexually or Physically Abusing Parent

The anger that mental health professionals feel toward abusing parents leads them to want to punish the parent by restricting or eliminating visitation altogether. The parent who wishes to kidnap the child (or has already done so) also presents a potential threat to the child's development. The parent cannot be punished by eliminating visitation, since the criterion for visitation patterns is the best interests of the child. Thus, the question becomes whether it is in the child's interests to have continued contact with the noncustodial parent.

---

*These criteria were suggested by Lanning Schiller, Ph.D. personal communication.

There are rare instances where such limitations are really appropriate, where the parent is so psychologically damaged that any contact is harmful. In general, however, the child benefits from having some contact with an abusing parent in several ways:

1. Many abusing parents can be quite loving and have a problem with self-control that is harmful to the child. If the child can be protected from the impulse control problem, there can be substantial benefits from the affection.

2. Prohibiting visitation can be damaging to the child's self-esteem in a variety of ways. "My parent is so damaged that he or she cannot see me," invites reduction in self-esteem through identification. In addition, the child's fearfulness of the pathology of the parent can increase through fantasy (Benedek and Benedek, 1977; Hoorwitz, 1983).

3. If the child decides that the decision to isolate the parent was inappropriate, the child may develop rescue fantasies. "My father would visit me and take care of me better (and not make me go to bed so early or restrict what I eat or restrict what I watch on TV) if they would just let him come." Normal resentment for age appropriate restrictions in freedoms can increase and be prolonged when such rescue fantasies are available.

While the foregoing arguments encourage some form of visitation even for abusing or psychopathological parents, such visitation should occur only if there are adequate safeguards to protect the well-being of the child. It would be better to have not visitation at all than to subject a child to a physically or psychologically dangerous home setting. Courts have a great deal of difficulty balancing these two values.

Armstrong (1985) documented several case histories of inadequate controls when the court gave what would appear to be excessive weighting to the value of noncustodial contact over child protection. For example, Armstrong gave case histories of courts ignoring reports from mothers of sexual abuse of the child, choosing to believe the denials of the father. In one case, a mother was sent to jail for refusing to send her children to visit the father who had repeatedly molested them. In another case, the father's mother was assigned supervision responsibility for the visitation of a 4-year-old daughter, a grandmother who apparently would not provide adequate controls. This supervision continued even with evidence of genital abrasions and labial burns. The same court ordered visitation even when the father was found to be sexually abusing the child, on the assumption that to terminate visitation would be harmful to the child. The court ordered treatment and supervision even when it was felt that neither would be effective. In all of the aforementioned examples, it is difficult to imagine that visitation value is more important than the damage done to the child. The child's welfare should take precedence and visitation is less important than protection from such abuse.

Who Should Supervise the Visit?

The child's welfare must be protected. A parent with impulse control problems cannot be permitted to impose those problems on the child. The most obvious protection of the child is to provide supervised visitation.

Family members may be unable or unwilling to control pathological inter-actions. This author recommends against using people who have emotional ties with either parent or teenager babysitters who may not be able to handle intimidation or recognize psychologically abusive behavior. Ringler-White (1982) noted that having a mental health professional available for supervision permits the court to have professional advice when the visitation pattern is too irregular to be useful to the child or the behavior during visitation cannot be controlled even under supervision.

The visitation supervision program at Children's Hospital in Denver, Col-orado was described in some detail by Ringler-White. The service provides feedback to the court on a regular basis (for example, every six months) about whether the visitation supervision plan should be changed. In addition, the visiting service has three different levels of supervision. First, the program provides a visitation exchange program. Children are dropped off and picked up under the supervision of a staff member. Parents never have to interact. This plan is helpful when parents cannot negotiate visitation plans, when one or more parents cannot follow the plans agreed on, and when the parents cannot control the anger that they feel toward one another. This plan is not used when the child's safety may be in question.

Second, monitored visits are provided. A staff member listens to the visit through microphones and observes the interaction from time to time through a one-way mirror. If necessary, the staff member can intervene directly with support, limit setting, or recommendations. This plan is used when limited supervision is sufficient to protect the child.

Finally, complete supervision is possible where a staff member observes and listens to the entire visit through a one-way mirror and audio system. With more severe problems, the staff member may be present in the room during the visit (a requirement that may be necessary when the child is exceptionally fearful and needs the reassurance of another person in the room). If there is significant risk of physical violence or self-destructive behavior even under this amount of supervision, the supervision is terminated and the hospital will not agree to supervision.

As can be guessed, such a program is expensive in staff time. Therefore, parents have to pay a significant amount for the service. When the choice is paying for supervision or not having any contact at all, the parent will often choose to have some contact. Abusing parents often have a significant amount of guilt about their past behavior and continued contact can reassure themselves as well as the children that the impulse control problem does not mean the child is unloved.

Lawyers looking for supervisors for visitation sometimes arrange to hire advanced graduate students in clinical psychology on an hourly basis. The graduate student is often less expensive than either a private practicing clinician or a public service facility. Retired teachers, social workers, or other retired mental health professionals may also provide lower cost supervision. The graduate student or retiree might welcome an opportunity to earn extra money. In addition, the graduate training means that the person can provide professional level input to the courts in determining whether supervision or visitation should be discontinued (although there are problems with such advice, as noted in the following section).

Stott, Gaier, and Thomas (1984) described a supervision program staffed by church-affiliated volunteers and another coordinated by staff of a Salvation Army Community Center.

Armstrong (1985) noted that there is some resistance by the court to ordering supervised visitation. It is, after all, babysitting of adults. In addition, it may represent prior restraint, that is, punishment for a crime that has not yet been committed (although in many cases, the abuse has occurred). The question of how long the supervision should continue is also raised.

Other problems with supervision of visitation have yet to be worked out. Since the supervision is costly, it is generally not possible to have extended visitation times. More importantly, it is difficult to know when to change the visitation pattern. Since the abuse may be a low frequency behavior, under conditions of frustration or being alone with the child, the absence of abuse in the supervised visits may not be a valid prediction of the likelihood of abuse occurring if supervision were terminated. Just because a parent is able to control the abuse for short visits when that parent knows that someone is watching (by being present or observing through a one way mirror) does not mean that such control would occur without the supervision. Behavioral scientists are not very good at predicting low frequency loss of control in people who have already demonstrated a tendency toward that behavior. No research has yet to be done on supervision of visitation.

Making the Transition to Less Control

If pathological behavior is not present during the observation, if the parent seems to be in better self-control, if the parent develops better understanding of child needs, it may be possible to make a transition toward less control, particularly for older children who are capable of reporting on the visit. Transitions might include: moving from the observation room or controlled playroom to the community with supervision continuing; moving to the home of the noncustodial parent with supervision continuing; having the supervision at the beginning and end of the visit, but having the middle of the visit unsupervised (permitting evaluation of the physical and psychological state of the children and parent, pre- and post-visit; moving to observation only at the end of the visit; moving to observation every other visit. If the children or either parent is substantially anxious about such transitions, continuing some structured supervision of the visitation is recommended.

The ability to predict future violent behavior is very poor. Supervisors should be very cautious in indicating that future violence or danger would not be likely to occur. For legal protection, supervisors of visitation should agree to participate only if there is a legal contract to prevent lawsuit if there is future damage. Such an agreement should also indemnify and hold harmless the supervisor of all costs that might occur as a function of any report or action on the part of the supervisor. While supervised visitation is a solution to the problem of potential harm to the child, moving toward unsupervised visitation is a much more complex problem. In some cases, supervision may have to continue indefinitely.

Hoorwitz (1983) suggested a gradual increase in visitation time with a recommendation as to the type of activities that would be preferable. For example if the child is fearful or angry, Hoorwitz suggested that the noncustodial parent be taught to "woo" the child with cards and letters.

If a child continues to show significant anxiety or acting out with supervised visitation, it must first be determined if the child is expressing the anxiety or anger of the custodial parent. If the custodial parent is having significant problems with the visitation, working with that parent may be helpful. If the anxiety or anger is not related to the behavior of the custodial parent, the child may be experiencing significant problems being with an abusing parent. Reduction in visitation time may be necessary or even elimination of visitation altogether may need to be considered under these conditions.

Visitation Supervision After a Long Separation

Ringler-White (1982) noted that some parents welcome supervision, particularly parents who are meeting their child for the first time after a long separation. The noncustodial parent can see the mental health professional as a resource for advice on how to handle the visitation. Often the custodial parent will be quite nervous when a noncustodial parent who has not seen the child in 5 or 10 years suddenly (at least suddenly from their point of view) asks for visitation. Supervised visitation can calm the custodial parents' fears. The child can also be quite fearful at such a meeting even when the child indicates interest. Having a chance to talk to a neutral party about those fears can be quite helpful.

When the parent has not seen the child for a long time (months or years), it is generally a mistake to make initial contacts all day or overnight. Trust builds extensively, not intensively. A child who has had a chance to have a brief contact of several hours (or all day, depending on the age of the child) with a chance to think about the visit and relax afterwards can benefit for additional contact the next day.

When there has been long periods without contact, even for older children, there should not be a sudden introduction of long visitations. Initial visitation should be relatively short, slowly increasing in duration to permit the development of a relationship without fear.

REDUCING VISITATION PROBLEMS

There are several strategies that can be used to reduce visitation problems.

1. *Definition of time.* Highly structured visitation agreements, specifying exact time and definition of terms, are recommended. A phrase can be added permitting "liberal visitation with the mutual consent of both parties." When one of the parents enters into a romantic relationship, liberal visitation often becomes less liberal. Vacations and school holidays need to be defined. When does spring vacation begin, 2:00 P.M. Friday before the vacation or 8:00 A.M. Monday when school would have been in session? Is a week long visitation seven or nine days long? If phone calls are permitted, how often, when, and for how long?

Johnston et al. (1985) noted that for the 44 children, aged 6 to 12 years in their study, with high levels of parental conflict, the children wanted set, regular visits. Children were upset by a chaotic schedule, particularly one that kept changing and was never made clear. Flexibility meant more fighting. Almost 60 percent of the children resisted changing from either parent and 40 percent had some somatic complaint at the time of transition.

With high levels of parental conflict, children benefit from highly predictable visitation. Flexibility can be built in once the stress conflict goes down.

2. *Build in consequences for minor breaking of the agreement.* One of the major problems is the limited sanctions available to the court. It is difficult and awkward to use contempt proceedings for being chronically a half hour late for picking up or delivering the child for visitation. Rules such as if either parent is more than one half hour late for picking the child up (or having the children ready) two times in a month, a $100 bond must be forfeited might be helpful. Since visitation is the right of the child and cannot be restricted because of the behavior of the parent, visitation time cannot be used as a consequence. The Uniform Marriage and Divorce Act (1970) on custody stated that the court could only modify an order granting or denying visitation rights when such modification would serve the best interests of the child and that the *only* reason visitation could be restricted is to protect the child.

3. *Use of a third party for transfer.* Reduction in angry communication and the use of an observer reduce irresponsible behavior. See the section on visitation and the physically or sexually abusing parent.

4. *Parent counseling.* Parents must be shown how the fighting hurts the

child and how the child needs positive relations with both parents to protect his or her self-esteem. Parents can be taught to reduce attacks on each other and to support the other parent's relationship with the child. Bentovim and Gilmour (1981) described a family therapy interactional approach to helping families deal with custody and access problems. Chapter 13 gives examples of other family therapy approaches.

5.   *Reduce stress on the child by increasing the commonality of rules at each household (e.g., when to go to bed, rules for television watching, sweets, etc.)* Children can learn that different households have different rules, but the more constant the environment across households, the less the stress.

6.   *Should a nonvisiting parent be punished for lack of visitation?* Since visitation is viewed as a right of the child rather than a right of the noncustodial parent, there is a question of whether it would be appropriate to provide sanctions against a nonvisiting parent. Seldom would such a plan be effective. Such a parent can be referred to a mental health professional for mediation or counseling as to why visitation is not occurring, but any parent who does not want to visit can insure that such visits are not helpful to the child.

7.   *Build in developmental needs of the child in scheduling visitation.*

8.   *Build in the use of mediation as a form of dispute resolution.*

9.   If one parent needs to move a long distance, parents should be required to mediate on a plan that will protect the access of the child to both parents, taking into account the developmental needs of the child.

10.   *Children can receive counseling or therapy to be taught how to protect themselves from psychological abuse.* For example it can be helpful to a child to understand that the problems come from the parent and are not their fault (if indeed, it is true).

Help parents anticipate problems prior to the onset of visitation. If the guidelines are anticipated, rather than introduced after problems exist, the severity of problems will be significantly reduced.

SUMMARY

Visitation should generally be encouraged and supported. Problems of visitation can often be solved by continued contact rather than limitation of visitation. Parent consultation, therapy, and mediation can be effective in reducing visitation problems. Access of some kind is beneficial to most children and frequent access is important in the absence of severe pathology. Supervision of visitation can protect the child from harm and reduce harmful fantasies. Anticipation and prior planning can help reduce visitation problems.

CHAPTER 8

Single Parenting: The Problems
of the Single Parent Household

Perhaps the most salient picture of single parenting in terms of its disadvantages is that it is exhausting. No child psychology book can prepare the single parent for the amount of effort that rearing children takes. The burden is difficult to imagine if one has not been through it (the author was raised in a single parent home). Even in homes where there is a relatively passive, inactive parent, that parent can take over occasionally if the other parent is busy. With single parenting, the single parent cannot afford to be ill. No matter how sick the parent, the children still must be fed and cared for. Also, when the child is ill, the single parent has few opportunities for help. Either the parent stays home (and possibly loses pay) or leaves the child alone. Two parent families in which both parents are employed have some of the same problems around child care, but at least they have the opportunity to spell each other.

The Census Bureau in the United States estimated that in 1984, 25.7 percent of the families with children under 18 were headed by single parents. It is predicted that by 1990, one out of every three families will be headed by a single parent and that half of all children born in the 1980s will live for some time in a single parent household before they become adults (Newsweek, July 15 1985 pp. 42–43). Given these statistics, it is remarkable how little this society is adapted to the needs of the single parent family.

This chapter will review some of the special problems of the single parent household. Chapters 2 and 3 reviewed the research and clinical evidence on the effect of divorce on child development. The purpose of those chapters was to evaluate the effects of exposure to chronic family conflict and loss of contact with one parent. This chapter will look at the longer term effects of single parenting. The clinician needs to remember that the effects of divorce are complex and some responses may be due to the stress of chronic conflict, to the strain of the divorce process, to the economic effects of divorce and to the effect of having only one parent.

There are a variety of reasons why single parent status is a problem.

1. The entire culture is organized around two parent families. School districts often do not have policies that permit mail outs to two different parent concerning school activities. The degree to which two parent

families are accepted as the norm is demonstrated by the fact that even in communities in which the majority of children are no longer living with both biological parents, the schools and child-oriented organizations are oriented toward two parent families.

2. Single parenting limits the wisdom of the family (Blechman and Manning, 1976). Since no parent can have a full range of competencies that can be provided by two parents, it is likely that the quality of problem solving will not be as good as in single parent families. The efficiency in problem solving is also reduced.

3. Emotional support may be more limited.

4. Sex role development can be impaired by the absence of one parent. While the absence of a parent can lead to more androgynous orientation, there is substantial evidence that a child's perception of the meaning of belonging to a particular biological sex (and feeling good about that belonging) is determined in part by exposure to warm close relationships with adults of both sexes. The issue of sex role will be discussed in detail later in this chapter.

5. The remaining parent may suffer from loneliness.

6. The child may show concern over separation and abandonment. If the divorce resulted in an abandoning parent, the child, particularly the young child from 3 to 7, may develop concerns about being left alone. This concern over abandonment may develop from fears that misbehavior or angry thoughts will lead to parental rejection. After all, if one parent gets rid of the other parent because of dissatisfaction with behavior, why shouldn't the same thing happen to the child? It is difficult for a child to understand that a parental relationship has different dynamics than a spousal relationship.

Concern over abandonment may be particularly acute for children from age 3 to 7. Magical thinking leads children of these ages to believe that angry thoughts can lead to severe retaliation. School phobias are often based on hostile, dependent relationships with a parent in which the child must protect the parent from the consequences of the angry thoughts. Children may need reassurance that parenting is forever and that they will not be abandoned. Children with concerns about the death of a parent may need information about what will happen to them should the death occur.

When a child shows concern over death, it is sometimes helpful to emphasize how the child will be cared for if the parent is "ill." (This wording is particularly helpful if death has not been articulated by the child.) If the noncustodial parent is involved with the child, abandonment fears due to death are less likely.

My mother informed me that when I was 6, I had intense anxiety anytime she was even mildly late from work. I was obsessed with the possibility that she might be killed in an automobile accident. (Death phobia, as has been mentioned, often shows up around 7 or 8). There was nothing she could do to reassure me that she sometimes had to work a few minutes late or that traffic was heavier than usual. One day, I asked what would happen to me. She informed me that she had a will and that I would live with an aunt and uncle. Since I liked that family, my anxiety disappeared! My mother said it was like turning off a spigot. The egocentrism of the young child is focused around "What will happen to me?" It does not occur to the child to worry about what the death would mean to the parent. Only with the empathy of later elementary years does the concern about the shortened life enter into the child's distress.

7. The parent's concern about the implications of child development of being raised in a single parent household can itself lead to problems in child rearing. Some parents raise the standards of strictness to protect the child from the tough world "out there." Others feel the need to compensate for the trauma of single parenthood by overindulging the child. Neither parenting style is in the best interests of child development.

8. Child care is a constant problem for young children. Finding high quality inexpensive child care can be a chronic problem. For the older child, the latch key may provide protection, but no supervision.

9. When the single parent is the mother, finances tend to be a major issue. The burden of single parenting requires more money, and yet women are less able to obtain it. Women earn about 65 percent of the amount earned by men.

10. Single parenting may encourage inappropriate use of the child as confidant or advisor.

THE STIGMA OF SINGLE PARENT FAMILIES

There is substantial evidence that there is significant stigma to belonging to a one parent family, even in this age of common divorce. Stigma tends to be greater for families of divorce than widowhood, where sympathy often plays a greater role (although sympathy itself can be a problem, as was discussed in Chapter 2).

A study on Head Start (Hodges and Kick, unpublished, see also Chapter 2) indicated that single parent status was not related to referrals for mental health consultation, in spite of the expectation of teachers that it would be. In the study on preschool children in Boulder, Colorado (Hodges, Wechsler and Ballantine, 1979), the preschool teachers informed us that the single parent families would represent the most disturbed children, and yet their own ratings did not agree with that judgment.

This author has heard many stories that emphasize the problems of being a single parent:

A single parent told the story of her son's experience in a scout troupe. The scoutmaster indicated that the family was like the tepee, with three poles holding it up, the father pole, the mother pole, and the child pole. Without each member of the family, the tepee could not stand! What a message to give a child from a single parent family. "You are flawed" or "There is something unnatural about your family."

In Boulder, another parent found it difficult to get church sponsorship for a single parent group. In Boulder, 60 percent of marriages end in divorce!

Other evidence of stigma for single parent families comes from research. Ferri (1976), in a study in England, asked teachers to rate parental interest in children. Teachers rated single parents as less interested in their children's performance, particularly for the divorced single mother. Single mothers who were widows were seen as just as interested as intact families. In spite of these attitudes, the frequency of school visits did not differ for single mothers as opposed to two parent families.

Single custodial fathers did have a lower level of parental school contact. Fathers on their own, in this case particularly widowers, were seen as less interested in their children's progress. When social class was controlled statistically, the significant differences disappeared suggesting that social class plays a major role in the bias against single parents.

As already discussed in Chapter 3, Santrock and Tracy (1978) found that teachers saw children from divorced homes as less happy, lower in emotional adjustment, and poorer in coping with stress as compared to children from intact homes. With similar findings, Kellam (1977) found that teacher ratings of children's social adaptation could be predicted from knowledge of the family background, in this case, income. Since single mothers have incomes 52 percent below the incomes of male headed, sole support families, this bias could also explain why children of divorce are more often seen as more damaged or poorly adjusted.

Ratings of children from single parent households may be biased. Children from single parent households due to death of a parent may receive sympathy while children from divorced homes may be stigmatized.

IS THE RESEARCH ON SINGLE PARENT HOUSEHOLDS BIASED?

Certainly, the previous discussion on stigma and single parent families suggests that research that is based on the judgments of teachers and others in the community about the adjustment level of children from single parent families as compared to intact families may have biased results. Research on single parent households may be biased for other reasons.

It is intriguing to discover that the literature on single parenting is relatively independent of the literature on divorce. This area of research is tremendously flawed. The most apparent flaw has to do with the fact that the research does not always indicate the reason single parent status occurred. Many studies treat single parent status as a unitary classification as if the psychological effects of death of a parent, divorce, desertion, or never-married were the same. As a dramatic example of the differences, when a parent is lost due to death, the remaining parent is able to participate in the grieving process. In divorce, the absent parent is likely to be seen as an enemy. In death, the absence parent is often idealized. The image of the absent parent can have profound impact on the family members. Research discussed later in this chapter will demonstrate that the cause of single parent status can make a significant difference in research findings.

Blechman (1982) has made a convincing argument that research on single parenting is so flawed that it is questionable what is really known about these families. Problems listed in this review include:

1. When income was statistically controlled, the relationship between family type and adjustment became trivial;

2. Cause and length of parent absence, sex of single parent, amount and type of contact with absent parent;

3. Income matching matched the upper income group of single families with the lower income group of intact homes. In another study, Blanchard and Biller (1971) obtained only 4 matched sets of 11 children from a pool of 297 children.

4. Other important variables were realized income, occupational prestige, availability of flexible working hours, perceived environmental control, precipitous drops in income, and drops in status; and

5. Unrepresentative samples.

THE SINGLE PARENT FAMILY FROM EACH MEMBER'S POINT OF VIEW

It is useful to review the perspective of each family member about the single parent family, beginning with the child.

The Child's Point of View

Blechman and Manning (1976) noted that the child has several disadvantages in a single parent family as compared to a two parent family. There is one less parent to help solve problems. There is no second parent to appeal unfair decisions. There is less time and attention available. The single parent provides less diverse view points and can train the child in fewer skills.

Schlesinger (1982) asked 40 children, averaging 14.9 year old and who had lived in a single parent household for an average of 4.7 years, their perceptions of the advantages and disadvantages of living in a single parent household. It is most interesting that the same items appeared on both lists:

Advantages	Disadvantages
Closer to mother	Not closer to father
More responsibility	Smaller dwelling
Helping in household	Helping in household
Get along with siblings	Coming home to empty house
More friends	More responsibility
Trusted more	Moving to new area.
Moving to new area	Not getting along with siblings
Closer to father	Less friends

It is clear from the above lists that single parenting status can lead to diametrically opposed outcomes. The child may perceive that the loss of a parent can increase or decrease the number of friends. Responsibility can be seen as a blessing or curse.

The Mother's Point of View

Phelps (1969), in a comparison of mothers' attitudes toward family life in one and two parent households with nursery school age children, found that one parent mothers tended to be more conservative in their attitudes on 23 attitudes than the two parent family mothers. One parent mothers were more rigid about allowing their children to express aggression, about learning about sex, and about willingness to expose the child to adult influences outside the home. They tended to blame adult males for their domestic problems. They expected more rapid physical and psychological development of their children than did the mothers in two parent homes. Many blamed their own parents' permissiveness for the failure of their own marriage.

Brandwein, Brown, and Fox (1974) noted that single parent mothers are at a disadvantage from several points of view. First, economic power is quite limited. Economic discrimination against women has been extensive documented. The majority of men do not continue support. The courts are reluctant to take legal action against nonpaying fathers. Second, the single parent mother commands less authority in society. They are taken less seriously and are less respected than men. Third, single parent mothers are less likely to obtain homemaking services.

The Father's Point of View

Relatively little research has been done on the single parent father since the frequency of such families has been relatively low in the past. Schlesinger (1982) listed the problems of single parent fathers, including:

1. Financial problems. (Public assistance may be unavailable);
2. Child care;
3. Social life (fathers rate problems around maintaining a social life while mothers do not);
4. Homemaking (learning basic housekeeping chores as an adult can be difficult, particularly for strongly stereotyped males);
5. Personal problems. (Men in general seldom seek professional help or friends to deal with role strain); and
6. Community support seems lacking to single fathers

Smith (1976) indicated that single fathers tend to adjust well if there is anticipatory socialization, prior experience in child rearing, education in child development, previous participation in household responsibilities, prior participation in child discipline, and prior experience in nurturing the children.

Bray and Anderson (1984) in discussing the problems of single parents regardless of sex of parent, noted that role overload was a common problem. Money was a constant problem. Groceries, meals, child care, and discipline all were demanding. Such parents also felt more intensely the fear, hurt and anger of the children, without the buffer of another parent.

Because there is not another parent to serve as a buffer or source of social support, single parents are more vulnerable to the hurt and anger experienced by their children. Such potential enmeshment may increase the pain of parenting and lead to inappropriate problem solving.

Keshet and Rosenthal (1978) studied 128 fathers with children under seven. These fathers were typically noncustodial, upper middle class professionals. They remained very active and in close contact with their young children. Their initial reaction to single parenthood was the feeling of having failed their children, regardless of whether they had initiated the separation. They experienced significant fear in learning the new roles. They felt overwhelmed at the thought of assuming the parental role on their own and questioned their competence as caretakers.

Frequently, the fathers did not know their children's likes or dislikes. They found planning, organizing, and anticipating the needs of the children to be difficult.

Ten fathers were studied more extensively. Fathers with less flexible work schedules felt more negative about child care. Initially, the fathers were dependent on the mothers for child care activities. It was not unusual for the mother to initially plan the father's time with the children and to monitor the activities. Gradually, the father became more independent of the mother. The father then monitored the children's reactions for validation of competence as a parent. Initially he often gave his children too much power in this transition. The father learned to take care of himself in order to create a comfortable environment for the children.

While the Keshet and Rosenthal study provided some information about single parenthood for fathers, it did not study custodial fathers and their role strain. In a study that did look at single parenthood in custodial fathers, Mendes (1976) studied 32 fathers, including 4 who were separated, 7 who were widowed, and 22 who were divorced. Mendes found that whether the father had chosen to be a single parent or not was the most salient factor in differentiating the fathers' experiences. Seekers of single parenthood had strong, positive feelings about being parents. These fathers had been involved in child care from their children's infancies. All but four of the fathers reported the mothers as inadequate. Mendes further broke the seekers into two groups, the aggressive seekers and the conciliatory seekers.

Aggressive seekers (i.e., those who had obtained custody in an assertive manner, often in disregard for the wishes of the mother) were under 35 and had children of preschool age. Keeping the child had important symbolic meaning for the fathers. This often stemmed from the father's own traumatic childhood experiences. (This author has noted that the most painful and vigorous responses to divorce and separation from children have occurred in parents who themselves experienced painful separations as children. The parents cannot tolerate doing to the child that which was done to them.)

Often the most aggressive fathers seeking custody are those who felt abandoned themselves as children.

Conciliatory seekers were typically over 30, and several were in their mid-40s. Most of the children were preadolescents. Most had sought custody while still living with their wives. The men were characterized as having few friends or close relationships. The wives had initiated the separation. The rejection by the wife was a narcissistic blow that weakened an already low self-confidence in their ability to establish and maintain a love relationship. By being custodial parents, these men were able to avoid the social isolation that would have occurred had the mothers obtained custody. They enjoyed being single fathers.

The fathers who did not seek custody were labeled "assenters." They agreed to custody, but had not initiated the process. They were older than the seekers, an average of 41 years old. Children ranged from preschool to adolescence. Widowers were included in this group. They did not necessarily enjoy being fathers. Relationships ranged from poor to excellent. Relationships typically change dramatically from the previously intact family.

One particularly angry group of assenters was a group of men who had been deserted by the wife (labeled aggressive initiation by Mendes). These men felt a sense of responsibility toward the children, guilt for former neglect of the children or wives, and fear of retaliation. If the preseparation relationship between the father and children was poor, the relationship was worse after the separation. These fathers had less interaction with their children and felt considerable anxiety about the father role.

Five fathers were categorized as in the conciliatory initiation category. Three of the fathers had always had good relationships with their children. All five maintained friendly relationships with their former wives.

This study raised some interesting questions about how single fatherhood started and had implications for father-child relationship postseparation. The study, however, was based on a very small sample, and breakdowns into four subgroups makes the ability to generalize very limited. While suggestive for further research, caution should be used before assuming that the data could be used for practice. One study that would be enormously useful would be a longitudinal study of how the children developed over time as a function of the type of single fatherhood.

TYPOLOGIES OF SINGLE PARENT LIFESTYLES

Mendes (1979) analyzed the lifestyles of single parent families and proposed five major lifestyles of parenting. These styles have not been related to child adjustment, but could provide a useful structure for considering how single-parent families function.

1. *Sole executive.* This parent is the only adult who feeds, clothes, shelters, nurtures, and socializes the young children. As might be expected, this parent tends to be enormously stressed.

   a. Tyrannized single parent. This parent was traumatized by the loss of the other parent and never feels complete or whole. This parents tries to be both parents to the child and to compensate to the child for the loss of the other parent. The impossibility of this role demand leads to stress, fatigue, anger, guilt, and failure.

Families in which the parent is trying to fulfilled all roles for the child needs help to attain a more realistic expectation about what is possible or reasonable. This parent needs help in more appropriate problem solving to solve the needs of the parent and the children.

   b. Single-parent family model. The single parent is a "contributing coordinator." The parent contributes what she or he can manage without undue stress and allocate the other roles to people both within and outside of the family. Children are also seen as contributors and are asked to assume responsibilities within the household. The children may also be given responsibility to meet needs outside of the home.

Given the findings that children from single parent homes tend to be more responsible and independent than children from two parent homes, it is clear that intact families in North America tend to underestimate the ability of children to assume responsibility in the family. It is helpful for single parents to see that single parent families have strengths that intact families do not have.

2. *Auxiliary parent.* The single parent shares the parental responsibilities with an auxiliary parent who does not live with the family. Usually this auxiliary parent is the father of one or more of the children. Part-time fathers often assume the role of visiting uncle. Decision-making, disciplining, socialization, and other child rearing functions are determined by the mother. With joint custody (but not joint time), the auxiliary parent may assume equal parental responsibility.

Mendes proposed that the more conflict that exists between the single parent and auxiliary parent, the more stressful the relationship between the single parent and the child. Certainly, the research is clear that the amount of conflict between the single parent and auxiliary parent, the poorer the adjustment of the child (see Chapter 3).

One special kind of auxiliary parent is the fantasized auxiliary parent in which the auxiliary parent has no contact with the children, but is kept alive in the memories of the family. The affection or authority of this absent parent can be invoked to help motivate or discipline the children. This fantasy is particularly common for families in which the parent is absent because of death. The use of an auxiliary parent may delay or prolong the grieving process.

3. *Unrelated substitute.* A live-in housekeeper who serves a mother surrogate role would fit this category. Friends of the family sometimes serve as surrogate parents.

4. *Related substitute.* Grandparents, aunts, uncles, cousins, or siblings may assume this role. If the sibling is the related substitute, the older child may assume the role of parental child. Mendes cited Minuchin (1974) about the danger of this role. Parents may abdicate the parental role and leave the older child with inadequate guidance.

Younger children can sometimes be very resentful of the authority of the older child, particularly when the ages are close or when the older child handles the authority in an arbitrary or hostile way.

When an older sibling is given parental responsibility for a child, the clinician should be sure that lines of authority are clear. In particular rules should be clear and authority to impose sanctions should be well defined. Neither child should be subject to the tyranny of the other. In particular the parent should be sure that the older sibling has adequate maturity to provide control and safety. Minuchin warned that such a role may clash with the older child's own developmental needs and be harmful to that child's development.

5.   *Titular parent.* In this category, the parent abandons the parental role altogether. The parent may act as one of the children. Severely disturbed parents may respond this way. Alcoholics and drug addicts may also be unable to maintain the responsibility of parenting.

THE EXPRESSION OF AFFECTION IN SINGLE PARENT HOUSEHOLDS

In a healthy two parent family, the bond between parents existed before the bond between parent and child. In healthy families, this bond is stronger than the parent-child bond. When the bond between one parent and a child is stronger, the parenting role can become lost and a coalition against the other "unreasonable" parent can develop. In single parent families, the absence of another parent tends to encourage a coalition anyway. Triads tend to prevent two person coalitions aligned against the third (Blechman and Manning, 1976). Divorce or widowhood intensifies the parent-child bond (Blechman and Manning, 1976). The loss of a parent can reduce competition, increase interactions, and improve the affection expressed between parent and child. This bond can become so strong that the child and parent will resist any intrusion and the parent is prevented from developing a successful remarriage.

One side effect of this intensification of the affectionate relationship between the parent and child is the parentification process discussed in Chapter 2. The child begins to care for the parent, cooking, cleaning, and providing reassurance. Young children may join the parental bed. Adolescents cannot separate from the parent, particularly if the parent is depressed. Parents begin the discussion of work related problems or discuss their love life. Blechman and Manning indicated that the intensification of the parent-child bond is particularly likely if the child is the same sex as the parent.

Single parents should be encouraged to maintain their parental roles. Parents should be encouraged to find an adult friend to share feelings about work or dating and to avoid sharing those feelings with the child. A peer relationship with a child can lead to premature adult responsibilities for the child and is sometimes quite anxiety provoking.

It would also seem that the increased bonding is more common between girls and their mothers as opposed to boys. Guidubaldi, Cleminshaw, Perry, and McLoughlin (1983) noted that girls of divorce were more likely to tell mothers about good events than were girls of intact families. However, boys of divorce were somewhat less likely to confide in their mothers than boys of intact families. The magnitude of these differences, while statistically significant, were small.

DISCIPLINE IN SINGLE PARENT FAMILIES

One common type of problem evidenced in the author's practice is the single mother who is angry at a 13-year-old son. The family was previously characterized as too lenient in terms of discipline. The child never learned self-control. When the child left the relatively tolerant, warm atmosphere of elementary school and entered junior high, his lack of self control became apparent. The child started failing in school work. The mother's response is excessive strictness, for example, long-term (one month or more) grounding. At the same time that the son developmentally needs to separate from the mother, she is trying to exert increased control. When this intervention is ineffective, the teenager either rebels by passively withdrawing from school and home or actively refusing to cooperate at any level. Not surprisingly, these families are difficult families to treat.

In the family where the discipline has broken down and the parent no longer has control over the child, individual treatment tends to be relatively ineffective. Family oriented therapy is more likely to return the control of discipline to the parent.

Blechman and Manning (1976) presented the point of view that two parent families have more reinforcement power than one parent families. They argued that children are involved in more aversive control of parents than positive control. This point of view confirms the author's view that parents who have children to satisfy their own needs at a concrete level are likely to be severely disappointed. Blechman et al. indicated that one problem that single parents have is the difficulty in diluting that aversive control on the part of children. If the child is successful in controlling the parent through tantrums, crying, misbehavior, or chronic illness, the parent finds parenting less rewarding and may actively resent the child. The parent begins to feel that the efforts at being good to the child results only in bad being given back. The danger of such a dynamic is the parent then is tempted to withdraw positive interactions. Blechman et al. felt that successful interactions in the single parent must be based on positive rewards. The fatigued parent can get in a coercive cycle with the child when the parent tends to ignore positive behaviors and respond only when the child has misbehaved.

Children who are ignored for positive behaviors can develop fears of nonexistance. Such a child will misbehave in order to get a response from a parent, reassuring themselves of their ability to have some impact in the world. Working with such parents requires intensive support from the therapist to energize the parents to provide support to the child.

Sack, Mason, and Higgins (1985) investigated the adult report of 802 noninstitutionalized adults about the use of abusive punishment in their own childhoods. The random sample of adults (an area probability sample in Oregon of adults 18 years of age or older) was asked about the ways in which they were punished as children, the reasons for punishment, and the age at which this punishment occurred. Abusive punishment was coded if the answer to ways in which they were punished included answers such as being hit with a fist or knocked unconscious and coded as serious but less severe if the report was answered with responses such as severe whippings in areas other than the buttocks.

Of the sample, 42 percent had had possible abuse and 6 percent had well-established abuse. Seventy-seven percent of the sample had lived with both their parents until 16, and 23 percent had not lived with either one or both parents for some time prior to 16. The father had left home in 56 percent of the cases for the latter group, the mother left home in 28 percent, and the child had left in 8 percent. Divorce and death were equally likely at about 40 percent as the cause for the parent leaving.

Abuse was more common in single parent households and more common in households that were single parent because of divorce. Either parent was equally likely to be the abuser. Well-established abuse occurred in 9 percent of single parent households and only 5 percent in two-parent households, a difference that was statistically significant. For divorced parents, the abuse level was 14 percent. The data did not provide information about whether the abuse occurred before or after the separation. Participants who said that they got along with their father best reported no well-established abuse regardless of the reason for the family breakup or sex of parent (although the father being the most compatible parent occurred in only 19 percent of the cases).

It is interesting that the data do not fit agency-based data that suggest that mothers are more likely to be abusers. This study looked at punishment, not abuse per se, and did not look at a clinical sample. The authors proposed that single parent mothers are more likely to request help for abuse and thus be identified.

Abuse is more likely to occur in families with rapidly accumulating stress. Single parenting would seem to produce sufficient stress as to increase the likelihood of abuse. Help the parent to avoid physical punishment and coercive hostile interactions. Impulse control and cooling off periods may be helpful when anger is out of control. Use of nonphysical punishment, rewards for appropriate behaviors, cognitive explanations for rules, and bonding facilitation are likely to be more effective.

FATHER ABSENCE AND DEVELOPMENT IN BOYS

As previously stated, much of the research on father absence is flawed in interpretation because the reason for father absence was not included as a variable.
In many of the studies, it is also impossible to determine whether there is any
contact with the father. As Biller (1981) has noted, many children whose fathers do not live with them have more actual contact with their fathers than
children in father present homes. As previously noted, children in divorce
homes benefit enormously from high levels of interaction with noncustodial
fathers. Biller also noted that father absent children may not be paternally
deprived if there is an adequate father surrogate. Competent mothers also
compensate for the lack of a father and may give a child a more positive view
of adult men than the family with a weak, ineffective, withdrawn, or passive
father in an intact home.

Masculine Sex Role

There is substantial evidence that masculine sex roles are affected by father
absence. Sears, Maccoby, and Levin (1957) found that father absent boys were
less aggressive and had less sex role differentiation in doll play activity than
father present boys. Many other studies (Biller, 1968, 1969, 1970, 1971, 1981)
indicate that father absent boys are seen as less aggressive, less masculine, and
more dependent.

   Hetherington (1966) felt that father absence before age 4 or 5 affected masculine developed. Nine- to 12-year-old father absent boys were less masculine,
more dependent on peers, and engaged in fewer physical contact games. Biller
(1969) set the age of importance of father absence for sex role development
at age 4 and 5. Santrock (1970) even found differences when separation occurred before or after 2 years of age in boys. Boys who became father absent
before age 2 were less trusting, less industrious, and had more feelings of in-
feriority than boys who became father absent between ages 3 and 5.

   Hodges, Wechsler, and Ballantine (1979) found that preschool age children
of divorce were less sex role stereotyped. Boys were less aggressive than the
comparison group of boys from intact families. Vess, Schwebel, and Moreland
(1983) found that the more postdivorce conflict the more feminine children of
both sexes were.

*There is nothing intrinsically valuable about appropriate sex role behavior.
Indeed it can be argued that defining appropriate behaviors by biological sex
only limits behavior. The evidence is overwhelming, however, that boys with
inappropriate sex role development have lower self-esteem and are more likely
to be rejected by peers. Therefore, anything that the mental health professional can do to foster positive images of being male in boys is likely to benefit
those boys. In addition, it would be valuable to provide a warm, caring, pos-*

itive adult male role model for boys without fathers to increase the chances of boys having high self-esteem for being male. Reinforcing assertive behavior can be of value to both boys and girls. Eliminating effeminate mannerisms in boys without fathers is helpful and does not indicate that important feminine sex role stereotyped behavior (such as interpersonal sensitivity) is undesirable.

One of the strange manifestations of effeminate behavior in boys is the development of stereotypic mannerisms. This author has not seen this discussed in the literature, but has observed it on numerous occasions. Such mannerisms clearly communicate an effeminate identification. They are strange because they are exaggerations of feminine behavior and do not often occur in that form. Some father absent boys exhibit a grossly exaggerated hip swing when they walk; this simply does not occur in girls in that form. Other boys develop the "limp wrist" that is the stereotype of homosexuality. This behavior does occur in some, but is not that common. These behaviors can be discouraged and more masculine behaviors supported without necessarily encouraging a "macho" orientation toward the world.

There are several studies that indicate that surrogate models make a difference in masculine development in boys. A brother, uncle, grandfather, or male boarder may provide a boy with the appropriate role model for heightened self-esteem. Vess, Schwebel, and Moreland (1983) reported that boys from divorced families with older brothers were more masculine than boys without older brothers. Boys with older brothers were also less dependent. If the mother encourages masculine behavior, the boys will behave in a more masculine way (Aldous, 1972; Biller, 1968, 1969, 1970, 1971).

One seventh grade boy had a pronounced sway in his walk. He had low self-esteem and was the object of harrassment by class mates. He had limited contact with a grandfather, but few other adult males. His mother was quite concerned about his emotional development, but was at a loss as to how to help him. She enrolled him in a martial arts class to give him greater self-esteem and reduce his sense of vulnerability. One day in gym, the boys were asked to sit in the bleachers to get a lecture from the physical education instructor. A boy behind the single-parent effeminate boy started poking him in the back with his foot, a typical harrassment in the school. Instead of taking it as he had done in the past, the single parent boy turned around and flipped the boy over his shoulder. The instructor had the two boys come down on a pad and fight. (This is a typically adult male solution to this problem. A woman instructor would not have used this solution). The single parent boy won and became a hero in the school! One of the more informative changes in the boy was that without any additional episodes, the walk changed to a more masculine walk. For junior high school age boys, the fear of fighting, rather than the fighting itself, is often a source of harrassment. While this author does not advocate fighting as a solution to boyhood problems, assertiveness is important. Children must be given a sense of the ability and right to stand up for themselves and to be free of intimidation.

Cognitive Changes in Father Absent Boys

The general assumption in the literature of the effect of father absence on cognitive development has led to the conclusion that boys from single parent families do worse in academic performance. Shinn's (1978) extensive review of the literature noted that 12 of 54 studies looking at general measures of cognitive ability found deficits in quantitative performance and only one found improvement.

In one of the few studies done on infants, Pedersen, Rubenstein, and Yarrow (1979) looked at the cognitive development of 55 black infants from 5 to 6 months old living in lower socioeconomic circumstances. Of these, 27 were in father absent homes. Male infants who had experienced minimal interaction with their fathers were significantly lower on the Bayley Mental Developmental Index and in measures of social responsiveness, secondary circular reactions, and preferences for novel stimuli. Female infants seemed to be unaffected by the father loss.

Pedersen et al. (1979) felt that alternative explanations such as socioeconomic status, an extended family household, and maternal behavior were ruled out. It is difficult, however, to come up with sensitive measures of socioeconomic status that reflect quality of living. The number of adults in the households were the same for father absent and father present homes. No true test of maternal behavior was made to eliminate this alternative explanation, although Pedersen et al. noted that substitute caregivers were common for both types of homes. On a very small subsample, direct observation was made of maternal behavior and no differences were found.

Blanchard and Biller (1971) found that with respect to both grades and achievement tests scores, early father absent boys were underachievers. Late father absent boys and low father present boys usually obtained somewhat below grade level scores. The high father present boys performed above grade level. The inclusion of low and high father presence as a control was a most helpful innovation. Too many investigators have treated father presence as if it were a unitary variable.

Overall, the amount of fathering in father present homes varies enormously. Kotelchuck's (1972) study of higher educated fathers found that about three-fourths of the fathers had no routine role in child care for children 6 months to 2 years of age. It is clear that the amount of fathering done in father-present homes may be quite low. One study cited by Shinn (1978) placed the average amount of quality time in which fathers were engaged in activities with the children at only two hours per week in father present homes (Szalai, Converse, Feldheim, Scheuch, and Stone, 1972). Thus, the norm of interaction with fathers is not high.

Given those findings, it is remarkable that father presence has been found to have any effect on cognitive development. Perhaps the effect of father presence on the mother is what mediates the effect of father presence for the child.

The reason for the father's absence also has an effect on cognitive functioning. While father absence due to divorce, desertion, or separation was found to have its most negative effect for the initial two years of life for boys and girls, father absence due to death was most negative in its effects in cognitive effects when it occurred from 6 to 9 years of age for boys (Santrock, 1972). These findings suggest that the effect of father absence is not simply the absence of a role model. Anger, grief, and the reaction of the remaining parent all may play a role in the effect of father loss on academic achievement.

Several investigators have proposed that father absence results in a "feminine" pattern of skills and deficits in cognitive functioning, with relatively higher verbal skills and lower quantitative skills. Shinn's (1978) extensive review of the father absent literature summarized four studies that found that pattern in boys. Because those studies were conducted at elite universities, it was not possible to tell whether the differences were relative or absolute, that is, do father absent boys score better than father present boys in verbal skills and worse than father present boys in quantitative skills. In Shinn's review, 12 studies were found in which specific decrements in quantitative performance was obtained for father absent children. Of 11 studies that reviewed verbal performance, five found improved verbal performance.

Lessing, Zagorin, and Nelson (1970), cited by Shinn, noted a socioeconomic effect of father absence. For working-class families, father absence was associated with generally lower IQ scores. For middle class families, father absence was associated with high verbal scores than father present children. Two performance scores were lower than for father present children. These results suggest that father absence has its effect in several areas: role modeling, cultural values, and economics.

Shinn came to the conclusion that sex role identification did not play an important role in academic performance. Financial hardship, high levels of anxiety, and low levels of parent-child interaction were seen as important causes of poor performance in children from single parent households.

Ferri (1976) in a longitudinal study done in England of 17,000 children, including 418 children in father absent homes, (discussed in more detail in the later section on mother absence), found that there was no differences in amount of school absence between those in fatherless as compared to two parent families, either before or after demographic variable were controlled. Children who were raised in father absent homes had lower arithmetic scores as compared to children in intact families, but not as low as children in mother absent homes. There was no sex difference in arithmetic ability. For reading ability, there was an apparent, strong negative effect of father absence, but this effect disappeared when the variable "free school meals" was controlled, suggesting that low income was a major contributing factor to low reading ability in father absent homes.

One of the most carefully done studies controlling for sample selection and socioeconomic factors is the study by Guidubaldi, Cleminshaw, Perry and Mcloughlin (1983) which was discussed in Chapter 3. This study evaluated school performance for first, third, and fifth graders from divorced and intact homes. Intact family children had higher full scale IQ's, Wide Range Achievement scores, and higher spelling scores. When socioeconomic factors were statistically controlled (remember, a weak indicator of socioeconomics was the only one available), all of the academic differences between children of divorce and intact families dropped out and only the full scale IQ difference remained in terms of cognitive factors.

Additional evidence for the effect of father absence comes from research of the effect of father surrogates on cognitive development. Shinn (1978) cited three studies in which father surrogates and stepfathers had a remedial effect on father-absent children. For example, Santrock (1972) found that remarriage of boys' mothers had a positive effect on academic performance. More recently, Guidubaldi et al (1983) found that the presence of a stepfather for children with early father absence led to no deficits in cognitive functioning as compared to children with early father absence and no stepfather, who did have problems.

The research is relatively clear that boys experience deficits in cognitive functioning as a function of father absence. For middle class boys, father absence may result in improved verbal skills, but quantitative skills tends to be lower for father absent boys regardless of socioeconomic level. Father surrogates and stepfather, particularly if present during early childhood, may negate the effect of father absence. Given the evidence that a close relationship with a father or father surrogate makes a difference in academic functioning, mental health professionals who wish to help families optimize cognitive functioning, should encourage warm, frequent father contact. If father abandonment has occurred, it is important to support a Big Brother or an adult male relative or friend.

Emotional Adjustment and Father Absent Boys

One 7-year-old boy was chronically afraid of trying out new activities. He was afraid to swim, to be alone in a room in his house, to bike, and to play soccer. He had a warm relationship with both parents who were divorced. Was his fearfulness related to specific parenting styles, modeling, or the fact that his parents had gotten a divorce?

There is evidence that emotional problems are more likely in single parent families. Felner, Stolberg, and Cowen (1975) found that children from single parent households were more likely to have school adjustment problems. If the parents were divorced, acting out behavior was more common. If the father had died, the child was more likely to show moody withdrawal.

Santrock and Wohlford (1970) found that for father absence due to divorce (as compared to father absence due to death), boys had more difficulty delaying gratification (e.g., waiting for a reward). Hoffman (1971) noted that father absent boys consistently scored lower than father present boys on a variety of indices of moral development. Socioeconomic status and reason for father absence was not controlled because data were not collected for the purpose of this particular analysis. The inability to determine the effects of the reason for father absence is a problem in many of the earlier father absent studies, and it is difficult to attribute the problems found to father absence, per se.

FATHER ABSENCE AND DEVELOPMENT IN GIRLS

There is some data that suggests that girls are less affected by father absence than boys. Other research studies, however, have indicated that girls are probably as much affected by father absence in terms of social development and heterosexual development as boys.

Sex Role Identification

Marino and McCowan (1976) found that for girls, father absence seemed to lead to a closer identification with the female role than for girls in father present homes. There was difficulty however in the development of male-female relationship after puberty. More negative attitudes toward males were likely in father absent homes than father present homes. In divorced families, college age girls with older brothers were less masculine than similar girls without older brothers (Vess, Schwebel, and Moreland, 1983). Girls with low father availability during childhood had less feminine self-concepts than those who reported high father availability (Fish, 1969). Jacobson and Ryder (1969) noted that many women who had father absence early in life had difficulties in achieving a satisfying sexual relationship with husbands. Hetherington (1972) found that father absent girls in adolescence had greater mother dependency. Girls had the most difficulties in their heterosexual interactions if the father absence had begun before age five. Vess, et al. (1983) found no differences in sex role identification for college students as a function of the earlier divorce of parents, so the effects of sex role identification may diminish over time. Hainline and Feig (1978) also found no differences by college age for girls with father loss.

Huston's (1983) review of sex-typing research came to the conclusion that fathers play an important though not irreplaceable role in girls' acquisition of heterosexual skills and sex-typed intellectual skills. Girls were given less emphasis in the father absent literature since it was assumed that identification with the same sex parent was crucial. Other theories have assumed a reciprocal interaction process between opposite sex parent and child that explains why father absence should influence girls' sex role development.

Ferri (1976) found no sex difference in adjustment as a function of father loss and both sex children from fatherless homes were seen by teachers as less well adjusted (remember potential teacher bias) than children from intact families. When other variables were controlled (i.e., economics, number of schools attended, free school meals, family size, social class, sex of child independent of family type, foster care, and parental aspirations), the relationship of family type and adjustment disappeared, again indicating that economics plays a major role in the relationship of adjustment and single parenting. As might be expected, regardless of family type, girls were better adjusted than boys.

Cognitive Changes in Father Absent

Shinn (1978) noted that in 12 of the 21 studies that included girls father absence had a detrimental effect on the girls' academic performance. This number of studies was about the same proportion of studies that found negative effects for boys. Marino and McCowan (1976) found that father absence enhanced verbal skills in girls and reduce quantitative skills. These effects were found for early, temporary, and permanent father absences. Lessing, Zagorin, and Nelson (1970) obtained lower ability in perceptual-motor and manipulative spatial skills for both sexes as a function of father absence. In Ferri's (1976) study for poor reading skills for boys and girls, low income was apparently a factor, but the poorer ability in arithmetic remained statistically significant even when "free lunch meals" was controlled.

MOTHER ABSENCE AND CHILD DEVELOPMENT

Research on mother absence is practically nonexistent. The frequency of mother absence is so low that obtaining samples permitting inferential statistics and generalization is almost impossible.

In a study already discussed for single fathers, Ferri (1976) reported on a British longitudinal study of 17,000 children born in Great Britain from March 3 to March 9, 1958. These children were followed-up at 7 years of age and at 11 years of age. The study included interviews with the custodial parent (usually the mother) and a teacher as well as a medical exam. While the original purpose of the study was a national perinatal mortality survey, the data provided an opportunity to study one parent families. At the same time, the data comes from a time that preceded the sharp increase in divorce rates in Western cultures, so that generalization to present day results may be somewhat limited. Certainly the degree of stigma or uniqueness may be less today.

At 11 years of age, 11,385 children were followed up. Of these, 88 were in motherless homes, about half by divorce and half by death of the mother. (This number compares to 418 in fatherless homes.) What makes this study particularly important is that it is one of the few studies with a substantial number of families that had mother absence. With more father custody, mother absence may be on the rise, permitting more research on the effect of mother absence.

Mother Absence and Development in Boys

School Performance

The Ferri (1976) study showed that motherless boys had statistically significantly better over all school attendance than boys from intact homes. There was no differences as a function of the cause of the mother absence. For arithmetic performance, boys from motherless families, due to divorce or separation, obtained lower arithmetic scores than boys from intact families. For reading, the data were difficult to assess, but Ferri concluded that the mother absent boys had significantly lower reading scores after other variables were controlled statistically. Economics, foster care, geographic mobility, parental aspirations, family size, and social class were all statistically significant variables. Although mother absence was significant, the amount of variance explained by mother absence was quite small compared to these other variables.

Social Adjustment

There was no evidence from the Ferri study that loss of a mother was in itself related to poorer over all adjustment. Loss of either parent through divorce was related to children of either sex being less well adjusted than if the child were from a widowed family or intact family. However, all statistical differences disappeared when other demographic variables were controlled. These findings are similar to those discussed in Chapter 3.

In the only other study that sheds light on adjustment and mother absence, Santrock and Warshak (1979), compared father and mother custody. Father custody boys were seen as more mature and sociable than mother custody boys. In terms of sex role identification, boys did not seem to suffer in mother absent homes.

Mother Absence and Development in Girls

The major concern for boys has been father absence and the effect of a lack of a adult male role model. However, the concern for mother absence could be focused on development in girls.

School Performance

In Ferri's (1976) study, girls tended to have better school attendance than girls from intact homes, although the differences were not statistically significant. Thus, the differences were not as pronounced as for boys. If the families were from working class backgrounds, the differences were even more pronounced and approached significance (although statistics were not summarized). Ferri suggested that one reason why school attendance may be better in mother absent homes is that the father was more likely to be employed and send the children to school when they were sick. Also, there was evidence from other studies that single parent fathers were less likely to see the children as ill than mothers or to be alarmed at minor ailments.

For arithmetic, the girls showed a lower performance for mother absent homes in which the mother absence was due to divorce or separation as compared to girls from intact homes. Foster care, family size, parental aspirations, and social class were more powerful predictors of arithmetic performance regardless of the sex of the child. There were no statistically significant differences by sex by 11 years of age. Lower arithmetic scores were obtained by children cared for by separated and divorced fathers than by the other groups, suggesting that the reason for mother absence may have some influence on arithmetic performance.

For reading, there was lower performance in reading with mother absence after other demographic variables were controlled, but the demographic variables accounted for more of the variance. The statistical analysis suffered from the small sample size. The results for both boys and girls were the same for both arithmetic and reading.

Social Adjustment

Again, the results for girls in the Ferri (1976) study mirrored the results for boys. Divorce was related to poorer adjustment as compared to loss of parent by death (regardless of sex of parent) and as compared to intact families. When demographic variables such as economics were controlled, the differences disappeared, suggesting that for girls the loss of a mother had no effect in and of itself on adjustment.

The Santrock and Warshak (1979) study on father-custody found that father-custody girls were less feminine, less independent, and more demanding than mother custody girls. This research suggests that girls may be less sex role stereotyped and not as mature if in mother absent homes, while boys do not seem to suffer.

Ferri (1976) noted that one reason why mother absence may have less apparent negative effects (the data are not completely in) may be due to the fact that mother absent homes suffer much less from financial hardship than do father absent homes. The standard of living was lower, however, when either parent was absent.

EMOTIONAL ADJUSTMENT AND SINGLE PARENTING

Rubenstein, Shaver, and Peplau (1979) looked at the adjustment of adults who had experienced parental divorce when children. The earlier the divorce the more likely the adults were to have low self-esteem and experience loneliness as adults. They reported worry, despair, feelings of worthlessness, fearfulness, and general separation anxiety.

A variety of clinicians have talked about the scapegoating that can occur in any family, intact or divorced, that may lead to one child being identified as the problem. Anxiety and anger can be displaced toward one child. In single parent families, where loss and anger are commonplace reactions to the divorce (or loss by death), transference of feelings from the absent parent to the child is more likely to occur if the child is somehow reminiscent of that parent. Often the basis of transference is toward the child of the same sex as the absent parent. This transference is even more likely if there is a strong physical resemblance. Several parents have reported difficulty in handling a particular behavior pattern in a child when that behavior pattern reminds them of the absent parent, particularly when that behavior pattern in the absent parent was a cause for the divorce. For example, one mother became incapacitated in the face of her son's lying because it reminded her of her ex-husband's lying. She had been unable to deal with her ex-husband's behavior and now could not deal with her son's.

Parents who have transference reactions to their children, in which they identify the behavior of the children as "identical" to the unacceptable behavior of the absent parent, can become ineffective. While it is possible that the child indeed picked up the unacceptable behavior through modeling, the needed response by the parent to a child is substantially different than to a spouse. Parents may need to be supported in reasserting their parental role. They may need to be reminded that some problems in childhood are typical childhood problems (such as lying and stealing) and not necessarily signs of inevitable undesirable adult outcomes. Family therapy may be needed to help the parent reassert the parenting role.

Blechman and Manning (1976) proposed that if the parent is persistently inefficient, the child may feel forced to take over that role often in a maladaptive fashion. The child may take the role of the "identified patient" in order to help the family unite to deal with the unacceptable behavior. In my experience, this role is considerably more likely if the child learns that intrafamily tension is substantially reduced when everyone is angry at that child.

The problem of transference for the parent is similar to the problem of identification by the child. Kaseman (1974) noted that if the identification of the child is with the devalued self of the remaining parent, the child could come to loath himself or herself. If the identification is with the absent parent, the child can carry unresolved feelings of pain.

Blechman (1982) argued that the effects of divorce or single parenting may not be maladjustment, but developmental lag. Santrock (1972), for example, found that while father-absent children had deficits in performance in the third grade, by the sixth grade there was only a nonsignificant trend. Vess, Schwebel, and Moreland (1983) looked at the effects of early parental divorce on the sex role development of college students. Of the sample, 84 had experienced the divorce of parents prior to the tenth birthday and 135 after the tenth birthday. There were no effects found of early divorce on sex role.

Blechman (1982) also noted that there have been suggestions that early parent loss may even lead to excellence among the highly gifted. Blechman also found that girls reared by a single mother may be better prepared for employment. Such girls may also suffer in preparation for traditional marriage. Blechman came to the conclusion that when multiple regression takes into account correlated variables, there is little relationship between adjustment and family type. Educational level, income, and quality of parenting are likely to be for more important.

DELINQUENCY AND DIVORCE

The Cambridge-Somerville study (Glueck and Glueck, 1950) was the historical antecedent to the assumption that "broken homes" cause delinquency. This study assumed that single parent families were characterized by family disorganization and that this disorganization caused delinquency. Bowlby (1946) stated that "broken homes" caused delinquency. A subsequent analysis of the Cambridge-Somerville data (Craig and Glick, 1963) indicated that family conflict and parental criminal activity were better predictors of delinquency than single parent homes.

Nye (1958) came to the conclusion that children from single parent homes committed only slightly more delinquent offenses than children from two parent homes, but were twice as likely to be institutionalized for such offenses when caught than were children from two parent homes. When the children in two parent homes are apprehended, they are more likely to seek psychotherapy as a solution for the problem and are more likely to convince the courts to provide warnings or probation. Whether the courts are more likely to see two parent families as able to solve the problem while single-parent homes are seen as less likely is unknown. In addition, if the court stigmatizes single parent households, the court may be less likely to suggest alternatives to incarceration.

In a study of 3700 high school students (Blechman, Berberian, and Thompson, 1977), self-reported student drug use was not related to family type. Instead, peer drug use, age, parental occupation, remarriage, sex, and parental unemployment were all important predictors. As additional evidence that single parenting may not cause delinquency, Schulz and Wilson (1973) found that frequency of drug use by peers accounted for 75 percent of the variance in adolescent drug use while family type accounted for a trivial amount of the variance. Maskin and Brookins (1974) noted that for 126 female delinquents in a girls treatment center, recidivism was more likely to occur in the two parent families. Marital adjustment of two parent families was a better predictor of successful treatment of the female delinquent than whether the girl came from a divorced home as compared to an intact home.

Cashion (1982), in a review of the literature from 1970 to 1980, concluded that delinquency is not associated with a child coming from a female headed family, while delinquency is clearly related to poverty. Violence was highest for delinquent boys from two parent families. While delinquent girls had negative perceptions of fathers, they were not more likely to come from father absent homes.

Finally, Blechman (1982) argued that cause and effect may be reversed. Temperamentally hard-to-handle children may increase the likelihood that parents will divorce by increasing stress on the family and may even encourage parents to divorce.

SUMMARY

Single parent families are likely to have significant problems, but the consequences of single parenting, such as lower income, play a major role. Discipline is more difficult in single parent households, particularly if enmeshment or disengagement is a problem. Sex role behaviors are likely to be affected. School performance is also likely to be lower, although lower income may play a major role in academic decline. For father absence, arithmetic skills may be lowered and adjustment in boys and girls affected. For mother absence, drawing conclusions are more difficult due to the limited number of studies, but reading skills may be affected and adjustment does seem to be poorer. Delinquency rates may not be greater in single parent families, but court involvement is greater for children of single parents.

In order to be effective in working with children of divorce, it is necessary to understand the impact of single parenting as well as the impact of the predivorce conflict, the separation and postdivorce behaviors of parents and children. Some of the stresses that children experience postdivorce are related to the problems of the single parent family.

In the next chapter, the additional stress of remarriage will be discussed.

CHAPTER 9

Remarriage: A New Time of Problems with Children

At the remarriage of one of the parents, a large number of children are referred for psychological evaluation and treatment. Given the data that 80 percent of divorced men and women remarry within three years of the divorce (Westoff, 1975), treatment of children of divorce is more often than not the treatment of children of remarriage.

At first glance, a chapter on remarriage may not seem to belong in a book on interventions for children of divorce. Certainly there are a variety of studies that include children of divorce only if they are presently living in a single parent household that was created because of marital disruption. Yet if the clinician wants to be effective working with children of divorce, the dynamics of stress associated with marriage must be addressed. While most parents expect difficulties with remarriage, many parents are surprised at how difficult the adjustment is (Messinger, 1976).

Indeed, how happy the new family is may be more dependent on the stepparent-stepchild relationship than on the marital relationship. Crosbie-Burnett (1984) obtained such results in a multiple regression analysis of the self-report of 87 Caucasian mother-stepfather households. The stepfather-stepchild relationship accounted for 59 percent of the variance in overall family happiness while marital happiness accounted for only an additional 10 percent. Discipline and nurturance between the stepfather and stepchild correlated with family happiness .62 and .45, respectively, but added no additional variance in predicting family happiness.

It is not unusual for a new family to want to exclude the other parent and to wish for a new "nuclear" family. The fact that a child has two families makes a step family significantly different from a nuclear family.

Because continued, warm, affectionate contact with both parents would seem to be supportive for the best adjustment in children, remarriage usually works best for children if both the biological parents and the stepparent do not try to exclude the other parent from the children's life. When the biological parent is abandoning, the stepparent may take a more active parental role, particularly if the children are young.

REMARRIAGE AS A STRESSOR

There are several reasons why the point of remarriage serves as a precipitating event in having a child identified as a problem. First, the remarriage is a concrete statement that the parents are not going to have a reconciliation. Given the frequency with which children harbor such fantasies, it is not surprising that even some years later, children have been able to keep such fantasies alive. While some children manage to continue to hope for reconciliation even after remarriage, many begin to give up hope at that point. Any repressed anger at the thought of the parents behavior then comes forth. In addition, the children may actively work toward breaking up the new marriage in order to make reconciliation possible.

The child may also have unresolved mourning of the previous relationship (Kleinman, Rosenberg, and Whiteside, 1979). Kleinman et al. argued that children are developmentally unable to mourn fully a loss prior to adolescence. The key word is "fully." Clearly children do mourn, but their cognitive functioning may be limited in terms of understanding the loss until they reach adolescence. Thies (1977) argued that remarriage usually occurs before the children have had an opportunity to resolve the grief associated with the divorce. According to Thies, the major determinant of whether the child will adjust to the remarriage is whether the divorce trauma is adequately resolved.

The child is placed in a position of significant stress. Having already lost a relationship, the child is now invited to attach and become vulnerable again to the possibility of going through another divorce. Given the fact that second marriages have a higher divorce rate than first marriages, such concerns are quite realistic.

Children may resist accepting a new marriage because they wish reconciliation of biological parents, fail to fully mourn the loss of the previous family, or fear experiencing a new loss.

According to Jacobson (1979), approximate 10 percent of the 66 million children in the United States are living with a stepparent. Yet the entire society is not developed for accepting stepfamilies. The previous chapter discussed the degree to which single parent families are not accepted by the culture as a whole. Stepfamilies develop somewhat greater superficial acceptance because those families resemble nuclear families. The problem the stepfamily has is that both they and society often wish to impose the same structure as the nuclear family and such a structure is malfunctional. This chapter will outline some of the dimensions that make it difficult for the stepfamily to survive.

Use of the Term "Remarried Family"

As with other subgroups of children of divorce, what labels are used can reflect or shape attitudes. The reconstituted family has often been used as a description of remarried families. While that label is accurate, it sounds a little like less-than-fresh orange juice! Satir (1972) used the words, blended family, which has a nice sense to what tasks the family has to address. Stepfamilies is a label used by many to refer to a family in which any person has a step role with anyone else in the family. For the purpose of this book the label, remarried family, will be used as potentially the most neutral.

Historical Antecedents of Stepfamilies

The word "stepparent" comes from middle and old English meaning "bereaved" or "orphaned." Prior to the commonality of divorce in western culture, the primary reason for remarriage was the death of a prior spouse. In fact, there is some evidence to suggest that the prestige of a family is increased by the death of a parent and decreased by divorce.

Prejudice Against Stepfamilies

Just as single families deal with being viewed as a deviant and pathological life style, stepfamilies also are the target of devaluation. Jacobson (1979) referred to the denigration of stepfamilies that is evident in the term "wicked stepmother." Jacobsen suggested that denigrating stepmothers is a socially supported way of handing ambivalence toward mothers.

WHY DO STEPFAMILIES HAVE GREATER STRAIN THAN OTHER TYPES OF FAMILIES?

When a nuclear family begins, the bonding occurs between the parents prior to the bonding between each parent and subsequent children. The ability of this bond to continue to grow and strengthen over time allows for stronger leadership and a united front for the children. In remarriage, reciprocal marital roles between husband and wife cannot be worked out prior to the parental roles (Fast and Cain, 1966). In dysfunctional families, one parent may permit a bond with a child to develop that excludes the other parent, but the structure of the nuclear family tends to discourage such a move.

The Slow Development of Roles

Duberman (1973) noted that the role of parent is learned gradually. Each person brings scripts based on their own childhood to the marriage. When children come, the parent either decides to apply that script spontaneously and usually without much consideration because "it feels natural" or to write a counterscript to do it better than was done for him or her. Such counterscripts are difficult to write and can never be done spontaneously.

My father died when I was three years old and my mother never remarried. When I became a parent, I was startled to discover how many decisions have to be made concerning child rearing, many of them trivial, but not irrelevant. I had no scripts for how to solve them and often did not know what was appropriate. How many cookies are appropriate after school? How much TV watching is harmful? Should there be a desert after every meal? When is the best bed time? There are no correct answers to these questions, but they must be addressed and, at some point, the answer can be important. Fortunately, my wife did not have the same combination of childhood scripts.

In remarried families, the slow evolution and negotiation around new scripts does not have the opportunity to take place. There is no time for the parental bond to solidify before dealing with the children. The children have already become used to the parenting style of the biological parents and it is almost inevitable that the old parenting style will not feel appropriate to the stepparent. Not only is there not time to gradually negotiate the blending of two parenting scripts, but (as will be discussed in more detail later) the children will mount substantial resistance to any changes in parenting style. The stepfamily is likely to judge the difficult individuation moves on the part of the child and show strong disapproval at the resistant behavior of the 2 year old or disrespectful challenge to authority of the adolescent. Messinger (1976) noted for first marriages, immaturity, sex, lack of readiness for marriage, and in-laws are mentioned as sources for concern. For remarried families, money and child-rearing are identified as the greatest problems. It is clear that for remarried families, parenting is a major source of concern.

In nuclear families, the more difficult developmental stages are sustained by the bonding that has occurred in previous stages. As Goldstein (1974) noted, a 2 year old's tantrum is easier to tolerate if the parent can remember the holding and snuggling that occurred during infancy. The stepparent that comes on stage when the child is 2 or a beginning adolescent has less reason to stay attached than does the biological parent.

Developmental stages of each family member may be different in remarriage. Unless each parent and stepparent have children of approximately the same age, it is likely that the developmental stages of the two parents will be different. The demands of family life may be incompatible with that person's life cycle position (Sager, Steer, Crohn, Rodstein, and Walker, 1980). A stepfather with older children may find that he does not want to repeat the dependency of very young children.

In counseling remarriage families, it is useful to help the family understand the resistance that may occur when parental figures are at different places in their life cycle. Parents who have already experienced a stage with their own children may resist having to go through the stage again with stepchildren. A stepparent without children of his or her own may regret missing stages of development.

Ghosts of the Past

Finally, no matter how much the remarried family would like to pretend that the previous relationship did not exist, its presence is always there. To deny its existence is to create pathology in the family.

Often, the ghosts of the past haunt the remarried family. At least one marriage has already failed. Remarried families are always born out of loss and expectations may be influenced by the hurt of the previous relationship (Whiteside and Auerbach, 1978). Will this marriage make it? Seldom do people enter any marriage with the expectation that the marriage will not last. For second marriages, the fantasy that one can always work it out has already been shattered. The ghost of previous relationships (just how attached is he to his former wife?) and concern about this relationship produces significant strain. Couples often do not argue about significant issues because they are phobic about any disagreement, fearing it is a sign that this marriage too is failing. Goldstein (1974) referred to this tendency as "pseudomutuality" and noted that there is often a denial of marital problems in remarriages and the behavior problems of the children are often the focus of the request for help.

Because remarried couple often have difficulty admitting to marital problems, they may use referral of the child for treatment as a source of asking for help. The clinician may want to change from child treatment or family therapy to marital counseling, if this dynamic is recognized.

Avoidance of Conflict

There is a strong tendency to avoid conflict in remarriages (Jones, 1978). Jones noted that jealousy is common in remarriages, particularly around feeling excluded and fear of loss.

Money may serve as a significant stress in remarriages. Messinger (1976) noted that financial problems often tie the remarriage to the first marriage. Mothers are sometimes embarrassed at the financial burden her children provide to the stepfather. Child support payments are notoriously underpaid, increasing the burden on the stepfather. Messinger noted that remarried women were sometimes secretive about their financial resources with the new spouse, indicating a lack of trust in the new relationship and the need to protect themselves from exploitation.

Role definitions are not clear in remarried families. While behavioral codes are well-defined for nuclear families, society does not have a tradition of behavioral codes on how stepfamilies relate to one another (Fast and Cain, 1966; Johnson, 1980). People do not know how they are supposed to feel so they do not know if what they do feel is normal or acceptable. Expecting to love another instantly or that the stepmother is likely to be wicked are examples of naive expectations.

Finally, the complexity of relationships is substantially greater than in nuclear families. Visher and Visher (1979) did an illuminating analysis of why stepfamilies have more complex relationship, independent of any of the complicating emotional factors, but just based on size. In a nuclear family with two parents, two children and four grandparents, there are 28 pairs and 247 different combinations. If one parent remarries a new partner with three children, there are now 136 pairs and 131,054 combinations. They also gave a typical example of a divorced man with two children who marries a widow with one child. His former wife marries a man who has three children by a former marriage (that wife did not remarry). Thus, in that fairly typical example, there are three families and six children. There are now 253 pairs and 8,388,584 combinations.

THE PROBLEM OF THE STEPFAMILY
FOR THE NONMARRIED PARENT

The biological parent who is not remarrying often has intense feelings about the remarriage of a former partner. Even when the remaining parent wanted or was the initiator of the divorce, there are usually ambivalent feelings about the attachment to the former spouse. Thus, the remarriage can raise feelings of rejection or loss. "She found someone else to love." "It really is over." Competition is not unusual, particularly around affection from the children. "She may replace me as mother." Such competition is more likely for the mother, whose stereotyped role is nurturance, than for the father who may not feel displaced. Fathers may feel relief because of lessened financial pressure or relief of guilt over inadequate financial support.

Remarriage can damage the relationship of the child to the remaining parent (Thies, 1977). The child may worry that giving affection to the stepparent will invite rejection (and indeed it can) from the biological parent of the same sex as the stepparent.

THE PROBLEM OF THE STEPFAMILY FROM THE FAMILY'S POINT
OF VIEW

Some of the stepfamily's problems are shared by the entire family. The entire stepfamily has to figure out how the sharply increased number of potential interactions can be handled, and other dynamics make the adjustment difficult.

The Myth of Instant Love

The hope of a new start can lead to unrealistic expectations for remarried families. Families often believe that because the two adults love each other and a new family is being formed, everyone in the family should love one another (Visher and Visher, 1978). Parents and children are often shocked to discover that such instant love does not occur. Indeed, unless the stepparent and stepchild have had a long-term relationship where affection developed prior to the remarriage, that affection may be a long time coming. Fast and Cain (1966) noted that some stepparents develop a hypersensitivity around whether they are accepted in the "parent" role. Such pressures make it difficult to have spontaneous interactions since all interactions are overinterpreted. There are several reasons why affection is likely, and appropriately, to be delayed:

1.   *The "burnt child."* The child has already lost contact with one parent due to divorce. The "burnt child" syndrome would lead the child to be cautious about developing feelings of attachment to the new stepparent until trust in the stability of the new relationship develops.

Stepfamilies should be encouraged to allow children to develop affection at their own pace, without pressure. Trust develops slowly, particularly for a child who has already had an involuntary loss.

2.   *There is ample evidence to demonstrate that the acceptance of the stepfamily by the child is inversely related to age.* The younger the child, the faster the acceptance of a stepparent in a parenting role. Preschool age children often accept the affection of a stepparent with little or no anxiety. Elementary age child are more cautious and may take some period of time. By late elementary age, the evolution of trust could take up to two years. Indeed, the child's self-esteem is related to the time of remarriage. Children were statistically more likely to be self-derogatory if they were over 8 years old when a parent remarried (Kaplan and Pokorny, 1971).

During adolescence, the resistance to the remarriage can be quite high for a variety of reasons. First, the adolescent often has a strong sense of loyalty to the nonremarried parent and sees the development of affection for a stepparent as disloyal. Second, the remarriage sexualizes the parent in a way that is often anxiety-provoking to the teenager. Finally, separation is the developmental task of the adolescent, and asking the adolescent to attach at the very time that he or she is working on psychological and physical leave-taking places them in a difficult bind. Indeed, it is not unusual for the adolescent to never develop affectional bonds with a stepparent.

The stepfamily needs to be warned that the older the child, the more resistance to bonding. In particular, adolescents need to have permission to avoid bonding altogether.

3.   *Loss of time and attention.* Another major source of resistance to bonding is the resentment that the stepchild may feel about the loss of time

and attention from the biological parent. The stepparent may represent an intrusion into what was a more intense relationship. Blechman and Manning (1976) noted that the triad in nuclear families (mother, father, and child) tends to dilute the intensity of parent-child relationships. Since the marital bond predates the parental bond, it tends to be stronger. After divorce, the triad becomes a dyad with the parent and each child. That dyad does not have the other relationship between parents and thus the parent-child relationship intensifies. In fact, the strength of the bond becomes so strong that it can be difficult for a stepparent to intervene. If the biological parent does transfer primary allegiance to the new partner, the child may feel an enormous loss and resent the stepparent.

4. *Given the nature of the strong bond, the stepparent also may have trouble with affection.* First, the strong bond between the biological parent and child can be difficult to break into, leading the stepparent to resent the presence of the child. Second, the resistance from a stepchild to the new relationship can be very difficult to tolerate over a long period of time. Several people have argued that particularly the stepmother has difficulty with this resistance. (See the discussion on the dilemma of the stepmother later in this chapter.) It is difficult to love a child who does not want to be loved.

The presence of a stepchild is a constant reminder to the stepparent that the remarried family is not a nuclear family. The child is a constant reminder of the previous relationship, particularly if the child is of the same sex as the absent parent, carries the same last name as the absent parent, or has a strong physical resemblance to the ex-spouse. Only when a couple without children remarry can the existence of the prior marriage be forgotten on a day-to-day basis.

5. *Sexuality can be a problem.* Stepfamilies can be often characterized as having a weakened incest taboo. Familiarity within the developing intact family tends to provide protection from inappropriate sexual relationships. With stepfamilies, that taboo has not had a chance to develop and parents and children can be distressed to discover "inappropriate feelings."

It is extremely important that families that are remarrying discuss sexuality. What may have been a comfortable level of casual undress in the previous family may no longer be appropriate. Even for preteen children, a family member walking around nude or partially clothed, or children bathing with parents, or playing or sleeping in the parental bed may be provocative. Especially for teenagers, the control of potentially stimulating behavior is important. Not only is it important to encourage stepfamilies to deal with this topic for stepparent-stepchild relationship, but also between stepsibling relationships. It can be very stimulating for a teenage boy to suddenly find himself with a fully developed stepsister!

This increased sexuality can be another reason for avoiding affection within the stepfamily. Stepparent and stepchild may feel increased attraction to each other and may handle that anxiety with pseudohostility (Goldstein, 1974). Schulman (1972) noted that many mothers are jealous of the relationship between their daughters and the girl's stepfathers.

The previous discussion should not lead stepfamilies to despair that affectional bonds are impossible. Duberman (1973) rated parent-child relationships in stepfamilies and rated 18 percent poor, 18 percent good, and 64 percent excellent.

6.   *Interrupted histories.* Visher and Visher (1979) noted that remarried families have difficulty recognizing the interrupted histories of the children. A child goes on a visitation with a noncustodial parent. Meanwhile, the family has gone on with its daily life. When the child returns, the family has difficulty remembering that the child does not know about events that have transpired since he or she left. Even when the family recognizes that the child needs to be reintegrated into the remarried family, the family members may be impatient and resentful of the need to habitually review events. When parent-child or stepparent-stepchild relationships are conflict filled, the interruptions are particularly destructive. For example, the child may leave on visitation in the middle of a fight. When the child returns several days later, the fight is forgotten. This type of pattern increases the likelihood of unresolved disagreement.

Absent family members need to be brought up to date on family history during absences.

7.   *Crowding.* Whiteside and Auerbach (1978) noted that remarriage often requires the juggling of bedrooms in order to find adequate space for everyone. The dining table may have less room and a family room may have too few chairs for television watching.

8.   *The problem of territory.* One major problem that stepfamilies have to solve is the problem of physical and role territories. With the blending to two families, space often becomes a problem. If two custodial parents marry, the need for space becomes critical as the family struggles to find room for all the children, often in a home designed to hold one set of children. Even when one parent is noncustodial, weekend visitations can be nightmares of space demands.

Family members who are asked to give up space for the remarriage are likely to be resentful. Children who remain in the same home are likely to resent step-siblings who move in and encroach on their territory. Families who are able to move to a new home at remarriage are likely to reduce feelings of encroachment for physical territory because both families are on an equal footing.

9.   *The problems of changing roles.* Roles change with the remarriage. The child who changes birth order is likely to be at risk for maladjustment after

a remarriage, since the demands and privileges for that child are likely to change radically. The youngest child who finds that there is now an even younger child in the family is likely to feel significant loss at no longer being the baby of the family. The oldest child, who is generally given the greatest amount of responsibility, may find that responsibility disappearing as an even older child moves in.

Clinicians should help remarried families facilitate the integration of children whose birth order changes with the blending of families. Particularly, families should try to maintain as many rights and privileges as possible for each child so that psychological loss is reduced. A child who has had some caretaking responsibilities for a parent (e.g., cooking, cleaning, or other chores) should be asked (unless there is reason to believe that only relief would occur with relinquishment) to continue those responsibilities at some level. The new stepparent may feel some irritation at not obtaining complete control over those roles, but integration of the children will be facilitated if the responsibilities are shared.

10.   *Discipline.* Hetherington, Cox, and Cox (1979) gave a vivid description of the degree to which preschool children, particularly boys, may receive inadequate structure when in mother custody. Parents may feel sorry for a child after a divorce and mistakenly believe that leniency will "make up for the loss." Parents often are lenient after a divorce because their own lives are chaotic and monitoring the children takes more energy than they have available at that time in their lives. Finally, there is evidence that when mothers make errors in parenting they tend to err in the direction of being too lenient. Remember the primary culturally defined role for mothers is nurturance, not discipline. When fathers make errors in parenting, they tend to make errors in the direction of being too strict. This dynamic is a set up for problems in the remarried family.

The lack of affectional bond and push for discipline may increase the likelihood of child abuse. Giles-Sims and Finkehor (1984) indicated that stepparents may be overrepresented among child abusers and proposed a variety of theoretical reasons to explain why.

The Shift From Single to Remarried Status

A common structure for remarried families is this: The mother has been too lenient and the children are out of control at some level. The mother has custody of the children and remarries a man who may or may not have children of his own, but does not have custody. The stepfather has standards of behavior control that lead him to be critical of the mother's parenting strategy. He makes the error of being too strict. He is rejected by the children as being unreasonable and depriving. He is rejected by the mother as being cruel and rejecting of the children. He abrogates his parenting role in anger and hurt.

The mother forms an unhealthy alliance with her biological children. The marriage continues in a cold war until the children are grown or the marriage ends in divorce.

This dynamic can be most unfortunate, particularly when the mother sees the remarriage as a rescue of children out of control and is therefore implicitly or explicitly asking the stepfather to immediately assume the discipline role. The stepfather who tries to move into a discipline role prior to the development of affection and trust will not be integrated into the family unit (Stern, 1978; Visher and Visher, 1979). Both the Stern and Visher and Visher studies have estimated that it takes between 1½ to 2 years for an affectional bond to develop. Stern also noted that the stepfather may sometimes need to take the child's side in the disagreement against the mother, provided it is an honest statement of beliefs.

The stepfather should not try to assume a discipline role until affectionate bonds have been developed. The stepparent who gives new rules to stepfamilies prior to the affectionate bonds developing will be hated. It does not help for the biological parent to introduce the new rules. Children are smart enough to know who caused the new rules to be developed. When the family is strongly in need of structure and limits, it may be appropriate for the divorced parent to consider family therapy to solve those problems prior to remarriage. Remarriage should not be used to solve discipline problems. The risk to the family is too great.

At the same time, the stepfather should not abrogate all parenting responsibilities. The development of an affectional bond and the assumption of disciplinary relationships should be a goal. Fast and Cain (1966) cautioned that the stepfather who behaves as a nonparent may not be helpful to a stepson who needs to have the intense mother-son bond weakened for adequate individuation.

The mother may be ambivalent about how much discipline she wants from the stepfather (Visher and Visher, 1978). The mother asks for discipline, but then is protective when the stepfather provides it. Stepfathers feel that they receive double messages in this situation.

Competition and Loyalty

As a part of the resentment and competition that a child may feel with a stepparent, the child may force the biological parent to choose between the stepparent and the child (Visher and Visher, 1978). A stepmother in this competitive bind will try to win the father over to her side. Visher and Visher noted that the stepmother usually succeeds. If the father sides with the children against the stepmother, the remarried family is in trouble. The marital pair needs to be the "architect" of the family with conscious executive control (Mills, 1984).

Johnson (1980) noted that if there is active dislike between the child and stepparent, the biological parent must assume most of the parenting responsibility including discipline. If the biological parent refuses to step in and assume this role, both the child and stepparent are likely to feel resentful. Mills (1984) suggested that requests for limits by the stepparent go through the biological parent. If the biological parent is to be temporarily absent, the biological parent should ask the stepparent to act like a babysitter with explicit rules to the children and stepparent.

Clinicians should monitor the relationship between the stepparent and stepchild. If the relationship is poor, the stepparent needs to withdraw from primary parenting responsibilities and let the biological parent assume most of that responsibility.

Lifestyle

Johnson (1980) felt that there are a variety of issues that have to be resolved when two families merge different life styles. Examples in this study included:

1. *Discipline.* This topic was discussed in the previous section.
2. *Eating habits.* Does the family eat together or separately? Can the TV be on during meals? Do the children have to eat everything on the plate, taste everything, or pick and choose?
3. *Division of Labor.* Who cooks, cleans, does the laundry, gets the car fixed, and balances the checkbook?
4. *Attitudes toward sex.* What is the appropriate level of dress around the house?
5. *Use of alcohol and drugs.* Is it acceptable for parents to use them? In front of the children? Are children allowed to use them?
6. *Attitudes toward obligations.* When are the bills paid? When do the children do their homework?
7. *Manners.* What behaviors are required to facilitate polite interaction?
8. *Household rules.* What are the rules for the phone? How are cleaning responsibilities allocated?
9. *Expression of hostility, aggression, or disagreement.* How much is accepted? Is expressing these feelings a sign of disrespect?

Surnames

When remarriage was a relatively uncommon event, children were sometimes self-conscious about the fact that their last name was different from that of their custodial biological parent and stepparent. Today, people have gotten so used to remarried families that school districts as matter of course will include last names of each family member on school records. Except in unusual geographic areas, it is the rare child who has to give a detailed explanation of why the last name is different from the parent. Indeed, last names have even become an issue for the remarried mother. The mother may choose to keep the previous, married last name, to resume the family-of-origin name, to assume a hyphenated name with the new spouse, or to assume the last name of the new spouse. Keeping the previous married name can sometimes create jealousy even when the reason is professional identity in the community, because the new spouse often sees the move as an indication of attachment to the previous relationship.

One-third of all adoptions in the United States are by stepparents. Particularly at the time of adoption, the question of names comes up. What shall the child be called? If abandonment by the noncustodial father has occurred, there may be little reason to keep the name of the father and the child should be encouraged to move on to more appropriate identities.

From a legal point of view, the question of who has the decision for name change of the child depends on the jurisdiction. Sometimes there is no state law to guide the judge's behavior. Different judges have different policies. Some judges believe that the last name is the property of the father and will not permit adoption or name change without the father's permission. Some judges believe that the custodial parent has the right of control of the name and that that person can make the decision without regard to the wishes of the noncustodial parent. While the choice of last names may seem trivial to some, it can have powerful symbolic meaning to everyone involved.

Families should be cautious about instigating name changes for the children after remarriage. If the child has continued contact with the noncustodial father, name changes can serve as a widening hurt that reduces contact with the father. Generally, a name change should not occur if there is any likelihood that the noncustodial father would withdraw and have less contact with the children after the change. Certainly, the meaning of the change should be discussed with children old enough to express an opinion. If total abandonment has occurred with a noncustodial father, the name change can encourage a child to loosen an identification with a rejecting parent and to turn to a stepparent for those needs.

Adolescents

It is clear from the research that the older the child, the more resistant the child is to the remarriage. Teenagers have particular difficulty with remarriage for a variety of reasons. First, there is often a loss of status with the remarriage with the adolescent losing responsibilities and freedoms that were previously available. Second, the stepfamily is asking the adolescent to bond at just the time in his or her life that she is trying to separate. Thus, the request from the stepfamily is opposite to the developmental needs. Third, it has been suggested that separating from two families may be more difficult than separating from one. Finally, the sexuality of remarriage and problems of mutual attraction discussed previously is more potent for adolescents. Indeed, hostility can serve as a defense against such unacceptable feelings.

The stepmother's role with adolescents may be particularly difficult (Walker, Rogers, and Messinger, 1977). She is more likely to spend time with the teenagers and may face more disciplinary problems.

In their struggle for autonomy, adolescents may use emotional blackmail for getting what they want. The threat of moving to the other family can lead an insecure stepfamily to give in to unreasonable demands (Whiteside and Auerbach, 1978).

While it may be reasonable for an adolescent to change residence, the clinician should encourage families to band together to prevent an adolescent from using the threat of moving from one family to the other as a ploy for manipulating reduced structure. Both families should be helped to provide a united front (if possible) concerning the conditions under which a change is appropriate.

Jones (1978) noted that the adolescent can also turn a younger sibling against the stepparent. The adolescent may view the affection that the younger sibling is likely to feel toward a stepparent as traitorous to the absent parent. The adolescent can place enormous pressures on the younger sibling.

Punishment of the adolescent for this provocative behavior can be particularly problematic. Each punishment is treated as an attack and the vicious cycle of provocation, punishment, and retaliation begins (Fast and Cain, 1966; Jones, 1978). Some teenagers bind the parents in such a way that no response is likely to reduce the level of anger. The provocation is so strong that parents cannot ignore it. Attempts to put the relationship on a more positive level is met with disdain. No attempts at giving are accepted. Attempts at ignoring the behavior escalate the battle. Family therapy may be helpful, but it may be difficult to get the teenager (particularly boys) to come in. Individual therapy is sometimes more palatable, but here too resistance can be high.

STEPFATHERS

A 9-year-old boy refused to eat off a plate if his stepfather was the one who had washed it. If the stepfather was the last one to take a bath, the boy would scour the tub again before using it. The message was clear, "you are poison to me." Fortunately, the stepfather was psychologically minded and, while annoyed, was willing to wait for affection to develop.

In spite of the foregoing example, stepfathers tend to have an easier time of the adjustment to the remarried family than do the stepmothers. Duberman (1973) has suggested that the stepmother may spend more time with the children since sex role stereotypes require that behavior. The expectation is greater on the stepmother to provide for affectional needs. Given the often abysmal parenting done by fathers, the family may expect less of him in terms of energy and affection. This lack of expectations may be why there are no stepfather myths.

The biological mother-stepfather combination is much more common than the biological father-stepmother family. Bowerman and Irish (1962) in a now dated study found that the mother-stepfather home ranged from 3.2 to 4.8 times more common than the father-stepmother combination.

Robinson's (1984) review of the research and clinical literature identified eight problem areas for stepfather: (1) uncertainty about the degree of authority that is acceptable; (2) how much affection to show to the children; (3) discipline; (4) money; (5) guilt over leaving biological children to another family; (6) loyalty; (7) sexual conflicts; and (8) conflicts over surnames.

In the Bowerman and Irish study, children in homes with a mother and stepfather had a slightly more distant relationship with their mother than children in intact families. They also had markedly lower levels of affection toward the stepfather. There was some evidence that marital discord may have offset the tendency toward greater bonding between mother and child. The same data demonstrated that marital discord was higher in the remarriage families than in the intact families.

Prior marital status of the stepfather predicts how well the stepfather gets along with the children (Duberman, 1973). If the stepfather was divorced, 54 percent had excellent relationships; and if never married, 85 percent of the stepfather-children relationships were excellent. According to Duberman (1973), the stepfathers feelings for the stepchildren were unrelated to the residence of his own children.

Perkins and Kahan (1979) examined the differences between 20 biological father families and 20 stepfather families. Family triads in which there was a husband, wife, and one child aged 12 to 15 were studied. If more than one child was in the designated age range, one was selected randomly. Typically, the custodial mothers in this study had been the initiators of the divorce and had three years between marriages. All of the children had maintained close contact with their natural fathers, seeing them on the average of twice a month. The fact that there was no abandonment suggests that the method of recruitment of participants did have some bias (although what the bias might be is unknown). These were college-educated, upper-middle class families. The question of whether the stepfather had other children was not included in the report, so the data are summarized here rather than in the following sections.

Adjustment scores and satisfaction scores were higher for biological father families than for stepfather families for all three family members. Biological fathers were seen as better and more powerful than the stepfathers. Perkin and Kahan (1979) felt that this result was counter to the prevailing belief that mothers tend to turn their children against the father after divorce.

Visher and Visher (1979) gave a useful discussion of the different constellations of stepparent as a function of who has children. It is clear that adjustment to remarriage is in part a function of the demands that different structures make. It is useful to describe each of these arrangements:

Stepfather with No Children and Custodial Mother with Children

According to Visher and Visher (1979), this dynamic produces the least difficulty for the stepfather. There is no guilt for having left behind other children.

There is difficulty with discipline because the stepfather has not had practice in doing it well and his expectations may be unrealistic. In addition, the stepfather may have difficulty understanding the children because of his lack of contact with children in general.

Since the stepfather does not have his own children who behave differently from the stepchildren, the conflict in values may not be as apparent (Visher and Visher, 1979). When the children are on visitation with the biological father, the stepfather and mother may have time to develop their own relationship. Bowerman and Irish (1962) found that the level of affection toward the stepfather is markedly lower than toward biological fathers.

Noncustodial Stepfather with Children and Custodial Mother with Children

The difficulty here is the guilt that the father may feel about giving the stepchildren more attention than his own children. These feelings may be increased by the jealously that the stepfather's own children may have. Sometimes, the father may feel so guilty about the abandonment of his own children that he is unable to establish relationships with his stepchildren (Visher and Visher, 1978).

Here, the stepfather does have some understanding of children. However, he may be relatively nonunderstanding about the different parenting styles of his new wife, because he is unaware of the slow negotiations that developed the discipline pattern for his own children.

However, Clingempeel, Ievoli, and Brand (1984) did not find that families of this type ($n = 16$) differed from families where the stepfather had no children ($n = 16$) on measures of stepparent behavior, child behavior, and family problem solving. Thus, it would seem that such noncustodial stepfathers, in general, do alright with the new family, in contrast to Visher and Visher's (1979) clinical experience.

Custodial Stepfather with Children and Custodial Stepmother with Children

Visher and Visher (1978) described this structure as being highly complex. There are many competing groups. Uninterrupted time between spouses may be limited and territory may be a constant problem.

Few families can afford a home large enough to handle such an increase in family size, particularly if there were more than one child in each family.

When two custodial parents marry, territory becomes particularly serious. Families are likely to do better if both families move in to a new home, rather than merge into an old home belonging to one of the families. Of course, such a move might not be financially feasible.

Does the Presence of Stepfathers Affect the Development of Stepsons?

In a study using an ego identity scale developed from Erikson's seven developmental stages, Oshman and Manosevitz (1976) found that mean scores for subjects in father-present families and stepfather families were higher than for the father-absent group on the scales of trust, industry, and total score. In no cases did the father present group differ from the stepfather group. In stepfather families, the reason for the absence of the biological father was not related to stepfather benefits. Oshman and Manosevitz felt that there were three reasons why stepfathers would produce benefits for stepsons: (1) The total amount of paternal deprivation may be reduced; (2) The quality of the relationship may be important; and (3) Mothers who remarry may have more adaptive psychological resources than mothers who do not remarry.

STEPMOTHERS

Numerous investigators have indicated that stepmothers have more trouble with adjustment to remarriage than do stepfathers (Kosinski, 1983). Duberman (1973) noted that the age of the child makes a difference (as it does for stepfathers) and that the adjustment is easier if the child is under 13. In Duberman's study, the age of the stepmother also made a difference. For stepmothers under 40, 70 percent had excellent relationships with their stepchildren. For stepmothers over 40, only 52 percent had good relationships. Education of the stepmother did not predict the quality of the relationship.

Prior marital status of the stepmother was a predictor. If the stepmother was previously divorced, 63 percent had an excellent relationship with stepchildren; if widowed, 76 percent had an excellent relationship; if never married before, only 55 percent had excellent relationships. Interestingly, stepfathers who were not married previously had the highest percentage of excellent relationship with stepchildren. For stepmothers, being widowed was the best predictor.

Duberman (1973) also found that a stepmother's feelings for her stepchildren were influenced by whether her own children resided with her. If they did, 67 percent had excellent relationship with the stepchildren. If the mothers had their own children reside elsewhere, only 44 percent had excellent relationships with the stepchildren. Perhaps guilt over not having her own children with her while caring for stepchildren led to these results. It is also possible that mothers who did not gain custody were somewhat poorer mothers as a group (and hence poorer stepmothers) than mothers who did obtain custody.

Stepmothers felt more anxiety, depression, and anger about the family than did biological mothers (Nadler, 1976). These stepmothers also had more interpersonal conflict in the family than did mothers not in a stepmother role.

Visher et al. (1979) felt that there are unrealistic expectations that drive the stepmother: the myth of instant affection, the need to have a new, close-knit, nuclear family, and the need to keep the family happy creates numerous problems.

Even an apparently simple problem, such as cooking meals can be a battleground. One six-year-old boy complained that his father's promise that the new stepmother was a terrific cook was not true. Reingold (1976) noted that it was axiomatic that children would not like their stepmother's cooking. Nothing tastes right. Even peanut butter and jelly sandwiches will invariably have too little peanut butter or too much jelly. Indeed, acceptance of a stepmother's cooking may be a sensitive thermostat of how the relationship is developing.

Draughon (1975) identified three models that a stepmother can use in the new family: (1) primary mother; (2) other mother; and (3) friend. Draughon felt that the primary mother role can be used only if the biological mother has abandoned the children and the mourning is complete. If there is a strong bond between the biological mother and the children, the friend could be the most useful model for a stepmother to follow.

The Wicked Stepmother Myth

Since a stepmother tends to spend more time with the children than a stepfather does, there is more opportunity for conflict (Duberman, 1975). Stepmothers are often quite sensitive about the "wicked stepmother" role and work hard to avoid it. As McGoldrick and Carter (1980) pointed out, the Brady Bunch myth is the alternative to the wicked stepmother myth. In the Brady Bunch myth (named after a television series of the same name), an integrated, loving family is obtained with minimal difficulty. In order to avoid the wicked stepmother and attain the Brady Brunch, the stepmother may then provide enormous affection on the stepchild to hasten bonding. According to Goldstein (1974), children will see this behavior as competing for the affection of the children with the biological mother. If the children allow themselves to accept the affection, they may feel disloyal to their biological mother. They will suppress feelings of tenderness to avoid this disloyalty. Walker, Rogers, and Messinger (1977) and Bernard (1971) felt that having a stepmother is particularly difficult for teenagers. The disciplinary problems are greater at this age and conflict with a stepmother may be greater than with the children's own mother.

The cruel or wicked stepmother is a ubiquitous figure in folklore around the world. The cruel stepmother myth exists in India, Hawaii, Chile, African countries, China as early as the year 863, Indonesia, Iceland, Apache, eleventh century Ireland, Greek mythology (Thomson, 1966) and, of course, in Cinderella in Europe and America. Given this overwhelming evidence for a common mythology, it is reasonable to assume that there is some cross-culture family dynamic that increases the likelihood of the stepmother having a difficult time. The wicked stepmother becomes a self-fulfilling prophecy: The stepmother tries to be very affectionate. The children reject the affection for what seem to them to be very good reasons. The stepmother feels rejected and withdraws. The children then find that they were right to be cautious and feel justified in their caution.

Stepmothers should particularly be encouraged to take time to develop affection and trust. There should be a requirement for cordial, polite interaction, but there should be explicit permission for stepchild and stepmother to not love one another.

Thomson (1966) said that the stepmother may be overeager to do a good job in parenting. This pressure can result in pushing too hard to teach the children to clean up or to improve their hair styles or dress. The children can interpret this as mean rather than helpful. Thomson also noted that the extended family is likely to be distrustful of the new stepmother. This distrust can set up that parent for failure. Another problem that stepmothers have is the wish to rescue the stepchildren in order to make up for the upset caused by the original divorce (Kosinski, 1983).

As for stepfathers, it is useful to follow the Visher et al. (1979) breakdown of types of stepmothers:

Custodial Mother with Children and Stepfather with No Children

This dynamic, which does not involve stepmothering, produces fewer conflicts than other arrangements. If there is visitation, the remarried mother has time to develop a relationship with the stepfather without the presence of other children.

Stepmother with No Children and Father with Children

Duberman (1973) indicated that stepmothers with no children of their own tend to have a more difficult time than either mothers, stepmothers with children of their own, fathers, or stepfathers. They have no experience to aid them in the tasks of being a stepmother. Bowerman et al. (1962) found that in these families the father is closer to his children than is the father in intact families. The affection level toward the stepmother tends to be quite low.

Jones (1978) noted that the stepmother-stepdaughter relationship was the most difficult. If the stepdaughter gets into a power play with the stepmother, it is important that the biological father communicate clearly and consistently the guidelines for appropriate behavior.

STEPSIBLING RELATIONSHIPS

Duberman (1973) found that 24 percent of stepsibling relationships were rated as excellent, 38 percent were rated as good, and 38 percent as poor. Cross-sex stepsiblings relationships seemed to be better than same-sexed stepsibling relationships. In those families in which there was a child as a product of the new marriage, 44 percent of the stepsibling relationship were excellent as compared to only 19 percent in which the remarriage was childless. Thus, with the birth of a new child, the stepfamily seems to do better. That information surprised this author, who expected that a new child in the stepfamily would leave the stepchildren feeling left out or in a competitive position. Duberman's (1975) later study confirmed the positive effect of a new baby in a remarried family. Seventy-eight percent rated the relationships between the stepparent and stepchildren as excellent, while 53 percent of families who had had no child together rated the stepparent-stepchild relationship as excellent. Perhaps, the new baby is a symbol to the stepchild that this relationship has developed a commitment. Certainly the birth provides a shared identity with the stepparent. "You are the parent of my half-brother."

The birth of new child will tend to increase integration within a remarriage family. Perhaps the children relax some with the expectation that this marriage is now more likely to last, given the commitment that a new child implies. In addition, the half-brother or half-sister is now a shared link with the stepparent. The stepmother is no longer just a stepmother any more, but the mother of a half-sibling.

Duberman (1975) also found that stepsiblings have a better relationship if their primary residence is in the same house. When the relationship is based on visitation times, the stepsiblings have less opportunity to interact and develop a relationship. In addition, visiting stepsiblings often are treated differently because they are not present as often, for example being exempt from household chores. Special preferences for visiting stepsiblings can create barriers that make it more difficult for relationships to develop.

To facilitate effective integration of stepsiblings, parents should review problems of preferential treatment.

CHILD ADJUSTMENT AND REMARRIAGE

The research is not clear concerning the effects of remarriage on adjustment of children. Langner and Michael (1963) found that children living in a remarriage family were less well adjusted than either children living in a family that had experienced bereavement or children living in a family of divorce without remarriage. A study by Walker et al. (1977) confirmed this finding.

Other studies have also looked at adjustment of stepchildren as a function of whether the previous marriage had ended in divorce or death. Duberman (1973) found that when the previous marriage had ended in death, the family was more likely to have good stepparent-stepchild relationships than when the previous marriage had ended in divorce.

Therapists should be particularly aware that remarriage after the death of a parent presents particular problems for the family as compared to remarriage after divorce. After divorce, the absent parent typically is the receipt of ambivalence or clear anger. After death, the absent parent tends to be idealized. Both the biological parent and children may have difficulties permitting another individual to break into that idealized image. Any affection toward the stepparent may feel like disloyalty after death.

Langner et al. (1963) also found that remarriage appeared to be most stressful for children of lower socioeconomic status. For middle class families, the older the child at the time of the remarriage, the more the stress. In a study of 89 remarried families out of a total of 1150 families, Bernard (1956) found no differences in adjustment level as a function of the type of family. As Walker et al. (1977) noted, the sample was based on college students and therefore biased toward a more affluent population which may have fewer problems with remarriage. Burchinal (1964) also found no effect of remarriage as compared to nuclear families.

Bowerman et al. (1962), in a large scale study of 2145 stepchildren, found that children residing with both biological parents felt rejection by either or both of them least often. In a stepparent home, the children were more likely to feel rejected by their biological parents and felt much more rejected by the stepparent. Boys were less likely to feel rejected than girls, regardless of the type of home. When asked whether they wished that they lived in a different home, children living with both biological parents together were least likely to wish for a different home, somewhat more likely if in a mother-stepfather home, and most likely to wish for a new home if in a father-stepmother home.

In the same study, Bowerman et al. found that if the previous home had been disrupted by divorce, the children were better adjusted toward the stepparent than when the previous loss was due to death of a parent. When orientation scores in terms of relationships between families members were evaluated, children of bereavement were both better and worse in their adjustment to stepparents than were children of divorce. The authors noted that the younger age and smaller number of children in the families of divorce may help to account for these differences. The intensity and content of the children's memories may also affect relationships to the stepparent.

In their review of the literature, Ganong and Coleman (1984) argued that more studies support stepchildren liking stepfamilies. In their own research (Coleman and Ganong, 1984), they compared intact, single parent and stepfamily structures and family integration with the effects on attitudes toward marriage and divorce for high school and college students. Children from mother-stepfather and mother-only families were more positive about divorce than were children from intact families. High family integration (as compared to low family integration), regardless of type of family, was related to positive attitudes toward marriage. Length of time in a stepfamily was unrelated to attitudes.

In the Clingempeel, Ievoli, and Brand (1984) study, girls in mother-stepfather families gave fewer positive verbal and more negative problem solving behaviors toward the stepfather than did boys, while the stepfather did not differ in the types of communications to stepsons and stepdaughters.

In another study looking at 16 stepmothers and 16 stepfathers (it is not clear whether the stepfathers were the same as in the previously described study) with three-and-a-half hour home interviews, self-report of stepchildren, stepparents, and biological parents indicated that stepparent-stepdaughter relations were more problematic than other relationships (Clingempeel, Brand, and Ievoli, 1984). Love was lower and detachment was higher for these relationships as compared to all the others.

In further research that looked at overall adjustment of children from stepfamilies as compared to children from nuclear families, Burchinal (1964) noted that child adjustment in personality and social adjustment was not different from a comparison group of children from intact families.

In a review of 38 empirical studies, Ganong and Coleman (1984) concluded that a majority of studies found no differences in self-image for children in nuclear or single parent families while one study found clear lower self-esteem in stepfamily children. Two studies found some lower self-concept as a function of remarriage when the children were adolescent or adults. For mental health, stepfathers seemed to mitigate the effects of father absence. The frequency of psychosomatic complaints were not different for stepchildren versus children from other types of families.

In our own research (Hodges and Bloom, 1984), we found that 18 months after the separation children living in divorced homes were better adjusted than children living in still separated homes. In turn, those children were better adjusted than children living in remarriage homes. Since our study was evaluating adjustment so close to the separation, the lower adjustment levels (as described by the parents) may have been due to the quick remarriage, rather than remarriage per se.

Wilson, Zurcher, MacAdams, and Curtis (1975) found that stepfamilies did not differ from nuclear families in crime, delinquency, child abuse, self-esteem, or independence. Adults who grew up in stepfamilies did obtain lower educational levels (perhaps due to lower income as a child), had lower family income as adults, and were less inclined to feel that most people were helpful and fair than were adults raised in a nuclear family. Adults raised in stepfamilies were also less satisfied with their own married life than adults raised in nuclear families.

Bernard (1971) also looked at the mental health of grown stepchildren. The subjects were university graduates. Bernard found no differences in the adjustment of adults who had grown up in stepfamilies as compared to adults from intact families in stability, self-sufficiency, or dominance.

Bohannan (1975) took a random sample of families and interviewed all members of 10 stepfamilies, 10 mother headed families, and 10 nuclear families. Stepchildren rated themselves as happy, successful, and achieving as children from nuclear families. The stepchildren also said they got along with their stepfathers as well as a child living with biological father. Bohannan also found that stepfathers were more negative about the stepchildren, rating them as less happy than the mothers and stepchildren rated themselves.

Given the information that remarriage may present problems to stepchild that may lead to maladjustment, it is particularly difficult to untangle why a problem may exist. As noted earlier in this chapter, a couple may identify a child as a problem to avoid working on the troubled marriage. The remarriage may present particular problems of adjustment to the child. However, just because a child has problems and lives in a remarried family does not mean a cause and effect relationship. As in the discussion on divorce and adjustment (see Chapters 2 and 3), it should not be assumed that all problems flow from remarriage.

The clinician needs to help families untangle stepfamily problems from normal developmental problems (Nichols, 1980). Recognizing that a problem is typical of adolescents and not "caused" by the remarriage may lead to a more relaxed level of problem solving.

Children in remarriage tend to be better adjusted to their biological parents than to their stepparents. They are also better adjusted to their stepfathers than their stepmothers.

DEATH OF A DIVORCED PARENT AND STEPFAMILIES

When a divorced parent dies, the children have more difficulty with the grieving process. The children usually recognize the ambivalence or clear anger of the remaining parent and often do not feel that that parent is available to aid in the mourning process. Particularly when it is the custodial parent that dies, the stepfamily comes under increased pressure. With the remarriage of the remaining parent, the child is particularly likely to see that parent as having changed allegiances (as indeed that parent has), and has difficulty talking to the parent about the grieving.

For the stepmother or stepfather who is in the family with death of the custodial parent, a problem of particular poignancy develops. Typically, the noncustodial parent obtains guardianship of the children with the death of the biological custodial parent. The stepparent who was quite comfortable (or more likely, somewhat comfortable) with the visitation, suddenly finds himself or herself with custody and full time parenting.

When a divorced parent dies, the need for therapy for the children may be quite high. Since the remaining parent is often seen as unavailable for mourning, a neutral person can facilitate that process. When the parent who died was custodial and the remaining parent has remarried, the stepparent may need support around the stress of obtaining full custody when that arrangement was not the original understanding.

Several stepparents in this situation show impressive forebearance for a situation that they did not count on. This author has seen many families in this situation. This suggests that this family dynamic is clearly at risk for problems. In one such family, the mother's death raised several issues. The father needed help in how to facilitate mourning for the son. The family needed help in integrating the son into a family with stepmother and stepsister. The father had created resentment in the family by being so concerned about the son's loss that he became quite permissive with the son while maintaining strict rules for the stepdaughter. The father was helped to recognize that permissiveness was not in the son's best interests. Indeed, some of the behavior problems that the son had were not in response to the mother's death and incomplete mourning, but to inadequate structure in the home. Once the rules were made uniform in the family, resentment was reduced, and the son became better behaved.

In another case, the boy in the family had experienced a series of deaths in the family including the custodial mother and had to be helped with mourning and fear of death itself. A chronic depression is also a not uncommon outcome of this family dynamic.

SHOULD THE CHILD PARTICIPATE IN THE DECISION TO REMARRY?

Reingold (1976) argued convincingly that it is a mistake to let the children decide as to whether a parent should remarry. In fact, this is similar to asking a child which parent to live with. Children often make such decisions without the perspective that permits them to make a wise choice. Since it may take one to two years for affectional bonds to develop, the parent is asking the child to make that decision without the opportunity to know whether affection is going to be possible.

In addition, the child who decides out of self-interest to recommend against remarriage may later feel guilt and remorse for denying the parent the opportunity for happiness. While the opinions about the potential stepparent should be taken into account, under no circumstances should it be the choice of the child. Parents should not abrogate their responsibility for making their own decisions and should avoid making the child a pseudoparent.

WHEN SHOULD REMARRIAGE OCCUR?

There is evidence to suggest that remarriage works best in terms of child adjustment if it occurs between two and four years after the breakup of the previous marriage. If the remarriage is too soon, the children are not given an opportunity to grieve the loss of the previous relationship. If remarriage occurs much later, habits of interaction become more difficult to break. The child has become used to the attention and roles assigned and resents to a greater degree the intrusion of the stepparent.

RELATIONSHIPS WITH STEPGRANDPARENTS

One problem that can arise in remarried families is the relationship of grandparents to their biological grandchildren as compared to step grandchildren. It is only natural for grandparents to have a greater bond with a biological grandchild than a steprelationship because there has been more time and contact (often from birth) to develop bonding and the biological relationship may lead to stronger identification. Particularly in families with both stepchildren and biological children, differential treatment (for example on birthdays and holidays) of the biological grandchild can unintentionally created feelings of rejection and abandonment by the stepchild.

If the grandparent is willing, it may be helpful for family unity and reduction of territorial feelings, to request that the grandparent provide similar gifts and time to biological and stepgrandchildren.

There are several bibliographies on stepfamilies for those who wish to systematically review the literature (Bergquist, 1984; Miller and Soper, 1982; Walker, Brown, Crohn, Rodstein, Zeisel, and Sager, 1979). The best overview of working with remarried families is Visher and Visher (1979).

THE PREDICTION OF DIFFICULTIES FOR REMARRIED FAMILIES

McGoldrick and Carter (1980) proposed nine warning signs for troubles for remarried families:

1. A wide discrepancy between family life cycle stages for the two families. When one parent has older children and the other either no children or very young children, the discrepancy will create new problems of adjustment. One parent will have to recycle over a previously accomplished stage, sometimes with strong reluctance.
2. Denial of prior loss or quick remarriage.
3. Failure to resolve the intense relationship issues of the first family.
4. Expectations that remarriage will be easily accepted by the children.
5. Inability to give up the ideal of the intact first family.
6. Forcing primary loyalty to the new family.
7. Exclusion of other parent or grandparents.
8. Denial of differences of a remarried family.
9. Shift in custody of children at time of remarriage.

THE PREDICTION OF SUCCESS IN REMARRIAGE

With the previous discussion, it is possible to be so discouraged about the ability of remarriage families to survive as to recommend against remarriage in any case where there are children, particularly older children. While the remarried family does have vulnerabilities that are unique to that structure, by no means are all remarrried families doomed. Numerous adults report strong feelings of affection toward stepparents and report parent-stepparent marriages that are strong and loving. There is also some research evidence to support the belief that stepfamilies can do very well.

Glenn and Weaver (1977), using survey data on the self-report of marital happiness of second married and first married couples, found no substantial differences. They concluded that if the second marriage does not end quickly, those marriages are probably almost as successful as first marriages.

Bernard (1971) looked at census data, case material, and questionnaires filled out by close acquaintances of 2009 remarried families. Although there were some people who went through serial marriages, one right after another, most people in the study were as successful in remarriages as first marriages. Bernard noted that in remarriages the strengths include greater motivation to resolve marital difficulties, age, maturity, and a new environmental situation. The variables that were associated with remarriage success were:

1. The partners were over 20 years of age in the first marriage.
2. Good first marriages.

3. College-level education of the spouses.
4. Either no children in the first marriage or wife having sole custody of her children.
5. Both sets of parents favorable to the remarriage.
6. The community favorable to the wife's remarriage.
7. An optimal time lapse between marriages.

Duberman (1973, 1975) found that the stronger the marital bond, the better the reintegration of the new family. These studies replicated Bernard's (1971) finding that a higher education level of the husband predicted a better marital relationship. Unlike Bernard, Duberman did not find place of residence of the stepchildren to predict the quality of the martial relationship. As noted by Sager, Steer, Brown, Crohn, Rodstein, and Walker (1980) in their review of the literature, the results of both the Bernard and Duberman's studies must be taken with caution. Bernard did not have a random sample and totally relied on informants for data. Duberman had a random sample but had only 88 couples that were primarily middle and upper middle class.

DEVELOPMENT IN STEPFAMILIES

Papernow's (1984) study looked at nine stepfamilies over time and concluded that the stepfamily experience involved seven stages of development:

1. *Fantasy.* Papernow suggested that mental health professional approach the stepfamily fantasies with gentleness and empathy. Fantasies included rescuing the children, healing the broken family, instant love and sharing the load. The child fantasy tended to be that if the stepparent (all stepfathers in this study) was ignored, he would go away.
2. *Assimilation.* The stepparent tries to enter the family, but cannot. The child rejects the affection of the stepparent.
3. *Awareness.* The stepparent becomes clear about a need for change. It is difficult for most biological and stepparents to understand each other's experience.

Restructuring begins with stage 4.

4. *Mobilization: Airing differences.* The stepparent begins to ask for changes. There can be support or opposition by the biological parent.
5. *Action: Going into business together.* Couples work together to solve differences, using old patterns and new rituals.

Then solidifying the new family begins.

6. *Contact: Intimacy in steprelations.* Steprelations now work on their relationship including names, honesty and discussion of feelings.
7. *Resolution: Holding on and letting go.* The fact of the steprelationship becomes background. Letting go of the children is the norm. The stepparent is an "intimate outsider."

COHABITING PSEUDO-STEPPARENTS

With the sharp increase in cohabiting relationships in the United States over the last decade more and more children are being exposed to a live-in relationship between one of their parents and a significant other. Some of these relationships represent serial monogamy, but only a series of short-term relationships. Children who attach to such "parenting" figures tend to give up trying to attach because the repeated sense of loss is too painful.

Relatively stable, enduring relationships in which the cohabiting partner is in a relationship similar to marriage are more common. However, such relationships lack the community sanctions for validity.

If the role of the stepparent is vague and ill-defined, the role of the cohabiting pseudo-stepparent is even more so. Since the relationship lacks community legitimacy, it is not unusual for the "stepparent" (there is no appropriate word to describe the role, perhaps, "nonstepparent" would do) to be significantly snubbed.

In one family, the father had joint custody and the father's woman partner played a significant role in child care, including feeding and babysitting the 3, 4 and 6 year-old children. While the woman partner became quite attached to the chldren, the community gave no legitimacy to her role. Other parents expressed disapproval when she showed up at school functions and snubbed her socially. She had to work significantly to define what kind of parenting role was appropriate and the reactions of her decision on the two biological parents.

In communities in which cohabiting is common, the cohabiting pseudo-parent may have an easier time. In most communities, however, the problems of the stepparents are compounded by the lack of definition of this new role.

The cohabiting pseudo-stepparent is likely to need significant help in defining that role. While many of the issues around parenting are the same as for stepparents, the lack of legitimacy may require more negotiations within the family to clarify and negotiate expectations. Family oriented therapy is likely to be helpful in this process.

SUMMARY

Clinicians working with families of divorce are often working with remarried families. Knowledge of development, potential problems in the area of affection, discipline, territory, loyalties, interrupted history, and the typical problems of each family member can facilitate effective interventions.

CHAPTER 10

School-Based Interventions and Other Group Approaches

Schools are a particularly useful arena for intervention. Such interventions are group oriented. This chapter reviews those strategies and other group based approaches.

SCHOOL-BASED INTERVENTIONS

Because of the concern that marital disruption and divorce is a significant stressor in the lives of so many children and because of the evidence that stress can result in poorer school performance (although there is some disagreement as to how much an academic problem is created; see Chapters 2, 3, and 8), school districts around the country have targeted the child of divorce for special interventions. Schools are a natural target for primary prevention. All children are available. Disruption is relatively easy to diagnose and intervention is relatively inexpensive to provide.

This section focuses on group therapy and instructional approaches to interventions in the schools. When the counselor provides individual psychotherapy, the strategies are covered in Chapter 12.

Interventions are generally broken down into age groups in order to take into account the different cognitive abilities of the children. A compromise with efficiency of presentation has led to grouping children in the following groups:

1. Preschool children (no programs discovered in the literature).
2. Early elementary school, grades 1–3.
3. Late elementary school, grades 4–6.
4. Early junior high school, grades 7–8.
5. High school, grades 9–12 (may be broken up into 9–10 and 11–12).

Preplanning for school based programs require covering some basic issues regardless of the age of the children:

Administrative Support

Any school-based intervention begins with the administration and staff of the school in which the intervention is to be based. It has been my experience that teachers already have a heightened concern for children of divorce. However, the feelings of both the administration and the teaching staff will help determine whether support or problems will be encountered as the program develops. Even if the school feels that there is a need and is willing to devote some resources to providing a program, there are likely to be several questions that need to be resolved prior to offering the program.

Getting Parental Permission

Is parental permission required for the child to participate? While school districts vary in policy for parental permission, particularly when counselors in the school are providing the service during normal school hours, permission should be obtained, however even if it is not legally required. For high school students, the ability to make a decision about participation in services without parental permission may be more appropriate, again depending on school policy. School districts are enormously vulnerable to angry parents and any upset from parents is likely to hurt the program.

Parents may be reluctant to provide permission because of concern that the child will reveal family secrets. Since no child is required to talk in the group and the focus of many of the groups is educational, it is often possible to reassure the parent that the purpose of the groups is to help the child think about the various aspects of the divorce experience, to explore common feelings, and to solve day-to-day problems. The group does not focus on highly personal issues. For the programs based on topic-oriented units, describing some of the units may reduce the parent's anxiety about allowing the child to participate. For example, parents may be informed that the program includes units on building self-esteem, understanding feelings about the self, understanding other people's feelings, and general problem solving that sounds less "loaded" than "why did your parents get a divorce?"

Some parents are reluctant to have their child participate because of concern that participation is an admission that the divorce was harmful to the child. Information sheets that depathologize the child are likely to be helpful. Parents who feel grievously harmed by the divorce and who want to prove that it was harmful to the child will often be eager to have their children participate.

When co-leading junior high school groups with school guidance counselors this author found that the level of problems was often significantly higher than for the children being seen in private practice. Upon reflection, this difference was easy to explain why. Parents who show sufficient concern to take their children to a therapist are already demonstrating several resources, that is, sufficient sensitivity to potential or actual problems that the child is having, financial availability, and the willingness to invest time and energy in finding and taking the child to a therapist. Parents are often willing to have a child participate in school programs because they involve no time, energy, or money. Therefore, children with less support than those who end up in private therapy may participate in school-based programs.

Timing

The issue of when the intervention will be provided raises questions: Will it be during school hours or before or after school? If the program is provided during school hours, how will the disruption to the school time be handled? Some schools have used a nonacademic activity time for the groups, such as lunch hour (where the students have brought their own lunches), and others have rotated the hour of the school day in which the groups meet so that the amount of time that the child misses of a particular academic activity is minimized. If the time is rotated, the child should not miss more than two class at a particular time of day for the entire program, which for most children is not likely to be a serious problem.

For school hour programs, many of the participants feel special getting out of class to come to the program. In fact, the opportunity to miss class was so powerful a special consideration, that perhaps that fact alone could account for placebo effects. Indeed, this author recently served on a dissertation committee in which the faculty requested that a study of the effectiveness of an elementary school-based intervention program include a control group consisting of children getting out of class for some other special activity. The control set-up (a very expensive control) was a program of career planning. Children either went to the divorce group or the career planning group. With this elimination of a powerful attention placebo, there were no benefits found in behavior for the children who participated. (Boren, 1982).

Before school or after-hour group programs will lose some of the special treatment for the children (an advantage if the response of the children is to feel stigmatized), but poses other problems. In schools in which a significant number of children arrive by school bus, extracurricular times are often impossible. In addition, if the parent has to provide transportation, defensive parents and those who work (a likely occurrence particularly in families of divorce) will be unwilling or unable to either bring the child in early or pick the child up after school.

If the teaching staff is willing to tolerate the disruption to the teaching schedule, groups provided during school time will increase the likelihood of children most needing the group participating.

There may be some concerns from the teaching staff about the effect of missing class, especially since some of the participating children are already having academic problems. The classroom teacher's flexibility around test times may result in the child either taking a make-up test or missing a group meeting. It does not help the child of divorce to antagonize the classroom teacher for participation in the program.

Classroom Teacher Involvement

Should the classroom teacher be involved in identifying the children who should be invited to participate? This question can best be answered by the teaching staff. Do they want to participate? Are they willing to participate in a program evaluation? What classroom problems concern them the most? Would they like a report back to the teaching staff about how well the groups work? That latter question raises the issue of confidentiality and how it will be handled in the school. It is this author's belief that confidentiality of the individual children should be protected. In other words, individual feedback about content of discussions should be avoided.

Schools often feel that any information about a child should be shared with all the staff. In a therapeutic situation, the question of limits of confidentiality should be made clear. If the teachers are going to be given feedback about individual children, parents and children should be informed at the time that informed consent is being acquired. Trust is basic to the therapeutic process, however, and school-based groups are more effective if the children are informed (truthfully) that all information is kept within the group. It may be useful to indicate that information about abuse cannot be kept a secret and should not be. It is also recommended that parents be told that individual feedback about what that parent's child discussed will not be available.

Parent Involvement

Certainly, if parents are showing enough concern to be willing to come into the school to discuss what the groups will do and what the issues of divorce are for children, the intervention is likely to be more powerful if pre- and post-treatment meetings are held. Parents who want help understanding their children, want suggestions about childrearing strategies and want to support their children getting help, are likely to support the groups.

Requirement of parent participation will increase the impact on those children who participate, but will decrease the number of children who are in the greatest need.

Sonnenshein-Schneider and Baird (1980) recommended obtaining basic information from parents of elementary age children. This information builds a communication channel with the parents and provides a realistic assessment of the child's situation. As the study noted, children can introduce fantasy as reality and the counselor can help the child separate these issues out.

How Many Therapists?

If possible, it is extremely helpful to have two therapists, rather than one, particularly if one is male and one is female. While having two therapists is expensive, it permits one therapist to focus on the child speaking and the other to watch for reactions among the other children. This author has been able to draw out relatively quiet children by noting that they seemed to be having a reaction to what another child was saying. If the group has trouble settling down, control of the group is easier if the two therapists sit apart. In addition, modeling of adults interacting without conflict and role playing for the adults around issues of the divorce become possible with two leaders.

Identifying Potential Participants

Drake (1981) suggested several criteria for identifying which children need additional help because they are at risk. The first criterion is identifying whether the child's adjustment problems are unusual: Are the problems typical reactions for a child of that age and gender? Are they reactions expected that will help the child recover his or her natural coping skills? The second criterion is length of time for crisis resolution: Has the child manifested the problems for more than one or two years? The third criterion is degree of problem, particularly depression and explosiveness. Drake noted that comments about self-harming behaviors should be given particularly notice. Additional assessments that follow Kelly and Wallerstein's (1976) model included obtaining a brief history indicating the child's understanding of the divorce and the available support systems.

ELEMENTARY SCHOOL INTERVENTIONS

Early Elementary School Interventions

Generally, it is recommended to have a somewhat smaller group for early elementary age children since the need for attention may be high, the need for structure may be greater, and the ability to wait for attention may be less. Groups of six or seven may be quite adequate. Sonnenshein-Schneider et al. (1980) recommended that sessions be limited to 15 or 20 minutes for younger primary groups.

Children need to have group rules explained. The concept of confidentiality should be explained. Elementary school age children are low on empathy for each other. The cruelty of teasing at this age can be extraordinary. There must be strong control by the leader or leaders to prevent the teasing that is common among children in primary school (and up to 15 years of age).

Keeping secrets must be emphasized. The leaders must explain rules to prevent teasing and attacking statements and exert control over the group to stop such statements should they occur.

Sonnenshein-Schneider and Baird (1980) noted that the competition for attention by telling war stories is a common part of the egocentrism of this age. Almost every child told and retold at least one story that was traumatic for them. The child expects the story to have the same shock value for all the other children. With the retelling, the story begins to lose its tragic power. The child gets the message that the event was not that bad and was survivable.

Early elementary school programs often focus initially on interventions that are not specific to divorce. Group building techniques, affective training, and general problem solving may all precede any discussion of divorce, per se. Later, the program may involve divorce-specific discussions.

Examples for group building include suggestions by Joan Levine and Norman Dewhurst of a Mental Health Team in the Cherry Creek School District in Colorado:

1. *The name game.* Add something to your name that says something about yourself. Then repeat what the previous person said about himself or herself.
2. *Car wash.* Form two lines. Each child goes down a line and looks at a person and says something positive (a potentially difficult exercise). The child being complimented can only say, "thank you."

More divorce specific exercises include:

1. *Reverse fantasies.* Draw four pictures: a happy time with your family; a sad time with your family; what would you like to happen now; what would you like to happen in two years. The pictures are used for discussion.
2. *Group murals.* Every child draws something important happening in their family on a large sheet of paper.
3. *Draw a family tree.*
4. *Children sit in a circle.* The therapist gives a topic and each child draws a part of the picture and passes it on. For example children may draw a composite picture of the day the family split up.
5. *Bibliotherapy.* Read from books that talk about children going through divorce.
6. *Discuss pictures relevant to divorce.*

To help children with understanding their family situation in a way consistent with their concrete operational thinking, Sonnenshein-Schneider and Baird (1980) suggested drawing family pictures with a separate picture of the absent parent. They also suggested brainstorming in conjunction with role playing and role rehearsal. When a group member expresses a problem, the group brainstorms possible solutions. When a possible solution is found, the children role play and rehearse the act of asking for what they want. Early brainstorming may have a funny and wild feeling that is part of the group cohesion. Wild solutions decline and the counselor can direct the discussion to form functional solutions.

Sonnensthein-Schneider and Baird also used storybooks, slide-tape programs, and movies. Puppets were employed to act out feelings and situations.

For younger elementary school children, Drake (1981) suggested play around family changes, using "dress-up" (i.e., adult-like clothes), doll houses and furniture, and household items that can provide props for common household scenes. Drake suggested an inflated plastic clown for punching, toy percussion musical instruments, and banging tools such as hammers as opportunities for sublimating aggression. Sports can also provide such an outlet. Creative opportunities, such as using clay, cutting and pasting, or finger painting, can also be used as outlets for feelings. These suggestions are similar to those that would be used by a play therapist in an individual setting, but clearly can be used in the school setting, either by a counselor in individual or group therapy or by the classroom teacher.

Drake also focused on helping the young child communicate feelings, particularly to provide an opportunity to release depression. Drake suggested a list of 48 feelings that a person might feel when parents separate or divorce that might be read to the child. The children could then be asked to choose the ones that they feel. Other feeling-eliciting activities included drawing pictures of feelings, teaching empathic assertion (Kessler and Bostwick, 1977), and role playing.

For children experiencing shame associated with the separation and divorce, Drake suggested pairing that child with a child who is openly accepting of the parent's divorce. Group work for children of divorce can also help such a child accept the divorce without shame.

Many of the Drake's suggestions are not differentiated for the younger elementary school children and can clearly be used for the later elementary school children as well.

Later Elementary School Interventions

It is easier to provide interventions for fourth, fifth, and sixth grade children because their higher verbal skills makes it easier for them to talk about the divorce. They are also significantly less egocentric than younger children and can recognize both similarities and differences with their experiences and the experiences of another child in the group. The children's attention span is significantly longer so that discussion can go for longer periods of time, perhaps 30 minutes to 45 minutes rather than 20 minutes. Groups can be slightly larger (seven to ten) since children are more likely to have some self control. Activities that have been suggested for this age include:*

1. Say three things about yourself. Make one of them false. Have the group guess which one. (This exercise is particularly good since it taps the game playing preference of this age group).
2. Role playing the courtroom divorce scene. Children who were there often have strong memories of the event and children who were not have strong fantasies. Reenactment can help the child think about and work through the feelings about the divorce.
3. Write a book about the divorce. One chapter per session is written. The therapist(s) suggests the topic. Topics might include: telling the children about the divorce; parent's dating; family secrets; family spying; remarriage; money; or visitation.

   A variation on this approach includes giving advice to other children going through divorce or giving advice to parents on how to help children.
4. Use of sentence stems to encourage verbalization of feelings. Stems might include statements like, "My mother gets angry at me when . . . " or "I get sad about. . . . " Each child writes their answers in private. The answers may be kept private if the child wishes. However, after the writing is finished the therapist brings up a stem and invites any child who wishes to read theirs aloud. Putting it in writing both reduces anxiety about saying it out loud and increases the chances that the child can discuss the issue raised.
5. Role playing. The therapists (particularly if male and female) role play a divorcing couple. The children write the script for the problem. The therapists can role play appropriate problem solving or have the children suggest solutions to the problem that the parent is struggling with.

Cantor's Groups

Cantor's (1977, 1979) program for children in third through sixth grades included many of the topics discussed below for secondary school students, including: eavesdropping, spying, being used by a parent, not liking to have to choose between parents, loss of a parent, relationships with stepparents, visitation, and court battles.

Cantor also used parts of the book, *The Boys and Girls Book About Di-*

---

*Suggestions 1 through 5 are suggested by Joan Levine and Norman Dewhurst.

vorce (Gardner, 1970) as a basis for stimulating discussion. One group wrote a play containing scenes of fighting, separating, going to court, and developing new relationships. The parents were contacted by questionnaire at the end of the groups to answer the following questions.

1.   Has your child talked to you about the groups? If yes, what was said?
2.   Has his or her behavior changed in any way?
3.   Has he or she discussed any issues or questions pertaining to the divorce that had not come up before?
4.   How did you, as a parent, feel about the group?

Generally, parents indicated that the children had not discussed the group with them; behavior changes were subtle; and parents liked the group concept and wanted it to continue. Children responded to the group by moving from feeling ashamed about being from a family of divorce to one of openness and a desire to share the experience.

Wilkinson and Bleck's Groups

Wilkinson and Bleck's (1977) children's divorce groups included the following exercises:

1.   Naming each other.
2.   Keeping secrets.
3.   An animal like you. Draw a picture of one animal that you feel is most like you.
4.   Pleasant and unpleasant feeling words. List as many feeling words as we can think of. Two lists are made, one for pleasant feelings and one for unpleasant feelings.
5.   Filmstrip entitled "Understanding Changes in the Family: Not Together Any More" (Guidance Associates, 1973).
6.   Personal shield. Draw a shield with four separate parts. In one part, draw a picture about a good time you had with your family. In another, draw a picture about an unpleasant time you had with your family. Draw a picture that shows why you think your parents got a divorce. Draw a picture of something you would like to see happen to your family next year.
7.   Role playing the problems of divorce. List as many problems of divorce as possible, pick the two or three most important by group vote and role play them. Then discuss the solutions.
8.   Puppet plays. Use puppets to dramatize the problems. One member is the director of the play. The counselor leads a group discussion of

the feelings, behaviors, and consequences of the characters. They then discuss alternate ways to solve the problems.

9.   Positive aspects of divorce. Cut out pictures in magazines that might stand for pleasant things that happened as a result of the divorce or draw pictures. Share the experiences.

10.   Positive feedback. Each person sit in a chair and the rest of the group says positive things to them.

11.   Each person related what they learned in the group.

The Helping Children of Divorce Groups

Green (1978) developed the HELPING Children of Divorce program. HELP-ING is an acronym for Health, nonjudgmental Environment, becoming aware of the Learning process, establishing Positive relationships, cultivating mental Images for happy lives, examining fundamental values and beliefs, and developing new behaviors. For each of these areas Green includes basic treatment strategies to help children.

The program is based on eight sessions, with each session having three components: (1) an icebreaker; (2) a stimulus activity; and (3) a closing time. A summary of the eight sessions are:

1.   *Introduction and getting to know you.* Icebreaker: Name tags with name, favorite thing, favorite TV show and star, three favorite foods, favorite color, and one word that describes him or her. After pairing children in dyads to discuss name tags, each dyad introduces themselves to the group.

Stimulus activity: Discussion of goals for the group.

Closing: Discusses privacy, confidentiality, rules for discussion, and future sessions. Each child is given a copy of *The Boys and Girls Book about Divorce* (Gardner, 1970) and is asked to read as much as they can by next session. Healthful refreshments are served. Then the children draw numbers indicating the session at which they will have time to share something of importance, such as a favorite game or special story, with the group.

2.   *Divorce and feelings.* Icebreaker: Either-or forced choice, a value clarifications exercise (Simon, Howe, and Kirschenbaum, 1972).

a.   *Stimulus activity.* Continued discussion about the book. Children pick out sections of interest to them. The group works on a poster that depicts feelings that come with divorce. The children then complete a personal set of "feeling gauges" indicating the intensity of several divorce-related feelings.

b.   *Closing.* Homework is finishing reading the book. The children write down feelings that they have during week.

3.   *Divorce and what to do about it.* Icebreaker: Each child divides a paper into four spaces and draws or writes something that they like to do alone, with

a friend/friends, with the family, and with one parent. Each child then shares the answers with the group.

a. *Stimulus activity.* Finishes the book. Brainstorm problems that children see about divorce and possible solutions.

b. *Closing homework.* Have children tell themselves and another person how they feel once each day for the next week.

4. *Talking about divorce.* Icebreaker: Self-portrait. Provide mirror.

a. *Stimulus activity.* Acting, feeling, choosing game (Keat, 1978). This is a board and card game designed to facilitate discussion about feelings through role playing, discussion, and making choices.

b. *Closing homework.* Have each child develop three cards of their own for the game.

5. *More about divorce.* Icebreaker: On the back of the self-portraits, have the children list positive, rational statements describing themselves. Have other children add to each child's list.

a. *Stimulus activity.* Continue game with greater focus on problem solving. Use the cards the children made. Add to group poster.

b. *Closing homework.* Increase list of positive self-statements. Tell someone what they like about that person once each day.

6. *Other children and divorce.* Icebreaker: Each child draws a family portrait, label the members, and discuss it.

a. *Stimulus activity.* Watch the filmstrip, "Understanding changes in the family: Not together any more" (Guidance Associates, 1973). Divide into dyads and role play the child and the child's friend in the film. Practice talking and listening about divorce, feelings, problems, and possible solutions. If videotaping is available, videotape the sessions and play back for the group.

b. *Closing homework.* Have each child talk to a close friend about the divorce and report back to the group about the experience.

7. *Divorce hits home.* Icebreaker: Each child writes positive, rational statements about the family on the back of the family portrait. Share.

a. *Stimulus activity.* Watch the television program, "Breakup" (National Instructional Television Center, 1973). Reinforce discussion with large poster boards.

b. *Closing homework.* Talk to one family member about the divorce and report back about the experience.

8. *Coming together.* Icebreaker: Each child is given a design (a star with a central circle) and asked to fill the spaces with pictures, words, or symbols. The center of the design is self-image and the outside points are learning,

friends, family, feelings, a positive thought kept all the time, a behavior that is enjoyable or has gotten under control.

    a. *Stimulus activity.* Round robin sentence stems involving learning, feeling, and self-description, that are both general and divorce related.

    b. Closing. Party.

Bowker's Groups

Bowker (1982) developed an intervention program in which elementary school children created and produced a sound filmstrip that told the story of separation and divorce from the child's point of view. Two groups of fifth grade children met weekly for one academic year to discuss issues and feelings about the family break-up. Unlike most groups previously described above, these groups were like-sexed group. Each child was interviewed individually, had the group explained, and invited to participate. Bibliotherapy was used more heavily than in other described programs, including *How Does It Feel When Your Parents Are Divorced?* (Berger, 1977) and *What's Going to Happen to Me? When Parents Separate or Divorce* (LeShan, 1978). They then developed a story line and prepared graphics. They worked on crayon and ink drawings to depict feelings. Magazines created word and picture collages. They selected background music, wrote dialogue, and taped the story. Classrooms of children who did not participate were invited to see the film and enter into discussion. A special viewing for parents was made available.

Hammond's Workbook

Hammond (1981a, 1981c) developed a workbook for children of divorce that provides structured activities for counselors working with groups of children of divorce. As with other approaches, warm-up activities and group rules were provided. Suggested activities included:

1. Getting to know others. Using cards to indicate name, favorite animal, and where they would like to go for a vacation.
2. Use of a filmstrip (the same as the one suggested by Wilkinson and Bleck). (1977).
3. Four pictures of families of divorce to be used to stimulate discussion about divorce.
4. House drawing. (also presented in Hammond, 1981b).
5. Value clarification related to divorce responding to 13 value-ladden statements about divorce (also in Hammond, 1981 b).
6. Family coat of arms. Similar to Wilkinson and Bleck's (1977) personal shield but provide a shield and add three words to describe the family.

7. Discussion of the Book *My Dad Lives in a Downtown Hotel* (Mann, 1973). This book is appropriate for fourth grade reading level. The manual provides discussion question for the group process. This activity covers two sessions.

8. Role play. Six role playing situations that are acted out and discussed.

9. The perfect marriage. Discussion of what makes a happy marriage (also in Hammond, 1981b).

10. Myths about step-parents. Using Cinderella to talk about fantasies or realities of stepparents.

11. Use the Movie *StepParents. Where is the Love?* and discussion (the reference for this movie was not given).

12. Use of a cartoon to discuss how they can change themselves, but not others.

13. Practice making decisions by giving exercises on peer pressure.

14. Exercise on assertiveness.

15. Exercise on group problem solving.

16. Wrap up in which group discusses what they like about the group and how to say goodbye.

The South Carolina Department of Education Groups

Bradford, Moore, Enwall, Taylor, Cooper, and Williams (1982) developed a counselor's guide for children of separation and divorce for the South Carolina Department of Education. This helpful document is known as EDRS document number ED 227391. The workbook included sample forms, a sample evaluation form, a student bibliography, a film, and filmstrip guide and references. While the workbook was designed for children from kindergarten to twelfth grade, the exercises seems best suited for children in late elementary and junior high school. Thus, they are summarized here. Warm-up activities included:

1. Houses my family live in. Drawing pictures of the houses including figures (stick figure are acceptable) of family members. Bradford et al. caution about protecting children who do not know where family members are or who have a parent in jail or a hopsital. They provided discussion questions about the different families.

2. Scrambled feelings. Unscramble letters of feeling oriented words. Discussion afterwards.

3. Coping with feelings. Helping children think about how to cope with different feelings in ways that do not cause problem or hurt anyone. The exercise involved providing each child with a paper cut in the shape of a cloud in which they list ideas. The study constructive coping and discussion.

Activities for the groups included:

1. *Getting to know you.* Find someone in the group that fits each of 13 categories (for example, "loves to eat vegetables"). Have that person sign the sheet. No person can sign the sheet more than twice. When you finish give the sheet to the leader for a check.

2. *Changes.* Listing changes in the family and self. List feelings about those changes.

3. *Things that bother me.* A list of 30 potential bothersome problems is provided. The child is asked to check those that bother him or her and circle the check for the three that bother the most. One problem is then selected to discuss how to solve it.

4. *Coping with feelings.* Discussion of displacement of angry or frustrated feelings and better coping.

5. *Communication.* This exercise is a list of nine questions about feelings about divorce such as whether parents divorce children, why divorce occurs, could the child get the parents back together, and whether the child gets caught in the middle.

6. *New rules since there has been a change.* Discussion of how things have changed since the separation.

7. *Happiness is. . . .* Discussion of what makes the child and parents happy.

8. *Mixed feelings.* The exercise provided a vignette about having mixed feelings and discussion of those feelings.

9. *From me to you.* Communication to parents through a note or picture to make them feel happy.

10. *Home responsibilities.* An exercise about who has what responsibilities at home.

11. *Make believe.* This exercise provides 10 short vignettes in which the child is asked to role play the situation and imagine how each person feels and acts.

12. *What should Sara do?* This exercise provided a vignette of a 12-year-old girl with mixed feeling about her mother's starting to date. The group is asked to answer questions as if they were "Ann Landers" or "Dear Abby."

The Children of Family Change Groups

The Children of Family Change program (Holdahl and Caspersen (1977) was developed for children from 8 to 12 years of age. The children met for five consecutive days for one hour per sessions. The program was designed to be educational in orientation rather than counseling. The five sessions were to:

1. Increase awareness of different kinds of families. Students constructed a model of their family in clay and shared the constructions with other members of the group.

2. Develop an understanding of the inevitability of family change and how to cope with that change. The children were encouraged to share personal experiences with loss such as a friend moving, the death of a pet or family member, divorce, and a new baby. Role playing the situation permitted exploring different ways of handling the situation. The book *The Tenth Good Thing About Barney* (Viorst, 1975b) was read and discussed.

3. Become aware of inevitability of family conflict and how to cope with that conflict. The children read the book, *Rosie and Michael* (Viorst, 1975a) to explore relationships. Using role play the children solved hypothetical family conflict. Often, an adult was invited to join the group and present a problem.

4. Identify mixed feelings and explore ways of expressing them. The children read the book *Where is Daddy?* (Goff, 1969) and parts of *The Boys and Girls Book About Divorce* (Gardner, 1970). The discussion focussed on emotional reactions of family members to change.

5. Explore new family structures and ways of coping with them. Children read *Gaston* (Saroyan, 1972). Using discussion and role play, they shared ways they have coped with the new family situations. Adults were also invited to share feelings.

The program used a model of training that led the children to identify life events that require readjustment, to personalize the events to their own lives, to integrate feelings with their knowledge and interpretation of stressful events, to apply skills to solve problems, and to practice those skills.

Kalter, Pickar and Lesowitz's Groups

Kalter, Pickar, and Lesowitz (1984) described a school-based program for fifth and sixth graders. Children met for one hour a week at school for eight weeks. Group leaders were one male and one female. The group was given four rules: (1) members would talk one at a time so everyone could be heard; (2) feelings would be respected; (3) if the member did not want to talk, that person could pass; and (4) everything said was private. The sessions had the following structure:

1. Group story. The children were asked to think about a family of two children in the fifth and sixth grades where the parents were thinking about getting a divorce. Each addition to the story was written on a large sheet of paper.

2. The group leader portrayed a predivorce argument between parents. The children would pretend to be in another room overhearing the argument. The role play was stopped from time to time for the group to discuss what was going on and feelings about it.

3–6. Skits were continued looking at postdivorce situations. The group members often took part in the role play. Skits included: "Custody and the Court," "A Daughter's Weekend Visit with Father," "Mother's Date," and "Boyfriend/Stepfather Discipline."

7. A Divorce Newspaper. Group members took turns being a reporter and interviewing the members about how children think and feel about divorce.

8. Each child received a copy of the newspaper and a photograph of the entire group with a group-ending party.

Kalter et al. (1984) noted that several themes were common: anxiety over parental battles; conflict over loyalties and anxiety over possible change in custody; sadness over the loss of the original family and less contact with the father; excitement and anxiety of the mother's dating; and anger at the mother's boyfriend or new husband over discipline.

Stolberg and Cullen's Groups

Stolberg and Cullen (1983) developed a primary prevention program for children from 8 to 13 years of age with three components. The Children' Support Group was a school-based educational program designed to help children with a supportive group experience. The intervention involved 12 weekly one-hour sessions led by one or two mental health professionals. The group experience included impulse-control training, communication skill training, anger-control skills, and relaxation techniques. Discussion, modeling, and role playing were used to teach children new ways of handling divorce-related situations. Children were selected who were not having significant behavior or emotional problems.

Each one-hour session was divided into two sections (Stolberg and Garrison, 1985). Part I was a discussion of a specific session-linked topics such as: "Whose fault is it?"; "What do I do on vacation?"; "Do I worry about my dad?" Part II of each session was the teaching, modeling, and rehearsal of specific cognitive-behavioral skills.

Other Groups

Two additional interventions were developed for parents: the Beyond Divorce program developed by Kessler (1977) which involved a 10-session adult education program; and Parenting Alone Together, a 10-session educational program developed for the project. This program provided single parents with support, information about divorce, strategies for increasing family cooperation, family communication skills, and child-management skills. Discussion of the effectiveness of these program is presented later in this chapter.

Roseby and Deutsch (1985) reported on a school-based program for fourth and fifth graders designed to provide training in cognitive social role taking and assertive communication. Rare for this type of study, a placebo control group was included that only discussed feelings about the divorce (a tough comparison indeed, since such a placebo group is also a treatment group.) Social role taking training produced more statistically significant positive changes in beliefs and attitudes about the divorce than did the discussion control group. Depression and school behavior were not affected by the cognitive therapy, leading Roseby and Deutsch to speculate as to whether a period of consolidation of changed attitudes might be needed. It is also possible that such generalization might not occur or that the two groups would be equally effective in inducing change.

SECONDARY SCHOOL INTERVENTIONS

Techniques for junior and senior high school students do not necessarily vary, although the psychological mindedness and maturity of the participants certainly does. Anxiety and self-consciousness may make junior high kids more reluctant to participate. Empathy is lower because of the shift from concrete operational thinking to formal operational thinking leaves the child losing the concrete empathy of late latency and not yet able to use the abstract ability of adolescence. Boys may show an increasing concern about participating because sex role is a central issue for adolescent boys and talking about problems is often not accepted by boys as way of handling upset. We found that seventh grade boys were more willing to participate. By ninth grade, boys were often reluctant to participate.

Group Composition

It is useful to build the group with teenagers at different levels of psychological mindedness. Asking some teenagers with good coping skills and relatively little upset about the divorce may provide good role models for the rest of the group. It is also useful to invite some teenagers who are both relatively verbal and comfortable with the adult leaders. Too many highly verbal members may lead to competition for center stage rather than providing some potential leaders for discussion. Highly aggressive, negativistic members should be avoided or limited to only one. To have more than one may permit feeding off each other in a synergistic way that would be destructive to group process.

Group Strategies

In the junior high schools where the author co-led groups (working with Barbara Kulton and Barbara Stiltner), we met for one period (40 minutes) each week. The techniques we used in those groups were developed by Kulton and Stiltner. Class time was set aside for the group and was rotated each week. In one group when two consecutive periods were tried at times, the 80 minutes sessions seemed too long for junior high kids.

The groups started by having each teenager draw a lifeline in which they drew a line, straight, jagged, or curved that represented the major events in their lives, that is, when they were born, where they lived, and what things happened to them in their life up to the present time. Kids typically mark moves, births, deaths, and accidents (e.g., "When I was six, I broke my arm"). This exercise gives them an opportunity to tell the group when the divorce happened and with whom they are presently living. In one group, several of the members got so upset telling the group about when the divorce occurred, that they had trouble continuing the discussion. Later, these same teenagers indicated that telling the group was the most useful experience they had had: it was the first time they had ever told anyone what had happened. The advantage of getting this information out first is to reduce secrets about living situations and to help the entire group know the living situation of each member.

There are several more likely problems in the junior high group:

1. Teasing can be vicious and must be prevented.
2. Confidentiality has to be stressed, given the tendency to gossip at this age. Kids who dominate the group should be given their chance to have their say, but they should be controlled.
3. Competition between kids should be discouraged. A child who says, "You think you have problems!" should be encouraged to first listen and then talk about his or her situation. Also, the leader must control tangential responses that take attention away from the original teen speaking either to reduce tension or to gather attention.

Do not worry about kids who seldom talk, but who are monitoring the process. It was clear that the quiet ones were watching and learning even though they did not feel comfortable speaking.

Nonverbal junior and senior high students may obtain significant benefits from group membership. These teenagers observe and model even when they do not contribute.

Empathy training is important with the egocentrism of early adolescence. Asking the group to paraphrase what was just said is helpful training.

Ventilation of feelings can increase self-esteem, but continued griping is not therapeutic. Focus on problem solving after ventilation is more helpful. Helping a child to discover when to give up on a particular problem and try to get those particular needs satisfied elsewhere can be helpful.

Less structure is needed for junior high school and senior high school groups than for elementary school children. Because the group can be more reflective, it is possible to use short vignettes to start the group and let group discussion carry the therapy. For example, a 5 to 10 minute narrative about problems of divorce that some children feel could be used to begin the discussion. Such a presentation can make it easier for the group to agree or disagree from their own experience. Some topics used in these groups include:

1. How did you hear about the divorce? How did parents tell you? Could they have done it better? Did you know what was going to happen? Was it hard or easy to ask questions? What questions did you have?

2. What would you like to say to your parents about the divorce? Do you think it was a good idea? Would you like them to get back together? Any advantages? Any disadvantages?

3. How do you talk with parents? How is anger handled? Is there a more constructive way to communicate anger?

4. Money (a frequent concern of teenagers). Is there enough? Is there child support? Is it predictable? Do parents fight over money?

5. What do you do about parents dating?

6. What are the problems of having a single parent?

7. What are the problems of remarriage?

8. How are holidays handled? These children often have significant concerns about where they will be on the holidays. Parents often avoid discussing this issue until late because they do not know that the teenager is worried. Kids should be encouraged to ask their parents when the switch will occur or even whether they will see the other parent during a particular holiday.

9. How do you feel about the future? Do you want to marry?

10. Do the parents want you to spy? How can you get out of the middle?

11. How do you pro and con problems? One major strategy that is helpful in group or individual work with adolescents is training them to look at both sides of an issue and to tolerate ambivalence about a problem. If the teen is able to list all the good and bad about a person or all the good and bad about the various alternatives for solving a problem, splitting is reduce and better problem solving results.

12. How much control do you want? How much control do you need? Do parents take your feelings into account enough? Too much?

These groups met for 10 weeks and celebrated the last session by going out to eat as a group. Group solidarity was strong. Friendships developed that went beyond the termination of the groups. There were numerous requests for continuation of the group. Unfortunately, they had to be turned down in order to give other children in the school an opportunity to participate.

Hammond's Groups

Hammond (1981b) developed a workbook for secondary school children. The exercises were similar to those used for elementary school children, although they were adapted for the age group. Hammond's process for group treatment for older children included:

1. *Introduction and group goals.* Use a card to describe self and favorite animal. Where would you like to go on next vacation?
2. *Value clarification sheet.* Again, as for Hammond's (1981a) groups 13 value-ladden divorce statements were used for discussion.
3. *Family coat of arms.*
4. *Bibliotherapy.* For older children she recommended *How to Get It Together When Your Parents Are Coming Apart* (Richards and Willis, 1976). Discussion questions were provided in her book.
5. *Family closeness and goal setting.* Drawing a family relationship chart.
6. *Empathetic assertion exercise.*
7. *Positive adjective sharing.* This exercise is design to help students think about strengths of family members.
8. *Challenge process.* This exercise is similar to Sonnenshein-Schneider and Baird's (1980) brainstorm, but includes a contract to work toward a solution.
9. *Review goals and music.* Hammond, the developer of these sessions, suggested three popular songs to be played. After each one, the group discusses the message. This exercise is probably very popular with teenagers.
10. *Stepparents.* Same movie as for younger children (*Stepparents: Where is the Love*?) with age appropriate discussion. Again, the resource for obtaining this movie was not given.
11. *Values around future marriage of student.*
12. *The ideal marriage relationship.* An exercise on what is important in a good marriage.
13. *Relationship value clarification.* An exercise on how the student feels about relationships.
14. *Saying goodbye and supporting group members.*

INTERVENTIONS WITH PARENTS

Drake (1981) suggested that school-based programs for parents can also be helpful. Programs on helping children with separation and divorce can be the basis of parent-teacher meetings. Information in Chapters 2 and 3 on typical reactions and concerns of children of different ages can be used, depending on the age level of the children in that particular school. Chapter 11 provides specific suggestions for information and strategies that can also be used when talking with parents. Bibliotherapy for parents, including lists of books that might be helpful to the child and to the parent, can be provided (Bernstein, 1977; Cantor and Drake, 1983; Fassler, 1978; McKay, Rogers, Blades, and Gosse, 1984).

INTERVENTIONS WITH TEACHERS

Given the information discussed previously, that is, that the classroom teacher may have a substantial bias that assumes that children of divorce are always going to be maladjusted, workshops for the classroom teacher can be helpful in reducing stereotypes. In addition, training the classroom teacher about how to provide help to parents undergoing marital separation, can provide additional avenues for getting information to parents. The classroom teacher can also evaluate when additional understanding and structure seem to be needed. A broader intervention and prevention program (of divorce-related problems prior to onset) at the classroom level may involve classroom reading and discussion on how different kinds of families work.

INTERVENTIONS AT THE SCHOOL SYSTEM LEVEL

School policy can make a significant impact on children of divorce. For example, is it the school's policy to provide information about the child to both biological parents, regardless of custody? Or is personal information about the child only provided to the custodial parent, unless a permission form is obtained from the custodial parent?

It is important for the schools to do what they can to keep both parents involved in the child and to provide support for the child in the school setting. Since the custodial parent may have sole authority to obtain school records, the schools should review the particular situation about access to school records. According to the Federal Educational Rights and Privacy Act, noncustodial parents have access to a child's school records unless there is a court ruling prohibiting it (Drake, 1981).

If the noncustodial parent does not have access to school records, the school could ask permission to send duplicate forms to the noncustodial parent that would increase the chances of keeping that parent involved with the child and provide an opportunity for both parents to support the child in relationship to school based problems. Schools can usually send newsletters about school activities, concerts, talent shows, and parent-teacher nights to noncustodial parents without permission of the custodial parent.

Drake (1981) noted that the staff of schools should review forms. If an emergency form does not provide an opportunity to indicate the special family circumstance for the child, the child may feel left out or ashamed. Having only one line for parents names is an example. Making provision for the child and the custodial mother to have different last names is another example.

RESEARCH ON SCHOOL–BASED INTERVENTION PROGRAMS

Pedro-Carroll (1983) and Pedro-Carrol and Cowen (in press) extensively evaluated the effectiveness of a school-based intervention program for 72 third through sixth grade children in four elementary schools. Of these children, 40 were assigned to an intervention group and 32 were assigned to a matched delayed treatment control group. Groups were similar in location, grade, sex, and length of time since the separation. Extensive evaluation materials were obtained, including teacher ratings of competencies and problem behaviors, children's perceived competence and trait-anxiety, attitudes about divorce and their experience in the group, parent ratings and group leader ratings.

The intervention program used by Pedro-Carroll followed Stolberg's and Cullen's (1983) 12-week Children's Support Group program, described in detail earlier in this chapter. The focus of this support group was to provide support for feelings and thoughts about the divorce and teach specific coping skills around personal problem solving, anger, self-control, and communication skills.

Positive changes in adjustment for children who participated in the intervention program as compared to the delayed treatment control were found in the teacher-reports (Pedro-Carroll, 1983). These changes included reductions in moody-anxious behavior, learning problems, and the overall school problem index. Teachers also rated the intervention children as having greater increases in total school competence scores and specific competencies of better peer sociability, frustration tolerance, compliance with rules, and adaptive assertiveness. Children in the intervention rated themselves as less anxious after the intervention than did the children in the delayed treatment control and their parents also rated them as better adjusted. Group leader ratings also saw the children in the intervention group as better adjusted at the end of treatment than the control with higher scores on total competence, total problems, and total ratings. Child-reported self-competence and self-esteem did not produce significant results.

While Pedro-Carroll's project presented an optimistic view of the effectiveness of school based intervention for children of divorce, there were some problems with the study (as is true for most studies). Pedro-Carroll was careful to acknowledge these problems. First, the raters were not blind to the category in which the child belonged. It took a tremendous amount of energy to perform this study. Teachers, therapists, and parents all knew which children were being treated and which were not. This problem is a potentially major one because the social demands of the study could have produced the positive results. Second, the sample was limited to a small, homogenous sample of predominately white, middle class, suburban children. Finally, not mentioned by Pedro-Carroll, the willingness to participate in the intervention and study may have produced unknown biases in the sample.

Kalter et al. (1984) evaluated their intervention program, which was summarized earlier in this chapter. Four of the six groups that received the school-based intervention were evaluated using a post-group evaluation only with no control group. The evaluation used parent reports, child questionnaires, and pre-post comparison on the Self-Competency Scales, the AML (Cowen et al., 1973), and the Divorce Perception Test (Plunkett and Kalter, in press). Parent reports were generally favorable and half reported observing specific changes. Interviews with the children suggested that the children experienced the groups as positive. Pre-post comparison on the Self-Competency Sales and the AML did not produce significant findings. On the Divorce Perception Test, 4 of the 25 items were significant including a reduction in wish for reconciliation, feelings of confusion about the divorce, feelings that the divorce was their fault, and a wish to perform better at school.

In the absence of a control group of children who had experienced the divorce of their parents, but who had not had the groups, the data is impossible to interpret. These feelings may decline over time as a natural process of working through the divorce. Children can work through the loss without therapy. In addition, one might expect two items (5%) to significantly change just by chance.

Stolberg and Garrison (1985) summarized the evaluation of group interventions for children of divorce. The four groups in their study were the Children's Support Group, the Single Parent's Support Group, a combined condition, with both children and parent groups and a no-treatment control group. A description of the single parents group is presented in Garrison, Stolberg, Mallonnee, Carpenter, and Antrim (1983). Data were collected pre-intervention, post intervention, and five months later. Measures included: The Fisher Divorce Adjustment Scale, the Single Parenting Questionnaire, the Life Experiences Survey, the Piers-Harris Children's Self-Concept Scale, and the Child Behavior Checklist.

Self-concept improvement was significantly higher in the Children's Support Group-Alone condition than for the children in either the combined intervention group or the no-treatment control group. Parent's improvement on the Fisher Divorce Adjustment Scale was significantly greater in the Single Parent Support Group-Alone condition than for parent's in the combined intervention. Improved social skills in children for the Children's Support Group-Alone condition were not statistically significant until the five month follow-up. The combined intervention was not more powerful than the separate interventions for the children and parents. These groups reported only two areas of improvement over the controls, fewer increases in negatively evaluated change events, and greater reductions in positively evaluated events. The surprising ineffectiveness of the combined interventions group may have been due to demographic differences for this group as compared to the others. Mothers in this group had been separated longer, had a lower employment status, and reported less time of visitation of the child with the noncustodial father than was true for the other groups. Stolberg and Garrison (1985) noted that there was no random assignment of people to groups. In addition, the reliance on self-report instruments limited the interpretation of data. In spite of those problems, this study and the Pedro-Carroll studies are important beginnings that would seem to demonstrate that school based interventions are useful to the children.

In the next section, other group techniques are presented. Clearly, school based group approaches and nonschool based techniques can be used in either setting.

OTHER GROUP TECHNIQUES FOR CHILDREN OF DIVORCE

Community based group intervention are sometimes sponsored by mental health centers, clinics, religious groups, colleges (workshops or courses through continuing education), courts, divorce support groups such as Parents Without Partners, and, more rarely, private practices. The power of group therapy, particularly for late latency and early adolescence where individual therapy is often more difficult, has clearly attracted attention as a major intervention approach.

Groups for Parents

Cantor and Drake (1983) described in some detail why a group approach can be helpful to parents. They noted that a group approach is particularly helpful to parents because the separation and divorce tends to generate loneliness and isolation. Working with other parents who have had life experiences that included divorce, visitation, and single parenting provides an opportunity to express feelings, share experiences, reduce feelings of uniqueness and incompetence, and support mutual problem solving. It is important to keep the focus on parenting in such groups, and not on the other concerns of the adults. As noted by Cantor and Drake (1983), the purpose of parenting groups is to benefit the children by helping the parents. Concerns such as financial concerns, the adult's sexuality, work and career concerns, and dating (except as it affects the children) are topics to be discussed in divorce groups rather than parenting groups.

Divorced parent groups have the advantage of keeping the topics focused their common experiences with their children. Divorce groups (not limited to parenting) are perfectly legitimate, but unlikely to be of as strong a benefit to the children, since the group is not uniformly parents and the focus is broader.

Cantor and Drake also noted several reasons why groups are a useful strategy: the opportunity for mutual support, the reduced costs, and the reduction in threat. They cautioned that some factors are counterproductive for effective groups. For example, group members with severe parental pathology, such as severe depression or psychotic thinking, are unlikely to benefit from a group experience and may have a negative impact on the group itself. Cantor and Drake recommended that such individuals seek individual therapy instead. They also noted that when parents have children with special concerns, such as adoption or major handicaps, the group may not be an appropriate place to air concerns.

The Post–divorce Parenting Program

Cantor and Drake (1983) described a structured group program for divorced parents. The function of the program was to prevent, reduce, or correct the postdivorce problems that children might experience. The sessions focused attention on the needs of the children around divorce-related issues such as custody and visitation and how to adapt parenting skills to the divorce situation. The program consisted of 8 1½ hour sessions with 8 to 12 participants. All ages of children were considered.

Each lesson consisted of educational materials, an opportunity for parents to identify examples from their own experience, and small group exercises. The small group exercises consisted of vignettes with incomplete endings. Parents were asked to respond to the incomplete endings with the questions, "What do you think the child is communicating by that behavior?" or "What should the parent do now?" The subgroups then reconvened into a larger group and shared the discussion. The eight sessons were:

1. You are still a parent.
2. How to be a good parent. This session focused on general rules of good parenting.
3. Four ways to minimize children's reactions to divorce. The four ways were: (1) Provide explanations for why one parent left. Help the child feel loved by both parents. Explain to the children that the divorce was not their fault. Use language appropriate to the age of the child. (2)

Help the child maintain contact with the noncustodial parent through visits, phone calls, and letters. (3) Avoid traingulating the child between parents. (4) Respond to changes in the behavior of the child that may be divorce-related.

The leaders then divided the groups up randomly. Four vignettes, involving children aged 3½, 6, 11, and 15, are given to each parents group and the parents are asked to choose three stories that match the ages of their children. The groups are asked to interpret the meaning of the behavior of the child and suggest solutions. After reporting to the group as a whole and summarizing the lesson, the parents are asked to rate themselves in terms of their perceptions of their effectiveness in these areas every day for a week.

4. Handling children's emotional reactions to divorce. The first part described the typical responses of preschool children and early latency children and suggestions about how to handle them.

5. Handling children's emotional reactions to divorce, Part II. The second part described the typical responses of later latency children and adolescents and suggestions about how to handle them.

6. Handling custody and visitation problems. This program was designed to help parents avoid acting out their negative feelings toward the ex-spouse through the custody and visitation.

7. Handling problems associated with parental dating and remarriages. The focus of this session was to help parents anticipate and respond effectively to the typical reactions of children to these situations.

8. Dealing with one's own feelings about marriage, divorce and parenting. Helping the parents understand their own feelings and how to avoid having those feelings hurt the child.

Cantor and Drake found that a support group with less structure was also helpful, provided some educational component was used.

Programs for Children

Beyond Divorce: Coping Skills for Minors

Kessler and Bostwick (1977) developed a small group experience for adolescents from 10 to 17 years of age. About 10 children met one Saturday for a six hour session. They limited the program to a single session because the adolescents had come from as far away as 150 miles to participate.

The program started with a short orientation for the parents to reduce their anxiety. The parents left and the adolescents were then asked to introduce themselves. They were then paired with someone that they did not know, and spent several minutes sharing information, including choosing two adjectives that best described themselves, the emotion hardest to express, and what they hoped to get from the workshop. Each person then had to introduce their partner to the group by talking to the partner.

The next activity was filling out a Sentence Completion Exercise alone. These stems were often divorce-related.

The next exercise was assertive training, including the use of "I" and "you" statements, empathy, listening to content, and working on action. This exercise was followed by the Film "Divorce: Part II." After each vignette, the film was stopped and discussion was held. After the film, the adolescents were encouraged to create their own vignettes and discuss them.

Divorce Experience Workshop

A court-mandated workshop for adolescents was described by Young (1980). A family relations court required adolescents from 12 to 17 whose parents had filed for divorce to attend one of seven workshops on divorce. At the beginning of each workshop, participants had to answer a four-part questionnaire involving demographic background, expectations and feelings about the workshop, concerns about the divorce, and assessment of "blame" for the divorce.

Participants then introduced themselves, age, school, and what they liked to do for fun. The leader gave follow-up questions to elaborate on the comments.

General discussion questions included: "Why do you think you are here?"; "What do you think divorce is?"; "How do families and people change when there is a divorce?" About 20 minutes were assigned to this task. The group then used a film, *What is a Family* that focused on an adolescent girl whose parents had divorced. Several discussion questions were provided about the film.

After a 10-minute break, the leader gave a presentation of the range of emotional reactions to parental separation and divorce. The eight areas of feelings were adapted from Gardner's (1970) *The Boys's and Girls's Book About Divorce.* The eight areas were: (1) experiencing a loss of control over parents' behavior; (2) feeling sadness; (3) being disappointed in parents; (4) feeling ashamed; (5) feelings that parents will stop loving you; (6) being angry; (7) feeling guilty; and (8) blaming one parent.

In a self-report evaluation of the program, the best predictor of the adolescent's feelings about coming was the parenting feelings about the program ($r(46) = .47, p < .001$). Afterwards, about half of the adolescents were very pleased with the workshop. About 20 percent were quite negative. Although helpful in terms of understanding the emotional reactions to the workshop, the evaluation did not answer the question as to whether such a program actually reduces negative reactions to divorce of parents. Young acknowledged that such an evaluation needs to have several control groups.

Programs for Parents and Children

Magid's Children Facing Divorce Progam

Magid (1977) described an innovative program for children of divorce that used role playing and videotapes of vignettes of common divorce situations. The program was designed to run for six weeks with members of several families meeting together once a week. Seven vignettes showing common family scenes were used as the basis for stimulating discussion. All the vignettes used children of divorced families. The vignettes noted by Magid included: "Who's to Blame?"; "Remember When"; and "Momma's New Boy Friend." Other topics (which may vary from group to group depending on need) include "Why Are We Here," "Divorce and the Variability of Human Perception," "Children Facing Guilt and Loneliness," "Children Facing New Step Relations," and "Looking Ahead."

Program goals, which were intended to break up inapproprite role patterns, included opening up feelings of anger, guilt, and rejection in a supportive atmosphere. Techniques used to break up these patterns included role playing, mirroring in psychodrama, training in "I" messages, and a magic circle technique in which children in the magic circle finish sentence stems. This latter technique is to encourage listening skills.

The therapists also tried to pair children in activities that would encourage role modeling. Children and parents were separated and saw the same vignettes in separate groups. The children watched part of the tape. The leader froze the tape and asked questions such as what the child in the story might be feeling. After some discussion, the story continued. The purpose of the tapes was to help the children see the divorce as terminating the relationship between parents, see their own role in the divorce, accept their feelings, and begin to talk about these feelings with their parents. Later the children were encouraged to develop their own vignettes. Because the sophistication level of the children, their attention spans, and the ability to abstract differ as a function of developmental level, children were grouped into two levels (older and younger).

Parents were shown the same vignettes with a focus on what the children might be feeling. Both parents were encouraged to attend unless the anger or hurt is so high as to interfere with their ability to focus on the program. For the first five weeks the parent sessions were separate from the children's. The final meeting was a joint session with the parents and children meeting together and sharing the experiences.

Magid proposed a variety of suggestions for the counselor, consultant to teachers, and consultant to parents. For the counselor, Magid recommended using value clarification. The counselor should use concrete explanations and avoid sarcasm or joking. Magid also suggested helping the child avoid the blame, supporting the full range of feelings, and not promising results that cannot be delivered. The counselor should also refer the child to a family therapist if necessary. Finally, the counselor is urged to review forms that could embarrass children of divorce.

For the consultation to teachers Magid's recommendations were: establish a library on children and divorce; plan classroom activities that help children understand divorce; help teachers understand therapeutic teaching; aid teachers in dealing with parent conferences; and encourage teachers to be supportive during the transition phases.

For parents, Magid recommended: keeping the focus on the children; reassuring the parents that the child is not alone and will recover; sharing resources of books, films, organizations, and referrals; and encouraging parents to be truthful without overburdening the children with details.

In a report of group therapy for 6 to 12 year olds, Bornstein, Bornstein, and Walters (1985) described a program of 1½ hour sessions provided weekly over six consecutive weeks. The first five sessions involved the children alone. The final session included the children and their parents. The sessions were described in some detail. Male-female therapists were used, and five to ten children were in each group. The sessions were:

Session 1:   Snacks were provided. Confidentiality was discussed. Common feelings about divorce were presented. A discussion was held about marriage and then about divorce, why it happens and how did it happen. Homework was to ask parents how they met and what they enjoyed doing together.

Session 2:   The session began with a discussion of the homework followed by a discussion on communication. Two role playing situations on divorce-related conflicts were provided by the therapists. Communication "stopping" and facilitative techniques were presented. A third role play with a therapist and child practiced positive communication skills. Homework involved calling an assigned buddy (another group member) and trying the "sandwich" technique with a parent (put a request or problem in between two positive, understanding remarks).

Session 3:   The session began with review of homework. The focus was of examination of feelings using the South Carolina, Department of Education exercises (Bradford, Moore, Enwall, Taylor, Cooper, and Williams, 1982) discussed earlier in this chapter. Children were then paired with their assigned buddies and asked to discuss one family situation that made them feel happy and one that made them feel sad. After a group discussion, thoughts and feelings were discussed and problems solving strategies developed.

Session 4:   A continuation of the discussion on problem solving characterized Session 4, using I BET E.T. as an acronym: identity the problem; brainstorm; evaluate; try it; evaluate the trial; and try another one.

Session 5:   This session reviewed buddy phone calls and problem solving. It was announced that parents were being invited to the next session. The rest of the session was on anger control.

Session 6:   All parents were invited. Three prepared videotapes were presented and discussed in small family groups. The parents were instructed to ask the child if the child had ever felt the feelings of the child in the videotape and they were encourage to discuss those feelings. A larger group discussion followed.

Programs Briefly Described in the Literature

The summer 1977 issue of the *Journal of Clinical Child Psychology* (1977, pp. 62–63) is devoted entirely to the impact of divorce on children. In that issue, eight programs are briefly described.

1. *Divorce Education Center.* This program in Toronto, Canada provided personal and group counseling to adults and children, audio and video resource material, crisis counseling, a speaker's bureau, and seminars and workshops for professionals. They developed an eight-hour cable television program for chidren.

2. *Children of Divorce.* A program in Pennsylvania to provide empathic training for children of divorce to help them share feelings with peers, develop a support system, and aid in problem solving within the family. A variety of visual aids were used including the "Acting, Feeling, Choosing" game, bibliotherapy, puppet play, role playing, and filmstrips.

3. *The Family Change Project.* This project, in the Minneapolis Public Schools, helped children recognize the inevitability of family change and how to cope with that change. The program was group oriented. Role playing, discussion, puppets, literature, and filmstrips were used.

4. *The Center for Children in Family Crisis.* This Pittsburgh-based program provided parents with information to ease the impact of divorce on children. Short-term primary prevention was the goal of the program. Training groups for children, parenting skills for custodial and noncustodial parents, and assessment were offered.

5. *Solo Center.* In Portland, Oregon, a resource group for single adults with rap groups for children of divorce from 8 to 12 were offered. Puppets, role play, games and movies were used with the children.

6. *Groups for Children of Divorce.* In Montreal, Canada a program was offered that was designed to help children of divorce with self-concept. Three groups of children separated by age (6 to 8, 9 to 11, and 11 to 13) and sex were used. Weekly hour-long sessions lasted for six to eight weeks.

7. *Parents Without Partners, Inc.* This group has sponsored training seminars, workshops, and conventions on helping the single parent.

8. *Divided Child Innovative Education Project.* In Oklahoma, a special counseling program within the elementary schools was set up. This program included small group discussions, in-class guidance activities, and teacher consultations. Stated objectives were increased school achievement, improved attitudes toward the home and family, improved self-concept and self-esteem, and general mental health.

SUMMARY

Group approaches for parents and for children of divorce would seem to be powerful intervention strategies. Intervention in the schools is particularly likely to reach children in need of help that are unlikely to receive help in other ways.

CHAPTER 11

Consultation with Parents

Usually the first contact between the clinician and the family is a meeting with the parents. Particularly useful are contacts where the parents are seeking advice prior to telling the children about the impending divorce and prior to the separation. There are no models for working specifically with parents around their concerns of their children. The most useful model this author has found is based on mental health consultation, an area that has not been traditionally applied to parent work. When parents are asking for advice and not wanting therapy or when the clinician is convinced that there are going to be only one or two contacts, a therapy model may be intrusive.

Parents do not want to be told that they are doing things wrong. They do not want to add to the burden of guilt around the separation and divorce. They may want to scapegoat the child, and thus may be defensive about any interpretation of their role in the problem. A family therapy model (see Chapter 13) tends to be more powerful than parent consultation in that the family dynamics can be observed and the clinician has the ability to intervene in an ongoing process. Often, one or two contacts are all that are needed or available. In addition, it is presumptuous to assume that all families are maladaptive or malfunctioning. Sometimes families need information and can utilize that information well.

This chapter is based on a mental health model developed by Saul Cooper and the present author and discussed in considerably more detail in *The Mental Health Consultation Field* (Cooper and Hodges, 1983). That book does not deal with either parenting consultation or divorce, but the principles of intervention are the same. In addition, many of the concepts in this chapter were influenced by the thinking of the most influential theorist in mental health consultation, Gerald Caplan (Caplan, 1970). There is no empirical research cited in this chapter because, to this author's knowledge, the consultation model has not been previously applied to working with divorced parents. The specific advice suggested for divorcing parents does draw on this author's experience and the literature.

Cooper et al. decided that conceptualizations of consultation could be based on the underlying reason(s) why the consultee (in this chapter, the parent) could not solve the problem of the child's behavior on their own. The first model, the educational model, assumes that the failure to solve the problem was lack of knowledge or skill. Mental health professionals who prefer this model are often oriented toward behavior modification. The second model, the individual process model, assumes that the difficulty on the part of the parent to solve the child's problems is due to the attitudes, motivation, intrapsychic conflicts, or personal style of the parent. Dynamically and humanistically oriented therapists are more likely to be drawn to this model of explanation in terms of how to help the parent. Theme interference (Caplan, 1970) and stereotyping (Heller and Monahan, 1983) are examples of concepts in this model.

The final model of conceptualization is the system model in which the problems of the parent are embedded in the characteristics of the family or the community in which the family belongs. Intervention in this model may focus around changing channels of communication, power, support and influence. While a systems oriented therapist may work with the parents alone, it is likely that the therapist will want to work with the whole system and see at least the family and maybe related figures that belong to the system, for example, grandparents, neighbors, and friends.

In order to develop an intervention strategy, the professional needs to conceptualize every problem brought to them by parents at each level of conceptualization. To what degree can this problem be considered a lack of knowledge or skill, an interpsychic or personality problem, or a family or community systems problem?

As intervention moves from education to process to systems, the intervention tends to become more powerful and long lasting and more difficult. The use of the first two models will be used in this chapter. Family therapy will be covered in Chapter 13.

GENERAL PRINCIPLES OF CONSULTATION

Consultation is not teaching. It is an interactive model in which the consultant helps the parent learn how to cope with problems that are unsolvable with the parent's present skills. It is not therapy. The function of consultation is to provide a supportive, noninterpretative environment in which parents can take the risk to change. Parents are not blamed for the difficulties. Such blame tends to increase guilt and withdrawal rather than constructive problem solving.

CONSULTATION PRINCIPLES

There are several basic principles in any consultation and particularly with parents.

1. The primary principle in any consultation is to start with the perceived needs of the parent (Caplan, 1970). Too frequently, mental health profession-

als identify an area in which work needs to be done and jump in to work on that topic. As stated in the previous chapters, parents will often use the child's acting out as the basis for avoiding their own issues. The child obliges by maintaining the misbehavior in order to reduce family anxiety.

Always begin the consultation by addressing the perceived needs of the parents. By responding to the perceived needs, parents are empowered, experience increased self-esteem, and feel more optimistic about the possibility of other changes.

Once perceived needs have been responded to, parents are more willing to permit the consultant to raise other important issues, such as the relationship between the parents.

   2.   It is the responsibility of the consultant to work with the parents to find a strategy of intervention that works for them. Mental health consultants should not present their favorite intervention, expecting the parents to adopt that strategy. The solution must fit the personality style. The parents must feel free to reject the advice the professional develops with them for whatever reason. If the parents feel pressured to try a particular intervention, they can make it fail. If the consultant has parents quote back things that were never said, it is likely that the solution did not fit the dynamics of the parents. It is the consultant's responsibility to (1) diagnosis why that intervention was inappropriate for those parents, and (2) help the parents find a solution.

   3.   The consultant's competence is demonstrated by the questions he or she asks (Caplan, 1970). The purpose of the intervention is to increase the competence of the parents in parenting, not to demonstrate the magical powers of the consultant. With questions, the parents are trained in how to think about their child's problems. In addition the use of questions involves the parent more actively, requiring them to engage in the issues, rather than passively tune out the consultant.

   4.   Respect the competence of the parent. Find areas of competence and use those areas as bases for developing solutions.

   5.   Do follow-up. Even a five-minute phone call after a single consultation sessions can uncover a reluctant or embarrassed parent who has not used the intervention or found that it did not work.

Follow-up diagnosis of problems, fine tuning of an intervention and the communication of caring.

   6.   Do not assume that the "bag of tricks" developed over time will work in every instance. This author tries to prepare parents for the possibility that a particular intervention will not work for this particular child. Temperament (in the child or parent), past history, poor implementation, or other unknown factors can all invalidate a seemly effective intervention. Set up the consul-

tation with initial advice given as a trial strategy. If the strategy does not work, even the failure is information. This attitude can lead the parents to return for more information, permitting a diagnostic as to whether the intervention plan was inappropriate or the parents were ineffective (or the suggestions were inappropriate for these parents).

7.   Prepare parents for the difficulty in implementing a plan. Not only does it take tremendous energy to treat a child differently from what feels natural and spontaneous (see the discussion on "parenting" scripts in Chapter 9, but the child is often disoriented by finding that the rules have changed.

Warn parents that when they are trying a new intervention for handling behavior, the behavior may get worse rather than better for a while. Children do what they know how to do best. When a parent changes the rules, the child has an investment in keeping the same pattern of interaction going. Tantrums become worse when parents change the script. The child tries to go back to the old script. Parents who are not warned of this intensification will prematurely abandon an intervention.

Tremendous social support for the parents may be needed during this time. Short five-minute phone calls encouraging parents to stay with the intervention and rewarding them for the investment in helping their children can be very helpful in maintaining the parents' behavior.

8.   Listen to how the parents symbolize the problem. Such a diagnostic can help in determining what kind of intervention is likely to be effective. Using the same symbolic language is likely to increase with the sense of being understood and accepted (Caplan, 1970). Ask the parents to describe the behavior and sequence of behaviors rather than use labels. When a parent describes a child as aggressive, ask the parent to describe some typical episodes, how they handled it and how the child responded to that handling. Parents tend to be better describers of behavior than diagnosticians.

9.   Consultation with parents has a strong primary prevention opportunity. The two ways in which consultation can efficiently help family is to reduce stress and to immunize the parent or child from the stress. Helping the parents anticipate the problems that might occur as a function of separation (or even the intervention) can be very helpful in preventing maladaptive responses on the part of the parent. For example, suggesting to parents that they provide explanations of the separation and clear information about the structure of access in the future will allow parents to reduce anxiety in the child. When parents are so concerned about their children's welfare to seek professional help prior to the separation, there are often strengths in the family that work in favor of good outcomes. The provision of information prior to the stressful event is what Caplan (1970) calls anticipatory guidance.

10.   Trust builds extensively over time rather than intensively in one sitting. It is better to have four, one-half hour consultations with parents spread

over two months than a two-hour marathon session. While extensive contact is not always available to the professional, particularly when the child has problems in several areas or skill training is involved, it is useful to encourage parents to come back on a regular basis for several consultation sessions.

WHO TO INVOLVE IN THE CONSULTATION

Single Parent Asking for Help

Often, one parent will be more psychologically minded and want help in parenting while the other parent is unwilling to participate. Refusal sometimes comes as a message, "It is your inadequate parenting that is causing the problem and I don't need help."

More often, it is the custodial parent who asks for help, because the almost constant child care responsibility makes them the target of the child's maladaptive behavior. Since the custodial parent is more likely to be placed in a position of enforcing discipline, requiring homework, insisting on a clean bedroom, and being involved in childrearing during the work week (when the parent is also tired from work and housekeeping), more conflict with child rearing occurs.

When the request for consultation occurs at the point of separation, the initiator and the "dumpee" are equally likely to request for help. The initiator asks for help because of guilt that the decision to separate is harmful for the children or because the problem that led to the decision to leave is from that person's point of view also damaging to the children. The dumpee asks for help because in addition to suddenly have to deal with abandonment, that person also has to deal with the emotional responses of the children. Sometimes the request for help exaggerates the harm to the children as "proof" that the leaving damaged everyone. Such manipulations at guilt toward the initiator lead to investments in maintaining the disruptive behavior and make consultation very difficult.

When the above factors are combined, it is more likely that when there is only one parent asking for help that it is the mother. The mother is twice as likely as the father to be the initiator (Bloom, Hodges, and Caldwell, 1982). The mother is also much more likely to be the custodial parent. Women are also more likely to seek professional help and seek talking to a professional as helpful.

Asking For Help or Ammunition?

The single parent asking for help presents a problem for consultation. It is easy for that parent to blame the absent parent for the problems with the child and to avoid changing behavior. The request of the absent parent's behavior is filtered through the eyes of a hurt or angry person. Also important is how often this combination is used to set up the mental health professional for custody or relitigation. Be careful when asked to evaluate certain child rearing behaviors. You may be receiving a partial or inaccurate description of the other parent's behavior.

When asked for advice by a single parent, particularly just after separation or just prior to litigation, avoid answering direct questions about the appropriateness of certain behaviors. Find out first who is perceived as having those behaviors so that you would know whether the person is asking for help for themselves or looking for ammunition against the absent parent.

This type of error can result in a subpoena to repeat that statement to a judge. Remember that descriptions of the other parent's behavior is hearsay and not evidence and may be substantially distorted. Since families are systems and not just a collection of unconnected behaviors, it is often the case that there are substantial omissions about the behavior of the complaining parent.

Both Parents

Unless one of the parents has remarried, which makes the decision as whom to include more complex, this combination is preferred. It is extremely important that the parent be required to put aside their ongoing battle to focus on the behavior of the child. If the consultant is not strict in demanding control of the session, the parents battle can erupt into rage. When the rage response is high, consultation can be used to help the parents accept the divorce and then focus on helping the child. Under such conditions it is difficult to tell when the intervention is consultation and when it is family therapy.

One major disadvantage in this combination when one of the parents has remarried or has developed a long-term, stable cohabiting relationship is that it denies the parenting role of the "stepparent." Often, the willingness to have the "other" woman or man involved in the consultation was a symbolic admission that the marriage was over.

Both Parents and One Cohabiting or Remarried Partner

Discussions of how the child interacts with everyone involved can be very useful. It is also helpful to have clear guidelines about how the child is to deal with a stepparent role. The information in the previous chapter can be helpful in defining problems for the stepparent.

Both Parents and Both Stepparents

While this is a potentially powerful combination, it is also problematic except for brief contacts. The stepparents (or cohabiting partners) often harbor chronic and intense rage at the other spouse motivated by jealousy or care for their partner who has hurt by this other person and a wish to maintain distance between the two families. The exspouses may have their rages mitigated by affectional ties (which may or may not be threatening). This author often starts the consultation with separate meetings with each of the two households in order to use the meetings to help each couple decide what issues need to be negotiated with the other family. After several separate sessions, a joint meeting of everyone can follow.

THE EDUCATION MODEL

Mental health professionals often overlook the power of education in helping others. It is presumptuous to assume that every problem is due to unresolved childhood conflict. Well meaning parents often do not know what else to do and are quite willing to assume a new intervention as soon as it is presented to them. Even if the effectiveness of this intervention is only 50 percent (a level this author has found to be true for parents handling aggression in the child with aggressive punishments), the results suggest that the educational model might be tried first.

The degree to which some mental health professionals forget what they have learned about learning principles in teaching parents how to deal with their children is surprising. Most mental health professionals know that lecture formats are not very useful in therapy. Yet when they work with parents in an educational mode rather than therapy, some mental health professionals give a long list of advice that the parent is suppose to follow.

Habitual ways of handling the child's problems are difficult to break. New learning follows well established patterns of behavior modification, reinforcement, and modeling. In addition, a significant amount of parent-child interactions are skills (i.e., knowing how to do something) rather than knowledge (i.e., knowing what needs to be done). Parents who do not know how to express affection, be sensitive to feelings, or reward appropriate behaviors need to develop those skills slowly and with successive approximations to the desired behavior. Such new learning takes tremendous energy and parents need significant social support to maintain that energy until the new behaviors become habitual.

Because the mental health professional is being asked to be the expert, there is a tendency to give advice too soon. By asking questions, the professional can assess the various needs of the parents, their repertoire of skills and the degree to which lack of knowledge or skill is involved. By careful assessment, the professional also models problem solving behavior for the parent. When a skill deficit is involved, there must be a careful plan of acquisition and support. For example, if one parent comes from a family of origin in which no one ever touched and where affection was seldom expressed, touching a child's shoulder or back for one second several times a day can change the pattern.

With successive meetings spread out over several months, the touch can last two or three seconds.

Kuehnel and Kuehnel (1983), in an excellent summary of educational model strategies, focused on behavioral approaches for helping consultees (in this book, parents) to develop knowledge or skills. They looked at instructions, modeling, shaping, and behavioral rehearsal with structured feedback and homework assignments. Prior to reviewing those techniques, it is useful to remind the reader of the following information for parents.

Advice for Parents

Specific Advice

Parents can be provided with potentially useful information about how children typically react to divorce. Given the child's age, gender, amount of conflict in the family, developmental history, finances, temperaments, reasons for the divorce, presence or absence of significant others, and psychological mindedness, the professional can develop ideas about what kind of information would be useful to the parents. Some of this information would have advice-giving implications. Chapters 2 and 3 of this book have a great deal of information that could serve as a base for information. However, some major areas will be highlighted here:

1. Provide predictability for the children. Children are very upset by having their view of the world destroyed. Parents are often insensitive to the need for child to understand what happens next. Where will the noncustodial parent live? How often will there be visits? How predictable will visits be? How will the family handle the old home? Will there be a move? The degree to which children feel that they know what will happen, the lower the level of anxiety, particularly as the parents' predictions unfold. According to Wallerstein and Kelly (1980c), however, 80 percent of parents do not provide the children with assurance of continuity of care.

2. Tell children that a separation or divorce is pending in the proper time and way. The time span of the child is the gauge for deciding how early to tell the children. Of course, when the separation occurs after a blow-up, no warning is possible. For very young children, a week to 10 days may be all that the child can handle. Excessive time beyond the ability of the child to comprehend could increase anxiety. For an adolescent, four to six weeks can be helpful in integrating and anticipating the event.

If parents are discussing the possibility of a separation, children should not be told of the possibility until the decision is made. Once the decision is made, at what point in time the child is told should be related to the child's time perspective. Children can usefully handle a period somewhat greater than their perspective.

Parents have difficulty telling the children about the divorce. They, themselves are upset and sometimes it is difficult to tolerate the anxiety and anger of the child. According to Jacobson (1978c), it is usually the mother alone who tells the child.

3.   Encourage the parents to be truthful about why the separation is occurring, but do not burden the children with details (Magid, 1977). Cantor and Drake (1983) noted that overdisclosure is confusing to children. They indicated that it is not good parenting to provide children with information that would lead them to turn against the other parent. They suggested that extramarital affairs, homosexuality, and impotence are best omitted from information given the children. Cantor and Drake also recommended that the older the child, the more complete the explanation for the separation needs to be.

While attacks on the other parent are harmful (see number 11), overconcern with protecting the image of the other parent can lead to confusion. When a parent only praises the absent parent, the question "If he's so great, why did you want him out?" is a reasonable one to ask.

4.   Tell the teachers that the child is going through a family divorce. This recommendation raises tricky problems. As mentioned in Chapters 2 and 8, there is reason to believe that teachers may stigmatize children of divorce. At the same time, a teacher is likely to be significantly more tolerant of a child's acting out when the behavior is put in context. While tolerance and understanding are desirable, permissiveness is not. Children need firm structure in the school setting with support and understanding when coping becomes difficult. In general, then, schools should be told.

5.   Reassure the child that the child is not alone (Magid, 1977).

6.   Use resources. There are books for parents and for children that can help in understanding divorce (Bernstein, 1977). There are a variety of organizations in many communities that can serve to provide information and social support (Magid, 1977).

7.   Do not allow the children to become messengers between families. Do not allow the children to become small adults (Magid, 1977).

8.   Do not isolate siblings (Magid, 1977).

9.   Do not allow children to become counselors to your problems (See Chapter 2 on parentification of children) (Magid, 1977).

10.   Do not promise children things and then not fulfill them. Children need predictability. Parents who easily promise outings or gifts and then forget can produce profound hurt and uncertainty about the future (Magid, 1977).

11.   Do not put the exspouse down in front of the children. The child typically identifies with each parent. When the children are invited to join in with a parent in attacking the other parent, self-esteem necessarily suffers. While it is quite appropriate for a parent to tell a child that the parent is angry at the exspouse, details as to why or frequent exposure to that anger hurts the child. The parent should avoid labels in particular. "Your father is lazy or irresponsible," is less helpful than "I don't know why your father did not show up for visitation. I know that it hurt your feelings" (Magid, 1977).

12. Do not argue about financial matters in front of the children. Magid's (1977) advice to specifically mention finances was wise since this area is one in which the intensity of anger is great and parents feel particularly justified in enlisting the child's loyalty. "We could buy you a new coat if your father wasn't so irresponsible."

13. Keep interparental hostility in check (Cantor and Drake, 1983). The parent should communicate respect for the child's feelings about the other parent.

14. Do not allow your own guilt to interfere with parental responsibility. Do not be overprotective or underprotective (Magid, 1977).

15. Protect the attachments of the children. Do not move unless you have to. Try to make it possible for the child to continue to see playmates.

16. It is not the child's fault that the divorce is occurring. The child is still loved even though the parents no longer love each other. Cantor and Drake (1983) indicated that young children need to have their specific concerns dealt with. Young children cannot use information that they are not responsible for unless it is specifically structured around their own fantasy. Older children will be able to separate out their own responsibility if they are given adequate information about why the divorce occurred.

For young children, it is useful to check back about their understanding about why the divorce occurred. If the child harbors a fantasy about causing the divorce, the child needs to have that fantasy disconfirmed.

17. The child will not be abandoned. (Provide this promise only if it is true that neither parent will abandon). The child may need information about family or friends that will serve as backups if parents are unavailable.

18. Parents can make mistakes. Children can learn from the mistakes that parents make.

19. The child need to be told that their lives will change (Cantor and Drake, 1983). Family structure, a change in residence, a mother going to work, less money, need for help with chores are some examples.

20. There is nothing the child can do to change the situation (Cantor and Drake, 1983). The child needs to be discouraged about trying to reunite the parents.

21. Encourage the child to talk about feelings and to ask questions. Jacobson (1978a) found that the more the child is encouraged to talk about the divorce, the better the adjustment. If the child has difficulty expressing feelings, use the techniques of Hiam Ginott and Carl Rogers to open up trust and self-confidence with expresion of feelings.

The following technique for helping parents help the child talk about feelings is outlined in Cooper and Hodges (1983, p. 31).

a. Tell the child how he or she feels several times a day. Try to focus on both positive and negative feelings. Try to make some of the comments in passing, on the way to another room or while the child is watching television or playing.

b. Make the comments short. Simply say, "You look bored." "You enjoyed playing with your sister." "I made you angry when I said that you had to go to bed now."

c. Do not use judgmental phrases, such as " . . . and if you felt that way more often you would get along better with your brother" or " . . . and if you weren't so angry, we would have more fun." It is surprising how often parents criticize children for having a good time by reminding them of all the bad feelings. Parents have a great deal of difficulty accepting feelings without judgements.

d. Do not pause. Children get so used to judgmental statements that if the parent leaves an expectant pause, the child will fill in the judgmental phrase themselves. By making the simple statement of feedback about feelings without a pause, the parent communicates acceptance without pressure to feel differently.

Experience with this technique indicates that initially the child shows no change in behavior (expect perhaps surprise at the parent's change in behavior). After about three weeks, the child will spontaneously elaborate on a feeling without any request from the parent. After six weeks, the child will talk about feelings prior to any reflection from the parents.

22.   Help the child understand the difference between destructive and constructive anger. Tantrums are destructive. They invite retaliation or withdrawal. The purpose of communicating angry feelings is to encourage effective problem solving around the problem that led to the anger in the first place. This approach implies encouraging children to control their anger rather than flooding.

Gordon (1970) talked about anger as an emotion that is secondary to other feelings of hurt, rejection, and fear. Gordon suggested that communication around those feelings tend to be more effective than around the anger. Particularly for younger children, anger and aggression are common responses to separation and divorce, it is useful to help parents cope with those responses.

Information Process

When giving parents advice about how to deal with children, particularly when specific intervention strategies are being suggested, it is useful to remember basic principles of learning. Break behaviors into small units. Use behavior shaping to help parents move toward the correct behavior.

Work on only a limited number of problems at a time. Start with the most intrusive problem where there is the greatest need. Once that problem is moving toward a solution and the particular parental problem solving behavior is becoming more habitual, then move to the next problem. Mental health professionals who try to give multiple solutions to problems are increasing the likelihood of failure.

Work on solving only a limited number of child behavior problems at one time. Parents become overwhelmed with too many solutions and will not implement any of them. Begin with parental perceived needs and then move to other problem areas as the parent becomes more successful.

Parents, like other people, have a limited ability to remember a large number of interventions. Try to provide social support for the effort that is required to implement the intervention. For example, a teacher might be told to call the parents daily to report on the stealing and lying behavior of the parent's child and to provide support for the consistency with which the parents were following through. Five-minute phone calls several times during the first few weeks give the parent an opportunity to ask questions, fine tune an intervention, and receive emotional support for the effort in changing behavior. To further build in support, the consultant can call the teacher once a week to support her support of the parent.

Skill Training for Parents

Kuehnel and Kuehnel (1983) suggested several techniques for facilitating skill learning:

1. *Role playing.* It is helpful for the parent to try the behaviors in a role playing situation with a dry run with feedback from the consultant. Behavior shaping can be used.
2. *Modeling.* Modeling can be a powerful technique for helping parents understand how to do a particular behavior. In this case the parent can play the role of the child and the consultant the role of the parent. By demonstrating the behavior in a role playing situation, the parent may feel less stress and see the exact behavior that is being discussed.
3. *Homework assignments.* The parent is asked to try out the behaviors in real life. It is important that the parent has sufficient skills to carry out the behavior successfully. Encourage the parent to work on only one child behavior that is relatively circumscribed.
4. *Dependency.* Pay attention to *fading* in which the parent is encouraged to maintain the behaviors without the constant support of the professional. Making meetings shorter and shorter and taking longer between meetings reduces dependency.

INDIVIDUAL PROCESS CONSULTATION

When the analysis of the reason why the parent cannot solve the problem presented by the child leads the mental health professional to the conclusion that intrapsychic dynamics, unconscious motivation, or problems in objectivity play a major role, the professional may utilize individual process consultation. This strategy of consultation is similar to what Caplan (1970) called consultee-centered case consultation.

When parents come in asking for professional advice about how to handle their children, they are generally not asking for psychotherapy. Attempts on the part of the professional to suggest that therapy would be appropriate may be met with anxiety and rejection. Many families prefer to keep the identified problem as the child and not the parents. When there are individual processes problems and resistant parents, a consultation model can be much more effective in changing behavior than a psychotherapeutic one.

Caplan proposed a category of individual process problems called theme interference. In theme interference, the parent has a syllogism in which if a child belongs to an initial category there is an inevitable undesirable outcome. Parents carry with them many themes around the topic of divorce: "A child from a broken home is doomed to become delinquent." "A child of divorce will inevitably hate his or her parents." "Children cannot be angry at parents after divorce or they will grow up warped in terms of their identity." Heller and Monahan (1983) proposed that Caplan's concept of theme interference is identical to the concept of stereotyping: prejudging that if a child belongs to a group, there will be inevitable outcomes.

Caplan proposed that a major error in handling this problem is what he called "unlinking" in which the consultant indicates that the child doesn't really belong to the initial category. An example of unlinking in this situation would be a comment like, "This child isn't really like a child of divorce, because there is frequent contact with both parents." While such a removal from the initial category may temporarily solve this problem, the theme has not been touched and remains to affect other behaviors. In addition, if the parent received other information that suggests the child really is a child of divorce, the theme interference immediately takes over.

Caplan (1970) proposed that role of the consultant is to invalidate the theme, by breaking the inevitable link between the initial category and outcome. To simply disagree with the parent is ineffective. The parent "knows" the theme at an emotional level and is likely to disqualify the expert if such a simple solution is tried.

Since such "stereotypes" can rarely be changed by direct confrontation, Caplan (1970) proposed that the professional agree that the outcome feared (or wished for in the case of the angry parent) is indeed a possible outcome, but that other outcomes are possible and indeed might be facilitated. Heller and Monahan (1983) also suggested focusing on unrecognized assets in the child as a way of helping the parent open up other, more desirable outcomes.

Stereotypes or theme interferences by parents of divorce can be invalidated by demonstrating that other desirable outcomes are possible and that a change in behavior can facilitate those outcomes.

Reframing by Focusing on the Child

Another technique for handling theme interferences is to reframe the problem as one that the child has rather than one that the parent has. Since the parent is likely to be defensive about direct confrontations about what they are doing wrong, the parent can listen more easily to suggestions that the reaction of the parent is a natural response to the behavior of the child (which from a systems analysis is perfectly true). By reframing the problem as that of the child, other individual process problems such as overinvolvement or underinvolvement, explosive anger at the child, and chronic anxiety in the parent can all be addressed without attacking the defenses. For example:

1. *Chronic anger at the child.* "The problem your child has, is that she is going around making people angry all the time. How can we help her not do that?" The focus is now on helping the child, rather than the chronic anger of the parent.

2. *Disinterest.* "This child's problem is that he pushes people away from him so that they don't want to interact with him. We need to help him with his need to have distance from others." Again the parent can look at withdrawal in the child, but does not get labeled as having that problem except as a reasonable response to the child's behavior.

3. *Dependency.* "She is constantly giving messages for people to take care of her, even when she doesn't need the help. We need to help her be more independent."

Reframing a parent's problem as a natural response to the child's problem can be helpful in getting a parent to consider behaving differently in order to help the child. The technique avoids direct confrontation with the parent's defensive process and permits movement. Do not use this technique dishonestly. Use it only for those problems in which a true interaction between the parent's behavior and the child's behavior is likely to be maintaining the problem. Given the frequency of this dynamic, such a caveat is not much of a restriction.

Reframing by Focusing on a Different, Underlying Problem

Another reframing technique is to translate what is seen as a motivational problem into a skill problem. Parents often are immobilized by a belief system that indicates that a child should want to behave. A child that doesn't behave is flawed and therefore there is nothing effective that the parent can do. By reframing the problem as one which the child doesn't know how to do, rather than too lazy to do, helps the parent think about how to help the child move from the place that they are, to a more adaptive position.

This technique has been helpful in working with the problem of attention span ("She doesn't know how to attend for long periods of time"), self-control ("He hasn't the skill to control himself"), study habits ("She hasn't learned good study skills and how to work for long periods of time''), aggression (''He needs to learn how to control his anger and use it effectively''), and trust (''She needs to learn to trust the world again'').

Parental Support

A procedure that is helpful in working with parents is role enhancement. Anything that the consultant does that aids the parents in having more motivation and energy for working with the child is likely to be helpful to the child. Helping the parents be more effective in general as parents is likely to help generalize to many parenting areas. Caplan (1970) suggested that using the same symbolism as the consultee is useful in helping the parent hear the intervention. For example, if a parent uses the word, ''respect,'' frequently, the clinical intervention will likely work better if the word ''respect'' is used in the solution.

Caplan identified several cues that an intrapsychic problem may be present. These cues include overidentification with the child, transference, and characterological distortions. Generalizing inappropriately from previous experience is a cue. Omitting key facts in presenting the situation of the child, facts discovered much later or only by accident, are also cues of interpersonal interferences.

Omitting key figures in the child's life is a cue. A grandparent with whom the child has frequent contact, who is not mentioned, may be the source of conflict.

THE SYSTEMS INTERVENTION MODEL

When working with parents in consultation, there are two systems to keep in mind, the family as a system and the broader community in which the family exists.

When the family as a system is the target of intervention, the system approach is basically family therapy (see chapter 13). While a system approach may be used to interpret to the parents why the child may be behaving in a particular way, a systems intervention is more likely to be effective if the entire family (or two sets of families) are seen in therapy.

In terms of a broader community intervention, the consultation can have contact with a variety of individuals in the family's life, including significant others, teachers, grandparents, child care workers, medical professionals, and any others who affect how the family responds to the stress of divorce.

Broadly speaking, a systems intervention may include increasing community tolerance and support for single parents, reducing stigma, increasing legal structures to provide a stable financial basis for families, increasing mediational services and reducing adversarial divorce procedures, providing Big Brother and Big Sister programs in the community, providing recreational facilities for families, increasing coping skills in children and parents, or providing informational services for marriage, marital counseling, divorce counseling, single parent family support, and remarriage.

SUMMARY

In conclusion, working with parents can be facilitated by using a consultation model. Parents are likely to provide less resistance when defenses are protected rather than challenged. Parents can be helped with developing effective interventions by the use of an educative model, an individual process model or a systems model. All consultation problems should be reviewed at all three levels of intervention prior to making a decision as to which level(s) for the professional to intervene.

CHAPTER 12

Individual Psychotherapy with Children of Divorce

The first part of this chapter describes play therapy strategies for young children. The second section summarizes other programs designed to help children of divorce.

Individual child therapy (always combined with work with one or both parents) is the treatment of choice in these types of situations: when parents are psychologically unavailable for working in family therapy; when the child's maladaptive behavior is related to past misinterpretations of events and is not corrected by less stressful interactions ongoing in the present; when the child needs to learn to separate his or her identity and problems from that of the parents; when the child could benefit from a consistent, predictable therapist in the midst of a chaotic family life; and when the child needs someone who does not have divided loyalties and provides a unique advocacy.

Work with the parents is always necessary (except possibly for teenagers who need to be separated from the family). There are always pressures within the family to maintain the status quo. The family will always show some resistance to changes in the child.

Cantor and Drake (1983) advised that family therapy is the treatment of choice when the child's problems appear to develop from continued family conflict or family avoidance of problems. Family therapy can be a very powerful intervention and is useful not only for helping families with divorce issues, but also for working with single parent problems and with remarriage. Chapter 13 on family therapy will deal with all these issues.

Cantor and Drake also noted that group therapy is the treatment of choice when peer issues predominate or when the child may benefit from modeling by peers for talking about problems. Group therapy is also of benefit when prevention of future problems is the goal, as the child can see other children problem solving issues that that child has not yet faced.

PLAY THERAPY

Erikson (1963) said that children find self-cure in the activity of playing. There is ample clinical evidence (although difficult to demonstrate empirically) that children express their preoccupation, concerns, and competencies in play. When the child is faced with unpleasant stressful situations over which mastery is incomplete, play provides an opportunity to rework the meaning of the stress and to practice solutions. Numerous clinicians have remarked about how restricted is problem solving in a child who does not have play or fantasy available as a problem solving tool.

The young child is limited in perspective taking (i.e., seeing the world from various points of view) that would be helpful in gaining alternative ways of coping with the stress of the divorce. Introspection is difficult for school age children and very limited in preschool age children. It is the rare child that can talk for long about the separation and divorce or upset over the chronic battling of the parents. Even the child who can talk about it at all is likely to exhaust the range of cognitions in a very short time. When a child is able to talk about the divorce and maintain the anxiety about the topic at manageable levels, the therapist should encourage the discussion of feelings and problem solving.

This author had one extremely bright 8-year-old boy who was able to talk extensively about his unhappy feelings about the divorce. Even with him, play became an adjunct for exploring alternatives without undue stress. For the average child, play provides an avenue for communication in a safe, trusting environment. Some child therapists believe that the Rogerian qualities of accurate empathy, nonpossessive warmth, and genuineness is necessary and sufficient for change to occur for children as well as for adults. Axline (1969) provides an example of a study of such noninterpretative therapy.

The relationship with the therapist is crucial, particularly with children undergoing the stress of marital separation, instability of postseparation lifestyles, and chronic upset between parents.

Often, the therapist is the only significant adult that is constant, accepting, and consistently caring. That stability alone is likely to be therapeutic. The caring from the therapist is also likely to help the child experience himself or herself as worthwhile.

The Effects of Caring

This author's private practice is in Boulder, Colorado, which is a relatively small town. Clinicians in small towns recognize that it is difficult to keep one's personal and professional lives completely separate. One day, a 10 year old girl in play therapy happened to see me in a shopping center with one of my daughters. At the next therapy session, I expected some reaction about finding out something personal about me and perhaps jealousy about having a daughter. The girl's actual reaction was unexpected: "I can't get over the fact that you are a father." When asked whether she had noticed my wedding ring, she said "yes." It had never occurred to her that I might be a father, however, "because *you* enjoy playing with me." Even if the content of the play had not been useful to her, the awareness of having an adult enjoy being with her was an important experience.

Does the Therapist's Gender Make a Difference?

The example just given raises the question of whether the gender of the therapist should be taken into account. Generally the answer is no, children will work on whatever they need to work on. The only exception to that rule is when the child has had no close experience with an adult member of that gender.

If the noncustodial parent is abandoning and the child has had no experience with an adult the same gender as the abandoning parent, there is a decided advantage in picking a therapist with that gender. This gender match would give the child the potential experience of having a warm relationship with a person of that gender. In other cases, the gender of the therapist is not relevant.

One mother suggested a woman therapist would be better for her daughter since the mother felt that the primary conflict was with her. This author felt that the child would likely work on whatever she needed to work on despite the therapist's gender. Indeed, within three sessions, I was playing a female role in our play, suggesting that the mother was correct in her perception of the conflict.

The Play Therapist's Role

Play therapy is much more difficult than adult therapy. There are several primary reasons why play therapy presents difficult work. In fact, there is some evidence that burn-out is relatively high among play therapists. Burn-out may be avoided by not doing play therapy exclusively. By mixing adult, couple, family, and play therapy, the therapist can avoid the exhaustion that can occur in working intensively with children. Play therapy is so exhausting because:

1. Play therapy is much like thinking in one language and talking in another. The child expresses a conflict or stress in symbolic language through play. The therapist must first translate that play into a conceptual understanding of the underlying conflict and then decide whether to provide a direct or metaphorical response that the child can understand. This response has to be

done while the child is still expressing that theme and has not moved on to another. Interpretation will be discussed later.

2.   The feedback as to whether the interpretation was useful is often delayed. Adults will give the therapist clues as to how useful a particular interpretation is by either accepting and using it, demonstrating a variety of defensive responses to it, or indicating why it is not useful. While children will also indicate at times that an interpretation is useful, it is not unusual for the therapist to have to wait several sessions to see whether a particular interpretation resulted in changes in the child's perceptions of the world.

3.   The therapist needs to be loose, playful, able to laugh, enjoy the child, and provide energy. The therapist needs to be able to enjoy the child. Therapists who had a restricted range of emotional experience in their own childhood may have difficulty loosening up with a child in a way that helps the child experience life in a new way. The ability to have a range of emotional experience is, of course, important to all therapy regardless of the age of the client. However, many therapists-in-training who are relatively effective with adult clients find it difficult to make the transition to child therapy.

4.   Because the child usually is not the person to make the decision for therapy, the child often does not understand the purpose of therapy and will not help in providing the focus. Resistance to the therapy may occur because the child fears that the therapist is an agent for the parents rather than an advocate for the child. In addition, the child is usually not capable of understanding the link between having personal problems and playing with a therapist. The child who does not want to play may create special problems for the therapist. The therapist must be creative to support play and in providing play settings that are going to be helpful for supporting change.

5.   The therapist must be supportive to parents as well as to the child in therapy. Some child therapists maintain chronic anger at parents, seeing them as the enemy who "damaged" the child. When the therapist identifies with the child and sees the parent as the enemy, the therapeutic stance is lost and the therapist is likely to be less effective.

6.   The system with which the therapist interacts is far more complex than is typically the case in adult therapy. Working with a child should always involve at least one parent, and optimally both. It may involve working with two families, stepparents, classroom teachers, day care providers, or even grandparents. Play therapy is seldom limited to one contact a week with just the child.

Goals of Play Therapy

All play therapies, regardless of theoretical orientation, have the following goals:

1.   *Increase recognition and acceptance of feelings.* Almost all therapy for children place value in helping the child understand what the feelings are. Ax-

line (1969), Ginott (1965) and Gordon (1970) all have focused on acceptance as a major goal of therapy. There is an apparent paradox in child psychology around the acceptance of feelings. It is clear that sometimes acceptance of feelings helps a child to feel more accepted, increases self-esteem, and improves problem solving. At other times, acceptance seems to reinforce the expression of negative feelings so that the child who is sympathetically responded to for angry expression of feelings may increase that expression. Certainly learning theory suggests that sometimes attention can reinforce the expression of negative feelings and experience suggests that sometimes parents reinforce whining or anger by responding to it. It is this author's personal experience that while recognition and expression of feelings is necessary for therapy, it is not sufficient.

The child must experience the therapist as warm and accepting of the child (but not necessarily of the behavior). Helping the child understand what feelings are being experienced and that those feelings are acceptable is a basic prerequisite to therapy occurring. With very bright children, this acceptance may be sufficient for change to occur, but most children need additional help to understand what the implications of having those feelings are.

2.   *Change acting out to talking out.* One major function of therapy is to help the child learn to use verbal symbols for problem solving. Helping the child think about the conflicts in life rather than behaving automatically to them can improve the child's adjustment.

Thus, one function of play therapy is to give identification to feelings of play figures, to talk about how they feel and why they feel that way rather than simply letting the figures continue to be destructive, withdrawn, or scared. When a child starts hitting the large punching doll, therefore, the therapist could start hitting the doll too. After a while, the therapist could start to tell the doll using themes that are likely to be of concern to the child, why he or she is angry at the doll. Later, the therapist could talk to the doll directly and with little aggression. Such a sequence also demonstrates the ally role discussed later in this chapter.

3.   *Improve problem solving.* It is this author's position that all feelings are perfectly logical. The feelings are logically connected to the underlying perceptions of the world. There are only incorrect premises about the nature of the world. Helping the child see that there are alternative ways of perceiving the world and that there are alternative ways of coping with problems will improve problem solving.

4.   *Direct the child toward getting needs met.* Erikson (1963) noted that cultures are designed to protect the family and the family is designed to protect the child. Every family is expected to provide nurturance and protection to children. When, for whatever reason the family or environment does not per-

form that function, the child may have to solve the problem normally solved by the family.

5. *Increase discrimination so that problem solving and getting needs met are more appropriate.* If a child feels attacked, he or she needs to learn that he or she is not being attacked by everyone. If the child feels abandoned, he or she needs to understand that there are people who are willing to stand by him or her. One 10 year old boy, for example, came in very angry and refused to interact. A good reaction was this: "When you come in here angry with me, I feel that you are angry at grown-ups and I am one more grown-up."

Diagnosis in Play Therapy

The Initial Parent Interview

Prior to seeing the child for the first time, a meeting with both parents (if available) is essential. Whether it is better to meet with the parents together or separately may depend on the quality of the relationship between them. It is important to evaluate the quality of the relationship between the parents. If the requesting parent indicates that such a joint meeting would be extremely difficult, the therapist should readily agree to separate meetings.

If the noncustodial parent has regular contact with the child, meeting with that parent might be considered as a condition of accepting a therapeutic contract. If the parent rarely sees the child or is an abandoning parent, such a requirement may not be necessary. However, if it is possible for a therapist to re-engage an abandoning parent with support for adequate parenting, such a strategy should be considered.

In that session, a discussion of the concerns of the parent(s) are obtained, followed by a developmental history, starting with the conditions of conception, pregnancy, delivery, infancy, and present development. Informed consent for contact with the schools should be obtained if it is appropriate. However, it is best to not contact the schools until after the diagnostic play therapy sessions. It is particularly interesting to note those areas in which each parent sees the facts as different. Retrospective reports are notoriously inaccurate, therefore *both* parents may be wrong and such reports should be taken with a grain of salt and considered tentative.

The initial contact with the parents will also explain how play therapy works and what would be the next steps. The parents should be given an explanation to give to the child about why they are coming (a surprising number of parents will bring the child with no explanation of why they are going to see this strange man). Instructing the parents what to tell the child about therapy is creating a model of the importance of providing explanations to the child. In addition, the therapist will be able to assess the degree to which they are able to follow-up on such suggestions.

The parents should be told the rules of confidentiality, that is, that the child will be told that the sessions are confidential and that the parents will not be informed on anything that the child tells the therapist or of the content of the play. Exceptions to this rule involve abuse or situations where the child may be potentially harmful to self or others. They are warned that a child choosing to not tell them the content of the play is a good sign for positive outcomes, since the child may be indicating a willingness to work on meaningful material.

The therapist should only provide information about the general areas of problems that the child is having and whether the therapy is able to provide help in those areas. It should be noted that many child therapists do not maintain such a confidentiality orientation and believe that parents should be informed on the ongoing therapy content. Parents should be seen on a regular basis depending on an assessment of how much they need to change their behavior in order to facilitate the therapy and how resistive they are likely to be to the changes in the child.

To reduce competition between the parents and the therapists, the parents should be told that the reasons why a therapist can often be helpful when it is difficult for a parent are twofold:

1. The therapist is not important enough. Children can afford to take chances with the therapist because they simply do not care that much how the therapist feels. Children can have difficulty talking to parents because they do care about how the parent feels.
2. The therapist only has the responsibility of understanding and being helpful. The major responsibility of physical protection and providing structure for the child's emotional and physical well-being belongs to the parents. Therefore, the therapist does not have to say "no" as often.

Play Therapy Evaluation

The first few sessions in play therapy provide the therapist with an opportunity to understand the symbols that the child uses, how much fantasy is available as a problem solving tool (or escape), and where the child is developmentally. The play room should have eliciting materials that encourage the child to enter play. Appropriate materials include a doll house with family figures, puppets, play clothes, balls, blocks, crayons, paper, and a wide range of toys. Toys should be selected that may be too young and too old for the child, as well as age appropriate (to evaluate developmental level). Toys should also be appropriate and inappropriate from a sex-role perspective. It is important to have eliciting materials. Because aggression is a common problem, materials that are aggression-eliciting are important. Punch dolls (which must be quite durable) that are similar in height to the child are useful. Foam rubber bats and pretend swords and knives can also be helpful. Avoid materials that can cause harm such as darts, plastic swords, and hard plastic toys.

The child should be told that there are five rules in the playroom:

1. They may not hurt themselves.
2. They may not hurt me.
3. They may not damage the room.
4. They must end on time.
5. The room must be in order at the end of the session so that other children can use it.

Other eliciting materials include dolls and family figures with a house. Younger children often prefer more fanciful houses such as castles. Some people have argued that if the therapist is working with children of divorce, it is appropriate to have *two* doll houses, on the grounds that it is more likely to reflect the reality of the child. It is, however, extremely rare for a child to provide a fantasy involving two homes. Often children identify one home as primary or are manifesting the wish for reconciliation by using a single home. Fantasy seldom demonstrates an identity with two home settings. With the recent increase in joint residential custody, this dynamic may change.

If the child is reluctant to separate from the parent in the waiting room, the parent may accompany the child and the therapist to the play room and stay a few minutes. If there is any show of anxiety about separation, the child should be told that the parent will remain in the waiting room. (Parents should stay in the waiting room for the first few sessions.) Children can check on seeing the parents at any time during the session. The ability to return to the parent is usually enough reassurance. Few children actually check out the presence of the parent (although a request to go to the restroom may have the function of checking on the parent's presence).

During the first session, the therapist should spend some time with the child explaining who he or she is and why the child is there. Since parents all too often do not provide any explanation to the child as to why the child is suddenly seeing this strange person in this strange setting, it is important to provide a truthful (although not necessarily exhaustive) explanation. For very young children, an appropriate explanation is that the therapist is like a worry doctor and that worry doctors talk about worries and do not use medicine or shots. The child could be told that someone in the family is worried. The parents may be worried about the child. They may see the child as worried about stresses in life.

Older children should be told that everything that they say is secret. Parents will not be told about play or discussions unless the child might hurt himself or herself. Other people will not be told unless the child is being hurt. The children should know that parents are very curious about what happens in play therapy. They should be given permission to tell the parents if they wish.

However, the therapist should also say that it is appropriate to tell the parents, that "the therapist said I don't have to tell."

It is this author's experience that children who choose to keep the content of the therapy secret from parents are often more serious about using the time effectively. While nothing may have happened yet in therapy that could remotely affect the parents, the wish to keep the content of the therapy secret has two functions: (1) it is a healthy statement of individuation from the parents and (2) it can be a recognition that future sessions may move into meaningful material.

During the first session or two, the therapist should play a more passive role in order to see how the child handles the therapist's presence, the new room, and which of the toys he or she prefers. Fantasy play is encouraged by having the therapist participate in the fantasy. During the diagnostic phase, however, no interpretation is made and only elaboration based on the child's leads are used. Children are sometimes reluctant to enter into play because they either do not have fantasy as a resource (indicating fewer problem solving skills in a child) or because they are self-conscious about letting an adult into the play. The degree of enjoyment that most children experience once joint play occurs is profound and aids the development of the therapeutic alliance.

Therapists who enter into and participate in the play therapy rather than remain a passive observer help facilitate the therapeutic alliance. Only therapists with a degree of playfulness should try this strategy however, since a stilted participation will be experienced by the child as rejecting.

Play Interpretation

There are two stages in the creative aspect of play therapy. The first stage is to propose a series of hypotheses about the symbolic meaning of the play. The following questions are useful in proposing hypotheses:

1. What is the cognitive understanding of the world? From Piaget's theory comes the questions about object permanence, time perspective, egocentrism, and cause-effect thinking. From Erikson comes questions about basic trust, autonomy, and industry. From Freudian developmental theory comes questions of psychosexual development, and from object relations theory comes questions about attachment, individuation and separation.

2. How is the view of the world distorted and how is it accurate? The context of the developmental history is important in making initial estimates of the accuracy of the world view. How dangerous is it? If parents report child or spouse abuse or severe battles with yelling and screaming, a child who views the world as a violent place is pretty understandable.

Assessment of play therapy candidates may require two or three sessions. Toward the latter part of this time, the therapist will see the degree to which the child can tolerate mild changes in the play through interpretation. The second or third session may begin with an invitation to talk about the child's life, and whether the child has any worries. Later, interpretations that encourage the child to change that cognitive understanding and develop new coping strategies should be provided.

The Role of Interpretation

Central to play therapy is the role of interpretation. How is the therapist helping the child change that cognitive understanding of the nature of the world? Once hypotheses are developed concerning what the cognitive understanding of the world is and how it is distorted or accurate, two additional questions are required in order to develop effective interpretation:

1. What would be adequate coping for this child? The therapist has to determine what world view would be more helpful than the one the child has.

2. How can that change in cognitive understanding be presented to the child within the context of play? One major dimension on which therapists who do interpretative play therapy differ is the degree to which they give interpretations within or outside of the metaphor. The therapist can have another character in the fantasy present alternatives (within the metaphor). The therapist can comment on the feelings or options of the protagonist in the play (again, within the metaphor). Finally, the therapist can note the similarities of play characters with real events in the child's world (out of the metaphor).

The degree to which the symbols are disguised, the greater the defensive structure of the child. Some defensiveness is healthy. The child with no defenses is likely to be quickly overwhelmed by stress. Some children draw a parallel between their lives and the characters in the play. This author once took the role of a hated gym teacher with one child and he proceeded to joyously attack me. For older children, taking nonhuman figures or highly developed fantasy figures may be an expression of the need to have greater distance from the emotionality of the play.

The more the child is able to tolerate the anxiety associated with an interpretation, the better able the child is to develop adequate coping strategies for the problem at hand. It is generally useful to provide as direct an interpretation as the child is able to utilize. For example, talking to the child about real events, if tolerated, may be more useful than talking about characters in a fantasy. If not tolerated, talking about the fantasy is far more useful.

Sometimes the child will begin talking about a problem, but cut off discussion because the anxiety level is too high. The child may be able to deal with the issues involved by disguising the anxiety-provoking elements to a greater degree, thereby reducing the associated anxiety.

For example, in a case of a child of divorce that this author supervised, the mother informed the therapist that her 6 year old son had gotten into a fight with a girl in his class at school. When the therapist asked the child what had happened, the child was unwilling or unable to discuss it. The therapist then asked whether the child could show her what had happened with the dolls. By using the dolls (and only slightly disguising the figures since the child was indicating that he was reporting on a factual event) the child was able to depict what had happened. The enactment was abbreviated, but complete. Later in the same session, the child gave a rich story of a boy who had been attacked by a girl and had to defend himself. That story was not presented as factual, but gave details about how the child had experienced and justified his behavior.

Greater abstraction in symbolization in an interpretation can be helpful if the child is still overwhelmed by anxiety.

For example, particularly for younger children, the symbolization can be expressed with animals rather than people as actors in the play. Even greater distance can occur when more primitive symbols such as bombs, explosions, or other inanimate objects express feelings.

When the child is incapable of discussing a particular issue, the therapist can give permission for a range of emotions and cognitions by discussing what "some children" feel in similar circumstances and asking whether this child has similar experiences.

The therapist should be concerned when a child does not maintain some distance. The child who uses real names of family members for actors in a play may not be establishing enough distance to effectively manipulate the symbols for useful problem solving. If the therapist feels that the child is not learning to cognitively manipulate symbols and learn symbolic problem solving, the child could be encouraged to distance the symbols.

The therapist should monitor the level of abstraction in the symbols that the child uses in play therapy in order to optimize the level of problem solving. As therapy progresses, and problem solving becomes more effective the child will often lower the levels of anxiety associated with symbols. The therapist may then be able to be more direct in the interpretations given to the child. Completely effective therapy can be obtained, however, without ever directly interpreting the meaning of the symbols to the child.

In order to do effective play therapy, it is necessary for a play therapist to watch the favorite movies and television shows of children, at least once. For some therapists this may be an onerous chore. For others it may be an excuse to see some movies that they would otherwise not see. After the *Star Wars* movies came out, numerous children in play therapy introduced star war themes. When *Willie Wonka and the Chocolate Factory* came out in movie form on television, this author had two children introduce chocolate factory stories in therapy. Not only is it important to know what stories "hook" the child, but it is also very important to spot changes in the story that fit the child's needs. Popular television shows including super powers are often incorporated into the fantasy.

Generally the more adjusted the child and the older the child, the greater the ability to use interpretation that draws the parallel with the child's life. Often later therapy sessions will include more direct interpretation.

How to Tell When an Interpretation Is Helpful

Since the therapist is dealing with symbolic imagery, there is no procedure to determine whether the hypothesis concerning the meaning of the symbol is correct. Interpretations can only be useful or not useful to the child. In order for an interpretation to be useful, it must be at least in some way at a level of cognitive complexity that the child is capable of utilizing. In addition, in order to utilize the information, the child must not be overwhelmed with anxiety.

There are several indicators that the interpretation is helpful:

1.   If the child incorporates the comment into the context of play or is willing to use the suggestion with the characters in the play, the interpretation may have been useful. If the child spontaneously incorporates the suggestion in the play in future sessions, the interpretation has been demonstrated as useful.

Children will sometimes indulge an adult without developing cognitive schemas associated with the interpretation. The failure to incorporate an interpretation in future play is likely to be an indication that the interpretation was not useful at the present time, either because the hypothesis is wrong or because the timing was wrong.

When an interpretation is very reasonable, but is not effective in changing the content of play, it is useful to turn around the potential way in which the symbols are being used. For example, it may be useful to propose that the symbol is a defense rather than a wish. A 9-year-old boy had a fantasy using building blocks and toys trucks in which a building caught on fire and a fire truck had to come and rescue the boy off the burning building. Low level interpretations about an out-of-control world, the need to be rescued, and even metaphoric suggestions that it was nice to have a rescuer (the therapist) around when things were not going well were accepted, but did not change the play over several weeks. Assuming that these interpretations were not useful, a reinterpretation that the person was setting the fire in order to force the firemen to prove that they still cared changed the play. Ultimately, the theme of having problems as a way of getting people to care was a recurrent symbol.

2.   If the child refuses to include a suggestion in the play, the interpretation is not useful.

3.   If the child stops the play and requests to play something else, there may have been an error in therapy. Such actions are usually responses to intense anxiety. Such disruptions are extremely useful, however, since they indicate clearly what symbols are being used. The therapist should permit the disruption, and then either use a less direct method of introducing the interpretation in the future or determine the smaller steps that the child needs to be able to accept the interpretation.

Process Themes in Play Therapy

A variety of content themes have been observed in working with children of divorce and are useful to expect. The utility of knowing specific symbolic content areas for children of divorce is that such areas form initial hypotheses about the meaning of specific fantasy material. Since children form idiosyncratic meanings, the therapist must be ready to abandon a hypothesis if the data indicate that interpretations based on that hypothesis is not useful.

The sequence of themes provides a useful indicator of the psychological development of the child. One child built forts which were immediately destroyed by the enemy. The inability to protect himself was a recurrent theme. The therapy explored both why the enemy was so powerful and how a stronger fort could be built. Could there be negotiations with the enemy? Why does the enemy want to destroy us? Is there help to make us stronger? These questions also raise another important principle of play therapy. In participatory play with the child, play the role of friend and let the enemy be imaginary.

When the play therapist is entering the play with the child, it is better to play the role of an ally of the child, rather than the enemy. There are two reasons why that role works better. First, the child is more willing to let an ally have alternative solutions to the problem than an enemy. Second, the child will often object when the enemy behaves less like an enemy. The child will then try to exert greater control over the script. With the therapist as an ally, the therapist can raise questions about the motives of the enemy and possible alternative ways of handling the enemy that model more effective problem solving.

An example of sequencing is a child who began with building laser beams that would destroy the galaxy. This child had major problems with aggression in school. Indeed the hypothesis was developed that this child felt the need to destroy everything before it destroyed him. As we worked together to destroy the galaxy, the anger gradually become more circumscribed from destroying the solar system, to the world, to attacking aliens and to finally providing protection so that attack was not necessary. Questions about why they were out to get us and whether perhaps they were scared of us were raised. Finally we developed ways of protecting ourselves without attack. There was a similar reduction in the use of aggression outside of therapy.

Common Themes of the Play Therapy of Children of Divorce

There are several common themes in play therapy.

1. *Anger.* An angry child is more intrusive than a grieving, withdrawn one. Acting out anger in school or home (or both) is a common impetus for parents seeking therapy for the child. Thomas Gordon (1970) identified anger as a secondary emotion. Thomas felt that children were most helped when the underlying feeling that generated the anger was identified to the child.

Since acting out of anger is a common response of preschool and early elementary school age children, helping the child to deal with the expression of anger is important. First linking the aggression to feelings of abandonment, unfairness, being attacked, of deprivation, and of not feeling loved is helpful to the child. The process then is to help the child see that the tantrum behavior evokes attack or withdrawal, but not negotiation. Talk and negotiation is likely to be more helpful. If negotiation is not helpful, the child must then turn to others to get needs met. Constructive anger addresses the cause of the anger and negotiates reduction in that cause. The child must learn self-control as part of that negotiation.

2. *Abandonment.* The child must decide whether true abandonment has occurred, how to ask for more support, how to gain reassurance that remaining people will not abandon, and how to get needs partially met.

3. *Loss.* Toomin (1974) proposed that loss is a basic issue for the child and that the process of coping with loss is the same, whether the loss is due to death, divorce, or a widening of psychosocial distance. Losses must be mourned in order for the child to separate from the absent person and develop new relationships.

Toomin's therapeutic approaches (either by working with parents or with the child) all imply working with the child around mourning, that is, helping the child over and over again express feelings of sadness and anger. Defenses against loss must be dealt with, including premature detachment and excessively close relationship with the other parent, or internalization of the lost person as a way of avoiding loss. Toomin felt that internalization of negative qualities occurs when the absent parent is feared. Identification with the aggressor is a common defense against overwhelming anxiety. Toomin noted that it was more common to internalize an idealized positive image of a separated father, even when the father was cruel.

While conceptualizing loss as an underlying construct for divorce is consistent with Bowlby's (1969) theoretical view of grief in childhood, there is some question in my mind about whether the child responds to all loses with the need for mourning. Mourning is significantly more difficult when the absent parent is either partially absent or completely absent, but alive. This author questions whether children conceptualize loss of a relationship as a loss requiring mourning. The egocentrism of children may lead to internalized feelings of rejection, but not grieving. Certainly the research discussed in Chapters 2 and 3 indicates that prior losses do not predispose a child of divorce to greater distress to the separation and divorce of parents.

Gardner (1976) also noted that grief and depression were common thematic issues for children of divorce and focussed in his book on *Psychotherapy with Children of Divorce* on several other common themes:

4. *Denial.* All therapists of children of divorce note that denial of the underlying feelings around the divorce process is a common response of children who have difficulty and are in need of psychotherapeutic help.

5. *Blame and guilt.* This theme is discussed in detail in Chapter 2.

6. *Immaturity.* Regression can be a response to overwhelming stress or can be an attempt to draw attention away from parental conflict to the child as the identified patient. Children can wish to be younger in order to return the family to the predivorce stage of development.

7. *Hypermaturity.* Pseudomaturity has already been discussed in detail in Chapter 2.

8. *Reconciliation preoccupation.*

9. *Self-esteem.*

10. *Sex role identification and sexual identity.* For children dealing with Oedipal issues (and unlike classical analytic theory, this author does not believe in the inevitability of the oedipal conflict), the separation of parents can be either the winning of the conflict so that the child has overwhelming anxiety or the losing of the conflict and the child feels rejected at a basic level.

As noted in Chapter 2, parents can feed these fantasies by allowing the child into the parental bed. Numerous families have participated in seductive behaviors in the name of sexual openness in the family. Nudity, family bathing, family "beds," and exposure of children to sexual material or sexual intercourse are common. Late latency and adolescent children can be identified as the "man" or "woman" of the house. It is important that parent consultation strongly deal with these problems.

11. *The quest for the wanted person.* Tessman's (1978) book on therapy with children of divorce mentioned the quest for the wanted person as an additional theme for children of divorce. Tessman was struck by the frequency by which children of divorce develop a quest for the lost parent. This quest may be a wish to merge with the wanted person or to be like that person. It may be a way of dealing with loss. This quest obviously prevents mourning and development of new attachments. This theme has also been addressed in other parts of this text.

12. *Cinderella.* The author's own experience in play therapy has indicated another common theme, Cinderella. The feeling of deprivation while others are allowed to go to the ball is a common theme. If played out in its entirety, the Cinderella theme offers the child hope of rescue, and love. Other ways in

which this theme of deprivation gets played out includes stealing themes and starving themes. Concern with lack of nurturance is developmentally more advanced than another common theme I have observed, annihilation.

13.   *Annihilation.* One of the most primitive themes is the total destruction of self. When a child repeatedly comes up with themes of self-destruction, it gives a clear picture of the panic that the separation has created for the child. Indeed, as noted in the examples in the previous section, rage on the part of the child may be a defense against this fear of self-destruction: kill before being killed.

14.   Feelings of guilt, responsibility of fear of retribution (Derdeyn, 1977).

15.   Feelings of devaluation (Derdeyn, 1977).

16.   Wishes for reconciliation (Derdeyn, 1977).

Techniques for Encouraging Fantasy Play

Some children are quite resistant to fantasy play either because they do not use fantasy in their lives or are scared of the implications of sharing their fantasy. Late latency boys particularly have difficulty getting into fantasy play. Gardner (1976), discussed in some detail later in this chapter, has developed numerous games to entice the child into trying fantasy.

One technique that this author has found useful for children who are resistant to fantasy play is "radio announcer." When a child is shooting foam basketballs, I will pick up a block or racket and pretend that it is a microphone and start announcing the shots as a sports announcer. The "basketball player" is then interviewed about how he feels about winning or losing or what happens when he misses a shot.

This author played news and weather program with a resistant 11-year-old girl. Headlines were made up to fit her problems, that is, "Guru found in cave up in mountains. He doesn't want to interact with anyone. Says that no one can hurt him up there." The weather report she gave was revealing about the turmoil she felt. "The weather in Alaska is most unusual today. There is a line down the middle of the state. On one side it is 50° below zero and on the other 110°. Down the middle, there are earthquakes and wind storms."

With another child this author played fortune teller. The child's fortune was told including stress lines and coping.

This author will use any available technique. One child was unwilling to stay in the play room. We roamed around the building. He asked if he could learn the key punch machines. The key punch machines were used to encourage him to deal with me in the play rooms. If the child played with me in the therapy room, we could spend 10 minutes on the machine. While he punched "secret" codes, I punched interpretations.

Another useful strategy for getting children to get involved in fantasy is Winicott's (1971) squiggles game. The squiggles game is one that absorbs children over a wide range of ages. This author has used it successfully from ages 6 to 12.

This technique involves having the therapist give a random (and rather simple) set of lines on a piece of paper. He tells the child that he will shut his eyes and make a mark on the paper. The child must then turn it into something. Then the child is asked to do the same thing while the therapist turns it into something. The therapist should continue the theme introduced by the child, usually with little elaboration. Interpretation should be avoided until the therapist feels that the child and he are talking about the same theme and that the child is able to use the interpretation. Winicott's examples indicate that interpretation was given both within and outside of the metaphor.

This therapist used the squiggles game to evoke themes of danger. My drawing involved having a big fish chase a little fish that was swimming into a hole too small for the big fish. My message to the child was that there are ways in which a little fish can be safe from danger. If the drawing had occurred at another point in therapy, a second big fish might have been drawn to help the little fish from danger (either an alliance with a supportive parent or the therapist).

Termination of Play Therapy

The imagery of play can tell the therapist when termination is near. The degree of conflict in the imagery will be significantly less. Acting out behavior is significantly reduced in the nontherapy world, and self-control and higher self-esteem seem to have some stability. Sometimes the imagery itself tells the therapist that the time to stop has come.

THERAPIST: Pretend we are in a domed city.

CHILD: OK

THERAPIST: We are looking out a round window. [A pretend window opens up]

CHILD: What we see is poisonous gas. You know, I used to think that poisonous gas was miles and miles thick. But I recently discovered that it is only a foot thick and on the other side there are birds, and trees, and flowers.

Clearly, this child is saying that he was ready to stop therapy. Termination in play therapy with children of divorce is particularly problematic.

It is important that the termination not reinstate a sense of parent loss and rejection that the child has already experienced. The termination should not become one more adult abandonment.

There are several good strategies that this author uses:

1.   Try to give the child some control over the quitting time. The therapist may indicate that life is going so well now that it is getting time to stop. The child should decide the exact date, given a small range of times in the near future. Children who have completely finished and show high levels of adjustment will often pick the closest time. Also children that find coming painful because of their concern about the stigma of being in therapy will often terminate as soon as possible. Children who pick the middle date are often showing the ability to compromise between their wants and their needs. Finally, the child who hangs on to therapy as long as possible may still be expressing dependency needs or strong attachment to the therapist. Regardless of when the child picks, this choice is one termination of a relationship in life where the child had some control over the ending.

2.   Indicate to the child that while the relationship will end, the caring will not end. They will be remembered forever. "Forever?" One 11-year-old girl asked me. "I will never forget you," I said. Three years later, she wrote me a letter that began, "Did you forget?"

The therapist wants to do everything possible to encourage object permanence. An 11-year-old boy who was terminated a month previously knocked on my office door. I was in conference with students and could not spend time with him. However, I stopped for 5 minutes to express pleasure at seeing him. He seemed enormously relieved that I still cared, smiled happily, and ran off satisfied. The child never again contacted me. That 5 minute contact was reassurance enough that I still cared after the therapy was over.

Such reassurance is particularly important when the child has experienced abandonment by the noncustodial parent or death of a parent. Establishing a belief that caring continues beyond the contact gives them the opportunity to hold on to the gains received from the therapy and use the identifications and bondings that they have not only with the therapist, but with other, more important people in their lives.

GARDNER'S MUTUAL STORYTELLING TECHNIQUE

Gardner (1976) developed a therapeutic technique for many children in therapy. His book, *Psychotherapy with Children of Divorce,* described the techniques in detail for that population of patients. The therapeutic techniques are not used for borderline or psychotic children or any child in which elaboration of fantasy is contraindicated. He focused on individual child therapy with parental observation and intermittent participation. The younger the child, the more parental involvement might occur.

The Mutual Storytelling Technique involves having the child tell a made-up story with a moral. The therapist then tells the same story with similar settings and the same characters, but with healthier adaptations and resolutions. Gardner uses humor and drama to encourage a therapeutic alliance. The technique is a more structured form of play therapy. It is completely compatible with my own view of what children need and the prior discussion in this chapter. By using fantasy, Gardner allows children to talk indirectly about what is bothering them and provides new cognitions about the perception of the world and what would be better coping strategies for coping with that stress.

The technique requires the same task of the therapist as play therapy: What is the theme that the child is presenting in the story? Which figures in the story represent the child and which represent significant others? What retelling of the story would provide the child with a different view of the world and better coping with it?

An example from Gardner's book provides a clear picture of how he uses the technique.* Kenneth, a 10-and-a-half-year-old boy whose parents had separated about six months prior to referral, told this story during his third week in treatment:

PATIENT (P):   Once there was a boy named Bill. He went with his parents on a picnic and, um, his parents gave him permission to walk—go down— this is up in the mountains—this is all taking place.

THERAPIST (T):   His parent gave him permission to do what?

P: Go around and look in the woods.

T: Yeah.

P: So his brother and sister were down by the lake and since he loves forest creatures . . . (mumbles) . . . .

T: Wait. His brother and sister did what now? Went down with him to the lake?

P: Yeah. And he was spying around and he saw some raccoon footprints.

T: Hh hmm.

P: And he being a very great lover of animals, um, followed them.

T: Yeah.

P: He kept on following them and following them, and following them until finally he saw that it was getting dark and it was getting cold. In the mountains it gets quite cold at night and he only had a thin jacket. And all of a sudden it was getting cold and it was getting really dark, and he couldn't follow the tracks back to the lake. And he started getting scared. He panicked and he went round and around in circles and circles for a few hours until he realized that he was going around in circles. Then he came back around and sat down and went to sleep. He could imagine his father and mother would go down to the sheriff's office and look for him. He would probably find his way back.

*Richard A. Gardner, Psychotherapy with Children of Divorce, 1976, reprinted with permission of Jason Aronson, Inc.

T: Yeah.

P: So he went to bed. And when he woke up he followed the tracks back and he walked back to the picnic grounds.

T: When he woke up he followed the tracks back. Yeah.

P: And he found the picnic grounds and he found his mother and father.

T: Hh hmm. I see. And that's the whole story?

P: Yeah.

T: And the lesson of that story?

P: There is none.

T: Aw, come on. Usually there is a lesson to every story. What's the lesson of that story?

P: Um, never follow a trail that isn't suited for the . . . (mumbles) . . . .

T: That isn't what?

P: That isn't marked for the night.

T: Okay. Now it's time for me to tell my story.

Gardner's analysis of that story focused on the view of the child that if he were abandoned by both parents, he could not count on them to seek him out. Gardner saw the child as believing that he would have to rely on his own resources to protect himself from abandonment. Gardner noted that there were strengths in the story in that the child was willing to assume responsibility for his own care. Gardner felt that there was less abandonment from the parents that the child thought. Both parents seemed to deeply care about the children.

Here is Gardner's retelling of the story:

THERAPIST: Once upon a time there was a boy and he was out with his mother and his father on a picnic. And he decided that he was going to do some scouting around. Now he knew that his mother and father were not fully capable of finding him were he to get lost. Although they were good at many things, they were not good at finding him if he was lost, because they themselves had trouble finding their way about in the forest. He knew he could count on them somewhat, but he knew that he couldn't count on them completely. Anyway, he knew that at times he could count on them to help guide him through the forest, but he knew that at other times he would have trouble.

So he decided to take a little can of paint and about every three or four hundred feet he would paint a little yellow spot on a tree so that he kind of made a trail for himself and would be able to find his way back. And in that circumstance he didn't get lost and if he got far away he had no trouble getting back. At other times he didn't have to take the can of paint because he knew that he could count on his parents when the forest was less dense and when there were standard markers and things like that.

So the lesson of that story is: if you can't count on your parents to guide you at certain times you may have to guide yourself. At other times when they can guide you then it's okay to count on them. The end. Anything you want to say?

PATIENT: Uh uh.

T: Okay. Any comments about that story?

P: Uh uh.

T: Okay.

In the example above, Gardner demonstrated both how he retells a story and the cognitive reorientation provided the child about the nature and degree of abandonment by the parents. Note how Gardner did not give unrealistic expectations about how much parents are able to give. Such a technique obviously works only to the degree that the therapist has a clear picture of family dynamics in order to determine what would be more effective coping.

Gardner's book on therapy for children of divorce is particularly useful in describing the cognitive reorientations that such children tend to need. Examples of such changes in world view include:

1.   If the theme of the story is to keep secrets, the child is given the message that children are better off when information is not kept secret.

2.   If the child gives a story of being alone, the message is that life is easier with help.

3.   If the story is that the child is fragile, the counter-message is that the child is not so fragile.

4.   Change acting out to talking out (note that this message is common to all interpretative and existential child therapies).

5.   Get needs met where appropriate, from other members of the family or friends. Do not keep asking for needs to be met from a parent who cannot meet them.

6.   Partial solutions are better than no solutions. Accept partial happiness and partial meeting of needs.

7.   Everyone is both good and bad. As previously noted in this book, children often split as a way of handling their ambivalence about their parents. The child who chooses one parent over the other is engaging in maladaptive problem solving and inviting self-rejection through the identification with that parent.

8.   Reduce identification with acting out parents.

9.   Reduce fantasy of reconciliation and get on with life.

10.   Do not become a parent surrogate.

11.   Do not win the oedipal conflict.

Much of Gardner's book on therapy with children of divorce presented techniques for helping children get into fantasy material. The child of divorce who has fantasy available is more likely to do effective problem solving. Examples from Gardner on how to help children get into story telling include:

1. Make Up a Story Television Program (kindergarten through second grade). There are 64 squares on a board. The squares have miniature toys including family members, zoo animals, farm animals, cars, and common objects such as baby bottle, knife, gun, lipstick, trophy and clay. A pair of dice with one red side are used. If one red side is up (one-third of the time), then the child selects an object. If the child can say anything about the object, he or she receives one reward chip. If a story is provided, then the child gets two reward chips. The person with the most chips at the end of the day (apparently usually the child, not the therapist) wins a prize.

2. Bag games. The child removes an object from a bag with the same reward system as in the previous game. There is a bag of toys, of things, and of words. The child gets two extra chips for picking the bag of words and telling a story. Words in the bag include "breast," "anger," "mother," "father," "love," and "hate."

3. *Scrabble for Juniors** (late first grade to fifth grade). Pick up seven tiles. The therapist and child play two letters at a time, building toward a word. Completing a word earns a reward chip. If the player says anything about the word, another reward chip is earned. If a story is given, there are two extra reward chips.

4. Alphabet Soup Game. The child is shown a plastic bowl with plastic letters. The child scoops up letters with spoons and is given one chip if the child can form a word, two chips if the child can comment on the word, and three chips if the child tells a story. The child can pay two chips and rescoop for letters.

5. The Talking, Feeling, Doing Game (third grade to sixth grade). This is a game that Gardner has made available for purchase. Cards involve talking about something, talking about feelings, and pretending doing something. The cards are divided into low anxiety instructions and moderate anxiety provoking comments. An example of a low anxiety provoking card for talking is "What food do you hate the most? Why?" An example of a moderate level of anxiety on a card is, "A child is ashamed to tell his father about something. What is it?"

TESSMAN'S ANALYTICALLY ORIENTED THERAPY

Another major description of therapy is Tessman's (1978) book, *Children of Parting Parents*. This book is rich with case history material about children

---

*Manufactured by Selechow and Richter, Bayshore, New York.

dealing with the separation and divorce of parents. From Tessman's point of view, the therapy is to help the child make peace with the loss so as to not lose the capacity for loving. When the child cannot share the sense of loss with others and substitutes symptoms for grieving, then psychotherapy is indicated.

The quest for the absent person is one way in which the child avoids dealing with the loss. As previously mentioned, the quest may be a searching for the rejecting or abandoning parent with a wish to merge or identify with that parent. The child may search for faces at shopping centers, looking for the parent, even when the abandonment has been so long ago that the child no longer knows what the parent looks like. The quest prevents grieving of the lost relationship and according to Tessman, "constriction of further growth is most clearly associated with situations in which the quest emerged predominantly as a defense against loss, unbolstered by sufficiently positive realities in the previous relationship and by an adequate human support network at the time of the loss" (p. 557).

When therapy begins, Tessman cautioned that the child should not be asked to separate from a therapist too quickly. If an intake evaluation is being done prior to starting therapy, she recommended that no more than two evaluation sessions be used if transfer to another professional might follow.

For services provided in an agency or institutional setting, the evaluation procedure should not risk an increase in feelings of abandonment. A child can quickly attach to a person doing assessment and find a transfer to a therapist another loss.

Tessman also warned the therapist to avoid counter-transference issues of wanting to be the person to fill the void for the child. The loss is real and substitution of the therapist as a pseudo-parent is not adaptive. The child must experience the loss of the therapist at some time in the future. The role of the therapist is to help the child deal with that loss. Therapy provides a reliable relationship with sufficient support to allow the child to risk sadness.

Tessman saw the task of confrontation in therapy as twofold. The first type of confrontation is the "effort to unmask denial." This area of confrontation is less often needed because the problem of the child is less often denial of inner impulses than it is denial of the reality of the loss of love of the absent parent. The child must give up an omnipotent self-image or parent-image that could make everything come out all right.

The second type of confrontation involves depression around abandoning the quest for the absent wanted person. Anger toward the therapist is a likely dynamic in this stage. Giving up such wishes for having the pleasure of the intact family was seen by Tessman as similar to giving up of all infantile wishes. Being able to make choices for himself or herself can be enormously freeing up to the child who no longer behaves in such a way as to bring back the absent parent.

Tessman cautioned the therapist to not become so intrigued with the imaginative nature of play therapy to lose sight of the goal of utilizing the material for ego-building. Ego-building occurs when the therapist supports the child's interest in sublimation and gratifying realities rather than interpreting underlying libidinal significance. When Tessman discussed interpretation at this stage, she was describing a process of problem solving very similar to my own cognitive orientation and totally consistent with Gardner's ego supportive reorientation toward reality.

Tessman also noted that rapid "transference cure" based on the positive relationship with the therapist is common with neurotic children. I have received reports from parents of sudden improvement of behavior on the part of the child long before I have provided reinterpretations of the cognitive orientation of the child. While Tessman feels that some children have gained enough inner freedom from such transference cure to be able to continue growth, it has been my experience that the child usually needs continued help with working through the experience of the divorce and what it meant.

Transference cure can only occur with the neurotic child. The impulse-ridden child cannot develop such identification with the therapist. Anxiety about wishing restitution of a deserting or depriving parent and fear of abandonment can lead such a child to act out the fear by breaking appointments, stealing, and being unresponsive or avoiding involvement. Countertransference issues here are particularly dangerous to the therapy. The therapist may be led to overpunitive or overpermissive reactions. Fantasies of rescuing the child from rejecting parents may motivate the therapist. Given the rejection by the child of this fantasy, the therapist can then become disenchanted and be either depressed and angry about the treatment.

The psychotic child also does not develop a "transference neurosis," but may play out merging with or destruction of the therapist. The core here is annihilation anxiety. Here the therapist interprets reality, demonstrating that it is not necessarily destructive and refuses to participate in the distortion of the psychotic fears. From my own point of view, the annihilation fantasy is also common is fairly distrubed, but nonpsychotic, children and the intervention is the same.

HOZMAN AND FROILAND'S LOSS MODEL

Hozman and Froiland (1976) developed a theory of therapy based on the assumption that children of divorce must grieve the loss of the parental relationship in the same way that children of parental death must grieve that loss. Using Kubler-Ross' (1969) concept of loss, they proposed that children had to go through the same five stages:

1. *Denial.* Children try to eliminate thinking about the separation and divorce and associated loss. Manifestations include withdrawal and isolation from peers, teachers, and environment. Tantrum behavior can be designed to push others away. The therapist needs to directly confront the behavior. Leg-

itimize feelings. Help the child come to express feelings as an aceptable part of the personality. Role playing can be used to help the child accept feelings. Play therapy also encourages children to express their reality. Hozman and Froiland also suggested providing role models, helping the child observe people who have experienced a divorce and accepted the reality with appropriate behaviors. Bibliotherapy, records, or tape recording can have that releasing effect.

2.   *Anger.* The child responds at this stage by striking out at anyone involved in the separation and divorce or against parent surrogates such as teachers. Hozman and Froiland assumed that the underlying dynamic was a feeling of guilt for having caused the divorce. (As mentioned in Chapter 2, the apparent frequency of this response to the divorce is age specific. There is some doubt about how common the response of guilt is.) The first therapeutic move is to help the child recognize and focus the anger and understand its origins. The child is given unconditional positive regard while experiencing the anger so that the child can accept that emotion as part of the self. The second phase would be to channel the anger, to limit the expression to appropriate ways. The therapy may have a releasing effect on the aggression, using displacement or symbolic expression (hitting a stuffed animal or blowing up a balloon. They recommended the kit, *Developing Understanding of Self and Others* (DUSO, 1970). Hozman and Froiland noted that owning feelings is not an end in itself, but a prerequisite to better functioning.

There is substantial evidence from learning theory research that catharsis is not adequate therapy. Encouraging a child to express angry feelings without providing the training for self control and better negotiation, may encourage tantrum behavior rather than better functioning. While Hozman and Froiland give recognition to that process, the article does not indicate how to support that next step.

3.   *Bargaining.* The child at this stage attempts to reunite the parents. The child may try to be particularly good if the perception is that the parent left because of the bad behavior of the child. The therapist's role is to help the child see the lack of personal responsibility for and control of the situation. The basic therapy strategy is to initiate interactions where the child is responsible for his or her own behavior and not for the behavior of others. Problem-solving games and puzzles and construction toys were seen as promoting that self-concept.

While a provocative idea, it would be difficult to determine if the symbolic content was in the mind of the therapist or child. There is substantial reason to believe that constructive interactions in the context of a stable, caring therapist may help the child, independent of the process of interpretation or constructive reconceptualization. My own preference is to gain evidence for how the child symbolizes and to use that symbolism for communicating more effective ideas to the child.

4.   *Depression.* When the child realizes that bargaining will not work to reunite the parents, the child may feel badly about past behaviors or missed

opportunities. Mourning may occur. The child needs help in owning the feeling of depression. Allowing the child to cry and otherwise express emotion may be helpful. The child should then be encouraged to reinitiate activities. Peers may be used to draw the child back into social activity.

5. *Acceptance.* The final stage of mourning the loss of the intact family is acceptance with a lack of despair. Individual worth is intrinsic, not determined by the divorce. The child is able to accept ambivalence toward parents.

Hozman and Froiland noted that not every child would go through these stages and the order is not invariate. Given that view, the question can be raised as to how helpful such a model is. It is clearly the case that the feelings addressed are more or less common for children of divorce, but as indicated many other responses also occur. They do suggest some potentially useful strategies for helping children cope with the loss, although the guiding theoretical bases are not clear.

DERDEYN'S CRISIS INTERVENTION MODEL

Derdeyn's (1977) model of therapy for children from 3 to 8 years of age is basically a description of therapy for the mother, father and child, given in general terms rather than specific techniques.

Assistance for the child included play therapy with interpretations to the child's feelings about the divorce, family group therapy, and individual work with the father and mother. Derdeyn spoke of concern over the blurring of generations boundaries, the need for structure and authority, the identification by the parent of the child with the absent parent, and depression due to unresolved loss. Themes of concern that could impede the therapy included sensitivity to parental anger, feelings of guilt, responsibility and fear of retribution, feelings of devaluation, guilt as a defense against existential anxiety, fear of abandonment, and the wish to reunite the parents.

THE DIVORCE AND MOURNING PROJECT OF MARIN COUNTY, CALIFORNIA

Given the extensive publications by Wallerstein and Kelly, (Kelly and Wallerstein, 1976, 1977a, 1977b; Wallerstein 1984; Wallerstein and Kelly, 1974, 1975, 1977, 1980a, 1980b, 1980c) about the 131 children of divorce that they studied, it is easy to overlook the fact that the study occurred in the context of therapy services. Three reviews summarized that service (American Institutes for Research, 1980; Wallerstein and Kelly, 1977, 1980c).

The direct services involved providing counseling for the family members affected by the divorce with an emphasis on short-term crisis intervention.

Family members were generally seen for individual sessions, although occasionally family therapy was performed.

Stages of Assessment

Three stages of assessment were used to determine the child's needs that needed to be addressed in the short term treatment.

1.   Development assessment was obtained by getting a detailed history from the parents, detailed information from the school, and direct observation of the child for several hours.

2.   Divorce-specific assessment was determined by focusing on the child's response to the divorce or separation situation. Thoughts, fantasies, affect, and behavioral responses to the divorce were included. The degree to which pain and anxiety were consciously experienced, defensive mechanisms were evaluation, as was the degree to which these responses were influenced by conscious or unconscious pressure from the parents. The child understanding of the divorce and what the child had been told were also determined. Wallerstein and Kelly found that the children, particularly preschool children, were very confused about the meaning of divorce and the reasons for the divorce.

As noted in Chapter 2, many preschool children had been given no explanation for the divorce at all. When affective reactions were assessed, the following questions were evaluated: How much pain is being experienced? Are irritability and aggressive behavior present? Are overt or underlying depressive reactions present. Defensive mechanisms to cope with the pain of divorce were evaluated. How contained was the response to the divorce? Finally an inquiry into the appearance of new symptoms was made.

3.   Social system assessment was the final area of assessment and included parent-child relationships, siblings, extended family, school, peers, and other activities. Lack of support was particularly a concern.

The Intervention

The first question of intervention was with whom will the intervention take place? First, the mother was usually seen, followed perhaps by the father. Then the children were seen individually. Most clients were seen for three months or longer rather than six weeks which was suggested in the original crisis model. Three different intervention types were included:

1.   *Child-centered.* Parents were encouraged to provide explanations to the child about the divorce. Children needed assurance of continued contact and support. Encouragement to the noncustodial parent to continue contact was given. Specific advice was given to parents about how to handle age-appropriate responses of the children to the divorce, help the parent understand the child's anger and what common responses to divorce were.

2. *Child-parent relationship intervention*. This intervention was to help parents with their capacity to respond effectively to the child. This approach helped the parents understand the child's dynamics and themselves, and why it was difficult to perform parental functions. Parents were helped to regain parental control.

3. *Adult-centered*. These interventions were designed to help parents with needs beyond the parental ones.

Children were seen for varying amounts of individual therapy. Children under 8 were generally seen only once or twice. Children from 9 to 12 were usually seen for three or four times. Teenagers often were hesitant to come in. Not surprisingly, girls were more willing to talk about their problems than boys, particularly for teenagers. At risk children were seen as those who felt responsible, who strongly reminded a parent of the other spouse, and who were caught up in a custody battle.

Wallerstein and Kelly (1980c) did not feel that there was an observable progression of defined stages in the child's response to the divorce, an observation at odds with Hozman and Froiland's grief model, discussed previously. Wallerstein and Kelly (1980c) felt that the response to the divorce was more related to the developmental stage, environment, and parent-child relationship than to predictable stages of response to divorce.

One model in working with the children involved utilizing the divorce-specific assessment. This approach usually involved three to four one hour sessions, centering on exploration, clarification, and some education and was combined with intensive work with parents. While Wallerstein and Kelly (1980c) did not provide information about the format of the intervention with the children, examples provided suggest that interpretative play therapy and direct discussion about the divorce issues with the child were used. The play therapy included doll house play and drawing. This intervention was used with very young children and with children unable or unwilling to use the therapist to explore their feelings.

Preschool children needed repeated explanations over a long time about the meaning of the divorce. Given the extended time period, parents were in a better place than the therapist for making these explanations. Wallerstein and Kelly (1977) felt that the interventions with the preschool children were not particularly useful. Intervention with the parents seemed to be far more effective for these young, preschool children.

The second model was an extended, focused crisis intervention. This model was more commonly used with school age children. For early latency children, denial was not as available as for younger children. These children had a great deal of difficulty talking about the divorce. Indeed, talking about the divorce seemed to sharply increase the pain, sometimes almost unbearably. Wallerstein and Kelly (1977) found a "divorce monologue" useful, in which the therapist discussed typical responses of other children without asking the child to discuss his or her own experience. Formats such as "many kids your age whose parents are divorcing, feel . . . '' permit the child to listen without revealing personal pain. When appropriate, details of the child's own situation were included in the monologue. In the example given by Wallerstein and Kelly (1977), the purpose seemed to be to permit the release of feelings, reduce the sense of loneliness ("other kids have felt the way I do"), and open opportunities for further exploration. Clearly this technique could be used to suggest different ways of responding to the stressors, providing alternative solutions similar to Gardner's Mutual Story Telling Technique. For children able to discuss their feelings, such techniques were not needed.

For later latency and preadolescent children, the brief intervention model was particularly helpful. Three or four sessions were usually sufficient. Helping the child to see the realities of the situation, to stay out of situations that were not for the child to solve, and specific advice related to that child's situation were used. Longer interventions were needed for severe guilt over causing the divorce, guilt over being the favored child, and intense loyalty alignment between the child and one parent against the other parent.

Goals of both models and across all ages included reduction of suffering, reduction in cognitive confusion, increase in psychological distance from the divorce, and successful resolutions of various idiosyncratic issues, that is, a mentally disturbed parent or the dilemma of choosing between parents.

While little of the effectiveness of the Marin County project is mentioned in the publications, Wallerstein and Kelly (1980c) did note that, of the children who were damaged by the conflicts of the unhappy marriage or the neglect of unhappy parents, 75 percent improved at five years and one-half of those accomplished that improvement with the help of therapy. How this improvement was assessed was not discussed. Of the parents who received counseling, 40 percent of the men and a higher percent (unspecified) of the women felt that the counseling was very useful and were still following suggestions five years later.

Given that the publications from this project focused on typical responses of children shortly after the separation and 1-, 5-, and 10-years later, it is not clear to what extent the therapy changed those views. The impression is clear that some children perceived the therapy as useful. Without a control group, it would be difficult, if not impossible, to determine if the therapy was helpful in a long term sense. Of course, the same can be said for all the therapies discussed in this chapter.

DLUGOKINSKI'S DEVELOPMENT APPROACH

Dlugokinski (1977) proposed an engagement-disengagement process for children of divorce. The children must go through a three-step process of orientation, integration, and consolidation:

1. *Orientation.* The divorce is a shock to the lifestyle of the child. In order for the child to have time to catch and respond, blocking of some of that stress

may occur. Anxiety is disowned. Sad feelings are not really experienced or grieved over. The counselor's demonstration of concern is essential.

2. *Integration.* Following a few weeks or months after the divorce, feelings about the divorce become personalized and the child responds with anger, sadness, excitement and some degree of disorientation. Fusion of parent and child identities may be a way of denial of the new reality. Depression may blunt the anxiety and lead the child to avoid establishing a new identity. The therapist must help the child experience and accept the self. The therapist must tolerate without running, strong emotions so that the child can accept them and avoid self-escaping alternatives.

3. *Consolidation.* Tools for effective daily living are incorporated. At this point regular sessions can cease.

LATE LATENCY THERAPY

There are no individual therapies that are designed specifically for the late latency (10 to 12 year olds) children of divorce.

Whether the child is willing to participate in fantasy material or able to maintain a discussion of feelings and problems in life may depend in part on the developmental level of the child.

Children of this age who began therapy at a younger age are quite willing to continue fantasy work. Children beginning therapy at this age are often reluctant to participate in fantasy material.

One subgroup of children of this age are more interested in games. Games can be used to strengthen the therapeutic alliance. Therapy can be successful with some game playing and some talking about problems. Certainly, games with discussion of feelings as a theme can be mixed with games of chance or skill. Since it is important to give the child some chance of winning, if the child is not particularly good at games, it is better to encourage some games that involve elements of chance so that the child can experience success.

This author does not believe in letting the child win, although the child may be permitted to make up rules that give them a handicap. When the child cheats to win, I have permitted the cheating, but comment on the importance to the child of that child's winning. The child should be encouraged to see the game as a sharing experience rather than competition.

Some children can talk about their problems while engaged in playing games. I was able to carry on a long discussion with one child while playing checkers. As soon as the game was over, the discussion stopped. Eye contact and the absence of a distractor was simply too anxiety provoking.

ADOLESCENT THERAPY

Work with adolescents in individual therapy is particularly taxing. The testing of limits, negativism, the lack of trust, and the need to individuate even at the cost of adaptive functioning makes the adolescent a particularly difficult client.

Adolescent Resistance to Therapy

Because the adolescent is likely to see the therapist as an agent of the parent and be highly resistive to treatment, it is important to return the control to the adolescent. Earlier in my professional career, I was willing to see children against their will. My view was that the success rate for resistant children was quite low. Now it is my practice to inform adolescents that I will see them three times at the requirement of their parents. After that time, I will not see them unless they are willing to continue with me. Whether the parents require the adolescent to continue in treatment is between the adolescent and the parents, but the adolescent has complete control after three sessions as to whether *I* am the therapist.

Teenagers are more likely to accept a therapeutic alliance if given some control on who the therapist is. Giving the teenager control over choice of the therapist after three sessions places some control back to the teenager and reduces resistance to treatment. If a therapeutic alliance cannot be established in three sessions, there is little likelihood of ever getting one established. For very disturbed teenagers, inpatient treatment without choice may be required. If the teenager refuses to accept anyone, the parent with consultation must decide whether to continue with a therapy with a low probability of being helpful.

Since using this strategy, the ability to develop a therapeutic alliance has gone up substantially. About 90 percent of the adolescents given this choice decide to continue. However, it does mean accepting the "no" from some teenagers.

Avoiding the Parent Role and Accepting Feelings

A major focus of working with adolescents is to increase a sense of being understood both in terms of feelings and why those feelings exist. As for younger children, the strategy is then to increase the quality of problem solving for the adolescent. The therapist must not provide answers to problems as that move reinstates for the adolescent a parental role that they are likely to be already fighting.

Attitudes toward the therapy indicates to some degree where the teenager is developmentally. Seventh and eighth graders are often humiliated at the idea of seeing a "shrink" even in Boulder, Colorado, where the use of therapy is quite common. These teenagers are preoccupied with belonging and not being different from the cliques to which they belong. Fear of being seen and of someone from school finding out may haunt early adolescents. Older teenagers may feel ambivalent. Mature teenagers are more likely to accept the idea that they have problems for which they need help and to acknowledge that need with peers. I had one teenager in treatment who went out of her way to be with a group of peers just before treatment so that she could say that it was time to go to see her "shrink." To have someone there just to listen to her was a source of prestige, not shame. Obviously, that open attitude was a good predictor of openness to help.

It is important for the therapist of the adolescent to avoid the parental role.

This author tells teenagers that the role of the therapist is to help them, not to force them to become what their parents want. The limits of confidentiality are explained, as is the fact that the parents must be seen from time to time (unless the adolescent has already separated from the parents). The adolescents are reassured that they have veto power over what the parents will be told about the therapy (except for those categories of things that *must* be told to the parents for the physical protection of the client or the parents). Even when confidentiality must be broken (for example for child abuse), the adolescent will be told first that the authorities must be informed.

The amount of testing adolescents do can be trying. I have had adolescents who want to smoke in my presence (I do not permit it, but make it clear that the cause is my allergy to smoke). Some teenagers have used curse words to see if I will admonish them. One 14-year-old girl came in with an incoherent, rambling, upset story of drinking beer over the weekend and losing her virginity. Working hard all through the session, I tried to help her to understand why she did it and what coping she wanted to do in the future. I was quite concerned, but did not contact the parents. During the next session, I learned that she had made up the whole story (and very convincingly, I might add) to see if her parents would be told. (She was in a position to prove that the incident had not happened.) Because her parents did not know about the story, she then decided to trust me with a discussion of a less stressful and loaded an area of some concern to her.

Another teenager took me for my word that the time was hers to use as she wished and spoke not one word to me for three sessions. (I learned to bring a book to read). After three sessions, she began to talk about her anger. Exhausting therapy!

Because teenagers use resistance and negativism as part of their strategy to affect separation and individuation, getting an alliance that is helpful in the working of problems can be particularly difficult. Use of the therapeutic double bind or paradoxical intervention can be useful in breaking up that resistance. In this technique, the adolescent is encouraged to increase the resistance. One girl cursed me in detail at every session, thus expressing her anger at being in therapy and how much she hated all adults. Finally, at the beginning of a session, I encouraged her to tell me to go to hell in as vivid and colorful language as she could, to really give it to me. This paradoxical intervention places the client in a bind. To refuse to fight me would be to cooperate. To tell me to go to hell would be to go along with my suggestion and cooperate. Her response was, "Why would I want to do that?"

The Use of Pro and Con; the Reduction of Splitting

One major problem that teenagers have is the tendency to split and see things in black and white terms. The difficulty in tolerating ambivalence is, of course, not restricted to adolescents, but is particularly troublesome to this age group. When a teenager proposes to do something that is forbidden by parents, the parents take the opposite side and indicate all the reasons why the child should not be permitted to do the particular action. The teen then increases the pressure on the positive side.

No effective problem solving is being internalized by this process. When a teenager proposed to do something that I think is not well thought out (a not unusual event), I will first ally myself with the side of the teenager. For example, one 15-year-old girl announced that she was thinking of running away. When asked why, she indicated that she was mad at her mother for making her wear dumb looking clothes to school. When asked whether there was any other reasons why she wanted to run away, she said, "no." My reaction was to tell her that I could think of at least a half-dozen reasons why she might want to run away. (This approach has a paradoxical intervention quality since she is being allied with, not attacked.) After spending 15 minutes going over all the reasons why it might be useful to run away, I asked then for reasons why it might not be a good idea. She came up with all the reasons and decided that running away was not a good idea.

If I had started with the reasons why she should not run away, she would have resisted me and might have even tried to run away as an expression of her resistance. By indicating that I was there to help her make her own decisions and to have things work out better for her, she was able to develop more effective problems solving.

I have even used this technique by instructing teenagers on deliberately using pro and con with parents as a way of increasing the chances of getting their way. When parents see a child look at both sides of an issue and carefully weigh the pros and cons, they are more likely to permit a previously forbidden activity. Of course, being able to look at the pros and cons and weigh the advantages and disadvantages of outcomes is one aspect of what maturity is all about.

In working with adolescents, use of the pros and cons reduces splitting and supports problem solving that is not based on one side of an ambivalence.

SUMMARY

Almost all forms of individual psychotherapy with children of divorce involves acceptance and clarification of feelings, assessment of cognitions, and support for more effective problem solving. For young children, fantasy is particularly helpful in providing a low anxiety forum for exploring ideas. For adolescents, trust and problem solving more directly seem to be helpful.

CHAPTER 13

Family Therapy and Group Therapy for Families

Family therapy has been argued to be the most powerful therapeutic technique for helping children of divorce, because the intervention is with the entire system in which the children have interactions.

WHEN FAMILY THERAPY IS THE TREATMENT OF CHOICE

Cantor and Drake (1983) proposed that family therapy is the treatment of choice in helping children of divorce. Since divorce is an interpersonal problem and children's anxieties, frustrations, and angers are focused around feeling about family members, family therapy provides a power technique for working through those feelings. Cantor and Drake recommend against family therapy when custody is in question, when one parent is unavailable because of abandonment, prison, or heavy substance abuse, and families in which the danger of violence exists.

Family system theory argues that individual therapy with children may be ineffective because the family needs to have the child have the symptoms to avoid resolving other anxiety provoking issues. As the child learns new means of coping through individual therapy or group therapy, the family becomes threatened and works to reinstate the homeostasis that was present prior to the therapy. This author is reminded of a mother who brought her 14-year-old son to therapy because he was immature and dependent. As he worked through his dependency and became more autonomous, the mother complained vigorously that he now stood up to her (which she interpreted as disrespectful and obstinate). She did not like it at all.

Family therapy makes the assumption that symptoms have functions within the family. Both the child with the problem and the family have an investment in keeping the very behavior that they are asking to get rid of.

Divorce is a family problem. Systems theory indicates that the family has an investment in maintaining the homeostasis that includes that problem. When the child is treated individually, the family will often develop counter-moves to maintain that homeostasis. Even with individual treatment, work with the parents is essential. It is generally more effective to assess and intervene with the family directly, rather than work with individuals within the family.

FAMILY THERAPY SYSTEMS

There are a wide variety of family therapy systems. For the purpose of this chapter, however, four primary ones will be reviewed:

1.   Psychoanalytically oriented family therapy with strong interest in multigenerational lines founded by Bowen (1976). Bowen's therapy is to help people understand family themes over generations that influence behavior.

2.   Strategic intervention is based on the paradoxical methods of Erickson and Haley (Haley, 1963). Paradoxical treatment involves encouraging the symptom as a way of handling the defensive style. Asking someone to resist has the effect of forcing cooperation, regardless of what the person is doing.

3.   The structural therapy of Minuchin (1974). This may be the most useful of the family therapy approaches. The focus of the therapy is to determine the boundaries, rules, and hierarchies that exist in the family.

All forms of family therapy, regardless of orientation, would seem to be concerned with boundaries. Are parents playing a parental role? Are the children allowed to continue to be children and are they provided proper guidance and support? The structural approach refers to boundaries and the behavioral approach refers to executive subsystems.

Minuchin is interested in how the family uses space and the degree to which the family is enmeshed or disengaged from one another. Not infrequently, the two styles occur in alternation. The only way some people can leave an enmeshed family is to completely disengage.

Minuchin disrupts the family process by redefining sick or maladaptive behavior as positive or as serving a positive function. In this way, destructive motives are eliminated. For example, when the complaint is overcontrol a therapist might say, "You are asking her to protect you." Minuchin also focused on complementary behavior. One person is encouraged to behave in a certain way by the behavior of the other. In addition, motivations are phrased in a positive way, for example "You protect him even when he does not need it."

4.   Behaviorist family therapy has as its focus reciprocity and exchange of benefits, as opposed to coercion. This form of therapy encourages communication with "I" messages and avoids labeling the feelings of the other person (a central focus in most family therapies). Thus, an atmosphere of support, understanding, problem solving, and behavior exchange is provided. Contracts and homework are common techniques.

Several problems are presented with working with divorced families that make them more complex than nuclear families (Cantor et al., 1983). Confidentiality is a particularly difficult problem. In addition to the legal problem, if there are separate sessions with individual subsets of the family system, it is important that secrets not be permitted.

Therapists should not permit members of the family to share secrets that cannot be discussed with other family members. Such secrets can result in collusion of the therapist with one or more of the family members and sabotage the therapy.

On more than one occasion, this author has seen a family member who felt grievously hurt that the therapist knew all along that there was an extramarital relationship, while that family member was operating on the assumption that good faith chances of reconciliation were possible.

Therapists should be cautious in indicating agreement with any family member. The therapist should support process and communication. Family members should be encouraged to ask questions, not have the therapist do it. Asking questions and indicating agreement can also result in apparent alliances with family members that can be destructive to the process.

Some states give legal confidentiality to family therapy, others do not. When future litigation occurs, having established the limits of confidentiality initially will avoid hurt and outraged feelings.

FAMILY THERAPY WITH DIVORCING FAMILIES

Kaplan's Family Therapy with Divorced Families

Kaplan (1977) provided some excellent examples of the use of structural family therapy for children of divorce. He suggested working with the subgroups of the family that seem the most stressful for the child. Kaplan's case histories give examples of diagram analysis of boundaries, illustrating excessive closeness or distance. One case history outlined the interaction in a family with an overprotective custodial mother and her child. The interaction was initially diagrammed as in Figure 1.

Figure 1. A mother (M) and child (C) in an enmeshed relationship in which the noncustodial father (F) is excluded. (From Kaplan, S. L. (1977). Structural family therapy for children of divorce: Case reports, *Family process, 16,* 75–83. Reprinted with permission of S. L. Kaplan and Berkshire Medical Center).

In Figure 1, the dotted line indicates excessive closeness and the vertical lines indicate excessive distance. As can be seen in Figure 1, the mother has inadequate separation from the child, a 9 year old girl, and the father is excluded from both. The child was having trouble in the classroom, with daydreaming, thumbsucking, and poor school work. She did not interact with her peers. The mother was overprotective, not allowing the child to go to the store a few yards from her home or play on the sidewalk in front of the house. The child was not allowed to see the father. In an individual session with the child, bizarre behavior was apparent and the child repeatedly requested to see the mother.

For 20 sessions, the mother and child were seen together. Initially the child played as if the therapist were not in the room. During this time, the therapist met with the father alone and had some sessions with the mother and father together. After four months of treatment, the child and the father had a session. They had a long talk in the presence of the therapist. The child complained about a variety of appropriate issues.

After the father-daughter sessions, the child was able to tolerate being with the male therapist, and the therapist and child played while the mother read in another part of the room. Finally, the mother was able to leave the therapist and child together. During this time, the behavior at home and school was significantly better. Figure 2 illustrates the goal for therapy.

In Figure 2 the barrier between mother and father is maintained as is appropriate for divorced parents. The boundary between child and each parent is of an appropriate closeness and the child moves back and forth between parents. Kaplan gave useful examples of a mother who becomes a child with her child and her own parents, and another example of a helpless and neglectful mother.

In any family therapy approach, it is recommended that the therapist(s) graph the dynamic of boundaries, hierarchy and disengagement that may exist in the family. The therapist should then graph the theoretical ideal relationship that takes into account healthy family functioning and appropriate distance between the divorcing spouses while protecting the relationship of the child with each parent, if possible.

Figure 2. Theoretical goal for therapy for the families of the custodial mother (M), noncustodial father (F) and nine-year-old daughter (C). (From Kaplan, S. L. (1977). Structural family therapy for children of divorce: case reports. *Family Process, 16,* 75–83. Reprinted with permission of S. L. Kaplan and Berkshire Medical Center).

Goldman and Coane's Family Therapy

Goldman and Coane (1977) also discussed strategies in working with families of divorce. Their model of intervention involved four parts:

1. Redefine the family as including both parents, regardless of the divorce. They cautioned about families talking about the absent parent as he or she were dead. Once both parents are included, the therapists then work on the difficult process of clarifying generational boundaries. Similar advice about including the father was given by Leader (1973) for many of the same reasons. Peck (1975) also insisted that every family remnant member come to the interviews. According to Peck, the mother-and-child "marriage" can have extraordinary homeostasis that is difficult to change. When parents move into roles of appropriate parental responsibilities, it tends to reduce the acting out of the children. As the generational boundaries are established, each parent can then work on relational ties with each child. The child is then given the opportunity to separate and individuate in a safe environment.

Goldman and Coane noted that the family suffers from "the guilt of omnipotence." The divorce is everyone's fault. Each parent feels threatened by the other parent and the children feel it is their responsibility to promote reconciliation.

2. Firm generational boundaries, reducing parentification of the children and encourage the parents to fight battles without involving the children.

3. The family need to experience a "replay of the history of the marriage." This replay permits a correction of the distortions of the marriage.

4. Help the parents divorce emotionally. The therapist may need to help the parents do their own separation and individuation.

Peck's Family Therapy

Peck (1975) recommended using a co-therapist to reduce the loneliness of working alone. From Peck's theoretical position, cotherapists work best if of the opposite gender. The therapist couple serves as a surrogate marital dyad that "adopts" the mother and children. The transference is reduced and the single parent is less likely to look to two therapists as a potential marital partner or rescuer.

Peck's position is that the family is having trouble because of the incompleteness of the divorce (almost by definition since the family is having trouble). The therapists refuse to solve the battle between the parents. The therapists use child's play to get the children to be just children. They model moving in and out of child's play without losing respect. The therapists support the mother as she separates from the children and gives up her love-hate battle with her former husband.

Isaac's Recommendations

Like Peck, Isaacs (1981) believed that families may get stuck because one or more of the family members cannot leave the experiences of the old family and are unwilling or unable to develop new arrangements and life-patterns in the new family. Isaacs also pointed out that other strategies, needs, and desires may influence the difficulty in resolving the divorce process. The theory of intervention then is to assess the individual strategies, determine how these strategies block the divorce process, and develop a counterstrategy to help the family develop a more productive future. As with other therapies, the counterstrategy is to encourage the parents to abandon secret agendas (such as covert strategies to force reconciliation) and retaliation and have as a primary goal the protection of the children.

Interventions given in case histories focused on such problems as: the role of helplessness as a strategy for keeping the other parent involved with the family and recreating a "phantom" family of the past; tolerating tantrums to maintain love; reducing guilt; poor boundaries about time, space, and control; protecting a parent from angry or avoidant feelings; and a family in which everyone was inappropriately disengaging from each other.

Moreland, Schwebel, Fine and Vess' Postdivorce Family Therapy

Moreland, Schwebel, Fine, and Vess (1982) have, as their postdivorce family therapy, an orientation of helping both parents stay involved with the children. Based on a review of the literature they concluded that postdivorce therapy should have as its goals: (1) to increase exspouse cooperation in parenting; (2) to improve the quality and effectiveness of parent-child communication; and (3) to train the mother and father in behavioral management techniques.

They noted that ideally exspouses should develop "circumscribed mutuality" around parenting. The avenue to such mutuality involves helping the parent express feelings, explore competencies, choices, and opportunities for growth, relate current hurts and angers to past rejections, recognize their own contribution to the conflict, and learn from past mistakes. Parents are encouraged to initiate discussion with the other parent.

If one parent has severe pathology, it may be difficult to obtain the circumscribed mutuality. The addition of a new emotional relationship will also place limits on the ability to co-parent.

Family Therapy With Very Young Children

In a very different kind of family therapy, Rosenthal (1979) reported on therapy with families of divorce with children two and four years of age. The child is given an explanation as to why the child and family needs help. The therapist tells the child that the parent and therapist will help the child with play and with talking about his or her upsetting feelings. The therapist sees the family in a large playroom. Interpretative play therapy then is accomplished in the presence of the parent and with the parent joining in.

Conjoint Mother-Daughter Therapy

Kalter (1984) described a conjoint mother-daughter treatment program in working with adolescent girls. These girls frequently presented a sexualized, pseudomature quality. Although demanding greater independence, Kalter felt that their actions were in fact indicating a wish for greater supervision. These girls viewed the mother as unfair and tyrannical and were quite resistive to beginning treatment. The girls had intense separation conflicts and would have been quite resistive to individual treatment. Self-esteem problems were intense and individual treatment was seen as stigmatizing and a derogation. Kalter felt that the two developmental issues that had to be addressed were (1) separation from the mother and (2) the damaged sense of femininity. While highly sexualized, the girls did not feel worthwhile as women. They felt unattractive, but longed to be loved. The daughter experiences the loss of the father as personal rejection around being lovable and feminine.

Adolescents are often particularly resistant to individual therapy. They see the move as defining them as the ones with the problem and view it as a putdown. While adolescents are also quite resistant to family therapy, they often will accept a family approach easier than individual work.

A Multiple Impact Therapy Approach

Multiple Impact Therapy has been used with divorced families in the treatment of adolescents (Ritchie and Serrano, 1974). The technique uses two therapists with team-family sessions, individual sessions, and various combinations. The different structures for therapy were seen by the authors as providing the opportunity for improving communication and for assessing, clarifying and redefining goals. The adolescent is seen as fixated in ego development because of the inability of the family to facilitate growth.

The theory proposed four positions of functioning in the family: (1) aggressive (leadership); (2) passive-aggressive (criticism); (3) emotional unstable (spontaneity); and (4) the passive-dependent (passivity-cooperation). When a family functions well, these roles work with cooperation and flexibility. Maladaptive families choose roles that are inconsistent with their personality or stage of development.

The initial strategy in the therapy is to shift the parents from fighting with each other to being concerned with the welfare of the child. The past is defined as secondary while the here-and-now and future are given primary importance.

Then, mutually agreed-upon goals are developed. The goal of the therapy is to provide some consistency and security for the child or children.

The adolescent is encouraged to understand his or her role in the parental conflict and to mourn the loss of the relationships. The adolescent is also encouraged to give up any omnipotent fantasies and manipulations about reconciliation or retaliation. The authors presented a fairly detailed case history illustrating the analysis of family dynamics and the changing structure of meetings with different configurations of family meetings including a stepparent and future stepparent.

Issues For Family Therapy After Divorce

Cantor and Drake (1983) gave the following lists of issues to be addressed in family therapy:

For parents:

1. Transition to single parent status
2. Child care and discipline
3. Dating, remarriage, stepchildren
4. Loneliness
5. Different relationship with former spouse, relatives, and children
6. Finances
7. Housing
8. Anger and other unresolved feelings
9. Childnapping
10. Grieving
11. Employment
12. Custody
13. Communication problems
14. Loss of generational boundaries

For the children:

1. Change of status
2. Adjustment to visitation
3. Loss of family life and contact with parent
4. Step-parent, stepsiblings, halfsiblings
5. Moving
6. Change of schools, friends
7. Loyalty
8. Involvement with custody issues

FAMILY THERAPY WITH SINGLE PARENT FAMILIES

Most of the therapies for families of divorce focus on the divorcing and recently divorced family and attempt to include both parents. What about families in which the absent parent is unavailable, either because of geographic distance, uninvolvement, or a wish to be excluded?

Bray and Anderson (1984) described one of the few case histories of working with single parent families in therapy. The therapy is based on strategic intervention. As noted in the chapter on single parent families, Bray and Anderson assumed that role overload, economic hardships, isolation, and feelings of loss and grief are common problems of single parent families. The parenting role of the noncustodial parent must also be resolved.

Bray and Anderson used reframing to have the family view the symptoms of the child (a suicide attempt in one case history) as a wish to help the family. In another case they complimented a mother on her unconscious knowledge of the danger of getting a divorce. In another family in which tantruming of a 3½ year old was the presenting problem, the therapist congratulated the mother both for doing such a fine job in such difficult circumstances and for helping her child to be strong-willed and independent. The reframing was to help the child express this strong-willed personality appropriately. They supported the mother in how to handle tantrums. They also reframed the child's tantrum behavior as expression of anger for the mother at the father for leaving. The child was also presented as interfering with dates because the child knew that the mother was not yet ready to date. Such an interpretation would encourage the mother to see the child's behavior as positively motivated and encourage her to assume responsibility for her own behavior.

GROUP THERAPY WITH STEPFAMILIES

One of the earliest writings of working in a family therapy setting with stepfamilies did not include the children and is not family therapy in the traditional sense, but focused on the relationship between the stepfathers and their wives (Mowatt, 1972). The couples had sought help with their children's behavior problems. The group consisted of three stepfathers and their wives which met for 1½ hours a week for six months. The children involved ranged from 10 to 17. As explained in Chapter 9 on stepfamilies, older children tend to have more trouble with remarriage and this study's target group is consistent with that view. Problems included truancy, vandalism, underachievement, and running away from home for boys and sexual promiscuity in the case of the one girl. Children were seen once at intake.

The purpose of the group was to provide peer group and identification models. As might be expected from the literature on problems of remarriage, the stepfathers were not clear about how far to go in assuming the role of father. All three of the fathers had moved from a "pal" relationship prior to marriage to a parent after the marriage. How much affection to show was another question and the fathers were uncomfortable about expressing affection. Disciplining and enforcing rules was the major focus of attention. All the children resented the mother showing attention to the stepfather. Mothers tended to blame the stepfathers since the problems tended to start after the marriage. Mothers criticized the fathers for not being rescuers while the fathers criticized the mothers for poor management of the children. The stepfather often seemed rivalrous of stepsons and potentially attracted to the stepdaughters. Part of the rivalry with the stepsons may have been the physical resemblance with the biological father. As part of the group process the mothers started to realize that they were pushing the stepfathers away from the children.

Nadler (1983) described a group program for stepfamilies that involved a six-week didactic and discussion group to help families understand the problems of remarriage, stepchildren, childrearing and discipline, and difficulties with the exspouse and visitation. The program involved six, one-and-one-half hour sessions, each focused on a separate problem. Groups were generally 8 to 10 people. The structure of the program was as follows:

Session 1. Introduction. Exploration of the commonality of stepfamily problems. All the stepparents were having trouble coping and many blamed the children for the problems. The myth of instant love was explained.

Session 2. Roles and conflicting loyalties. The second session tried to help families understand how conflicting loyalties generate problems. Alignments based on biological lines threatened family integration.

Session 3. Communication skills. This session stressed the open expression of feelings. There was discussion of the "stepparent disavowal syndrome" which occurs when the stepparent initially invests in the child and then is hurt by the rejection and finally feels rage and avoidance.

Session 4. Problems concerning the stepchild. Focussing on the stepchild situation and how to deal with childrearing and discipline was the theme of the fourth session. Hostility toward the stepparent was explained to be a function of feelings of abandonment, loss of security, resentment over the divorce, rivalry for affection, and feelings of disloyalty.

Session 5. Problems in marital interaction. Stepparents often feel the least cared for in the family. The natural parent does not tend to support the stepparent. Sometimes the problem is the demand from the stepparent to have the biological parent always confirm their point of view.

Session 6. Problems of visitation and the exspouse.

FAMILY THERAPY WITH STEPFAMILIES

After presenting a detailed model of stepfamily dynamics, McGoldrick and Carter (1980) presented models of family therapy with remarriages. The three key emotional issues that they felt required resolution were (1) the emotional attachment to the exspouse(s), (2) giving up attachment to the nuclear family concept and accepting a different model, and (3) accepting the time, space, ambivalence, and problems of remarried families.

Similar to Bowen (1976, 1978), they recommended going back several generations to evaluate the parental marriage. Rather than the classic triangle in nuclear families with the parents and children, McGoldrick and Carter felt that there were six common triangles in remarried families. McGoldrick and Carter coached the adults to differentiate from families of origin. They worked on nuclear family problems if the clients are motivated to do so.

The spouse may be coached in the presence of the new spouse to work out the relationship with the old spouse. In cases where the new couple get along well, a severely misbehaving child may be engaged in a conflict with the other parent. They proposed that under this condition, it is important to get the stepparent in a neutral position rather than against the child. The biological parent is put in charge of managing the child's behavior. This technique was frequently used in the examples given. They did note that such a technique was difficult to implement if the biological parent worked long hours and the stepparent was home with the children.

McGoldrick and Carter (1980) had as general goals of therapy:

1. Forming an open coparenting relationship between the biological parents.
2. Working out the emotional divorce.
3. Firming up parental boundaries and not giving children the power of deciding on remarriage, custody or visitation.

McGoldrick and Carter (1980) got a three-generational genogram. They tried to be particularly sensitive to family members in different life cycle stages. Helping the child handle the loss of any exceptionally close single-parent/child relationship was also emphasized.

Kaplan's (1977) description of structural family therapy, described previously, also gave case histories of remarried families. In one case, a 7 year old boy was having severe temper tantrums. The therapist first worked on an excessive boundary and disengagement problem of the biological mother with the child, and then worked on reducing the boundary with the stepfather.

Crohn, Sager, Rodstein, Brown, Walker, and Beir (1981) from the Remarried Consultation Service of the Jewish Board of Family and Children's Services in New York City discussed the clinical experience with a program specifically designed to help remarried families. From 1977 to 1979, the service treated 213 remarried families with 367 children. Impulse control problems characterized 38 percent of the children, school problems 36 percent, and pseudo-independence 23 percent. A large 83 percent were described as having dysfunctional relations with a parent or stepparent. Only 9 percent were considered free of problems. Of course, if these families were not having some problems they would not have sought the services of the clinic.

In the initial contact, the therapists works to stay neutral and not allied with any part of the family system. Family members from both households were invited to the first session. The evaluation sessions took from one to four visits and lasted from one-and-one-half hours to two hours each.

Crohn, Sager, Rodstein, Brown, Walker, and Beir (1980) utilized multiple impact family therapy based on McGregor (1964). Multiple impact therapy implies that different families members may be seen in different combinations as the therapist identifies areas that need work. Sager, et al. also recommended against seeing the child alone in individual treatment too early in the course of treatment. The danger is that the child will be scapegoated as the problem and the parents will withdraw from the treatment process. Later in treatment, child work is more appropriate and likely to be more successful.

Avoid beginning treatment of a family by seeing the child in individual therapy first with the intent of moving to family therapy later. Always start with the entire family or with the parents. Often the family would much prefer that the child be seen as the problem and want the child to be seen first. In addition, the child who forms a therapeutic alliance with the therapist can feel betrayed by the move to family therapy, both by the experienced reduction in support and concerns of confidentiality.

During evaluation the therapist has the family draw a genogram of the family, a process that is relative nonthreatening and permits even very young children to participate. Issues such as unresolved mourning, fights, secrets, illness, and divorce and remarriage histories are revealed. This genogram allows the therapist to understand the family dynamics. The genogram is left on the table during each session and added to as new information is gathered.

The genogram is central to assessment because history is central in working with remarried families and the authors argued that history is even more vital in treating remarried families than in treating nuclear families. Specifically cross-generational alliances are major blocks to shifting relationships to a more appropriate level of interaction.

The issues of system oriented therapy for remarried families not surprisingly deals with those issues that remarried families tend to have (see Chapter 9). Unresolved mourning is a major blockage in many remarried families. The therapist then focuses on the mourning process and the symptoms in the family that are an indicator of the unfinished work that needs to be done.

Exposing myths is a part of the work with remarried families, myths already discussed in some detail in Chapter 9. Myths of the wicked stepmother, instant love, the perfect mate, the idealized (or monster) absent parent, and the perfect family are all problems with which the therapist must deal. Thus, one major focus is refocusing the problems and redefining the child's problems as problems of the family. Then the family is helped to understand the system. Stressing differences between family members rather than similarities seems to facilitate growth.

Johnson (1980) proposed several areas that clinicians should evaluate as part of working with stepfamilies:

1. Unclear expectations
2. Losses and gains
3. Questions of physical and emotional turf
4. Differences in life style
   a. Discipline
   b. Eating habits
   c. Division of labor
   d. Attitudes toward sex
   e. Use of alcohol and drugs
   f. Attitudes toward obligations
   g. Manners
   h. Household rules
   i. Expression of hostility, aggression, or disagreement.
5. Benefits, including relief from child care, sharing stepsibling relationships, harmonious family life, an increase in emotional giving, and extended circle of friendly, giving adults.

In stepfamilies, the development of boundaries may include a greater distance in the boundary between the stepparent and child than between the biological parent and child. Particularly for children who are of school age, the stepparent needs to wait for the affectional bond to develop before a discipline role can be assumed (see the extended discussion of this issue in Chapter 9)

Johnson (1980) noted that when there is active dislike between the stepparent and child, the biological parent should assume most of the parenting responsibilities, particularly discipline. If the biological parent avoids this responsibility, both the child and stepparent are likely to feel angry and abandoned.

Problems for the Therapist in Stepparent Therapy

Sometimes the therapist has a problem deciding which family system to treat. For example in a residential treatment setting, Weisfeld and Laser (1977) focused on the original parents in treating the child and felt that inclusion of stepparents could (although not necessarily) hinder the therapeutic process.

The advantage of multiple impact therapy is that the therapist can consider working with each of the separate systems that may be disordered.

In family therapy with remarried families, the therapist should consider carefully the effect of constituting therapy based on the original nuclear family with the exclusion of stepparents. The stepparent may already be significantly excluded. Multiple impact therapy strategies would permit working on each system and also has the advantage of treating them as separate systems.

Crohn et al., (1981) described several problems that therapists for families of remarriage tend to have. Counter-transference and burnout are frequent problems. Therapists can have unrealistic expectations about how a remarried family should work, with either the nuclear family or the Brady Bunch as models. (Of course, remarried families get in trouble when they have the same expectations.) Therapists join the denial system of the family and avoid taboo topics. Therapists have sometimes not paid sufficient attention to protecting positive images of both biological parents. The therapist can be drawn into wanting to be the "good" parent, particularly when the absent parent has abandoned the children. Therapists who are overwhelmed by the complexity of stepfamilies sometimes move toward overcontrol. Having a co-therapist is one way to guard against some of the problems previously described.

SUMMARY

Family therapy with divorcing families, single parent families, and remarried families provides a powerful way to restructure self-defeating interactions. Clinicians should have a clear understanding of the dynamics of family therapy and of each type of family before intervening in this manner.

CHAPTER 14

Postscript

THE GOAL OF THIS BOOK

The purpose of this book is to provide mental health professionals, lawyers, and judges with principles of working with children of divorce. The hope is that social changes, education, and therapy intervention can help families cope more adequately with the painful process of marital dissolution and provide for children of divorce. As mental health professionals, lawyers, and judges become more aware of the developmental needs of children of divorce and their families, the original process of divorce may be more humane and the subsequent structure supportive of all members of the family.

Mediation as an alternative to adversarial court battles is an excellent example of such a new process. Early evidence suggests that it might be a major preventive procedure. Further explorations in joint legal and residential custody are other examples of structures that seem to facilitate continued contact and bonding between the children and each of the parents and may reduce continued conflict. No fault divorce and conciliation court counseling also reduce harmful family conflict. More subtle changes are evolving in the community around the attitudes of school teachers, the clergy, and other important social support key figures. These attitudes can reduce stigma and improve coping. Education for divorcing parents and children concerning the family's needs around divorce and ways of providing support, information, and adequate coping as well as maintaining dignity and integrity of each family member, are also important strategies for supporting the family through divorce.

Primary prevention in which problems are anticipated and avoided will become important for the future. Changes to increase financial support to children and maintain as much as possible the predivorce quality of life for the children is likely to lower subsequent maladjustment. In addition, early detection of problems and effective intervention techniques can serve as remediation when the structure of society fails to provide adequate support to children to prevent the problems in the first place.

This book cites a large number of studies, most descriptive and few that are methodologically adequate. The recommendations in this book are tentative, based on my best understanding of the state of the art at the time of publication. If we are to improve the quality of life for divorcing couples, that state of the art must improve and the recommendations in this book are likely to undergo modification.

WHAT IS NOT YET KNOWN ABOUT HELPING CHILDREN OF DIVORCE?

The list of what has not yet been empirically determined that would be of vital importance in helping children of divorce is surprisingly basic. The following is a nondefinitive list of important issues, yet to be determined:

1. How effective is custody and access assessment? Is there a basis for deciding what the standards for assessment should be?

2. What is the best visitation pattern by age of the child?

3. In joint residential custody, what is the optimal switch for residence as a function of the age of the child? Is there a destructive pattern that should be avoided?

4. How should society handle geographic moves for joint residential custody? Should best interests of the child determine which parent now gets primary residential care? Should the moving parent be penalized for the move by not being given one-half of shared access? Some of these questions are clearly value laden rather than empirical.

5. What is the best way to handle long distance visitation with low frequency and long duration?

6. What are the conditions under which joint legal or joint residential custody are not in the best interests of the child?

7. How can joint residential custody work well with infants and toddlers?

8. Does mediation help child adjustment? Are there situations in which mediation does not help the family?

9. Should the courts limit access under adverse situations such as psychopathological noncustodial parents, abusive noncustodial parents, psychopathological reactions to visitation by the custodial parents, and severe conflict between parents?

10. How much risk for negative outcomes is acceptable? In terms of determining best interests of the child, the court is asked to guess what will happen rather than what has happened. Some jurisdictions are more willing than others to accept relatively low probabilities of negative outcomes while others are more concerned about avoiding harm.

In spite of this long list of unknowns, those working with children of divorce continue to use theory, the limited research available and their best judgment based on clinical experience to try to help the family adjust to these stressful life events. Theory and research, limited as it is, will likely improve the quality of services provided.

REFERENCES

Abarbanel, A. (1979). Shared parenting after separation: A study of joint custody. *American Journal of Orthopsychiatry, 49,* 320–329.

Adam, K. S., Lohrenz, J. G., & Harper, D. (1973). Suicidal ideation and parental loss: A preliminary research report. *Canadian Psychiatric Association Journal, 18,* 95–100.

Adams, M. (1984). Kids and divorce: No long-term harm. *USA Today,* December 20, 1984, p. 1, 5D.

Ahrons, C. R. (1979). The binuclear family: Two households, one family. *Alternative Lifestyles. 2(4),* 499–515.

Aldous, J. (1972). Children's perceptions of adult role assignment: Father absence, class, race, and sex influences. *Journal of Marriage and the Family, 9,* 55–65.

American Institutes for Research (1980). *Helping youth and families of separation, divorce, and remarriage.* Washington, D.C.: U.S. Department of Health and Human Services (DHHS Publication No. (OHDS)80–32010).

APGA *Guidepost* Staff (1980, September 4). One-parent kids troubled.

APGA *Guidepost* Staff (1984, September 18). NCCE hits single-parent students.

Armstrong, L. (1985, March/April). Daddy dearest wins the day. *New Directions For Women, 1,* 11.

Ash, P., & Guyer, M. (1984). Court implementation of mental health professionals' recommendations in contested child custody and visitation cases. *Bulletin of the American Academy of Psychiatry and the Law, 12*(2), 137–147.

Atwell, A. E., Moore, U. S., Nielsen, E., & Levite, Z. (1984). Effects of joint custody on children. *Bulletin of the American Academy of Psychiatry and the Law, 12*(2), 149–157.

Ault, R. L. (1977). *Children's cognitive development: Piaget's theory and the process approach.* New York: Oxford University Press.

Awad, G. A. (1978). Basic principles in custody assessments. *Canadian Psychiatric Association Journal, 23*(7), 441–447.

Awad, G. A., & Parry, R. (1980). Access following marital separation. *Canadian Journal of Psychiatry, 25*(5), 357–365.

Axline, V. M. (1969). *Play therapy* (revised ed.). New York: Ballantine.

Bahr, S. J. (1981). An evaluation of court mediation: A comparison in divorce cases with children. *Journal of Family Issues, 2*(1), 39–60.

Bales, J. (1984). Parents' divorce has major impact on college students. *APA Monitor, 15*(8), 13.

Bane, M. J. (1976). Marital disruption and the lives of children. *Journal of Social Issues, 32*(1), 103–117.

Benedek, E. P. (1972). Child custody laws: Their psychiatric implications. *American Journal of Psychiatry, 129,* 326–328.

Benedek, E., & Benedek, R. (1979). Joint custody, solution or illusion. *American Journal of Psychiatry, 136,* 1540–1544.

Benedek, R. S., & Benedek, E. P. (1977). Post-divorce visitation. *Journal of the American Academy of Child Psychiatry, 16,* 256–271.

Bentovim, A., & Gilmour, L. (1981). A family therapy interactional approach to decision making in child care, access and custody cases. *Journal of Family Therapy, 3,* 65–77.

Bernard, J. (1956). *Remarriage: A study of marriage.* New York: Dryden.

Bernard, J. (1971). *Remarriage: A study of marriage (2nd ed.).* New York: Russell and Russell.

Berger, T. (1977). *How does it feel when your parents get divorced?* New York: Julian Messner.

Bernard, J. M., & Nesbitt, S. (1981). Divorce: An unreliable predictor of children's emotional predispositions. *Journal of Divorce, 4*(4), 31–42.

Bernstein, J. E. (1977). *Books to help children cope with separation and loss.* New York: Bowker.

Berquist, B. (1984). The remarried family: An annotated bibliography, 1979–1982. *Family Process, 18,* 107–119.

Biller, H. B. (1968). A note on father absence and masculine development in lower-class Negro and white boys. *Child Development, 39*(3), 1003–1006.

Biller, H. B. (1969). Father absence, maternal encouragement and sex role development in kindergarten-age boys. *Child Development, 40*(2), 539–546.

Biller, H. B. (1970). Father absence and the personality development of the male child. *Developmental Psychology, 2*(2), 181–201.

Biller, H. B. (1971). The mother-child relationship and the father-absent boy's personality development. *Merrill-Palmer Quarterly, 17*(3), 227–241.

Biller, H. B. (1981). Father absence, divorce, and personality development. In M. E. Lamb (Ed.), *The role of the father in child development (2nd ed.).* New York: Wiley, 489–552.

Blanchard, R. W., & Biller, H. B. (1971). Father availability and academic performance among third-grade boys. *Developmental Psychology, 4,* 301–305.

Blechman, E. A. (1982). Are children with one parent at psychological risk? A methodological review. *Journal of Marriage and the Family, 44,* 179–195.

Blechman, E. A., Berberian, R. M., & Thompson, W. D. (1977). How well does number of parents explain unique variance in self-reported drug use? *Journal of Child Clinical Psychology, 45,* 1183–1187.

Blechman, E. A., & Manning, M. (1976). A reward-cost analysis of the single-parent family. In E. J. Mash, L. A. Hamerlynck, & L. C. Handy (Eds.), *Behavior Modification and families.* New York: Brunner/Mazel.

Bloom, B. L. (1975). *Changing patterns of psychiatric care.* New York: Behavioral.

Bloom, B. L., Asher, S. J., & White, S. W. (1978). Marital disruption as a stressor: A review and analysis. *Psychological Bulletin, 85,* 867–899.

Bloom, B. L., Hodges, W. F., & Caldwell, R. A. (1982). A preventive intervention program for the newly separated: Initial evaluation. *American Journal of Community Psychology, 10,* 251–264.

Bloom, B. L., Hodges, W. F., & Caldwell, R. A. (1983). Marital separation: The first eight months. In E. J. Callahan & K. A. McKluskey (Eds.), *Life-span developmental psychology: Non-normative events.* New York: Academic Press, 218–239.

Bloom, B. L., Hodges, W. F., Caldwell, R. A., Systra, L., & Cedrone, A. R. (1977). Marital separation: A community survey. *Journal of Divorce, 1,* 7–19.

Bloom, B. L., Hodges, W. F., Kern, M. B., & McFaddin, S. C. (1985). A preventive intervention program for the newly separated: Final evaluations. *American Journal of Orthopsychiatry, 55*(1), 9–26.

Bohannan, P. J. (1975). *Stepfathers and the mental health of their children* (final report). La Jolla, CA: Western Behavior Sciences Institute. As cited in Sager, C. J., Steer, H., Crohn, H., Rodstein, E., & Walker, E. (1980). Remarriage revisited. *Family and Child Mental Health Journal, 6*(1), 19–33.

Booth, A., Brinkerhoff, D. B., & White, L. K. (1984). The impact of parental divorce on courtship. *Journal of Marriage and the Family, 65*(4), 85–94.

Boren, R. (1982). The therapeutic effects of a school-based intervention program of the divorced. Unpublished doctoral disseration. School of Education. University of Colorado.

Bornstein, M. T., Bornstein, P. H., & Walters, H. A. (1985). Children of divorce: A group treatment manual for research and application. *Journal of Child and Adolescent Psychotherapy, 2*(4), 267–273.

Bowen, M. (1976). Principles and techniques of multiple family therapy. In P. Guerin (ed.), *Family Therapy,* New York: Gardner Press.

Bowen, M. (1978). *Family therapy in clinical practice.* New York: Jason Aronson.

Bowerman, C. E., & Irish, D. P. (1962). Some relationship of stepchildren to their parents. *Marriage and the Family, 24,* 113–121.

Bowker, M. A. (1982). Children and divorce: Being in between. *Elementary School Guidance and Counseling, 17,* 126–130.

Bowlby, J. (1946). *Forty four juvenile thieves: Their characters and home life.* London: Ballice, Tindall, & Cox.

Bowlby, J. (1969). *Attachment and loss:* Vol. 1. *Attachment.* London: Hogarth.

Bradford, A., Moore, R. S., Enwall, B., Taylor, J., Cooper, S. B., & Williams, C. G. (1982). *Parting: A counselor's guide for children of separated parents.* Columbia, South Carolina: South Carolina Department of Education.

Brandwein, R. A., Brown, C. A., & Fox, E. M. (1974). Women and children last: The social situation of divorced mothers and their families. *Journal of Marriage and the Family, 36*(3), 498–514.

Bray, J. H., & Anderson, H. (1984). Strategic interventions with single parent families. *Psychotherapy: Theory, Research and Practice, 21*(1), 101–109.

Bronson, G. W. (1972). Infants; reactions to unfamiliar persons and novel objects. *Monographs of the Society for Research in Child Development, 37*(3).

Brown, D. G. (1982). Divorce and family mediation: History, review, future directions. *Conciliation Courts Review, 20*(2), 1–44.

Burchinal, L. G. (1964). Characteristics of adolescents from unbroken, broken and reconstituted families. *Journal of Marriage and the Family, 26,* 44–51.

Caldwell, R. A., & Bloom, B. L. (1982). Social support: Its structure and impact on marital disruption. *American Journal of Community Psychology, 10(6),* 647–667.

Caldwell, R. A., Bloom, B. L., & Hodges, W. F. (1984). Sex differences in separation and divorce: A longitudinal perspective. In A. U. Rickel, M. Gerrard, & I. Iscoe (Eds.), *Social and Psychological Problems of Women: Prevention and Crisis Intervention.* Washington, D.C.: Hemisphere.

Cantor, D. W. (1977). School-based groups for children of divorce. *Journal of Divorce, 1(2),* 183–187.

Cantor, D. W., & Drake, E. A. (1983). *Divorced parents and their children: A guide for mental health professionals.* New York: Springer.

Caplan, G. (1970). *The theory and practice of mental health consultation.* New York: Basic Books.

Cashion, B. G. (1982). Female-headed families: Effects on children and clinical implications. *Journal of Marital and Family Therapy, 8(2),* 77–85.

Charnas, J. F. (1981). Practice trends in divorce related child custody. *Journal of Divorce, 4(4),* 57–67.

Chasin, R., & Grunebaum, H. (1981). A model for evaluation in child custody disputes. *American Journal of Family Therapy, 9(1),* 43–49.

Chess, S., Thomas, A., Korn, S., Mittelman, M., & Cohen, J. (1983). Early parental attitudes, divorce and separation, and young adult outcome: Findings of a longitudinal study. *Journal of the American Academy of Child Psychiatry, 22,* 47–51.

Clawar, S. S. (1984). How to determine whether a family report is scientific. *Conciliation Courts Review, 22(2),* 71–76.

Cline, D. W., & Westman, J. C. (1971). The impact of divorce on the family. *Child Psychiatry and Human Development, 2(2),* 78–83.

Clingempeel, W. G., Brand, E., & Ievoli, R. (1984). Stepparent-stepchild relationships in stepmother and stepfather families: A multimethod study. *Family Relations, 33,* 465–473.

Clingempeel, W. G., Ievoli, R., & Brand, E. (1984). Structural complexity and the quality of stepfather-stepchild relationships. *Family Process, 23,* 547–560.

Clingempeel, W. G. & Reppucci, N. D. (1982). Joint custody after divorce: Major issues and goals for research. *Psychological Bulletin, 91(1),* 102–127.

Coddington, R. D. (1972a). The significance of life events as etiologic factors in the diseases of children. I. A survey of professional workers. *Journal of Psychosomatic Research, 16,* 7–18.

Coddington, R. D. (1972b). The significance of life events as etiologic factors in the diseases of children. II. A study of a normal population. *Journal of Psychosomatic Research, 16,* 205–213.

Coleman, M., & Ganong, L. H. (1984). Effect of family structure on family attitudes and expectations. *Family Relations, 33,* 425–432.

Colletta, N. D. (1979). The impact of divorce: Father absence or poverty? *Journal of Divorce, 3(1),* 27–35.

Conger, J. J., & Petersen, A. (1984). *Adolescence and youth: Psychological development in a changing world* (3rd ed.). New York: Harper & Row.

Coogler, O. J. (1978). *Structured mediation in divorce settlement: A Handbook for marital mediators*. Lexington, MA: Lexington Books.

Coogler, O. J., Weber, R. E., & McKenry, P. C. (1979). Divorce mediation: A means of facilitating divorce and adjustment. *The Family Coordinator, 28,* 255–259.

Cooper, S., & Hodges, W. F. (1983). *The mental health consultation field.* New York: Human Sciences Press.

Copeland, A. P. (1985). Individual differences in children's reactions to divorce. *Journal of Clinical Child Psychology, 14*(1), 11–19.

Cowen, E. L., Dorr, D., Clarfield, S., Kreling, B., McWilliams, S. A., Pokrachi, F., Pratt, D. M., Terrell, D., & Wilson, A. (1973). The AML: A quick screening device for early identification of school maladaptation. *American Journal of Community Psychology, 1,* 12–35.

Craig, M. M., & Glick, S. J. (1963). Ten years experience with the Glueck Social Prediction Table. New York: New York City Youth Board.

Crohn, H., Sager, C. J., Rodstein, E., Brown, H. S., Walker, L., & Beir, J. (1980). Understanding and treating the child in the remarried family. In I. R. Stuart & L. E. Abt (Eds.), *Children of separation and divorce: Management and treatment.* New York: Van Nostrand Reinhold.

Crook, T., & Raskin, A. (1975). Association of childhood parental loss with attempted suicide and depression. *Journal of Consulting and Clinical Psychology, 43,* 277.

Crosbie-Burnett, M. (1984). The centrality of the step relationship: A challenge to family theory and practice. *Family Relations, 33,* 459–463.

D'Andrea, A. (1983). Joint custody as related to paternal involvement and paternal self-esteem. *Conciliation Courts Review. 21*(2), 81–87.

Derdeyn, A. P. (1975). Child custody consultation. *American Journal of Orthopsychiatry, 45*(5), 791–801.

Derdeyn, A. P. (1977). Children in divorce: Intervention in the phase of separation. *Pediatrics, 60*(1), 20–27.

Derdeyn, A. P. (1985). Grandparent visitation rights: Rendering family dissension more pronounced? *American Journal of Orthopsychiatry, 55*(2), 277–287.

Derdeyn, A. P., & Scott, E. (1984). Joint custody: A critical analysis and appraisal. *American Journal of Orthopsychiatry, 54*(2), 199–209.

Desimone-Luis, J., O'Mahoney, K., & Hunt, D. (1979). Children of separation and divorce: Factors influencing adjustment. *Journal of Divorce, 3*(1), 37–42.

Dishon, M. (1985). Psychological aspects and factors in planning visitation. *Family Law News* (Official publication of the State Bar of California Family Law Section), *8*(3), 36–39.

Dlugokinski, E. (1977). A developmental approach to coping with divorce. *Journal of Clinical Child Psychology, 6*(2), 27–30.

Dorpat, T. L., Jackson, J. K., & Ripley, H. S. (1965). Broken homes and attempted and completed suicide. *Archives of General Psychiatry, 12,* 213–216.

Drake, E. A. (1981). Helping children cope with divorce: The role of the school. In I. R. Stuart & L. E. Abt (Eds.), *Children of Separation and divorce: Management and treatment.* New York: Van Nostrand Reinhold.

Drake, E. A., & Shellenberger, S. (1981). Children of separation and divorce: A review of school programs and implications for the psychologist. *School Psychology Review, 10*(1), 54–61.

Drapkin, R., & Bienenfeld, F. (1985). The power of including children in custody mediation. *Journal of Divorce, 8*(3/4), 63–95.

Draughon, M. (1975). Stepmother's model of identification in relation to mourning in the child. *Psychological Reports, 36,* 183–189.

Duberman, L. (1973). Step-kin relationships. *Journal of Marriage and the Family, 35,* 283–292.

Duberman, L. (1975). *The reconstituted family: A study of remarried couples and their children.* Chicago: Nelson-Hall.

DUSO (1970). *Developing understanding of self and others.* Circle Pines, MN: American Guidance Service.

Emery, R. E. (1982). Interparental conflict and the children of discord and divorce. *Psychological Bulletin, 92,* 310–330.

Erikson, E. (1963). *Childhood and society.* New York: Norton.

Evans, A., & Neel, J. (1980). School behaviors of children from one-parent and two-parent homes. *Principal, 60*(1), 38–39.

Farber, S. S., Felner, R. D., & Primavera, J. (1985). Parental separation/divorce and adolescents: An examination of factors mediating adaptation. *American Journal of Community Psychology, 13*(2), 171–185.

Farber, S. S., Primavera, J., & Felner, R. D. (1983). Older adolescents and parental divorce: Adjustment problems and mediators of coping. *Journal of Divorce, 7,* 59–75.

Fassler, J. (1978). *Helping children cope: Mastering stress through books and stories.* New York: Free Press.

Fast, I., & Cain, A. C. (1966). The stepparent role: Potential for disturbances in family functioning. *American Journal of Orthopsychiatry, 36,* 485–491.

Federico, J. (1979). The marital termination period of the Divorce Adjustment Process. *Journal of Divorce, 3*(2), 93–106.

Felner, R. D., Stolberg, A., & Cowen, E. L. (1975). Crisis events and school mental health referral patterns of young children. *Journal of Consulting and Clinical Psychology, 43,* 305–310.

Felner, R. D., Terre, L., Farber, S. S., Primavera, J., & Bishop, T. A. (1985). Child custody: Practices and perspectives of legal professionals. *Journal of Clinical Child Psychology, 14*(1), 27–34.

Felner, R. D., Terre, L., Goldfarb, A., Farber, S. S., Primavera, J., Bishop, T. A., & Aber, M. S. (1985). Party status of children during marital dissolution: Child preference and legal representation in custody decisions. *Journal of Clinical Child Psychology, 14*(1), 42–48.

Ferri, E. (1976). *Growing up in a one-parent family: A long-term study of child development.* Windsor, Berkshire, England: NFER Publishing.

Fine, S. (1980). Children in divorce, custody and access situations: The contribution of the mental health professional. *Journal of Child Psychology and Psychiatry, 21,* 353–361.

Fine, M. A., Moreland, J. R., & Schwebel, A. I. (1983). Long-term effects of divorce on parent-child relationships. *Developmental Psychology, 19*(5), 703–713.

Fish, K. D. (1969). Paternal availability, family role structure, maternal employment, and personality development in late adolescent females. *Dissertation Abstracts International, 30*(9–B), 4369.

Flynn, T. (1984, March 25). Single parenthood. *The Sunday Denver Post, Contemporary,* p. 2.

Folberg, H. J., & Graham, M. (1979). Joint custody: Myth and reality. In A. L. Milne (Ed.), *Joint custody: A handbook for judges, lawyers and counselors.* Portland OR: Association of Family Conciliation Courts.

Foster, H. H. (1973). Divorce reform and the Uniform Act. *Family Law Quarterly, 7,* 170–210.

Foster, H. H., & Freed, D. J. (1978). Life with father: 1978. *Family Law Quarterly, 11*(4), 321–342.

Franklin, R. L., & Hibbs, "B" (1980). Child custody in transition. *Journal of Marital and Family Therapy, 6*(3), 285–291.

Fulton, J. A. (1979). Parental reports of children's postdivorce adjustment. *Journal of Social Issues, 35*(4), 126–139.

Galper, M. (1978). *Co-parenting: Sharing your child equally,* Philadelphia: Running Press.

Ganong, L. H., & Coleman, M. (1984). The effects of remarriage on children: A review of the empirical literature. *Family Relations, 33,* 389–406.

Gardner, R. A. (1970). *The boys and girls book about divorce.* New York: Bantam Books.

Gardner, R. A. (1974). "The mental health professional and divorce litigation." Cassette recording. New York: Psychotherapy Tape Library.

Gardner, R. A. (1976). *Psychotherapy with children of divorce.* New York: Jason Aronson.

Garrison, K. M., Stolberg, A. L., Mallonnee, D., Carpenter, J., & Antrim, Z. (1983). *The single parents' support group: A procedures manual.* Unpublished manual, Divorce Adjustment Project, Virginia Commonwealth University, Richmond.

GAP (Group for the Advancement of Psychiatry) (1981). *Divorce, child custody, and the family.* San Francisco: Jossey-Bass.

Gersick, K. (1979). Fathers by choice: Divorced men who receive custody of their children. In G. Levinger and O. C. Moles (Eds.), *Divorce and separation: Context, causes, and consequence.* New York: Basic Books.

Giles-Sims, J., & Finkelhor, D. (1984). Child abuse in stepfamilies. *Family Relations, 33,* 407–413.

Ginott, H. G. (1965). *Between parent and child.* New York: Macmillan.

Girdner, L. K. (1979). On some contradictory aspects of child custody policy (with emphasis on the expert witness). Paper read at the Annual Meeting of the National Council on Family Relations, August 17, 1979 in Boston, Massachusetts.

Girdner, L. K. (1985a). Adjudication and mediation: A comparison of custody decision-making processes involving third parties. *Journal of Divorce, 8*(3/4), 33–47.

Girdner, L. K. (1985b). Strategies of conflict: Custody litigation in the United States. *Journal of Divorce, 9*(1), 1-15.

Girdner, L. K. (in press). Child custody determination: Ideological dimensions of a social problem. In J. Rappaport & E. Seidman (Eds.), *Redefining social problems,* New York: Praeger and Plenum.

Glenn, N. D. & Weaver, C. N. (1977). The marital happiness of remarried divorced persons. *Journal of Marriage and the Family, 39*(2), 331-337.

Glenn, N. D., & Shelton, B. A. (1983). Pre-adult background variables and divorce: A note of caution about overreliance on explained variance. *Journal of Marriage and the Family, 45,* 405-410.

Glueck, S., & Glueck, E. (1950). *Unraveling juvenile delinquency,* Boston: Harvard University Press.

Goff, B. (1969). *Where is daddy? The story of a divorce.* Boston: Beacon.

Goldman, J., & Coane, J. (1977). Family therapy after the divorce: Developing a strategy. *Family Process, 16,* 357-362.

Goldstein, H. S. (1974). Reconstituted families: The second marriage and its children. *Psychiatric Quarterly, 48,* 433-440.

Goldstein, J., Freud, A., & Solnit, A. (1973). *Beyond the best interests of the child.* New York: Free Press.

Goldstein, S., & Solnit, A. J. (1984). *Divorce and your child.* New Haven, CT: Yale University Press.

Goldzband, M. G. (1982). *Consulting in child custody: An introduction to the ugliest litigation for mental health professionals.* Lexington, MA: Lexington Books.

Goode, W. J. (1965). *Women in divorce.* New York: Free Press.

Gordon, T. (1970). *P.E.T.: Parent Effectiveness Training.* New York: Van Rees Press.

Green, B. J. (1978). HELPING child of divorce: A multimodal approach. *Elementary School Guidance and Counseling, 13*(1), 31-45.

Gregory, I. (1965). Anterospective data following childhood loss of a parent: II. Pathology, performance, and potential among college students. *Archives of General Psychiatry, 13,* 110-120.

Gregory, I. (1966). Retrospective data concerning childhood loss of a parent. *Archives of General Psychiatry, 15,* 362-367.

Greif, J. B. (1979). Fathers, children, and joint custody. *American Journal of Orthopsychiatry, 49,* 311-319.

Greif, J. B., & Simring, S. K. (1982). Remarriage and joint custody. *Conciliation Courts Review, 20*(1), 9-14.

Grossman, S. M., Shea, J. A., & Adams, G. R. (1980). Effects of parental divorce during early childhood on ego development and identity formation of college students. *Journal of Divorce, 3*(3), 263-272.

Guidance Associates. (1973). "Understanding changes in the family. Not together anymore." Filmstrip. Pleasantville, NY.

Guidubaldi, J., Cleminshaw, H. D., Perry, J. D., & Mcloughlin, C. S. (1983). The impact of parental divorce on children: Report of the nationwide NASP study. *School Psychology Review, 12,* 300-323.

Guidubaldi, J., & Perry, J. D. (1984). Divorce, socioeconomic status, and children's cognitive-social competence at school entry. *American Journal of Orthopsychiatry, 54*(3), 459–468.

Hainline, L., & Feig, E. (1978). The correlates of childhood father absence in college-aged women. *Child Development, 49,* 37–42.

Haley, J. (1963). *Strategies of psychotherapy.* New York: Grune & Stratton.

Hammond, J. M. (1979). Children of divorce: Implications for counselors. *School Counselor, 27*(1), 7–14.

Hammond, J. M. (1981a). *Group counseling for children of divorce,* Ann Arbor, MI: Cranbrook.

Hammond, J. M. (1981b). *Divorce group counseling for secondary students.* Ann Arbor, MI: Cranbrook.

Hammond, J. M. (1981c). Loss of the family unit: Counseling groups to help kids. *Personnel and Guidance Journal, 59,* 392–394.

Hansen, C. M. (1982). The effects of interparental conflict on the adjustment of the preschool child to divorce. Unpublished doctoral dissertation, University of Colorado.

Hare-Mustin, R. T. (1976). The biased professional in divorce litigation. *Psychology of Women Quarterly, 1*(2), 216–222.

Haynes, J. M. (1981). *Divorce mediation: A practical guide for therapists and counselors.* New York: Springer.

Heller, K., & Monahan, J. (1983). Individual process consultation. In S. Cooper & W. F. Hodges (Eds). *The field of mental health consultation.* New York: Human Science Press.

Hepworth, J., Ryder, R. G., & Dreyer, A. S. (1984). The effects of parental loss on the formation of intimate relationships. *Journal of Marital and Family Therapy, 10*(1), 73–82.

Herzog, E., & Sudia, C. E. (1973). Children in fatherless families. In B. M. Caldwell & H. N. Ricciuti (Eds.), *Review of child development research: Volume three: Child development and social policy.* Chicago: University of Chicago Press.

Herzog, J. M. (1980). Sleep disturbance and father hunger in 18- to 28-month old boys: The Erlkoenig syndrome. *Psychoanalytic Study of the Child, 35,* 219–233.

Hess, R. D., & Camara, K. A. (1979). Post-divorce family relationships as mediating factors in the consequences of divorce for children. *Journal of Social Issues, 35*(4), 79–96.

Hetherington, E. M. (1966). Effects of parental absence on sex typed behaviors in Negro and white preadolescent males. *Journal of Personality and Social Psychology, 4,* 87–91.

Hetherington, E. M. (1972). Effects of paternal absence on personality development in adolescent daughters. *Developmental Pathology, 7,* 313–326.

Hetherington, E. M., Cox, M., & Cox, R. (1979). Beyond father absence: Conceptualization of effects of divorce. In E. M. Hetherington & R. D. Parke (Eds.), *Contemporary readings in child psychology.* New York: McGraw-Hill.

Hetherington, E. M., Cox, M., & Cox, R. (1978). The aftermath of divorce. In J. H.

Stevens, Jr. & M. Matthews (Eds.), *Mother-child, father-child relations.* Washington, DC: National Association for the Education of Young Children.

Hirst, S. R., & Smiley, G. W. (1984). The access dilemma—A study of access patterns following marriage breakdown. *Conciliation Courts Review, 22*(1), 41–52.

Hodges, W. F. (in press). Problems of visitation post divorce. In W. Witlin & R. Hinds (Eds.), *The child custody handbook.* New York: Irvington Press.

Hodges, W. F., & Bloom, B. L. (1984). Parent's report of children's adjustment to marital separation: A longitudinal study. *Journal of Divorce, 8*(1), 33–50.

Hodges, W. F., & Bloom, B. L. (1986). Preventive intervention for newly separated adults: One year later. *Journal of Preventive Psychiatry 3*(1), 35–49.

Hodges, W. F., Buchsbaum, H. K., & Tierney, C. W. (1983). Parent-child relationships and adjustment in preschool children in divorced and intact families. *Journal of Divorce, 7*(2), 43–58.

Hodges, W. F., Tierney, C. W., & Buchsbaum, H. K. (1984). The cumulative effect of stress on preschool children of divorced and intact families. *Journal of Marriage and the Family, 46,* 611–617.

Hodges, W. F., Wechsler, R. C., & Ballantine, C. (1979). Divorce and the preschool child. *Journal of Divorce, 3,* 55–69.

Hoeffer, B. (1981). Children's acquisition of sex-role behavior in lesbian-mother families. *American Journal of Orthopsychiatry, 51*(3), 536–544.

Hoffman, M. L. (1971). Father absence and conscience development. *Developmental Psychology, 4,* 400–406.

Holdahl, S., & Caspersen, P. (1977). Children of family change: Who's helping them now? *Family Coordinator, 26,* 472–477.

Hoorwitz, A. N. (1982). "Extraordinary circumstances" in custody contests between parent and nonparent. *Journal of Psychiatry and Law, 10,* 351–361.

Hoorwitz, A. N. (1983). The visitation dilemma in court consultation. *Social Casework, 64*(4), 231–237.

Hozman, T. L., & Froiland, D. J. (1976). Families in divorce: A proposed model for counseling the children. *Family Coordinator, 25*(3), 271–276.

Huston, A. C. (1983). Sex-typing. In P. H. Mussen (Ed.), *Handbook of child psychology* (E. M. Hetherington, Vol. Ed.). New York: Wiley, 387–467.

Ilfeld, F. W., Ilfeld, H. Z., & Alexander, J. R. (1982). Does joint custody work? A first look at outcome data of relitigation. *American Journal of Psychiatry, 139*(1), 62–66.

Irving, H. H. (1980). *Divorce mediation: The rational alternative.* Toronto: Personal Library.

Irving, H. H., Benjamin, M., & Trocme, N. (1984). Shared parenting: An empirical analysis using a large data base. *Family Process, 23,* 561–569.

Irving, H. H., Bohm, P., MacDonald, G., & Benjamin, M. (1979). A comparative analysis of two family court services: An exploratory study of conciliation counseling. Toronto, Canada: Welfare Grants Directorate, Department of National Health and Welfare and the Ontario Ministry of the Attorney General.

Isaacs, M. B. (1981). Treatment for families of divorce: A systems model of prevention. In I. R. Stuart & L. E. Abt (Eds.), *Children of separation and divorce: Management and treatment.* New York: Van Nostrand Reinhold.

Jacobson, D. S. (1978a). The impact of marital separation/divorce on children: I. Parent-child separation and child adjustment. *Journal of Divorce, 1*(4), 341–360.

Jacobson, D. S. (1978b). The impact of marital separation/divorce on children: II. Interparent hostility and child adjustment. *Journal of Divorce, 2,* 3–19.

Jacobson, D. S. (1978c). The impact of divorce/separation on children: III. Parent-child communication and child adjustment and regression analysis of findings from overall study. *Journal of Divorce, 2,* 175–194.

Jacobson, D. S. (1979). Stepfamilies: Myths and realities. *Social Work, 24,* 202–207.

Jacobson, G., & Ryder, R. G. (1969). Parental loss and some characteristics of the early marriage relationship. *American Journal of Orthopsychiatry, 39*(5), 779–787.

Jauch, C. (1977). The one-parent family. *Journal of Clinical Child Psychology, 6*(2), 30–32.

Johnson, H. C. (1980). Working with stepfamilies: Principles of practice. *Social Work, 25,* 304–308.

Johnston, J. R., Campbell, L. E. G., & Mayes, S. S. (1985, in press). Latency children in post-separation and divorce disputes. *Journal of the American Academy of Child Psychiatry, 24*(5).

Johnston, J. R., Gonzalez, R., & Campbell, L. E. G. (1985). Ongoing post-divorce conflict as predictor of child disturbance. Paper presented at the Annual Meeting of the American Psychological Association, Los Angeles, August, 1985.

Johnston, J. R., Campbell, L. E. G., & Tall, M. C. (1985). Impasses to the resolution of custody and visitation disputes. *American Journal of Orthopsychiatry, 55*(1), 112–129.

Jones, S. M. (1978). Divorce and remarriage: A new beginning, a new set of problems. *Journal of Divorce, 2*(2), 217–227.

Kagan, J., Kearsley, R., & Zelazo, P. (1978). *Infancy: Its place in human development.* Cambridge: Harvard University Press.

Kalter, N. (1977). Children of divorce in an outpatient psychiatric population. *American Journal of Orthopsychiatry, 47,* 40–51.

Kalter, N. (1984). Conjoint mother-daughter treatment: A beginning phase of psychotherapy with adolescent daughters of divorce. *American Journal of Orthopsychiatry, 54*(3), 490–497.

Kalter, N., Pickar, J., & Lesowitz, M. (1984). School-based developmental facilitation groups for children of divorce: A preventive intervention. *American Journal of Orthopsychiatry, 54*(4), 613–623.

Kalter, N., & Rembar, J. (1981). The significance of a child's age at the time of parental divorce. *American Journal of Orthopsychiatry, 46,* 20–32.

Kaplan, H. B., & Pokorny, A. D. (1971). Self-derogation and childhood broken home. *Journal of Marriage and the Family, 33,* 328–337.

Kaplan, S. L. (1977). Structural family therapy for children of divorce: Case Reports. *Family Process, 16,* 75–83.

Kaseman, C. M. (1974). The single-parent family. *Perspectives in Psychiatric Care, 12,* 113–118.

Keat, D. B. (1974). *Fundamentals of child counseling.* Boston: Houghton Mifflin.

Keat, D. B. (1978). The acting, feeling, choosing game: A multimodal game for children. Harrisburg, PA: Professional Associates.

Kellam, S. G., Ensminger, M. E., & Turner, R. J. (1977). Family structure and the mental health of children: Concurrent and longitudinal community-wide studies. *Archives of General Psychiatry, 34,*(9), 1012–1022.

Kelly, J. B. (1981). The visiting relationship after divorce: Research findings and clinical implications. In I. R. Stuart & L. E. Abt (Eds.), *Children of separation and divorce: Management and treatment.* New York: Van Nostrand Reinhold, 338–361.

Kelly, J. B., & Wallerstein, J. S. (1976). The effects of parental divorce: Experiences of the child in early latency. *American Journal of Orthopsychiatry, 46,* 20–32.

Kelly, J. B., & Wallerstein, J. S. (1977a). Brief interventions with children in divorcing families. *American Journal of Orthopsychiatry, 47*(1), 23–39.

Kelly, J. B., & Wallerstein, J. S. (1977b). Part-time parent, part-time child: Visiting after divorce. *Journal of Clinical Child Psychology, 6*(2), 51–54.

Keshet, H. F., & Rosenthal, K. M. (1978). Fathering after marital separation. *Social Work, 23,* 11–18.

Kessler, S. (1977). *Beyond divorce: A divorce primer.* Atlanta: National Institute of Professional Training.

Kessler, S., & Bostwick, K. S. (1977). Beyond divorce: Coping skills for children. *Journal of Clinical Child Psychology, 6,* 38–41.

Kirkpatrick, M., Smith, C., & Roy, R. (1981). Lesbian mothers and their children: A comprehensive survey. *American Journal of Orthopsychiatry, 51,* 85–100.

Kleinman, J., Rosenberg, E., & Whiteside, M. (1979). Common developmental tasks in forming reconstituted families. *Journal of Marital and Family Therapy, 5,* 79–86.

Koch, M. A., & Lowery, C. R. (1984). Visitation and the noncustodial father. *Journal of Divorce, 8*(2), 47–65.

Koopman, E. J., Hunt, E. J., & Stafford, V. (1984). Child related agreements in mediated and non-mediated divorce settlements: A preliminary examination and discussion of implications. *Conciliation Courts Review, 22*(1), 65–70.

Kosinski, F. A. (1983). Improving relationships in stepfamilies. *Elementary School Guidance and Counseling, 17*(3), 200–207.

Kotelchuck, M. (1972). The nature of the child's tie to his father. Unpublished doctoral dissertation, Harvard University.

Krantz, S. E., Clark, J., Pruyn, J. P., & Usher, M. (1985). Cognitive and adjustment among children of separated or divorced parents. *Cognitive Therapy and Research, 9*(1), 61–77.

Kubler-Ross, E. (1969). *On death and dying.* New York: Macmillan.

Kuehnel, T. G., & Kuehnel, J. M. (1983). Mental health consultation: An educational approach. In S. Cooper & W. F. Hodges (Eds.), *The mental health consultation field.* New York: Human Sciences Press.

Kulka, R., & Weingarten, H. (1979). The long-term effects of parental divorce in childhood on adult adjustment. *Journal of Social Issues, 35,* 50–78.

Kurdek, L. A., & Berg, B. (1983). Correlates of children's adjustment to their parents' divorces. In L. A. Kurdek (Ed.), *Children and divorce: New directions for child development* (No. 19). San Francisco: Jossey-Bass.

Kurdek, L. A., Blisk, D., & Siesky, A. E. (1981). Correlates of children's long-term adjustment to their parents' divorce. *Developmental Psychology, 17*(5), 565–579.

Lamb, M. (1981). The development of father-infant relationships. In M. Lamb (Ed.) *The role of the father in child development (2nd ed.).* New York: Wiley, 459–488.

Landis, J. T. (1960). The trauma of children when parents divorce. *Marriage and Family Living, 22,* 7–12.

Langner, T. S., & Michael, S. T. (1963). *Life stress and mental health.* New York: Free Press of Glencoe.

Leader, A. L. (1973). Family therapy for divorced fathers and others out of home. *Social Casework, 54,* 13–19.

LeShan, E. (1978). *What's going to happen to me? When parents separate or divorce,* New York: Scholastic.

Lessing, E. E., Zagorin, S. W., & Nelson, D. (1970). WISC subtest and IQ score correlates of father absence. *Journal of Genetic Psychology, 117,* 181–195.

Levin, M. L. (1984). Sequellae to marital disruption in children. NIMH Workshop on Divorce and Children, June 14, 15, 1984, 29 pages and tables.

Lewis, M. (1974). The latency child in a custody conflict. *Journal of the American Academy of Child Psychiatry, 13,* 635–647.

Lewis, M., Feiring, C., & Weinraub, M. (1981). The father as a member of the child's social network. In M. E. Lamb (Ed.), *The role of the father in child development.* New York: Wiley, 259–294.

Longfellow, C. (1979). Divorce in context: Its impact on children. In G. Levinger & O. C. Moles (Eds.), *Divorce and separation: Context, causes, and consequences.* New York: Basic Books.

Lowenstein, J. S., & Koopman, E. J. (1978). A comparison of the self-esteem between boys living with single-parent mothers and single-parent fathers. *Journal of Divorce, 2*(2), 195–208.

Lowery, C. R. (1981). Child custody decisions in divorce proceedings: A survey of judges. *Professional Psychology, 12*(4), 492–498.

Lowery, C. R. (1984). The wisdom of Solomon: Criteria for child custody from the legal and clinical points of view. *Law and Human Behavior, 8*(¾), 371–380.

Lowery, C. R. (1985a). Child custody in divorce: Parents' decisions and perceptions. *Family Relations, 34,* 241–249.

Lowery, C. R. (1985b). Child custody evaluations: Criteria and clinical implications. *Journal of Clinical Child Psychology, 14*(1), 35–41.

Lowery, C. R. (1985c). Child custody in divorce: Parents' decisions and perceptions. *Family Relations, 34,* 241–249.

Luepnitz, D. A. (1982). *Child custody: A study of families after divorce,* Lexington, MA: Lexington Books.

MacGregor, R., Ritchie, A. M., Serrano, A. C., & Schuster, F. P. (1964). *Multiple impact therapy with families.* New York: McGraw-Hill.

Magid, K. M. (1977). Children facing divorce: A treatment program. *Personnel and Guidance Journal, 55,* 534–536.

Mahler, M. S., Pine, F., & Bergman, A. (1975). *The psychological birth of the human infant.* New York: Basic Books.

Mann, P. (1973). *My dad lives in a downtown hotel,* New York: Scholastic.

Marino, C. D., & McCowan, R. J. (1976). The effects of parent absence on children. *Child Study Journal, 6,* 165–182.

Maskin, M. B., & Brookins, E. (1974). The effects of parental composition on recidivism rates in delinquent girls. *Journal of Clinical Psychology, 30*(3), 341–342.

McDermott, J. F. (1968). Parental divorce in early childhood. *American Journal of Psychiatry, 124,* 1424–1432.

McDermott, J. F. (1970). Divorce and its psychiatric sequelae in children. *Archives of General Psychiatry, 23,* 421–427.

McDermott, J. F., Tseng, W., Char, W. F., & Fukunaga, C. S. (1978). Child custody decision making. *Journal of the American Academy of Child Psychiatry, 17,* 104–116.

McGoldrick, M., & Carter, E. A. (1980). Forming a remarried family. In E. A. Carter & M. McGoldrick (Eds.), *The family life cycle: A framework for family therapy.* New York: Gardner Press.

McGregor, R., Ritchie, A. M., & Serrano, A. C. (1964). *Multiple impact therapy with families.* New York: McGraw-Hill.

McKay, M., Rogers, P. D., Blades, J., & Gosse, R. (1984). *The divorce book.* Oakland, CA: New Harbinger Publications.

McLoughlin, D., & Whitfield, R. (1984). Adolescents and their experience of parental divorce. *Journal of Adolescence, 7,* 155–170.

Mendes, H. A. (1976). Single fatherhood. *Social Work, 21,* 308–312.

Mendes, H. A. (1979). Single-parent families: A typology of life-styles. *Social Work, 4*(1), 37–48.

Messinger, L. (1976). Remarriage between divorced people with children from a previous marriage. *Journal of Marriage and Family Counseling, 2*(2), 193–200.

Miller, J. J., & Soper, B. (1982). An emerging contingency, the stepfamily: Review of the literature. *Psychological Reports, 50,* 715–722.

Mills, D. M. (1984). A model for stepfamily development. *Family Relations, 33,* 365–372.

Milne, A. L. (1979). *Joint custody: A handbook for judges, lawyers, and counselors.* Portland, OR: The Association of Family Conciliation Courts.

Minton, M. H., & Elia, M. G. (1981). Jarrett v. Jarrett: The custody crossroads. *Journal of Divorce, 6*(3), 1–29.

Minton, M. H. (1983). Epilogue Jarrett v. Jarrett: The custody crossroads. *Journal of Divorce, 6*(3), 83–86.

Minuchin, S. (1974). *Families and family therapy,* Cambridge, MA: Harvard University Press.

Mitchel, A. K. (1983). Adolescents' experiences of parental separation and divorce. *Journal of Adolescence, 6,* 175–187.

Moreland, J., Schwebel, A. I., Fine, M. A., & Vess, J. D. (1982). Postdivorce family therapy: Suggestions for professionals. *Professional Psychology, 13*(5), 639–646.

Morley, I., & Stephenson, G. (1977). *The social psychology of bargaining.* London: Allen & Unwin.

Morrison, J. R. (1974). Parental divorce as a factor in childhood psychiatric illness. *Comprehensive Psychiatry, 15,* 95–102.

Mowatt, M. H. (1972). Group psychotherapy for stepfathers and their wives. *Psychotherapy: Theory, Research and Practice, 9*(4), 328–331.

Musetto, A. P. (1980). Evaluating families with custody or visitation problems. *Advances in Family Psychiatry, 2,* 523–531.

Mussen, P. H., Conger, J. J., & Kagan, J. (1979). *Child development and personality* (5th ed.). New York: Harper & Row.

Mussen, P. H., Conger, J. J., Kagan, J., & Huston, A. C. (1984). *Child development and personality* (6th ed.). New York: Harper & Row.

NAESP report. (1980). One-parent families and their children. *Principal, 60*(1), 31–37.

Nadler, J. H. (1976). The psychological stress of the stepmother. Unpublished doctoral dissertation. California School of Professional Psychology, Los Angeles, California.

Nadler, J. H. (1983). Effecting change in stepfamilies: A psychodynamic/behavioral group approach. *American Journal of Psychotherapy, 37*(1), 100–112.

National Instructional Television Center (1973). *Breakup.* Bloomington, IN: National Instructional Television Center.

Newman, G. (1981). *101 ways to be a long distance super-dad.* Mountain View, CA: Blossom Valley Press.

Newsweek Staff. (1985, July 15). Playing both mother and father. *Newsweek, CVL* (3), 42–43.

Nichols, W. C. (1980). Stepfamilies: A growing family therapy challenge. In L. R. Wolberg & M. L. Aronson (Eds.), *Group and family therapy, 1980.* New York: Brunner/Mazel.

Nye, F. I. (1958). Child adjustment in broken and in unhappy unbroken homes. *Marriage and Family Living, 19,* 356–361.

Oshman, H. P., & Manosevitz, M. (1976). Father absence: Effects of stepfathers upon psychosocial development in males. *Developmental Psychology, 12,* 479–480.

Ourth, J. (1980). Children in one-parent homes: The school factor. *Principal, 60*(1), 40.

Ourth, J., & Zakariya, S. B. (1982). The school and the single-parent student: What schools can do to help. *Principal, 62*(1), 24–26, 31, 38.

Papernow, P. L. (1984). The stepfamily cycle: An experimental model of stepfamily development. *Family Relations, 33,* 355–363.

Pearson, J. (1981). Child custody: Why not let the parents decide? *The Judges Journal, 20*(1), 4–12.

Pearson, J., Munson, P., & Thoennes, N. (1983). Children's rights and child custody proceedings. *Journal of Divorce, 7*(2), 1–21.

Pearson, J., & Thoennes, N. (1982). Mediation & Divorce: The benefits outweigh the costs. *Family Advocate, 4*(3), 26–32.

Pearson, J., & Thoennes, N. (1984). Mediating and litigating custody disputes: A longitudinal evaluation. *Family Law Quarterly, 17*(4), 497–524.

Pearson, J., & Thoennes, N. (1985). Research report: Mediation versus the courts in child custody cases. *Negotiation Journal, 1*(3), 235–244.

Peck, B. B. (1975). Psychotherapy with disrupted families. *Journal of Contemporary Psychotherapy, 7*(1), 60–66.

Pedersen, F. A. (1981). Father influences viewed in a family context. In M. Lamb (Ed.) *The role of the father in child development (2nd ed.).* New York: Wiley, 295–317.

Pedersen, F. A., & Robson, K. S. (1969). Father participation in infancy. *American Journal of Orthopsychiatry, 39,* 466–472.

Pedersen, F. A., Rubenstein, J. L., & Yarrow, L. J. (1979). Infant development in father-absent families. *Journal of Genetic Psychology, 135,* 51–61.

Pedro-Carroll, J. (1983). The children of divorce intervention project: An investigation of the efficacy of a school-based prevention program. Unpublished doctoral dissertation, Rochester, New York: University of Rochester.

Pedro-Carroll, J., & Cowen, E. L. (in press). The children of divorce intervention project: An investigation of the efficacy of a school-based prevention program. *Journal of Consulting and Clinical Psychology, 54.*

Perkins, T. F., & Kahan, J. P. (1979). An empirical comparison of natural-father and stepfather systems. *Family Process, 18,* 175–183.

Phelps, D. W. (1969). Parental attitudes toward family life and child behavior of mothers in two-parent and one-parent families. *Journal of School Health, 39,* 413–416.

Pitts, F. N., Meyer, J., Brooks, M., & Winokur, G. (1965). Adult psychiatric illness in family members: A study of 748 patients and 250 controls. *American Journal of Psychiatry, 121* (Suppl), i-x.

Plunkett, J., & Kalter, N. (in press). Children's beliefs about reactions to parental divorce. *Journal of the American Academy of Child Psychiatry.*

Polikoff, N. D. (1982). Why are mothers losing: A brief analysis of criteria used in child custody determinations. *Women's Rights Law Reporter, 7*(3), 235–243.

Porter, B., & O'Leary, K. D. (1980). Marital discord and childhood behavior problems. *Journal of Abnormal Child Psychology, 8*(3), 287–295.

Provence, S., & Lipton, R. C. (1962). *Infants in institutions.* New York: International Universities Press.

Rahe, R. H. (1968). Life-change measurement as a predictor of illness. *Proceedings of the Royal Society of Medicine, 61,* 1124–1125.

Rahe, R. H., Meyer, M., Smith, M., Kjaer, G., & Holmes, T. H. (1964). Social stress and illness onset. *Journal of Psychosomatic Research, 8,* 35–44.

Ramos, S. (1979). *The complete book of child custody.* New York: Putnam.

Raschke, H. J. (1977). Family structure, family happiness, and their effect on college students' personal and social adjustment. *Conciliation Courts Review, 15,* 30–33.

Raschke, H. J., & Raschke, V. J. (1979). Family conflict and children's self-concepts. *Journal of Marriage and the Family, 41,* 367–374.

Rebelsky, F., & Hanks, C. (1971). Fathers' verbal interaction with infants in the first three months of life. *Child Development, 42*(1), 63–68.

Reingold, C. B. (1976). *Remarriage,* New York: Harper & Row.

Reinhard, D. W. (1977). The reaction of adolescent boys and girls to the divorce of their parents. *Journal of Clinical Child Psychology, 6,* 15–20.

Reppucci, N. D. The wisdom of Solomon: Issues in child custody determination. In N. D. Reppucci, L. A. Weithorn, E. P. Mulvey, & J. Monahan (Eds.), *Children, mental health, and the law.* Beverly Hills, CA: Sage.

Rheingold, H. L. (1956). The modification of social responsiveness in institutional babies. *Monographs of the Society for Research in Child Development, 2*(2, Serial No. 63).

Rheingold, H. L., & Eckerman, C. O. (1970). The infant separates himself from his mother. *Science, 168,* 78–90.

Ricci, I. (1985). Mediator's notebook: Reflections on promoting equal empowerment and entitlements for women. *Journal of Divorce, 8*(3/4), 49–61.

Richards, A., & Willis, I. (1976). *How to get it together when your parents are coming apart.* New York: Bantam Books.

Rickel, A. U., & Langner, T. S. (1985). Short- and long-term effects of marital disruption on children. *American Journal of Community Psychology, 13*(5), 599–611.

Ricks, S. S. (1984). Determining child custody: Trends, factors, and alternatives. *Conciliation Courts Review, 22*(1), 65–70.

Ringler-White, M. (1982). Supervised visitation: Working with the most difficult parents. Presented at the Child Custody Conference. Visitation: From chaos to cooperation. The Interdisciplinary Committee on Child Custody and the Continuing Legal Education in Colorado, Inc. May 8, 1982. Boulder, Colorado.

Ritchie, A. M., & Serrano, A. C. (1974). Family therapy in the treatment of adolescents with divorced parents. In R. E. Hardy & J. G. Cull (Eds.), *Therapeutic needs of the family: Problems, descriptions and therapeutic approaches.* Springfield, IL: Charles C Thomas.

Robinson, B. E. (1984). The contemporary American stepfather. *Family Relations, 33,* 381–388.

Rohrlich, J. A., Ranier, R., Berg-Cross, L., & Berg-Cross, G. (1977). The effects of divorce: A research review with a developmental perspective. *Journal of Clinical Child Psychology, 6,* 15–20.

Roseby, V., & Deutsch, R. (1985). Children of separation and divorce: Effects of a social role-taking group intervention on fourth and fifth graders. *Journal of Clinical Child Psychology, 14*(1), 55–60.

Rosenthal, P. A. (1979). Sudden disappearance of one parent with separation and divorce: The grief and treatment of preschool children. *Journal of Divorce, 3*(1), 43–54.

Ross, G., Kagan, J., Zelazo, P., & Kotelchuck, M. (1975). Separation protest in infants in home and laboratory. *Developmental Psychology, 11,* 256–257.

Rubinstein, C., Shaver, P., & Peplau, L. A. (1979). Loneliness. *Human Nature, 2,* 58–65.

Rutter, M. (1971). Parent-child separation: Psychological effects on the children. *Journal of Child Psychology and Psychiatry, 12,* 233-260.

Rutter, M. (1979). Maternal deprivation, 1972-1978: New findings, new concepts, new approaches. *Child Development, 50,* 283-305.

Sack, W. H., Mason, R., & Higgins, J. E. (1985). The single-parent family and abusive child punishment. *American Journal of Orthopsychiatry, 55*(2), 252-259.

Sager, C. J., Walker, E., Brown, H. S., Crohn, H. M., & Rodstein, E. (1981). Improving functioning of the remarried family system. *Journal of Marital and Family Therapy, 7*(1), 3-13.

Sager, C. J., Steer, H., Crohn, H., Rodstein, E., & Walker, E. (1980). Remarriage revisited. *Family and Mental Health Journal, 6,* 19-33.

Sandler I. N., & Ramsay, T. B. (1980). Dimensional analysis of children's stressful life events. *American Journal of Community Psychology, 8,* 285-302.

Santrock, J. W. (1970). Influence of onset and type of paternal absence on the first four Eriksonian crises. *Developmental Psychology, 3,* 273-274.

Santrock, J. W. (1972). Relation of type and onset of father absence on cognitive development. *Child Development, 43,* 455-469.

Santrock, J. W. (1975). Father absence, perceived maternal behavior and moral development in boys. *Child Development, 46,* 753-757.

Santrock, J. W., & Tracy, R. L. (1978). The effects of children's family structure status on the development of stereotypes by teachers. *Journal of Educational Psychology, 70,* 754-757.

Santrock, J. W., & Warshak, R. A. (1979). Father custody and social development in boys and girls. *Journal of Social Issues, 35,* 112-125.

Santrock, J. W., & Wohlford, P. (1970). Effects of father absence: Influence of the reason for and the onset of the absence. *Proceeds in the 78th Annual Convention of the American Psychological Association, 5,* 265-266. (Summary).

Sarnoff, C. (1976). *Latency.* New York: Jason Aronson.

Saroyan, W. (1972). Gaston, In E. D. Landau, S. L. Epstein, & A. Platt-Stone (Eds.), *Child development through literature.* Englewood Cliffs, NJ: Prentice-Hall.

Satir, V. (1972). *Peoplemaking.* Palo Alto, CA: Science and Behavior Books.

Schulman, G. (1972). Myths that intrude on the adaptation of the stepfamily. *Social Casework, 49,* 131-139.

Schulz, D. A., & Wilson, R. A. (1973). Some traditional family variables and their correlates with drug use among high school students. *Journal of Marriage and the Family, 35,* 628-631.

Schlesinger, B. (1982). Children's viewpoints of living in a one-parent family. *Journal of Divorce, 5,* 1-23.

Schooler, C. (1972). Childhood family structure and adult characteristics. *Sociometry, 35,* 453-475.

Sears, R. R., Maccoby, E. E., & Levin, H. (1957). *Patterns of Child Rearing.* Evanston, IL: Row, Peterson & Co.

Seligson, M. (1977, June). The wicked stepchild. *Cosmopolitan,* 198-199.

Settle, S. A., & Lowery, C. R. (1982). Child custody decisions: Content analysis of a judicial survey. *Journal of Divorce, 6,* 125-138.

Shinn, M. (1978). Father absence and children's cognitive development. *Psychological Bulletin, 85,* 295–324.

Simmons, R. C., Rosenberg, F., & Rosenberg, M. (1973). Disturbance in the self-image at adolescence. *American Sociological Review, 38,* 553–568.

Simon, S. B., Howe, L. W., & Kirschenbaum, H. (1972). *Values clarification.* New York: Hart.

Skafte, D. (1985). *Child custody evaluations.* Beverly Hills, CA: Sage.

Slater, E. J., Stewart, K. J., & Linn, M. W. (1983). The effects of family disruption on adolescent males and females. *Adolescence, 18,* 931–942.

Smith, R. M. (1976). The impact of fathers on delinquent males. *Dissertation Abstracts International, 35*(10–A), 6487–6488.

Sonnenshein-Schneider, M., & Baird, K. L. (1980). Group counseling children of divorce in the elementary schools: Understanding process and technique. *Personnel and Guidance Journal, 59*(2), 88–91.

Sorosky, A. D. (1977). The psychological effect of divorce on adolescents. *Adolescence, 12,* 123–136.

Spitz, R. A. (1946). Hospitalism. *Psychoanalytic Study of the Child, 2,* 113–117.

Springer, C., & Wallerstein, J. S. (1983). Young adolescents' responses to their parents' divorces. In L. A. Kurdek (Ed.), *Children and divorce: New directions in child development* (No. 19). San Francisco: Jossey-Bass.

Sroufe, L. A. (1979). The coherence of individual development. *American Psychologist, 34,* 834–841.

Stein, M., Levy, M. T., & Glasberg, H. M. (1974). Separations in black and white suicide attempters. *Archives of General Psychiatry, 31,* 815–821.

Steinman, S. (1981). The experience of children in a joint-custody arrangement: A report of a study. *American Journal of Orthospychiatry, 51,* 403–414.

Stern, P. N. (1978). Stepfather families: Integration around child discipline. *Issues in Mental Health Nursing, 1*(2), 50–56.

Stolberg, A. L., & Bush, J. P. (1985). A path analysis of factors predicting children's divorce adjustment. *Journal of Clinical Child Psychology, 14*(1), 49–54.

Stolberg, A. L., & Cullen, P. M. (1983). Preventive interventions for families of divorce: The divorce adjustment project. In L. A. Kurdek (Ed.), *Children and divorce: New directions for child development.* San Francisco, CA: Jossey-Bass.

Stolberg, A. L., & Garrison, K. M. (1985). Evaluating a primary prevention program for children of divorce. *American Journal of Community Psychology, 13*(2), 111–124.

Stott, M. W. R., Gaier, E. L., & Thomas, K. B. (1984). Supervised access: A judicial alternative to noncompliance with visitation arrangements following divorce. *Children and Youth Services, 6,* 207–217.

Suarez, J. M., Weston, N. L., & Hartstein, N. B. (1978). Mental health interventions in divorce proceedings. *American Journal of Orthopsychiatry, 48*(2), 273–283.

Szalai, A., Converse, P. E., Feldheim, P., Scheuch, E. K., & Stone, P. J. (Eds.) (1972). *The use of time: Daily activities of urban and suburban populations in 12 countries.* The Hague, The Netherlands: Mouton, As cited in M. Shinn (1978). Father absence and child's cognitive development. *Psychological Bulletin, 85,* 295–324.

Tessman, L. (1978). *Children of parting parents,* New York: Jason Aronson.

Thies, J. M. (1977). Beyond divorce: The impact of remarriage on children. *Journal of Clinical Child Psychology, 6*(2), 59–61.

Thomas, A., & Chess, S. (1984). Genesis and evolution of behavioral disorders: From infancy to early adult life. *American Journal of Psychiatry, 141*(1), 1–9.

Thomson, H. (1966). *The successful stepparent.* New York: Harper & Row.

Tierney, C. W. (1983). Visitation patterns and adjustment of preschool children of divorce. Unpublished doctoral dissertation, University of Colorado.

Toomin, M. K. (1974). The child of divorce. In R. E. Hardy & J. G. Cull (Eds.) *Therapeutic needs of the family.* Springfield, IL: Charles C Thomas.

Tullock, J. D. (1976, May 22). Visitation: A view from the couch. Conference entitled: Divorce, children, attorneys, and clinicians. Sponsored by the Interdisciplinary Committee on Child Custody and the Continuing Legal Education in Colorado, Inc. Denver, Colorado.

Turner, J. R. (1984). Divorced fathers who win contested custody of their children: An exploratory study. *American Journal of Orthopsychiatry, 54*(3), 498–501.

Uniform Marriage and Divorce Act (1970). Chicago, IL: National Conference of Commissioners on Uniform State Laws.

U. S. Department of Health and Human Services (1980). *Helping youth and families of separation, divorce, and remarriage: A program manual.* Washington, D.C.: U. S. Government Printing Office (DHHS Publication No. (OHDS)80–32010).

Vanderkool, L., & Pearson, J. (1983). Mediating divorce disputes: Mediator behaviors, styles and roles. *Family Relations, 32,* 1–10.

Vess, J. D., Schwebel, A. I., & Moreland, J. (1983). The effects of early parental divorce on the sex role development of college students. *Journal of Divorce, 7*(1), 83–95.

Visher, E. B., & Visher, J. S. (1978). Common problems of stepparents and their spouses. *American Journal of Orthopsychiatry, 48,* 252–262.

Visher, E. B., & Visher, J. S. (1979). *Stepfamilies: A guide to working with stepparents and stepchildren.* New York: Brunner/Mazel.

Viorst, J. (1975a). *Rosie and Michael.* New York: Random

Viorst, J. (1975b). *The tenth good thing about Barney.* New York: Atheneum.

Volgy, S. S., & Everett, C. A. (1985). Joint custody reconsidered: Systemic criteria for mediation. *Journal of Divorce, 8*(3/4), 131–150.

Walker, L., Brown, H., Crohn, H., Rodstein, E., Zeisel, E., & Sager, C. J. (1979). An annotated bibliography of the remarried, the living together, and their children. *Family Process, 18*(2), 193–212.

Walker, K. N., Rogers, J., & Messinger, L. (1977). Remarriage after divorce: A review. *Social Casework, 58,* 276–285.

Wallerstein, J. S. (1983, September 10). Children of divorce: Findings from a ten year study; Parent-child relationships following divorce. Speeches at the Interdisciplinary Committee on Child Custody Annual Conference, Keystone, Colorado.

Wallerstein, J. S. (1984). Children of divorce: Preliminary report of a ten-year follow-up of young children. *American Journal of Orthopsychiatry, 54*(3), 444–458.

Wallerstein, J. S., & Kelly, J. B. (1974). Responses of the preschool child to divorce: Those who cope. In M. F. McMillan & S. Henao (Eds.), *Child psychiatry: Treatment and research.* New York: Brunner/Mazel.

Wallerstein, J. S., & Kelly, J. B. (1975). The effects of parental divorce: Experiences of the pre-school child. *Journal of the American Academy of Child Psychiatry, 14,* 600–616.

Wallerstein, J. S., & Kelly, J. B. (1976). The effects of parental divorce: Experiences of the child in later latency. *American Journal of Orthopsychiatry, 46,* 256–269.

Wallerstein, J. S., & Kelly, J. B. (1977). Divorce counseling: A community service for families in the midst of divorce. *American Journal of Orthopsychiatry, 47*(1), 4–22.

Wallerstein, J. S., & Kelly, J. B. (1980a, January). California's children of divorce. *Psychology Today, 67*–76.

Wallerstein, J. S., & Kelly, J. B. (1980b). Effects of divorce on the visiting father-child relationship. *American Journal of Psychiatry, 137*(12), 1534–1539.

Wallerstein, J. S., & Kelly, J. B. (1980c). *Surviving the breakup: How children and parents cope with divorce.* New York: Basic Books.

Waters, B., & Dimock, J. (1983). A review of research relevant to custody and access disputes. *Australian and New Zealand Journal of Psychiatry, 17,* 181–189.

Warshak, R. A., & Santrock, J. W. (1983a). The impact of divorce in father-custody and mother-custody homes: The child's perspective. In L. A. Kurdek (Ed.), *Children and divorce: New directions for child development* (No. 19). San Francisco: Jossey-Bass.

Warshak, R. A., & Santrock, J. W. (1983b). Children of divorce: Impact of custody disposition on social development. In E. J. Callahan & K. A. McCluskey (Eds.), *Life-span developmental psychology: Nonnormative life events.* New York: Academic Press.

Watson, E. (1979, June 23). Custody investigation as conducted by the Denver District Court Probation Department. Fourth Annual Child Custody Workshop sponsored by the Continuing Legal Education in Colorado, Inc. and the Interdisciplinary Committee on Child Custody, Keystone, Colorado.

Weisfeld, D., & Laser, M. S. (1977). Divorced parents in family therapy in a residential treatment setting. *Family Process, 16,* 229–236.

Weiss, R. S. (1979). Issues in the adjudication of custody when parents separate. In G. Levinger & O. C. Moles (Eds.), *Divorce and separation: Context, causes, and consequences.* New York: Basic Books.

Westman, J. C., Cline, D. W., Swift, W. J., & Kramer, D. A. (1970). Role of child psychiatry in divorce. *Archives of General Psychiatry, 23,* 416–420.

Westoff, L. A. (1975, August 10). Two-time winners. *New York Times Magazine,* 10–13.

Whiteside, M. F., & Auerbach, L. (1978). Can the daughter of my father's new wife be my sister? Families of remarriage in family therapy. *Journal of Divorce, 1,* 271–283.

Wilkinson, G. S., & Bleck, R. T. (1977). Children's divorce groups. *Elementary School Guidance and Counseling, 11,* 205–213.

Wilson, K. L., Zurcher, L., MacAdams, D. C., & Curtis, R. L. (1975). Stepfathers and step-childern: An exploratory analysis from two national surveys. *Journal of Marriage and the Family, 37,* 526–536.

Winnicott, D. W. (1971). *Therapeutic consultations in child psychiatry.* New York: Basic Books.

Wolchik, S. A., Braver, S. L., & Sandler, I. N. (1985). Maternal versus joint custody: Children's postseparation experiences and adjustment. *Journal of Clinical Child Psychology, 14*(1), 5–10.

Woody, R. H. (1977). Behavioral science criteria in child custody determinations. *Journal of Marriage and Family Counseling, 3*(1), 11–17.

Wyman, P. A., Cowen, E. L., Hightower, A. D., & Pedro-Carroll, J. L. (1985). Perceived competence, self-esteem, and anxiety in latency-aged children of divorce. *Journal of Clinical Child Psychology, 14*(1), 20–26.

Young, D. M. (1980). A court-mandated workshop for adolescent children of divorcing parents: A program evaluation. *Adolescence, 15*(60), 763–774.

Zakariya, S. B. (1982). Another look at the children of divorce: Summary report of the study of school needs of one-parent children. *Principal, 62*(1), 34–37.

Author Index

Subject Index

(continued from front)

Handbook of Research Methods in Clinical Psychology *edited by Philip C. Kendall and James N. Butcher*

A Social Psychology of Developing Adults *by Thomas O. Blank*

Women in the Middle Years: Current Knowledge and Directions for Research and Policy *edited by Janet Zollinger Giele*

Loneliness: A Sourcebook of Current Theory, Research and Therapy *edited by Letitia Anne Peplau and Daniel Perlman*

Hyperactivity: Current Issues, Research, and Theory (Second Edition) *by Dorothea M. Ross and Sheila A. Ross*

Review of Human Development *edited by Tiffany M. Field, Aletha Huston, Herbert C. Quay, Lillian Troll, and Gordon E. Finley*

Agoraphobia: Multiple Perspectives on Theory and Treatment *edited by Dianne L. Chambless and Alan J. Goldstein*

The Rorschach: A Comprehensive System. Volume III: Assessment of Children and Adolescents *by John E. Exner, Jr. and Irving B. Weiner*

Handbook of Play Therapy *edited by Charles E. Schaefer and Kevin J. O'Connor*

Adolescent Sexuality in a Changing American Society: Social and Psychological Perspectives for the Human Service Professions (Second Edition) *by Catherine S. Chilman*

Failures in Behavior Therapy *edited by Edna B. Foa and Paul M.G. Emmelkamp*

The Psychological Assessment of Children (Second Edition) *by James O. Palmer*

Imagery: Current Theory, Research, and Application *edited by Aneés A. Sheikh*

Handbook of Clinical Child Psychology *edited by C. Eugene Walker and Michael C. Roberts*

The Measurement of Psychotherapy Outcome *edited by Michael J. Lambert, Edwin R. Christensen, and Steven S. DeJulio*

Clinical Methods in Psychology (Second Edition) *edited by Irving B. Weiner*

Excuses: Masquerades in Search of Grace *by C.R. Snyder, Raymond L. Higgins and Rita J. Stucky*

Diagnostic Understanding and Treatment Planning: The Elusive Connection *edited by Fred Shectman and William B. Smith*

Bender Gestalt Screening for Brain Dysfunction *by Patricia Lacks*

Adult Psychopathology and Diagnosis *edited by Samuel M. Turner and Michel Hersen*

Personality and the Behavioral Disorders (Second Edition) *edited by Norman S. Endler and J. McVicker Hunt*

Ecological Approaches to Clinical and Community Psychology *edited by William A. O'Connor and Bernard Lubin*

Rational-Emotive Therapy with Children and Adolescents: Theory, Treatment Strategies, Preventative Methods *by Michael E. Bernard and Marie R. Joyce*

The Unconscious Reconsidered *edited by Kenneth S. Bowers and Donald Meichenbaum*

Prevention of Problems in Childhood: Psychological Research and Application *edited by Michael C. Roberts and Lizette Peterson*

Resolving Resistances in Psychotherapy *by Herbert S. Strean*

Handbook of Social Skills Training and Research *edited by Luciano L'Abate and Michael A. Milan*

Institutional Settings in Children's Lives *by Leanne G. Rivlin and Maxine Wolfe*

Treating the Alcoholic: A Developmental Model of Recovery *by Stephanie Brown*

Resolving Marital Conflicts: A Psychodynamic Perspective *by Herbert S. Strean*

Paradoxical Strategies in Psychotherapy: A Comprehensive Overview and Guidebook *by Leon F. Seltzer*

Pharmacological and Behavioral Treatment: An Integrative Approach *edited by Michel Hersen*